Keys to Learning Strategies for Success

Custom Edition

From works by Carol Carter, Joyce Bishop, Sarah Lyman Kravits, and Kateri Drexler

Taken from:
Keys to Success: Building Analytical, Creative, and Practical Skills,
Seventh Edition
by Carol Carter, Joyce Bishop, and Sarah Lyman Kravits

Cornerstones for Career College Success, Third Edition
by Robert M. Sherfield and Patricia G. Moody

Keys to Online Learning
by Kateri Drexler, Carol Carter, Joyce Bishop, and Sarah Lyman Kravits

Keys to Success: Cultural Awareness and Global Citizenship
by Carol Carter and Sarah Lyman Kravits

Power Up: A Practical Student's Guide to Online Learning
by Stacey Barrett, Catrina Poe, and Carrie Spagnola-Doyle

Cover Art: Courtesy of Columbia Southern University

Taken from:

Keys to Success: Building Analytical, Creative, and Practical Skills, Seventh Edition
by Carol Carter, Joyce Bishop, and Sarah Lyman Kravits
Copyright © 2012, 2009, 2006, 2003, 2001, 1998, 1996 by Pearson Education, Inc.
Published by Allyn & Bacon
Boston, Massachusetts 02116

Cornerstones for Career College Success, Third Edition
by Robert M. Sherfield and Patricia G. Moody
Copyright © 2013, 2010, 2006 by Pearson Education, Inc.
Published by Pearson
Upper Saddle River, New Jersey 07458

Keys to Online Learning
by Kateri Drexler, Carol Carter, Joyce Bishop, and Sarah Lyman Kravits
Copyright © 2012 by Pearson Education, Inc.
Published by Allyn & Bacon

Keys to Success: Cultural Awareness and Global Citizenship
by Carol Carter and Sarah Lyman Kravits
Copyright © 2013 by Pearson Education, Inc.
Published by Pearson

Power Up: A Practical Student's Guide to Online Learning
by Stacey Barrett, Catrina Poe, and Carrie Spagnola-Doyle
Copyright © 2009 by Pearson Education, Inc.
Published by Prentice Hall
Upper Saddle River, New Jersey 07458

Copyright © 2013 by Pearson Learning Solutions
All rights reserved.

Pearson Learning Solutions, 501 Boylston Street, Suite 900, Boston, MA 02116
A Pearson Education Company
www.pearsoned.com

Printed in the United States of America

4 5 6 7 8 9 10 V011   18 17 16 15 14

000200010271755682

JA/OP

ISBN 10: 1-269-15237-8
ISBN 13: 978-1-269-15237-2

BRIEF CONTENTS

chapter 1 | *Welcome to College*   1

chapter 2 | *Online Learning*   42

chapter 3 | *Values, Goals, and Time*   62

chapter 4 | *Learning How You Learn*   95

chapter 5 | *Learning Strategies*   119

chapter 6 | *Note Taking for Online Courses*   149

chapter 7 | *Memory and Studying*   171

chapter 8 | *Test Taking*   197

chapter 9 | *Critical Thinking*   219

chapter 10 | *Cultural and Global Awareness*   248

chapter 11 | *Careers and More*   281

chapter 12 | *Maintaining Your Online Success*   305

Appendices   311

Appendix A | *The Writing Process*   313

Appendix B | *Social Networking and Media*   319

CONTENTS

 chapter 1 *Welcome to College* 1

STATUS CHECK ▶ *How prepared are you for college?* 2

WHERE ARE YOU NOW—AND WHERE CAN COLLEGE TAKE YOU? 2
The culture of college 3
What are employers saying? 4

GAINFUL EMPLOYMENT 6
What strategies can i use to keep from being outsourced? 6

CREATING YOUR SUCCESS 7
Can you really create your future? 7

YOUR EDUCATION AND YOU 8
Why is it the partnership of a lifetime? 8
Your place in the world of work 9

HOW CAN SUCCESSFUL INTELLIGENCE HELP YOU ACHIEVE YOUR GOALS? 11
The three thinking skills 12
How thinking skills move you toward your goals 12

HOW CAN A "GROWTH MINDSET" MOTIVATE YOU TO PERSIST? 13

GET ANALYTICAL *Define Your "College Self"* 14
Build self-esteem with responsible actions 15
Face your fears 16
Learn from failure 16

WHY DO YOU NEED EMOTIONAL INTELLIGENCE? 17

GET CREATIVE *Consider How to Connect* 18
How emotional intelligence promotes success 18
The abilities of emotional intelligence 19

THE POWER AND PASSION OF MOTIVATION 20
What is the difference between internal and external motivation? 20

THE NEED TO BE MORE 21
What is the relationship between motivation and Maslow? 21

CONQUERING THE "FIRST-GENERATION GAP" 21
How do you make it and stay motivated when you're the first in the family? 21

ACHIEVING YOUR POTENTIAL AND INCREASING YOUR MOTIVATION 24
What are the cornerstones of personal and professional success? 24
Point 1: Develop a new attitude 24
Point 2: Make excellence a habit 25
Point 3: Overcome your doubts and fears 26
Point 4: Put adversity and failure into perspective 27
Point 5: Eliminate negative self-talk and the "I Can't" syndrome 28
Point 6: Identify and clarify what you value in life 29
Point 7: Take pride in your name and personal character 31
Point 8: Develop a strong, personal guiding statement 31

DID YOU KNOW 32
Point 9: Make a commitment to strengthen your self-esteem 33
Tips to enhance your self-esteem 34

Building Skills for College, Career, and Life 36

chapter 2 *Online Learning* 42

STATUS CHECK ▶ *Rate yourself as an online student* 43

Benefits of online learning 44
You Have Much to Gain from College 45

UNDERSTANDING THE ONLINE LEARNING ENVIRONMENT 45
Facts and fictions of online learning 45
Types of online courses 47
Types of assignments 48
Types of learning management systems 48

SETTING YOURSELF UP FOR SUCCESS: PRACTICES OF SUCCESSFUL ONLINE LEARNERS 49
Prepare for the path ahead 50
Structure your schedule 50
Set priorities 51
Develop discipline and accountability 51
Foster relationships 52

ONLINE OUTLOOK 53
Seek new skills 54
Manage your thoughts and emotions 54
Ask for help 55

E-MAIL 56
E-mail communication guidelines 56

Building Skills for College, Career, and Life 60

chapter 3 *Values, Goals, and Time* 62

STATUS CHECK ▶ *How developed are your self-management skills?* 63

WHY IS IT IMPORTANT TO KNOW WHAT YOU VALUE? 63
How values develop and change 64
How values affect your life experience 64
HOW DO YOU SET AND ACHIEVE GOALS? 64

GET ANALYTICAL *Explore Your Values* 65
Establish your personal mission 65
Set long-term goals 66
Set short-term goals 67
Set up a SMART goal-achievement plan 67

GET CREATIVE *Find Ways to Get Unstuck* 68

HOW CAN YOU EFFECTIVELY MANAGE YOUR TIME? 69
Identify your time profile and preferences 70
Build a schedule 71
Make to-do lists and prioritize 73
Plan and track 74
Confront procrastination 75

GET PRACTICAL *Conquer Your Time Traps* 76
Be flexible 78

MANAGE YOUR TIME IN ONLINE COURSES 79
Manage E-mail 79

ONLINE OUTLOOK 79
Manage discussion forums 80
Manage course resources 80
Manage your noneducational computer time 80
Put off procrastination 81
Develop good habits 81

HOW CAN YOU MANAGE STRESS? 83
Manage stress by managing time 87

Building Skills for College, Career, and Life 89

chapter 4 *Learning How You Learn* 95

STATUS CHECK ▶ *How aware are you of how you learn?* 96

WHY EXPLORE WHO YOU ARE AS A LEARNER? 96
Use assessments to learn about yourself 96
Use assessments to make choices and to grow 97

WE HOPE YOU LEARNED YOUR LESSON! 98
What is this thing called learning, anyway? 98
What do the experts say? 98

GIVE YOUR BRAIN A WORKOUT 98
Can i really learn all this stuff? 98

DID YOU KNOW 100

THE LEARNING PROCESS 100
What are the steps to active, authentic learning? 100

UNDERSTANDING YOUR STRENGTHS 102
What are the advantages of discovering and polishing your talents? 102

UNDERSTANDING MULTIPLE INTELLIGENCES 102
Why is it important to discover new ways of looking at yourself? 102

UNDERSTANDING LEARNING STYLES THEORY 106
Why is it important to know how i learn? 106

WANTED: A VISUAL LEARNER WITH TACTILE SKILLS 106
Do you know the differences between your primary learning style and your dominant intelligence? 106

SUCCESSFUL DECISIONS
An Activity for Critical Reflection 108

UNDERSTANDING PERSONALITY TYPE 108
Are you ENFJ, ISTP or ENTJ, and why does it matter? 108
E Versus I (Extroversion/Introversion) 112
S Versus N (Sensing/Intuition) 112
T Versus F (Thinking/Feeling) 112
J Versus P (Judging/Perceiving) 112

REFLECTIONS ON LEARNING HOW TO LEARN 114

Building Skills for College, Career, and Life 116

chapter 5 *Learning Strategies* 119

STATUS CHECK ▶ *How developed are your reading and information literacy skills?* 120

IS READING FUNDAMENTAL OR JUST PURE TORTURE? 120
Getting ready to read college-level material 120

DISCOVERING YOUR READING STYLE 121
Are you active or passive? 121

I FEEL THE NEED . . . THE NEED FOR SPEED! 121
Do you know your personal reading rate? 121

DEVELOPING A POWERFUL VOCABULARY 124
Do you have to be a logodaedalian to enjoy words? 124
Expand your vocabulary 125

LEARNING TO READ FASTER AND SMARTER 126
Can you improve speed and comprehension? 126
Learn to concentrate 126

DID YOU KNOW 126
Overcome fixation 127

HOW CAN SQ3R IMPROVE YOUR READING? 127
Step 1: Survey 128
Step 2: Question 128

GET ANALYTICAL *Survey a Text* 130
Step 3: Read 131
Step 4: Recite 135
Step 5: Review 135

GET PRACTICAL *Mark Up a Page to Learn a Page* 136

WHAT STRATEGIES HELP WITH SPECIFIC SUBJECTS AND FORMATS? 137
Math and science 137

GET CREATIVE *Use SQ3R to Make a Connection* 138
Social sciences and humanities 138
Literature 139

Multiple Intelligence Strategies 140
Visual aids 141

READING ONLINE MATERIAL 141
Do i need a new set of reading skills? 141

ONLINE READING CHALLENGES 141
Complex material 141
Eyestrain 142

ONLINE OUTLOOK 143
Reading strategies for different learning styles 144

Building Skills for College, Career, and Life 145

chapter 6 *Note Taking for Online Courses* 149

STATUS CHECK ▶ *How developed are your listening and note-taking skills?* 150

HOW CAN YOU BECOME A BETTER LISTENER? 150

THE IMPORTANCE OF LISTENING 150
Why does listening really matter in classes and relationships? 150

I THINK I HEARD YOU LISTENING 151
Is there really a difference between listening and hearing? 151
Listening defined 151

FOUR LISTENING STYLES DEFINED 153
What is your orientation? 153

LISTENING CAN BE SO HARD 154
Can you really overcome the obstacles to listening? 154
Obstacle 1: Prejudging 154
Obstacle 2: Talking 155
Obstacle 3: Becoming too emotional 155

GET ANALYTICAL *Discover Yourself as a Listener* 156

TAKING EFFECTIVE NOTES 156

HOW CAN YOU IMPROVE YOUR NOTE-TAKING SKILLS? 156
Record information effectively 157
Review and revise 157

WHAT NOTE-TAKING SYSTEMS CAN YOU USE? 157

GET PRACTICAL *Face a Note-Taking Challenge* 158
Outlines 158
Cornell T-note system 159

Multiple Intelligence Strategies 160
Think links 162
Other visual strategies 162

NOTE-TAKING FOR MULTIMEDIA PRESENTATIONS 163

ONLINE OUTLOOK 163

HOW CAN YOU TAKE NOTES FASTER? 164

GET CREATIVE *Craft Your Own Shorthand* 166

Building Skills for College, Career, and Life 167

chapter 7 *Memory and Studying* 171

STATUS CHECK ▶ *How developed are your memory and studying skills?* 172

HOW DOES MEMORY WORK? 172
The information processing model of memory 172
Why you forget 174

HOW CAN YOU REMEMBER WHAT YOU STUDY? 175

GET ANALYTICAL *Link Memory and Analytical Thinking* 176
When, where, and who: Choosing your best setting 176

GET PRACTICAL *Answer Your Journalists' Questions* 178
What and why: Evaluating study materials 178
How: Using study strategies 179

Multiple Intelligence Strategies 181

WHAT WILL HELP YOU REMEMBER MATH AND SCIENCE MATERIAL? 186

HOW CAN MNEMONIC DEVICES BOOST RECALL? 187

GET CREATIVE *Craft Your Own Mnemonic* 188
Create visual images and associations 188
Use visual images to remember items in a list 188
Make acronyms 189
Use songs or rhymes 191

WHAT STUDY STRATEGIES HELP YOU PUT IT ALL TOGETHER? 191
Create a summary of reading material 192

Building Skills for College, Career, and Life 193

chapter 8 *Test Taking* 197

STATUS CHECK ▶ *How prepared are you for taking tests?* 198

HOW CAN PREPARATION IMPROVE TEST PERFORMANCE? 198
Identify test type and what you will be expected to know 198
Determine where and how the test will be given 199
Create a study schedule and checklist 199
Use reading and studying strategies 200
Make and take a pretest 200
Prepare physically 200

GET CREATIVE *Write Your Own Test* 202

Make the most of last-minute cramming 202

HOW CAN YOU WORK THROUGH TEST ANXIETY? 203
Prepare well and have a positive attitude 203
Math anxiety 203
Test time strategies 204
Test anxiety and the returning student 205

WHAT GENERAL STRATEGIES CAN HELP YOU SUCCEED ON TESTS? 205
Test day strategies 205

GET PRACTICAL *Assess Test Anxiety with the Westside Test Anxiety Scale* 206

Multiple Intelligence Strategies 207

HOW CAN YOU MASTER DIFFERENT TYPES OF TEST QUESTIONS? 208
Multiple-choice questions 210
True/false questions 211
Matching questions 212
Fill-in-the-blank questions 212
Essay questions 213

Building Skills for College, Career, and Life 215

chapter 9 *Critical Thinking* 219

STATUS CHECK ▶ *How developed are your thinking skills?* 220

WHY IS IT IMPORTANT TO ASK AND ANSWER QUESTIONS? 220

HOW CAN YOU IMPROVE YOUR ANALYTICAL THINKING SKILLS? 221
Gather information 222
Break information into parts 222
Examine and evaluate 222
Make connections 225

HOW CAN YOU IMPROVE YOUR CREATIVE THINKING SKILLS? 227
Brainstorm 227

GET ANALYTICAL *Analyze a Statement* 228

Take a new and different look 229

GET CREATIVE *Activate Your Creative Powers* 230

Set the stage for creativity 230
Take risks 231

HOW CAN YOU IMPROVE YOUR PRACTICAL THINKING SKILLS? 231
Why practical thinking is important 232
Practical thinking means action 232

GET PRACTICAL *Take a Practical Approach to Building Successful Intelligence* 233

HOW CAN YOU SOLVE PROBLEMS AND MAKE DECISIONS EFFECTIVELY? 233
Solve a problem 235
Make a decision 235
Keep your balance 236

THINKING ABOUT COURSE CONTENT 236
Critical thinking 237
Ask questions 237

INTERNET RESEARCH 237
Search engines 238
Types of online searches 238
Boolean searches 239

THE CREDIBILITY OF INFORMATION ONLINE 241
Primary and secondary sources 241

ACADEMIC INTEGRITY AND PLAGIARISM 242
Looking closely at plagiarism 242
Citing sources 243

Building Skills for College, Career, and Life 244

chapter 10 *Cultural and Global Awareness* 248

STATUS CHECK ▶ *How prepared am I to be a culturally aware global citizen?* 249

STUDENT PROFILE 250

WHAT IS CULTURAL AWARENESS? 251
Defining culture 251
Four levels of cultural awareness 252
Know your culture first 253
Explore other cultures 255
Be receptive and respectful 255
The value of cultural awareness 256

HOW CAN YOU BUILD CULTURAL COMPETENCE? 256

SPEAK IT *Expand Your Perception of Culture* 257

Action 1: Value diversity 258
Action 2: Identify and evaluate personal perceptions and attitudes 258
Action 3: Be aware of what happens when cultures interact 261
Action 4: Build cultural knowledge 261
Action 5: Adapt to diverse cultures 262
The cultural components of communication 263

KNOW IT *How Can I Become More Culturally Competent?* 265

Barriers to intercultural communication 267

WHAT IS GLOBAL CITIZENSHIP? 269
Defining community 269
The global community 271
Being a global citizen 271

HOW CAN I TAKE ACTION AS A GLOBAL CITIZEN? 272
Global communication strategies 273

WRITE IT *Personal Journal and Real-Life Writing* 275

Building Skills for College, Career, and Life 276

chapter 11 *Careers and More* 281

STATUS CHECK ▶ *How prepared are you for workplace and life success?* 282

HOW CAN YOU PREPARE FOR CAREER SUCCESS? 282
Consider your personality and strengths 282
Be strategic 283
Build knowledge and experience 283
Investigate career paths 285
Know what employers want 286
Expect change 288

HOW CAN YOU CONDUCT AN EFFECTIVE JOB SEARCH? 288
Use available resources 288
Use an organized, consistent strategy 290
Your resumé, cover letter, and interview 290

GET PRACTICAL *Find Useful Keywords* 291

HOW CAN YOU CONTINUE TO ACTIVATE YOUR SUCCESSFUL INTELLIGENCE? 291

GET ANALYTICAL *Evaluate Your Development* 293

HOW WILL YOUR LEARNING IN THIS COURSE BRING SUCCESS? 294
Lifelong learning and the growth mindset 294

GET CREATIVE *Think Fifty Positive Thoughts* 296

Flexibility helps you adapt to change 297

Building Skills for College, Career, and Life 298

chapter 12 *Maintaining Your Online Success* 305

STAYING ORGANIZED 306
Computer files 306
Textbooks for future reference 306
Emergency backup 307

THE MASTER JUGGLER: YOU 307
Planning ahead 307
One class follows another and another 308
Celebrate your achievements 308

GOOD LUCK! 308

More Power To You 309

APPENDICES 311
APPENDIX A: The Writing Process 313
APPENDIX B: Social Networking and Media 319
INDEX 321
CREDITS 327

Welcome to College

*T*racy Barnes is an elite athlete who trains and competes in the biathlon, a winter sport that combines cross-country skiing with rifle marksmanship. Barnes, who shares her passion for the biathlon with her twin sister, has been competing for 11 years and both plan to participate in the 2014 Olympic Winter Games.

Barnes' love for the biathlon takes her many places. "I'm on the road for about eight months out of the year. I spend most of the winter (November through March) in Europe and travel to training camps all over the U.S. in the summer and fall," she explained. The travel, competition and travel have paid off for the Durango, Colo., native.

"Biathlon has such a unique combination of skill and endurance that makes it so challenging. And it's the No. 1 winter sport in Europe. It is so exciting competing in Europe in front of 20,000 screaming fans! And the biggest thrill for me is representing the U.S. in the Olympics. There's no greater honor," she said.

Another thrill for Barnes has been attending CSU in pursuit of an online bachelor's degree in business.

"A friend of mine was taking some courses and told me about CSU. I had wanted to finish my degree for some time and had attended colleges and universities all over the U.S.," she said. "But I hit a point where I was traveling too much and was unable to attend classes. CSU offered me the flexibility I needed to finish my degree and still pursue my athletic goals. I started taking classes in 2010 and hope to finish my degree before the next Olympics."

Barnes said that her desire for an education also has yielded some dividends for her athletic career. "I find that when I have my schoolwork to do, I'm more efficient with my time and that helps my training and competing. It's nice to have an outlet outside of my sport and it's always a fun challenge to continually expand the mind and learn all you can on a certain topic."

She added that feedback from professors and intriguing online courses have contributed to her enjoyment of CSU.

"My education has always been important to me and I always wanted to pursue a degree in business, but was having trouble attending classes being on the road for so long. CSU was a perfect fit for me because the classes were high quality and it has the flexibility to allow me to take classes from anywhere in the world. I'm very passionate about business and it's always exciting to learn everything I'll need to know to run my own business someday."

For those considering pursuing a degree, Barnes offers this advice: "Do it! Start now! You certainly won't regret it. No one can afford to pass up an opportunity to have a degree. Set your mind to it and you'll have a quality degree before you know it.

STATUS *Check*

▶ *How prepared are you for college?*

For each statement, circle the number that feels right to you,
from 1 for "not at all true for me" to 5 for "very true for me."

▶ I feel ready to handle college-level work.	1 2 ③ 4 5
▶ I can identify how college culture differs from high school and the workplace.	1 2 ③ 4 5
▶ I am aware of what it takes to succeed in today's technology-driven, ever-changing workplace.	1 2 3 ④ 5
▶ I believe my intelligence can increase as a result of my effort.	1 2 3 4 ⑤
▶ I use a combination of critical, creative, and practical thinking to reach a goal.	1 2 3 4 ⑤
▶ I believe that success demands hard work and practice no matter what my talents are.	1 2 3 4 ⑤
▶ I can explain the value of acting with academic integrity in college.	1 2 ③ 4 5
▶ I am able to perceive my own emotions accurately as well as those of others.	1 2 3 ④ 5
▶ I relate effectively to others and can work successfully in a team.	1 2 3 4 ⑤
▶ I know that I will need to learn throughout my life to succeed in the workplace.	1 2 3 4 ⑤

Now total your scores.

25
8
9
42

Each of the topics in these statements is covered in this chapter. Note those statements for which you circled a 3 or lower. Skim the chapter to see where those topics appear, and pay special attention to them as you read, learn, and apply new strategies.

REMEMBER: *No matter how prepared you are to succeed in college, you can improve with effort and practice.*

"Successfully intelligent people . . . have a can-do attitude. They realize that the limits to what they can accomplish are often in what they tell themselves they cannot do, rather than in what they really cannot do."

—Robert Sternberg

Where are you now—and **where can college take you?**

Think about how you got here. Are you going to college straight from high school or its equivalent? Or are you returning after working one or more jobs or completing a tour of duty in the armed forces? Do you have life skills from experience as a partner or parent? No matter what your background or motivation, you have enrolled, found a way to pay for tuition, signed up for courses, and shown up for class. You have earned this opportunity to be a college student.

If you are wondering how this or any other college course will make a difference for you, know that your experience in this course and during this term has the potential to:

- ▶ Allow you to discover more about how you learn and what you want
- ▶ Build academic skills as well as transferable life skills
- ▶ Help you set and reach your most important goals
- ▶ Increase your ability to relate effectively to others and work together

Now that you *have* the opportunity, you need to *use it*. This book, and your course, offer tools that will help you grow and achieve your goals, perhaps beyond what you've ever imagined. You will be able to make the most of them—if you start by believing that you can grow.

When a high jumper or pole vaulter gets over a bar of a certain height, someone raises the bar so that the athlete can work toward a new goal. The college experience will "raise the bar" for you with tougher instructors, demanding coursework, and fellow students whose sights are set high. Others' goals and expectations are only part of the picture, though. College is a place where *you* can raise the bar to reach your personal aspirations, whatever they might be. Think about how you want to improve *your* life. This book and course will challenge you to set the bar to the height that's right for you.

First, however, begin your transition to college by looking at the present— the culture of college, what you can expect, and what college expects of you. Then, consider the future—what a college education means for you in the workplace and life.

The culture of college

Whatever your age or stage of life, knowing what to expect in college will help you to transition more successfully. You are likely to experience most or all of the following aspects of college culture (spend some time with your college's student handbook to get informed about details specific to your school).

■ *Independent learning.* College offers you the chance to learn with a great deal of freedom and independence. In exchange, though, instructors expect you to function without much guidance. This culture requires strong self-management skills. You are expected to make the following—and more—happen on your own:

► Use syllabi to create, and follow, a schedule for the term
► Navigate course materials electronically (if your school uses an online course management system such as BlackBoard)
► Complete text and other reading with little to no in-class review of the reading
► Turn in projects and coursework on time and be prepared for exams
► Get help when you need it

■ *Fast pace and increased workload.* The pace of each course is typically twice as fast as high school courses and requires more papers, homework, reading, and projects. Although demanding, learning at this speed can also energize and motivate you, especially if you did not feel inspired by high school assignments. The heavy, fast-paced workload demands more study time. For each hour spent in class, plan two to three hours of study and work time outside of class. For example, if you are in class for nine hours a week, you need to spend at least twice that number each week studying and working outside of class time.

■ *Challenging work.* Although challenging, college-level work offers an enormous opportunity to learn and grow. College texts often have more words per page, higher-level terminology, and more abstract ideas compared to high school texts. In addition to difficult reading, college often involves complex assignments, challenging research papers, group projects, lab work, and tests.

■ *Diverse culture.* Typically, you will encounter different ideas and diverse people in college. Your fellow students may differ from you in age, life experience, ethnicity, political mindset, family obligations, values, and much more.

■ *Higher-level thinking.* You'll be asked to move far beyond recall in college. Instead of just summarizing and taking the ideas of others at face value, you will interpret, evaluate, generate new ideas, and apply what you know to new situations (more on thinking skills later in this chapter).

Courtesy of Shutterstock

You are not alone as you adjust. Look for support resources, including instructors, academic advisors, mentors, other students, or tutors; technology such as the Internet, library search engines, and electronic planning aids; and this book. And to give meaning to your efforts in college, consider how your efforts will serve you in the workplace.

What are employers saying?

According to the report *College Learning for the New Global Century* (2008), "Employers want college graduates to acquire versatile knowledge and skills. Fully sixty-three percent of employers believe that too many recent college graduates do not have the skills they need to succeed in the global economy and a majority of employers believe that only half or fewer recent graduates have the skills or knowledge needed to advance or to be promoted in their companies." Other skills listed as vitally important to employers include:

- ▶ Computer literacy
- ▶ The ability to learn new skills quickly
- ▶ Accuracy
- ▶ Attention to detail
- ▶ Self-confidence
- ▶ Tact
- ▶ Humor
- ▶ Character

Whether we like it or not, a massive transformation is going on all around us in this country, as well as all over the world. Thriving in the coming years is going to be more difficult than in the past and will require certain new and different abilities and attitudes. You will need to learn the skills that will make you competitive, give you an edge, and help you master a life filled with changes and challenges. Many of these skills are outlined in Key 1.1, Essential Cornerstones for Success in a Changing World. These skills will be needed for your success, personal independence, and growth in the new economy. Study them carefully as each one will help you create a positive transition to the world of work.

ESSENTIAL CORNERSTONES FOR **SUCCESS** IN A CHANGING WORLD

Seek Excellence as a Communicator

Writing, speaking, and listening skills are constantly listed by employers as mandatory for success in any profession. Few people actually possess these qualities, especially all three. If you want to put yourself ahead of the competition, then attend every class, every seminar, every meeting, and every function where you can learn more about effective writing, speaking, and listening skills.

Become a Desirable Employee

A strong work ethic will be another valuable quality that sets you apart from the other job seekers. A work ethic can include a variety of characteristics, including your pride, passion, professionalism, ability to work on a team, and ability to adapt, grow, and change. Your work ethic is how you perform at work without a job description, constant supervision, or someone threatening you. Your work ethic is not tied to what you do to get a raise or a promotion, but rather what you do because it is the right thing to do. In today's work environment, employers want to make sure that you are dedicated to your job, your company, and your colleagues. Our suggestion is to develop a strong work ethic that is healthy for you and your employer.

Practice Loyalty and Trustworthiness

Loyalty to your employer is a highly valued trait. However, one's loyalty cannot be measured by a resumé or determined by a simple interview. Proving that you have the characteristics of loyalty and trustworthiness comes over time. It may take years to establish loyalty and trustworthiness with your company and within your industry, but with hard work, dedication, and honesty, it can and will be achieved. Be forewarned, however: it may take years to build trust, but it only takes seconds to destroy it.

Walk with Confidence and Make Bold Decisions

Appropriate confidence and boldness are important to employers. There is a difference between having confidence in yourself, your work, and your decision-making ability and being cocky. Confidence comes from experience, calculated risk taking, and previous successes. Employers are looking for confident people who are not afraid to make hard decisions. They are also seeking individuals who have confidence through experience. There is a difference between bragging about doing something and actually doing it. There is a difference between being hard and making hard decisions. When you meet with the person(s) interviewing you, confidently steer the conversation toward your general and specific abilities and characteristics.

Use Critical-Thinking Skills

The ability to think your way through problems and challenges is highly valued by employers. Employers are looking for people who can distinguish fact from opinion; identify fallacies; analyze, synthesize, and determine the value of a piece of information; think beyond the obvious; see things from varying angles; and arrive at sound solutions. They also want people who possess the emotional intelligence to critically and creatively work to resolve challenges.

Manage Your Priorities Well

Setting priorities and managing time are essential to success in today's stressful workplace. Today, maybe more than any other time in human history, we are faced with more and more to do and what seems like less and less time in which to do it. Your success depends on how well you manage your priorities both personally and professionally. Priority management not only involves getting today's work accomplished, it also involves the ability to plan for your personal and professional future. Use your time wisely at work, at home, and in leisure.

Multiply by Multitasking

The ability to multitask, or accomplish several things at once, will serve you well in the workplace and at home. A recent newspaper cartoon suggested that you are too busy if you are multitasking in the shower. This may be true, but in keeping pace with today's workforce, this is another essential task—the ability to do several things at a time, and the ability to do them all very well. If you have not had much experience in multitasking, we suggest that you begin slowly. Don't take on too many things at one time. As you understand more about working on and completing several tasks at a time, you can expand your abilities in this arena. An example of multitasking at home is to have a casserole baking while clothes are washing at the same time you are researching a project on the Internet. To be successful in the fast paced world we live in today, you must be able to manage several tasks at once—without burning dinner.

Stay Current and Build Transferable Skills

Keeping your skills and knowledge current is essential to your success. Building skills that can be transferred from one position to another is essential in today's workplace. Fine tuning your computer skills can set you apart from many of today's applicants. Your skills need to include the ability to work with word processing programs, spreadsheets, databases, and PowerPoint. Some careers will require knowledge and expertise of industry software, and you will need to be an expert if this is true in your field. Learn to develop webpages, and create your own website that reflects a professional, career oriented person. Learn to use social media for more than socializing.

Continue to Get Experience and Education

Never stop learning! You may not want to hear it, but your education will never end. You will eventually complete your formal schooling, but as long as you are working in today's global economy, you will need to keep abreast of the changes in your field. Seek out opportunities to expand your knowledge base. Get certified in areas that will make you more marketable. Take a continuing education course to brush up on changing workplace skills. Make yourself the best, most knowledgeable, most well rounded applicant in the field.

Avoid Internet and Social Media Blunders

Don't let social media mistakes come back to haunt you and cause you to miss out on your dream job! What you post online today may very well come back to haunt you in the future—even if you remove it, it can still be accessed. You may not lose your current position over a crazy, spur of the moment posting, but it may cost you a future position. You may tell yourself that your Facebook, LinkedIn, or webpage is private and no one's business, but remember, nothing is private online and everything is someone's business in the world of business.

Watch Your Credit Rating

Building a good credit rating is one of the most important jobs you have. Really? My credit rating? What in the world does my credit score have to do with my employment? The answer: A great deal. More and more, employers are accessing your credit history and score as a part of the hiring procedure. Why? Because some employers believe that your credit history paints a clear picture of your working future. Bad credit history means a bad employee. Missed payments mean missed work. Low score means low morale. Careless errors mean careless job performance. This is just one of the many ways that your credit history and score can follow you for years.

Remain Open-Minded

The ability to accept and appreciate a highly diverse workplace and the inherent differences and cultures that will be commonplace is important. You will need to develop the ability to listen to others with whom you disagree or with whom you may have little in common and learn from them and their experiences. The ability to learn a new language (even if your mastery is only at a primitive, broken, conversational level) and conduct yourself in a respectable and professional style will set you apart from other employees.

Practice Accountability

The ability to accept responsibility and be accountable for all aspects of your future—including your psychological and spiritual well being, your relationships, your health, your finances, and your overall survival skills—is vitally important. Basically, you must develop a plan for the future that states, "If this fails, I'll do this," or "If this job is phased out, I'll do this," or "If this resource is gone, I'll use this," or "If this person won't help me, this one will."

Polish Your Human Relation Skills

Polish your people skills and learn to get along with people from all walks of life. We saved this one for last, certainly not because it is least important, but because this quality is an overriding characteristic of everything listed previously. Employers are looking for individuals who have "people skills." This concept goes so much further than being a team player; it goes to the heart of many workplaces. It touches on your most basic nature, and it draws from your most inner self. The ability to get along with grouchy, cranky, mean, disagreeable, burned out coworkers is, indeed, a rare quality. But don't be mistaken; there are those who do this, and do it well. Peak performers, or those at the "top of their game," have learned that this world is made up of many types of people and there is never going to be a time when one of those cranky, grumpy people is not in our midst. Smile. Be nice. Remain positive.

"You want to be the most educated, the most brilliant, the most exciting, the most versatile, the most creative individual in the world because then, you can give it away. The only reason you have anything is to give it away."

—Leo Buscaglia, Ph.D.

Gainful employment

What strategies can I use to keep from being outsourced?

Go where the puck is going! Sound crazy? The great hockey champ Wayne Gretzky made the comment that ***this one step*** had been his key to success. What does it mean? He said that when he was playing hockey, he did not skate to where the puck was at the moment; he skated to where the puck was *going*. He anticipated the direction of where the puck was going to be hit, and when it came his way, he was already there—ready to play.

Think of your career in this light. Go to where it will be bright in the future, not necessarily where it is bright at this moment. Look ahead and try to determine what is going to be "hot" in the coming years, not what is hot right now. Plan ahead. Look at trends. Read. Ask questions. Stay prepared. Think in the future, not the moment.

People holding degrees and certificates are a dime a dozen. This does not mean, however, that *you are* a dime a dozen. Herein lies the challenge. How do you distinguish yourself from the countless job seekers out there? What are you going to do that sets you apart from your competition? What do you have to offer that no one else can possibly offer to an employer? Later, we will discuss some of the talents and qualities that are becoming increasingly rare, yet constantly sought after, in today's "workquake." By understanding more about these qualities, you can put yourself miles ahead of the competition.

Take some time now and work through the exercise in Key 1.2. You will find several skills and traits for which employers are looking in the left-hand column. In the right-hand column, create two tips that outline ways ***you*** can impress a potential employer.

SKILLS FOR
GAINFUL EMPLOYMENT

SKILL/TRAIT EMPLOYERS SEEK	TWO TIPS TO IMPRESS
Priority/Time Management	1. 2.
Attitude	1. 2.
Written Communication	1. 2.
Interpersonal Communication/Relationships	1. 2.
Ethics	1. 2.
Dress/Personal Grooming	1. 2.
Computer/Technology Skills	1. 2.
Decision Making/Problem Solving Skills	1. 2.
Confidence	1. 2.
Advanced Training/Certifications	1. 2.

Creating your success

Can you really create your future?

Is it really possible to draft a blueprint of your own future? Is it possible to "create success?" The answer is yes. The process of creating success begins with an internal idea that you have the power, the passion, and the capacity to be successful—to reach your chosen goals. It has been said that those people who are not out there creating their own future deserve the future that will be handed to them. You can be a person who creates the future for yourself and your family. Your education is one of the most important steps in this process because your education will give you options and alternatives. It will also help you create opportunities, and, according to Leo Buscaglia, writer and speaker, the healthiest people in the world are the people with the most alternatives.

"So, how do I create a successful future with more options?" you may be asking. The formula is simple, but the action required is not—and have no doubt, ***action is required***. The formula consists of four steps:

1. The willingness to set clear, realistic goals and the ability to visualize the results of those goals

What is the most surprising thing you have learned about your institution's curriculum thus far? IndexOpen

2. The ability to recognize your strengths and build on them
3. The ability to recognize your weaknesses or challenges and work to improve them
4. The passion and desire to work at your zenith every single day to make your goals and dreams a reality

Simple? The first three are rather simple. Number four is the kicker. Truthfully, most people have little trouble with the first three; it is the work involved with number four that causes most people to give up and never reach their fullest potential—and to be handed a future over which they had little say in creating. You can create your own future, your own success, and your own alternatives.

Coming to the realization that there is no "easy street" and no "roads paved with good intentions" is also important to creating your success. In his landmark book, *Good to Great*, Jim Collins suggests that once you decide to be great, your life will never be easy again. Rid yourself of the notion that there is some easy way out, that school will be easy, or that your education will make your professional life easier. Success requires hard, passionate work on a daily basis. This passionate work may require you to change some of your thoughts, actions, and beliefs. That is what this chapter and indeed this entire course is about: Creating success through positive change.

Your education and you

Why is it the partnership of a lifetime?

What can a college education do for you? The list will certainly vary depending on whom you ask, but basically, career colleges can help you develop in the areas listed below. As you read through the list, place a checkmark beside the statements that most accurately reflects which skills you hope to gain from attending classes at your institution. If there are other skills that you desire to achieve from your education, write them at the end of the list.

_____ Grow more self-sufficient and self-confident
_____ Establish and strengthen your personal identity
_____ Understand more about the global world in which you live
_____ Become a more involved citizen in social and political issues
_____ Become more open-minded
_____ Learn to manage your emotions and reactions more effectively
_____ Understand the value of thinking, analyzing, and problem solving
_____ Expand and use your ethical and moral thinking and reasoning skills
_____ Develop commanding computer and information literacy skills
_____ Manage your personal resources such as time and money
_____ Become more proficient at written, oral, and nonverbal communication
_____ Grow more understanding and accepting of different cultures
_____ Become a lifelong learner
_____ Become more financially independent
_____ Enter a career field that you enjoy

Which skill is the most important to you?

_____
_____
_____

"Though no one can go back and make a brand new start, anyone can start from now and make a brand new ending."

—Carl Bard

Why?

_____

_____

_____

What plans will you put into action to hone
and master this skill?

_____

_____

_____

Getting through the day-to-day activities of college demands
basic computer know-how as well as an understanding of the
school's research and communication technology.
© iStockPhoto

Your place in the world of work

Although this is likely to be one of your first
courses, it can lay the foundation for career
exploration and workplace skill development. You
will learn to distinguish yourself in a global marketplace, in which North American workers often
compete with workers from other countries.
Thomas Friedman, author of *The World Is Flat*,
explains how the digital revolution has transformed the working
environment you will enter after college:

> It is now possible for more people than ever to collaborate and compete in real
> time with more other people on more different kinds of work from more different
> corners of the planet and on a more equal footing than in any previous time in the
> history of the world—using computers, e-mail, networks, teleconferencing, and
> dynamic new software.[1]

These developments in communication, combined with an enormous
increase in knowledge work such as Internet technology and decrease
in labor-based work such as factory jobs, mean that you may compete for
information-based jobs with highly trained and motivated people from around
the globe. The working world, too, has raised the bar.

What can help you achieve career goals in this new "flat" world?

> DIGITAL REVOLUTION
> The change in how people
> communicate brought on
> by developments in
> computer systems.

> KNOWLEDGE WORK
> Work that is primarily
> concerned with information
> rather than manual labor.

■ *College degree.* Statistics show that getting a degree increases your chances
of finding and keeping a highly skilled, well-paying job. College graduates earn,
on average, around $20,000 more per year than those with a high school
diploma (see Key 1.3). Furthermore, the unemployment rate for college graduates is less than half that of high school graduates (see Key 1.4).

■ *21st century skills.* Taking a careful look at what the current workplace
demands of workers and what it rewards, education and business leaders have
founded an organization called the Partnership for 21st Century Skills.
Together these leaders developed the Framework for 21st Century Learning
shown in Key 1.5, delineating the categories of knowledge and skills that successful workers need to acquire.

Looking at this framework, you will see that success in today's workplace
requires more than just knowing skills specific to an academic area or job.
Author Daniel Pink argues that the ability to create, interact interpersonally,
generate ideas, and lead diverse teams—skills all found in the Framework for
21st Century Learning—will be more and more important in the workplace.
Because coursework traditionally focuses more on logical and analytical skills,
building your interpersonal and creative skill set will require personal initiative
from you. Often, these skills can be developed through in-class collaboration
and teamwork as well as volunteer work, internships, and jobs.[2]

MORE EDUCATION
IS LIKELY TO MEAN **MORE INCOME**

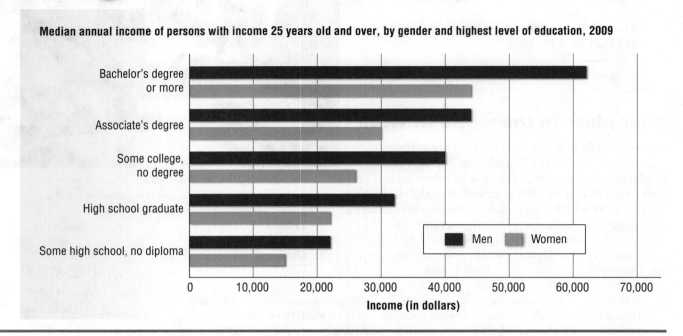

Median annual income of persons with income 25 years old and over, by gender and highest level of education, 2009

Source: U.S. Census Bureau, "Income, Poverty, and Health Insurance Coverage in the United States, 2009," *Current Population Reports,* Series P60-238, September 2010.

MORE EDUCATION
IS LIKELY TO MEAN **MORE CONSISTENT EMPLOYMENT**

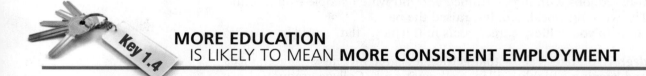
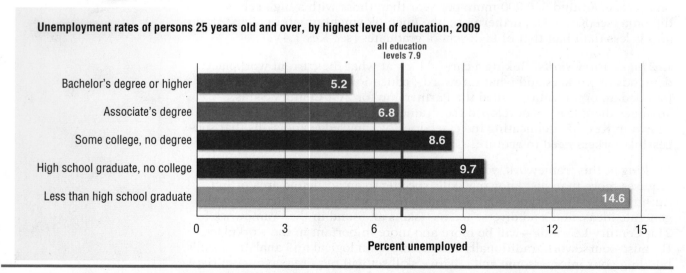

Unemployment rates of persons 25 years old and over, by highest level of education, 2009

Source: U.S. Department of Labor, Bureau of Labor Statistics, Office of Employment and Unemployment Statistics, "Current Population Survey," May 2010.

THE **FRAMEWORK FOR 21ST CENTURY LEARNING** SHOWS WHAT YOU NEED TO SUCCEED

Key 1.5

CORE SUBJECTS AND 21ST CENTURY THEMES	LEARNING AND INNOVATION SKILLS
• Global Awareness • Financial, Economic, Business, and Entrepreneurial Literacy • Civic Literacy—Community Service • Health Literacy	• Creativity and Innovation • Critical Thinking and Problem Solving • Communication and Collaboration
INFORMATION, MEDIA, AND TECHNOLOGY SKILLS	**LIFE AND CAREER SKILLS**
• Information Literacy • Media Literacy • ICT (Information, Communications, and Technology) Literacy	• Flexibility and Adaptability • Initiative and Self-Direction • Social and Cross-Cultural Skills • Productivity and Accountability • Leadership and Responsibility

Source: Adapted from Partnership for 21st Century Skills Framework, www.p21.org/index.php?option=com_content&task=view&id=254&Itemid=120.

As you read the content and do the exercises in *Keys to Learning Strategies for Success*, you will grow in every area of this framework. There are links between these 21st century skills and what you will be reading and doing in the weeks to come, and the Personal Portfolio activity at the end of each chapter indicates which 21st century skills it builds. In fact, the three thinking skills that take focus in this text—analytical, creative, and practical—are all included within the framework. These three thinking skills will help you achieve your most important goals because they are critical to delivering what the world needs workers to do.

How can successful intelligence help you achieve your goals?

How do you define *intelligence?* Is an intelligent person someone who excels in high-level analytical courses? A successful professional in science or law? Or a person who scores well on standardized tests such as IQ (intelligence quotient) tests? The idea of using an IQ test to gauge intelligence and predict success is based on the belief that each person is born with a fixed amount of intelligence that can be measured. However, cutting-edge researchers such as Robert Sternberg and Carol Dweck have challenged these ideas.[3]

When test anxiety caused Sternberg (a psychologist and dean of students at Tufts University) to score poorly on IQ and other standardized tests during elementary school, he delivered what was expected of him—very little. However, his fourth-grade teacher turned his life around when she expected more. Sternberg has conducted extensive research supporting his sense that traditional intelligence measurements lock people into poor performance and often do not reflect their potential.[4]

Stanford psychologist Carol Dweck also had a life-changing experience when, as a young researcher, she conducted an experiment to see how elementary school children coped with failure. She gave students a set of puzzles that grew increasingly difficult. To her surprise, certain students welcomed the tough puzzles and saw failure as an opportunity. "They knew that human qualities, such as intellectual skills, could be cultivated through effort. And that's what they were doing—getting smarter. Not only weren't they discouraged by failure, they didn't even think they were failing. They thought they were learning."[5] Dweck's research since then has focused on the potential for increasing intelligence and the attitude that fosters that potential (more on that attitude later in the chapter).

The research of Sternberg, Dweck, and others suggests that intelligence is *not* fixed; people have the capacity to increase intelligence as they learn. In other words, *you can grow what you are born with.* Studies in neuroscience support this perspective, showing that the brain can develop throughout life if you continue to learn. Recent brain research shows that when you are learning, your brain and nerve cells (neurons) are forming new connections (synapses) from cell to cell by growing new branches (dendrites).[6] These increased connections then enable the brain to do and learn more.

The three thinking skills

How can you unlock your potential and achieve your important goals in college, work, and life? According to Sternberg, it takes three types of thinking: analytical (critical), creative, and practical. He calls this combination *successful intelligence,*[7] and he illustrates it with a story.

> Two boys are walking in a forest. They are quite different. The first boy's teachers think he is smart, his parents think he is smart, and as a result, he thinks he is smart. He has good test scores, good grades, and other good paper credentials that will get him far in his scholastic life.
>
> Few people consider the second boy smart. His test scores are nothing great, his grades aren't so good, and his other paper credentials are, in general, marginal. At best, people would call him shrewd or street smart.
>
> As the two boys walk along in the forest, they encounter a problem—a huge, furious, hungry-looking grizzly bear, charging straight at them. The first boy, calculating that the grizzly bear will overtake them in 17.3 seconds, panics. In this state, he looks at the second boy, who is calmly taking off his hiking boots and putting on his jogging shoes.
>
> The first boy says to the second boy, "You must be crazy. There is no way you are going to outrun that grizzly bear!"
>
> The second boy replies, "That's true. But all I have to do is outrun you!"[8]

This story shows that successful goal achievement and problem solving require more than book smarts. When confronted with a problem, using *only* analytical thinking put the first boy at a disadvantage. On the other hand, the second boy *analyzed* the situation, *created* options, and took practical *action.* He knew his goal—to live to tell the tale—and he achieved it.

How thinking skills move you toward your goals

Sternberg explains that although those who score well on tests display strong recall and analytical skills, they are not necessarily able to put their knowledge to work.[9] No matter how high you score on a library science test, for example, as a librarian you will also need to be able to devise useful keyword searches (creative thinking) and communicate effectively with patrons and other librarians (practical thinking). Of course, having *only* practical "street smarts" isn't enough either. Neither boy in the bear story, if rushed to the hospital with injuries sustained in a showdown with the bear, would want to be treated by someone lacking in analytical skills.

What do each of the three thinking skills contribute to goal achievement?

■ *Analytical thinking.* Commonly known as *critical thinking,* analytical thinking starts by engaging with information through asking questions and then proceeds to analyzing and evaluating information, often to work through a problem or decision. It often involves comparing, contrasting, and cause-and-effect thinking.

■ *Creative thinking.* Creative thinking concerns generating new and different ideas and approaches to problems, and, often, viewing the world in ways that disregard convention. It often involves imagining and considering different perspectives. Creative thinking also means taking information that you already know and thinking about it in a new way.

■ *Practical thinking.* Practical thinking refers to putting what you've learned into action to solve a problem or make a decision. Practical thinking often means learning from experience and emotional intelligence (explained later in the chapter), enabling you to work effectively with others and to accomplish goals despite obstacles.

Together, these abilities move you toward a goal, as Sternberg explains:

> Analytical thinking is required to solve problems and to judge the quality of ideas. Creative intelligence is required to formulate good problems and ideas in the first place. Practical intelligence is needed to use the ideas and their analysis in an effective way in one's everyday life.[10]

Why is developing successful intelligence so important to your success?

1. *It improves understanding and achievement, increasing your value in school and on the job.* People with critical, creative, and practical thinking skills are in demand because they can apply what they know to new situations, innovate, and accomplish their goals.

2. *It boosts your motivation.* Because it helps you understand how learning propels you toward goals and gives you ways to move toward those goals, it increases your willingness to work.

3. *It shows you where you can grow.* Students who have trouble with tests and other analytical skills can see the role that creative and practical thinking play. Students who test well but have trouble innovating or taking action can improve their creative and practical skills.

Although thinking skills provide tools with which you can achieve college and life goals, you need (motivation) to put them to work and grow from your efforts. Explore a mindset that will motivate you to vault over that bar (and then set a higher one).

→ MOTIVATION
A goal-directed force that moves a person to action.

How can a **"growth mindset"** *motivate you to persist?*

Different people have different forces or *motivators*—grades, love of a subject, the drive to earn a degree—that encourage them to keep pushing ahead. Motivators can change with time and situations. Your motivation can have either an external or internal *locus of control*—meaning that you are motivated either by external factors (your parents, circumstances, luck, grades, instructors' feedback, and so on) or internal factors (values and attitudes).

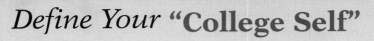

GET ANALYTICAL!

Define Your "College Self"

Making the most of the opportunities that college offers starts with knowing, as much as you can, about who you are and what you want. Analyze your "college self" using questions like the following to think through your personal profile. Write and save your description to revisit later in the course.

What is your student status—traditional or returning, full- or part-time?

_____

_____

How long are you planning to be in your current college? Is it likely that you will transfer?

_____

_____

What goal, or goals, do you aim to achieve by going to college?

_____

_____

_____

_____

What family and work obligations do you have?

_____

_____

What is your culture, ethnicity, gender, age, lifestyle?

_____

_____

What is your current living situation?

_____

_____

What do you feel are your biggest challenges in college?

_____

_____

_____

_____

What do you like to study, and why does it interest you?

_____

_____

_____

_____

Often, you will be motivated by some combination of external and internal factors, but internal motivation may have a greater influence on success. Why? Although you cannot control what happens around you, you *can* control your attitude, or *mindset*, and the actions that come from that mindset. Based on years of research, Carol Dweck has determined that the perception that talent and intelligence can develop with effort—what she calls a *growth mindset*— promotes success. "This view creates a love of learning and resilience that is essential for great accomplishment," reports Dweck. People with a growth mindset "understand that no one has ever accomplished great things—not Mozart, Darwin, or Michael Jordan—without years of passionate practice and learning."[11]

By contrast, people with a *fixed mindset* believe that they have a set level of talent and intelligence. They think their ability to succeed matches what they've been born with, and they tend to resist effort. "In one world [that of the fixed mindset], effort is a bad thing. It . . . means you're not smart or talented. If you were, you wouldn't need effort. In the other world [growth mindset], effort is what *makes* you smart or talented."[12]

For example, two students do poorly on an anatomy midterm. One blames the time of day of the test and her dislike of the subject, whereas the other feels that she didn't study enough. The first student couldn't change the subject or meeting time, of course, and didn't change her approach to the material (no extra effort). As you may expect, she did poorly on the final. The second student put in more study time after the midterm (increased, focused effort) and improved her grade on the final as a result. This student knows that "smart is as smart does."

You don't have to be born with a growth mindset. *You can build one.* "You have a choice," says Dweck. "Mindsets are just beliefs. They're powerful beliefs, but they're just something in your mind, and you can change your mind."[13] One way to change your mind is through specific actions that demonstrate your beliefs. Such actions include being responsible, practicing academic integrity, facing your fears, and approaching failure as an opportunity to learn and improve.

Build self-esteem with responsible actions

You may think that you need to have a strong sense of self-esteem to take action toward your goals. In fact, the reverse is true. Taking responsible action builds strong self-esteem because it gives you something to be proud of. Your actions change your thinking. Basketball coach Rick Pitino explains: "If you have established a great work ethic and have begun the discipline that is inherent with that, you will automatically begin to feel better about yourself."[14]

A growth mindset helps you build self-esteem because it encourages you to put forth effort. If you know you have the potential to do better, you will be more likely to try. A research study of employees taking a course in computer training supports this idea. Half the group, told their success depended on innate ability, lost confidence by the end of the course. By contrast, the other half, told their skills could be developed through practice, reported a good deal *more* confidence after they had completed the same course and made, in many cases, the same mistakes.[15]

Even simple responsible actions can build the foundation for powerful self-esteem. What actions will you take to build your confidence? Consider using Key 1.6 as a starting point for ideas. Taking daily responsible actions such as these will help you to succeed in any course. Your efforts will enable you to grow no matter what your starting point.

> **SELF-ESTEEM** Belief in your value as a person that builds as you achieve your goals.

Courtesy of Shutterstock

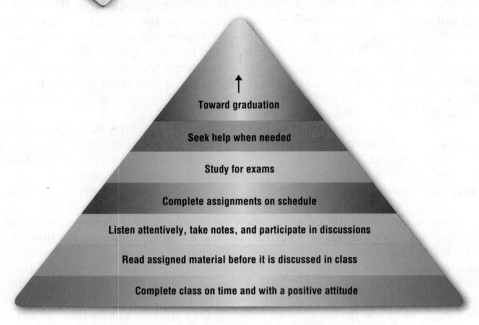

Toward graduation

Seek help when needed

Study for exams

Complete assignments on schedule

Listen attentively, take notes, and participate in discussions

Read assigned material before it is discussed in class

Complete class on time and with a positive attitude

Face your fears

Anything unknown—starting college, meeting new people—can be frightening. Facing fear with a growth mindset will allow you to proceed with courage as you reignite your motivation and learn. Following a step-by-step process can help you deal with otherwise overwhelming feelings.

1. *Acknowledge fears.*   Naming your fear can begin to release its hold on you. "I'm worried about understanding a Shakespeare play I have to read."
2. *Examine fears.*   Determine what exactly is causing your fear. Sometimes deeper fears emerge. "I feel that if I don't understand the play, I won't do well on the test and it will affect my GPA. That could cause trouble with my financial aid or my major."
3. *Develop and implement a plan.*   Come up with ways to manage your fear, choose how to move forward, and put the plan into action. "I will rent a film of the play and watch it after I read. I will talk to my instructor about my concerns."

When you've put your plan into action, you've done what a growth mindset gives you the power to do—take action and learn from the experience. Then perhaps next time you face a similar situation, your fear may not be as strong.

Learn from failure

Failure approached with a growth mindset can spark motivation, showing you what you can do better and driving you to improve. Increased effort in the face of failure is a hallmark of successful people—witness the fact that Michael Jordan got cut from his high school basketball team as a sophomore (and clearly took that as a cue to work harder).

However, for people with a fixed mindset, failure is evidence of low intelligence and ability and means that you should give up and try something else. "This mindset gives you no good recipe for overcoming it," says Dweck. "If failure means you lack competence or potential—that you are a failure—where do you go from there?"[16]

Approach failure as a "problem to be faced, dealt with, and learned from."[17] Employ analytical, creative, and practical thinking as you take action.

■ *Analyze what happened.* Look carefully at what caused the situation. For example, imagine that after a long night of studying for a chemistry test, you forgot to complete a U.S. history paper due the next day. You realize that your focus on the test caused you to neglect everything else. Now you may face a lower grade on your paper if you turn it in late, or you may be inclined to rush it and turn in a product that isn't as good as it could be.

■ *Come up with creative ways to improve the situation and change for the future.* In the present, you can request an appointment with the instructor to discuss the paper. For the future, you can make a commitment to set alarms in your planner and to check due dates more often.

■ *Put your plan into action now—and what you've learned into action in the future.* Talk with the instructor and see if you can hand in your paper late. If you decide you have learned to pay more attention to deadlines, in the future you might work backward from your paper due date, setting dates for individual tasks related to the paper and planning to have it done two days before it is due to have time for last-minute corrections.

People who can manage the emotions produced by failure learn from the experience. They also demonstrate the last of this chapter's ingredients in the recipe for success—emotional intelligence.

Why do you need emotional intelligence?

Success in a diverse world depends on relationships, and effective relationships demand emotional intelligence. Psychologists John Mayer, Peter Salovey, and David Caruso define *emotional intelligence* (EI) as the ability to understand "one's own and others' emotions and the ability to use this information as a guide to thinking and behavior."[18] Reading this definition carefully shows it isn't enough to just *understand* what you and others feel. An emotionally intelligent person uses that understanding to make choices about how to *think* and how to *act*.

In the past, and perhaps for some even today, the "head" (thought) was thought of as separate from, and perhaps more valuable than, the "heart" (emotion). However, modern science connects thought and emotion, and values both. "Emotions influence both what we think about and how we think," says Caruso. "We cannot check our emotions at the door because emotions and thought are linked—they cannot, and should not, be separated."[19]

Emotions also connect you to other people, as recent research has demonstrated. When a friend of yours is happy, sad, or fearful, you may experience similar feelings out of concern or friendship. Your brain and nervous system have cells called *mirror neurons* that mimic an observed emotion, allowing you to "participate" in the feeling even though it comes from somewhere else. An MRI brain scan would show that the same area of your friend's brain that lit up during this emotional experience lit up in your brain as well.[20]

GET CREATIVE!

Consider How to Connect

Making connections with people and groups in your school early can benefit you later on. Brainstorm how you would like to spend whatever time you have available outside of your obligations (class time, work, family). On paper or on your computer, list your ideas. Try one or more of the following questions as a starting point:

If you had no fear, what horizon-broadening experience would you sign up for?

_____

_____

When you were in elementary school, what were your favorite activities? Which ones might translate into current interests and pursuits?

_____

_____

What kinds of organizations, activities, groups, experiences, or people make you think, "Wow, I want to do that"?

_____

_____

Think about the people that you feel bring out the best in you. What do you like to do with them? What kinds of activities are they involved with?

_____

_____

How emotional intelligence promotes success

Two short stories illustrate the power of emotional intelligence.

The more able you are to work and communicate with others, the more you will learn as well as develop teamwork skills.
Courtesy of Blend Images/Alamy

■ *Two applicants are competing for a job at your office.* The first has every skill the job requires, but doesn't respond well to your cues when you interview him. He answers questions indirectly and keeps going back to what he wants to say instead. The second isn't as skilled, but you feel during the interview as though you are talking with a friend. He listens carefully, picks up on your emotional cues, and indicates that he intends to make up for any lack of skill with a willingness to learn on the job. Whom would you hire?

■ *Two students are part of a group you are working with on a project.* One always gets her share of the job done but has no patience for anyone who misses a deadline. She is quick to criticize group members. The other is sometimes prepared, sometimes not, but always has a sense of what is going on with the group and responds to it. She works to make up for it when she hasn't gotten everything done, and when she is on top of her tasks she helps others. Which person would you want to work with again?

To be clear: Skills are crucial. The most emotionally tuned-in person in the world, for example, can't perform surgery without medical training. However, the role of emotional intelligence in communication and relationships makes it a strong predictor of success in work and life, as indicated by the following conclusions of research using an assessment measuring EI (MSCEIT).[21]

▶ Emotionally intelligent people are more competent in social situations and have higher quality relationships.
▶ Managers in the workplace with high EI have more productive working relationships and greater personal integrity.
▶ Employees scoring high in EI were more likely to receive positive ratings from peers and salary raises.
▶ Lower levels of EI are connected to higher amounts of drug, alcohol, and tobacco use, as well as aggression and conflict in teens.

The bottom line: More emotional intelligence means stronger relationships and more goal achievement.

The abilities of emotional intelligence

Emotional intelligence is a set of skills, or abilities, that can be described as *reasoning with emotion* (an idea illustrating how thought and emotion work together). Key 1.7 shows how you move through these skills when you reason with emotion.

These skills allow you to create the best possible outcomes from your interactions. Given that you will interact with others in almost every aspect of school, work, and life, EI is a pretty important tool. You will see references to emotional intelligence throughout the text.

How might emotional intelligence fit into the rest of the skills discussed in this chapter? Think of it as *thinking skills applied to relationships*. Putting emotional intelligence to work means taking in and analyzing how you and others feel, shifting your thinking based on those feelings, and taking action in response—all with the purpose of achieving a goal.

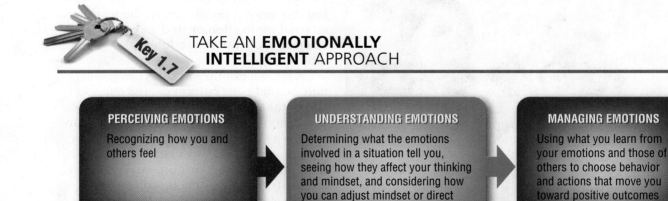

Key 1.7 TAKE AN **EMOTIONALLY INTELLIGENT** APPROACH

PERCEIVING EMOTIONS	UNDERSTANDING EMOTIONS	MANAGING EMOTIONS
Recognizing how you and others feel	Determining what the emotions involved in a situation tell you, seeing how they affect your thinking and mindset, and considering how you can adjust mindset or direct thinking in a productive way	Using what you learn from your emotions and those of others to choose behavior and actions that move you toward positive outcomes

Source: Adapted from John D. Mayer, Peter Salovey, and David R. Caruso, "Emotional Intelligence: New Ability or Eclectic Traits?" September 2008, *American Psychologist, 63*(6), pp. 505–507.

The power and passion of motivation

What is the difference between internal and external motivation?

Motivation can change your life! Read that statement again. *Motivation can change your life!* Ask any successful businessperson. Ask your favorite athlete or actor. Ask your classmates who ace every exam, project, or paper. It is their burning desire—their aspiration to succeed, to live an exceptional life, and reach their goals that changed their lives and got them to where they are today. Motivation is a force that can transform your attitude, alter the course of your performance, intensify your actions, and illuminate your future. Motivation can help you live a life that reflects your true potential. Motivation can help you live a life beyond your grandest dreams.

> The moment you begin to do what you really want to do, your life becomes a totally different kind of life."
>
> —B. Fuller

If you have a need or desire to change your motivation level or attitude toward personal and academic success, there are steps you can take to help you with this goal. Some of the steps we describe will be easy to implement and others will greatly challenge you, but taken seriously, each step can assist you in discovering who you really are and what you want in life and help you find the motivation you need to change. No one can do this for you.

There are two types of motivation: **external and internal**. *External motivation* is the weaker of the two because, as the title suggests, there are *external forces or people* causing you to do something. You do not own it. External motivators may be things or people such as your parents, spouse, or partner pushing you to complete your degree; your supervisor telling you to do "x, y, or z" or you will be fired; or even your instructors giving you an exam to make sure you have done the reading. You may do the things asked of you, but the reason for doing them is external. You do not necessarily choose to do them on your own.

Internal motivation is uniquely yours. It is *energy* inside of you—pushing you to go after what you want. Internal motivation is a strong and driving force because you own it. There are no external forces or people telling you that you must do it—it comes from your desire *to be something, to have something, to attain a goal that you truly desire, or to solve a problem.* Successful people live in the world of internal motivation or find ways to convert external motivation into internal motivation.

A simple example of this conversion may be that your current degree requires you to take classes whose value or purpose you cannot understand. You may ask yourself, "Why would an interior design major have to take an algebra class?" The class is hard, math is not your thing, the chapters are frustrating and difficult to read, and math has little to do with your interests, career goals, or overall life plan. The challenge for you is to find an internal reason to move forward—a rationale for how math is going to help you, now and in the future. This is called *internalizing.* Perhaps you

How can doing something you love and enjoy increase your motivation level?
Bananastock

want to own your own interior design business—a business that will require the use of math. Internalizing the content of this math class and it requirements can motivate you to do well.

By converting this external motivation (a requirement for your degree) into internal motivation (something that can help you run your business), the math class will become easier and more relevant, because you have found a way to link it to your success, your goals, your money, your health, your family, or your overall life plan.

By internalizing, you see that good math skills can help you land a work-study job in design shop. You find that good math skills can help you create an effective personal budget plan and help you save money. You find that the more you learn about the logic and process of math, the easier it is to solve problems and think more critically, thus helping you perform better in other classes. By silencing your negative self-talk about math (*"I hate math," "Math is so stupid," "I'm going to fail this class"*), you are able to internalize the rewards of the class and own the outcome. You have made a conversion.

The need **to be more**

What is the relationship between motivation and Maslow?

One important way to think about motivation is to consider the work of Abraham Maslow, a renowned psychologist who in 1943 introduced the **Hierarchy of Basic Needs** in his landmark paper, "A Theory of Human Motivation." His basic premise is that every human being is motivated by a set of basic needs and we will do whatever it takes to have these things in our lives. The bottom four levels are what he calls *deficiency needs,* and they include things such as the need for food, air, water, security, family, health, sexual intimacy, self-esteem, achievement, and respect from others. The top level is called a *psychological need,* and it involves self-actualization, personal growth, and fulfillment. See Key 1.8.

Self-actualization, the top level, is perhaps the most obscure and abstract to understand, but it is the most important when it comes to motivation. Maslow suggests that we all have a basic, driving desire to matter—to have a life where we are doing what we were meant to do. Self-actualization can also be described as living at our "peak" and to be fully ourselves. The renowned psychologist, author, and speaker Dr. Wayne Dyer describes self-actualization as meaning "You *must* be what you *can* be." By this he suggests that if you know you are living a life that is "less" than what you know you are capable of living, true happiness will never be yours.

Conquering the **"First-generation gap"**

How do you make it and stay motivated when you're the first in the family?

Many college students are first-generation students, meaning that their parents' highest level of education is a high school diploma or less. This may not seem like such a big deal, but it can be on many levels. If you are a

SELF-ACTUALIZATION
Personal growth, fulfillment, reaching your potential socially, compassion

ESTEEM NEEDS
Self-esteem, achievement, recognition, earning the respect of others, independence

LOVING/BELONGINGNESS NEEDS
Friendship, family, affection, relationships, belonging in work groups, sexual intimacy

SAFETY NEEDS
Security of body, security of employment, having resources, protection from the elements, law, order, stability

PHYSIOLOGICAL NEEDS
Basic life needs such as air, food, water, sleep, shelter, warmth, sex, excretion

first-generation student, you may not have the support and understanding of family members who know firsthand the pressures of what you're going through. It may seem as if they are not supportive. This could be true, but more than likely, they are unaware how to offer support because college is new for them, too. Therefore, it is so very important that you find support beyond what your family may be able to offer. You will encounter many people at your college who are first-generation students and they can help guide you. Many non-first-generation students, faculty, staff, and personal friends will be able to offer you support, too.

In a personal survey, first-generation students responded that their reasons for attending college were to be well off financially and provide their children with better opportunities than they had.

Statistics from years of research with first-generation students also show that many are more likely to have families of their own (spouses and children), are more likely to be older (over 30), come from families with lower incomes, work more full-time hours off campus, enroll part time, be less academically prepared, and attend community colleges. It was also found that first-generation students drop out more frequently than non-first-generation students (U.S. Department of Education, 1998).

Don't despair, however. These statistics do not have to predict your future, who you are, or where you are going. You are not tied to what others have or have not done. This is your life, your future, your beginning. Being a first-generation student can have many rewards, such as an esteemed sense of accomplishment, the ability to serve as a mentor for family and friends, and the ability to increase your socioeconomic status.

As you begin your studies, however, you may find that you face some resistance from some friends and family members. You may even find that some relationships suffer or end because of your pursuit of self-improvement. Don't let this discourage you. Again, this is one of the many changes that may occur in your personal life as you embark on your college journey. Before ending a relationship, try talking to the other person and letting him or her know that you still care, while holding fast to the notion that your own life and your own future is of great importance, too. You may find that some people leave you. You may also find that you have to leave some people. Some friends may not be able to rejoice in the fact that you are going to college because they feel that you are leaving them behind; others will simply be jealous of the fact that you are bettering yourself and they are not. If those around you do not support you and your dreams and they cannot be reasoned with, you may have to part company for the sake of growth and future security.

As you begin your studies, let yourself undergo the whole spectrum of the college experience. Get involved with your classmates. Use college resources to your best advantage. Establish meaningful relationships, and enjoy the ride. Yes, you may face challenges on a day-to-day basis, but growth and change include challenges. It only means you are moving. Expanding! Growing!

If you are a first-generation student, you can do many things to help ensure your success and graduation. They include the following:

What support groups exist on your campus to help first generation students?
Courtesy of Shutterstock

▶ Deal with family conflicts and misunderstandings early and quickly. Talk with them about your plans, daily schedules, and college culture. Keep family members involved so they don't feel left out or that you are abandoning them.

▶ Don't let feelings of guilt or "selling out" derail your goals and plans. Yes, you may be the first in your family to attend college, but with your guidance and mentoring, you will not be the last.

▶ Work hard to find a support group, advisor, counselor, peer, or professor who understands your situation and ask them for advice. Talk to people. Make friends. Associate.

▶ Try to meet people who have been at your institution for at least one term so that you can learn "survival tips" from them.

▶ Immerse yourself socially and academically at your institution. Make use of every source of academic, financial, career, and cultural assistance possible.

▶ Find a healthy balance among your work, family, and college studies. Remember, this is your future. One way to look at this is to ask yourself, "Is my current job my future? Is it my destiny? Can I do what I am doing right now for the next 25 years?"

▶ Involve your family and friends in your education as much as possible. Ask them to attend events with you. Encourage them to begin their studies, too.

▶ Don't be ashamed of what you are doing and for trying to improve your station in life. Dimming your own light does nothing to help others see more clearly. This is a major step forward, and you should be proud of yourself for taking it.

▶ Have an open mind and enjoy the process. This is the time to learn, grow, explore, and prosper.

Achieving your potential and increasing your motivation

> "Watch your thoughts, they become words. Watch your words, they become actions. Watch your actions, they become habits. Watch your habits, they become character. Watch your character, it becomes your destiny."
>
> —Frank Outlaw

What are the cornerstones of personal and professional success?

"I am a winner."
"I fail at everything I do."

"I am a dedicated person."
"I don't really care about anything."

"I hate getting up in the morning."
"I can't wait for my day to start."

As you can see by the two different perspectives above, your attitude about how you approach life, relationships, problems, and goals can mean the difference between being a motivated, inspired, and successful person or a weary, frightened, and unsuccessful person.

The reason that we have included the following *Strategies for Lifetime Success* is to help you see that by focusing on you—becoming a person who knows where you're going, what you want, and what you have to offer—your motivation and passion for learning and growing will flourish. By knowing more about yourself, you can then establish a clearer vision of your true potential. Take your time and read each point carefully. Consider the questions asked and complete the chapter activities to assist you with your motivation plan.

Point 1: Develop a new attitude

Your attitude—new or old, good or bad—belongs to you. If your attitude needs changing, no one can do it for you. Now is the perfect time to begin changing your attitude if it needs an adjustment, because small changes in the way you approach life can mean major changes to your success throughout your college career.

Just as some people embrace the attitude of *learned helplessness* (letting your past or other people's failures dictate your future), you can just as easily embrace the attitude of learned optimism. A *pessimist* finds bad news in most situations; he or she lives in a world that has a cloud over it all the time. *Optimists,* on the other hand, can handle bad news and difficult challenges because they have a positive way of viewing the world. Optimists learn how to determine why things went wrong and can adjust and fix the underlying problem.

People actually create their own success, reach their goals, and become successful by embracing a positive outlook on life. Conversely, a great deal of personal misery and failure is caused by adopting a bad attitude and by embracing negative feelings and *self-defeating behaviors*. Take the assessment in Key 1.9 to determine your current attitudes.

Select one of the self-defeating habits that you checked from the list and state exactly what your behavior is and why you think you are experiencing this problem.

Do you think that surrounding yourself with optimistic, motivated people will help you succeed? Why or why not?
Courtesy of Shutterstock

_____

_____

_____

_____

_____

Review the checklist below of typical self-defeating habits that can be changed by adopting the right attitude. Place a check by the ones that relate to you and your behavior:

☐ I am frequently depressed, lonely, sad, frustrated, worried, or frightened.

☐ I spend a lot of time with people who aren't very motivated to excel in college.

☐ I waste a lot of time watching TV, playing video games, texting, scanning Facebook, and so on.

☐ I get very uptight and negative when I have to take a test.

☐ I am more worried about associating with friends than I am about my grades.

☐ I spend money that I shouldn't spend and charge things on my credit card that I can't afford.

☐ I eat too much junk food when I get stressed.

☐ I don't exercise properly when I feel depressed.

☐ I procrastinate a lot and I lose my temper quickly when I am under pressure.

☐ I tend to give up easily when things get hard.

☐ I am having trouble with my living arrangement.

☐ I have trouble making it through the day without some form of stimulant such as coffee, cigarettes, drugs, or alcohol.

☐ I daydream in some of my classes.

☐ I turn in my assignments late and make up excuses as to why.

☐ I daydream a lot about how things used to be.

☐ I cut class when I feel depressed or unprepared.

☐ I don't feel comfortable talking to my advisor and instructors.

☐ I don't feel like I am making many friends here, and I often feel lonely and discouraged.

☐ I do not participate in any co or extracurricular activities.

☐ I spend a lot of my time doing nothing.

☐ I hate my job.

☐ Some of my classes are awful, and I cut them often.

If you checked off five or more statements on this chart, you may be experiencing self defeating behavior. You will need to consider carefully how to eliminate these behaviors from your life as you work on a personal attitude adjustment.

Develop five action steps to help you change your attitude and overcome this self-defeating behavior.

1. _____

2. _____

3. _____

4. _____

5. _____

Point 2: Make excellence a habit

As you work to change some of your habits and become a highly motivated person, one practice you need to embrace is excellence in everything you do. The average person is happy doing just enough to get by. Those who excel and succeed demand excellence from themselves in everything they do. If you don't think excellence matters, consider these points: Would you want a doctor who

"NEVER leave well enough alone. If it ain't broke, fix it; take fast and make it faster; take smart and make it smarter; take good and make it great."

—Cigna Advertisement

If 99.9% were good enough, then:

- 12 newborns would be given to the wrong parents in the United States every day.
- 7 people would be buried in the wrong graves or cremated incorrectly daily in the United States.
- 292 book titles published in the United States would be shipped with the wrong covers on them this year.
- 400 entries in Webster's Dictionary would be misspelled.
- 1,200,000 credit cards held in the United States would have incorrect cardholder information on the black magnetic strip on the back of the card.
- 79,000 drug prescriptions would be written incorrectly this year in the United States
- 32,000 of the Library of Congress's books would be filed on the shelves incorrectly.

EXCELLENCE MATTERS!

cheated his or her way through medical school to operate on you or your child? Would you want a pilot who didn't perform very well on the simulated crash test to fly your plane? Would you want to cross a bridge every day that was designed by an engineer who cheated his way through design class? Excellence matters! Key 1.10 illustrates the importance of excellence in several real-life situations.

Point 3: Overcome your doubts and fears

Success is a great motivator, but so is fear. Actually, fear probably motivates more people than anything else. Unfortunately, fear motivates most people to hold back, to doubt themselves, to stay in their comfort zones, and to accomplish much less than they could have without the fear.

Your own personal fears may be one of the biggest obstacles to reaching your potential. If you are afraid, you are not alone; everyone has fears. Isn't it interesting that *our fears are learned?* As an infant, you were born with only **two fears:** a fear of falling and a fear of loud noises. As you got older, you added to your list of fears. And if you are like most people, you may have let your fears dominate parts of your life, saying things to yourself like: "What if I try and fail?" "What if people laugh at me for thinking I can do this?" or "What if someone finds out that this is my dream?" You have two choices where fear is concerned. You can let fear dominate your life, or you can focus on those things you really want to accomplish, put your fears behind you, and *go for it.*

Dr. Robert Schuller, minister, motivational speaker, and author, once asked, *"What would you attempt to do if you could not fail?"* This is an important question for anyone, especially someone trying to increase his or her motivation level. In the spaces below, work through this idea by answering the questions truthfully. We have adapted and expanded this question for the purpose of this exercise.

1. What would you attempt to do if you could not fail?

   _____

   _____

   _____

   _____

   _____

"People become who they are. Even Beethoven became Beethoven."

—Randy Newman

2. Beyond the answers "I'm afraid" or "Fear," *why* are you not doing this thing?

_____

_____

_____

_____

3. If you did this thing and were successful at it, how would your life change? Be specific.

_____

_____

_____

_____

_____

Point 4: Put adversity and failure into perspective

Thomas Edison was once asked how it felt to fail over 1,000 times at making the light bulb work. He reportedly responded, "I have never failed at making the light bulb work. I successfully identified over 1,000 ways that it would not work." Edison looked on his unsuccessful attempts to build the electric light bulb positively. He saw it as eliminating ways that it would not work, not as failure. Failure is just a temporary byproduct of the success that lies ahead if you persevere. A part of being motivated means learning to deal with failure and setbacks. Most people compile a string of failures before they have great success.

Have you ever given up on something too quickly, or gotten discouraged and quit? That feeling is quite different from completing a goal and getting an adrenaline rush from success. Can you think of a time when you were unfair to yourself because you didn't stay with something long enough? Completing a goal feels much different than giving up. Have you ever stopped doing something you really loved because somebody laughed at you or teased you about it? Doing what brings you joy in the face of adversity gives you a feeling much different than caving in to peer pressure. Overcoming failure and learning from mistakes make victory much more rewarding. Motivated people know that losing and making mistakes are necessary aspects of winning: the difference between winning and losing is the ability to get up, stand tall, and try again. Winning is getting up one more time than you are knocked down. A successful person is successful because he or she hung on **just one moment longer** than the person who gave up.

"If you fall down or if you're knocked down, try to land on your back because if you can look up, you can get up."

—Les Brown

When faced with adversity, what techniques have you used in the past to survive and move on?

Michael Ventura/Alamy

Point 5: Eliminate negative self-talk and the "I Can't" syndrome

Try as you might, sometimes harmful emotions, fear of the unknown, and that nagging little voice inside your head (negative self-talk) can cause you problems. Negative self-talk usually appears when you are afraid, uneasy, hurt, angry, depressed, or lonely. By the time you read this, you may have experienced these feelings. When you experience change, your body, mind, and soul typically go through a process of physical and emotional change as well. Learning to recognize these symptoms in order to control them can help you control the stress that can accompany change. You may have to develop a new attitude.

Your attitude is yours. It belongs to you. You own it. Good or bad, happy or sad, optimistic or pessimistic, it is yours and you are responsible for it. However, your attitude is greatly influenced by situations in your life and by the people with whom you associate. Developing a winning, optimistic attitude can be hard yet extremely rewarding work and beneficial to the change process. Motivated and successful people have learned that one's attitude is the mirror to one's soul.

Listen to yourself for a few days. Are you more of an optimist or a pessimist? Do you hear yourself whining, complaining, griping, and finding fault with everything and everybody around you? Do you blame others for things that are wrong in your life? Do you blame your bad grades on your professors? Is someone else responsible for your unhappiness? If these thoughts or comments are in your head, you are suffering from the ***"I CAN'T" Syndrome*** (**I**rritated, **C**ontaminated, **A**ngry, **N**egative **T**houghts). This pessimistic condition can negatively influence every aspect of your life, from your self-esteem, to your motivation level, to your academic performance, to your relationships, to your career success.

If you want to eliminate ***I CAN'T*** from your life, consider the following tips:

▶ Think about the many positive aspects of your life and show gratitude for them.

▶ Work every day to find the good in people, places, and things.

▶ Eliminate negative thoughts that enter your mind before you begin your day.

▶ Discover what is holding you back and what you need to push you forward.

▶ Visualize your success—visualize yourself actually being who and what you want to be.

▶ Locate and observe positive, optimistic people and things in your life.

▶ Make a list of who helps you, supports you, and helps you feel positive; then make a point to be around them more.

▶ Take responsibility for your own actions and their consequences.

▶ Force yourself to find five positive things a day for which to be thankful.

You've seen the difference between an optimist and a pessimist. They are both everywhere—at work, at school, and maybe in your own family. Think of the optimist for a moment. You've probably sat next to him or her in one of your classes or seen him or her at work—the person who always seems to be happy, motivated, bubbling with personality, organized, and ready for whatever comes his or her way. Optimists greet people as they enter the room, they respond in class, they volunteer for projects, and they have a presence about them that is positive and lively. You may even look at these people out of the corner of your eye and ask, "What are they on?"

Positive, upbeat, and motivated people are easy to spot. You can basically see their attitude in the way they walk, the way they carry themselves, the way they approach people, and the way they treat others.

Be wary, however, of "the others." The ones you need to avoid. Whiners. Degraders. Attackers. Manipulators. Pessimists. Backstabbers. Abusers. Cowards. Two-faced racists, sexists, ageists, homophobes, ethnocentrists. These people carry around an aura so negative that it can almost be seen as a dark cloud above them. They degrade others because they do not like themselves. They find fault with everything because their own lives are a mess. They do nothing and then attack you for being motivated and trying to improve your life. We call them **contaminated people.** Contaminated people are unhappy with who they are. To make themselves feel better, they try to tear down people who are the opposite of what they are. They belittle your positive actions and try to make your life as miserable as their lives are.

Sure, everyone has bad days and bad stretches in his or her life. **This is not the person** we are talking about here. With contaminated people, being negative and trying to bring you down is epidemic in their lives. It is the way they operate all the time. It is constant. Having a bad day and complaining is normal for some people at various times, but contaminated people see life (and you) as negative and bad on an hourly and daily basis.

Point 6: Identify and clarify what you value in life

If you have been highly motivated to accomplish a goal in the past, this achievement was probably tied to something you valued a great deal. Since most of what you do in life centers on what is truly important to you, you need to identify and then clarify what you value in your life—what really matters to you.

Values, self-esteem, motivation, and goal setting are all mixed up together, making it difficult to separate one from the other. The things you work to accomplish are directly connected to the things you value. Therefore, your *attitude* and *actions* are tied to your *values*. If you value an attitude or belief, your actions will be centered on these ideals. If you love to spend time with your friends and this is valuable to you, you will make the time for this on a regular basis. Why? Because having friends is a fundamental part of your value system. You like it and get pleasure from it, so you are motivated by it and you do it. It is that simple. Our values influence our actions. It is, once again, tied to Maslow's Hierarchy of Basic Needs.

Below, you will find a wide and varied list of personal qualities. Read over them carefully and circle the ones you truly value. Be careful and selective. Do *not* just randomly circle words. As criteria for each word you circle, ask yourself, "Can I defend why I value this in my life?" and "Is this truly something I value, or something I was told to value and never questioned why?" If you value something and it is not on the list, add it to one of the spaces at the end.

"Our souls are not hungry for fame, comfort, wealth, or power. These rewards create almost as many problems as they solve. Our souls are hungry for meaning, for the sense that we have figured out a way to live so that our lives matter."

—H. Kushner

Honesty	Affection	Punctuality	Respect
Frankness	Open-mindedness	Reliability	Trustworthiness
Sincerity	Wit/Humor	Spontaneity	Devotion
Frugality	Justice	Creativity	Caring
Spirituality	Friendliness	Energy	Intellect
Attentiveness	Conversation	Money	Security
Beauty	Enthusiasm	Positivism	Commitments
Foresightednes	Organization	Learning	Listening
Control	Comfort	Knowledge	Success
Athletic ability	Thoughtfulness	Independence	Courage
Safety	Fun	Excitement	Partying
Love	Friendship	Writing	Speaking
Reading	Family	Dependability	Teamwork
Time alone	Time w/friends	Phone calls	Walks
Exercise	Problem solving	Empowerment	Integrity
Service to others	Modesty	Strength	Tolerance
Imagination	Self-esteem	Food	Power
Winning	Goals	Risk taking	Change
Self-improvement	Forgiveness	Fairness	Optimism
Motivation	Trust	Direction in life	Giving
Working	Hobbies	Stability	Mentoring

_____ _____ _____ _____

_____ _____ _____ _____

_____ _____ _____ _____

_____ _____ _____ _____

Now that you have circled or written what you value, choose the five that you value the most. In other words, if you were *only* allowed to value five things in life, what five would you list below? In the space to the right of each value, rank them from 1 to 5 (1 being the most important to you, your life, your relationships, your actions, your education, and your career).

Take your time and give serious consideration to this activity, as you will need to refer back to this exercise later in this chapter.

LIST   **RANK**

✓ _____   _____

✓ _____   _____

✓ _____   _____

✓ _____   _____

✓ _____   _____

Now, look at your #1. Where did this value originate?

_____

_____

_____

_____

Defend why this is the one thing you value more than anything else in life.

_____

_____

_____

_____

How does this one value motivate you?

_____

_____

_____

Point 7: Take pride in your name and personal character

"My name?" you may ask. "What does my name have to do with anything?" The answer: At the end of the day, the end of the month, the end of your career, and the end of your life, your name and your character are all that you have. Taking pride in developing your character and protecting your good name can be a powerful motivational force.

Imagine for a moment that you are working with a group of students on a project for your English class. The project is to receive a major grade and you and your group will present your findings to a group of 300 students at a campus forum. Your group works hard and when you present the project, your group receives a standing ovation and earns an A. The name of each individual group member is read aloud as you stand to be recognized. Your name and project are also posted in a showcase. You are proud. Your hard work paid off. Your name now carries weight with your peers and among the faculty. It feels good.

Conversely, imagine that your group slacks off; the project is poorly prepared and received by the audience and your instructors. Your group earns an F on the project. Your name is associated with this project and your name and grade is posted with every other group. Your group is the only group to receive an F. It doesn't feel good.

Basically, it comes down to this: Every time you make a choice, every time you complete a project, every time you encounter another person, your actions define your character and your name. People admire and respect you when you make an honorable and moral choice, especially if it is a difficult decision. Both your character and your name are exclusively yours, and you are responsible for their well-being. When you care this passionately about your reputation and character, your life is governed by protecting your name. Your actions, beliefs, and decisions are all tied to this one belief: "My name and my reputation matter and I will do nothing to bring shame or embarrassment to my name."

Point 8: Develop a strong, personal guiding statement

You're wearing a t-shirt to class. It is not your normal, run-of-the-mill t-shirt, however. You designed this t-shirt for everyone to see and read. It is white with bright red letters. On the front of the t-shirt is

"Your character is determined by how you treat people who can do you no good and how you treat people who can't fight back."

—Abigail Van Buren

How can damage to your name and reputation negatively affect your overall success?
Courtesy of Shutterstock

written your **personal guiding statement**—the words by which you live. The words govern your life. What would your t-shirt say? Perhaps you will use the golden rule, "Do unto others . . ." It might be an adaptation of the Nike slogan, "Just Do It," or it might be something more profound such as, "I live my life to serve others and to try to make others' lives better," or "Be a blessing," or "Live, love, laugh."

Whatever your guiding statement, it must be yours. It can't be your parents', your professor's, or your best friend's statement. It must be based on something you value, and it must be strong enough to motivate you in hard, tough times. Your guiding statement must be so powerful that it will literally "guide you" when you are ethically challenged, broke, alone, angry, hurt, sad, or feeing vindictive. It is a statement that will guide you in relationships with family, friends, spouses, partners, or would-be love interests. It is a statement that gives direction to your daily actions. Think about how different your life would be if you woke up each morning and lived your guiding statement to the fullest.

One of the best ways to start working on your guiding statement is to look back at those values you earlier circled as important to you. If you value something, it may appear in your guiding statement. For example, if you circled the words *respect*, *giving*, and *optimism* among those you value, this is a basis for your statement. A guiding statement based on these words might read:

"I will live my life as a positive, optimistic, upbeat, motivated person who respects others and enjoys giving to others on a daily basis."

did you know

Tim McGraw

Tim McGraw, recording artist and country music sensation, was born in Louisiana in 1967. When he was 11 years old, he discovered that the man he believed to be his father was not and that his father was actually the famous New York Mets baseball player Tug McGraw. Tug denied that Tim was his son for seven years. When Tim was 18, Tug finally admitted that he was Tim's father.

During Tim's early recording years, his first series of singles failed so badly that he was told to give up his dream of becoming a country recording artist. One producer even told him, "You'll never make it, son. Go on home and find yourself a job."

As of today, he has sold over 40 million CDs and has 31 number one hits. His last 11 CDs debuted at number one on the Billboard charts. He has won three Grammy awards, 14 Academy of Country Music Awards, 11 Country Music Association Awards, and three People's Choice Awards. He is also married to another famous country music singer, Faith Hill (TimMcGraw.com, n.d.; Wikipedia, n.d.).

PHOTO: AllStar Picture Library/Alamy

If your circled words included *integrity, honesty,* and *fairness,* your statement may read:

"My integrity is the most important thing in my life, and I will never act in any way that compromises my integrity. I will be truthful, fair, and honest in all my endeavors."

More simply, your guiding statement may read something like:

"Be reliable," "Live optimistically," or **"Never give up."**

In the space below, transfer the most important words from the value list on pages 71–72 and then work to develop your guiding statement.

The most important values were:

_____   _____

_____   _____

_____   _____

_____   _____

Using these words, draft your guiding statement. (Take your time and be sincere. You will need this statement later in the chapter.)

_____

_____

_____

_____

Point 9: Make a commitment to strengthen your self-esteem

If you were asked to name all the areas of your life that are affected by self-esteem, what would you say? The correct answer is, "Everything." Every area of your life is affected by your self-esteem.

Self-esteem and self-understanding are two of the most important components of your personal makeup! To be truly motivated, you have got to know yourself and love yourself. Many people who are in therapy are there simply because they cannot accept the fact that they are OK. Self-esteem is a powerful force in your life and is the source of your joy, your productivity, and your ability to have good relationships with others.

You might think of self-esteem as a photograph of yourself that you keep locked in your mind. It is a collective product—the culmination of everyone with whom you have associated, everywhere you've traveled, and all of the experiences you have had. William James, the first major psychologist to study self-esteem, defined it as "the sum total of all a person can call their own: the Material Me (all that you have), the Social Me (recognition and acceptance from others), and the Spiritual Me (your innermost thoughts and desires)."

Stanley Coopersmith, noted psychologist and developer of the most widely used self-esteem inventory in the United States, defined self-esteem as "a personal judgment of worthiness." Psychologist and author Nathaniel Branden defined self-esteem as "confidence in our ability to cope with the basic challenges of life." And finally, psychologist Charles Cooley called it "the looking glass." Perhaps in everyday terms, we can define healthy self-esteem as "I know who I am, I accept who I am, I am OK, and I'm going to make it."

Self-esteem has five basic characteristics based on Maslow's Hierarchy of Basic Needs. They are:

▶ A sense of **security** (I am safe and have the basics of life—food, water, etc.)
▶ A sense of **identity** (I know who I am and where I'm going)
▶ A sense of **belonging** (I know how to love and I am loved)
▶ A sense of **purpose** (I know why I'm here and what I am going to do with my life)
▶ A sense of **personal competence** (I have the ability to achieve my goals and grow)

These characteristics are considered key to a person's ability to approach life with motivation, confidence, self-direction, and the desire to achieve outstanding accomplishments.

Tips to enhance your self-esteem

■ *Take control of your own life.* If you let other people rule your life, you will always have unhealthy self-esteem. Get involved in the decisions that shape your life. Seize control—don't let life just happen to you!

■ *Adopt the idea that you are responsible for you.* The day you take responsibility for yourself and what happens to you is the day you start to develop healthier self-esteem. When you can admit your mistakes and celebrate your successes knowing you did it your way, loving and respecting yourself become much easier.

■ *Refuse to allow friends and family to tear you down.* Combat negativity by admitting your mistakes and shortcomings to yourself (without dwelling on them) and by making up your mind that you are going to overcome them. By doing this, you are taking negative power away from anyone who would use your mistakes to hurt you.

■ *Control what you say to yourself.* "Self-talk" is important to your self-esteem and to your ability to motivate yourself positively. If you allow negative self-talk into your life, it will rule your self-esteem. Think positive thoughts and surround yourself with positive, upbeat, motivated, happy people.

■ *Take calculated risks.* If you are going to grow to your fullest potential, you will have to learn to take some calculated risks and step out of your comfort zone. While you should never take foolhardy risks that might endanger your life or everything you have, you must constantly be willing to push yourself.

■ *Stop comparing yourself to other people.* You may never be able to beat some people at certain things. Does it really matter? You only have to "beat yourself" to get better. If you constantly tell yourself that you are not "as handsome as Bill" or "as smart as Mary" or "as athletic as Jack," your inner voice will begin to believe these statements, and your motivation and self-esteem will suffer. Everyone has certain strengths and talents to offer to the world.

■ *Keep your promises and be loyal to friends, family, and yourself.* If you have ever had someone break a promise to you, you know how it feels to have your loyalty betrayed. The most outstanding feature of your character is your ability to be loyal, keep your promises, and do what you have agreed to do. Few things can make you feel better about yourself than being loyal and keeping your word.

How can actively participating in class help build your self-esteem?

Image 100

" To every person there comes that special moment when he is tapped on the shoulder to do a very special thing unique to him. What a tragedy if that moment finds him unprepared for the work that would be his finest hour."

—Winston Churchill

■ **Win with grace, lose with class.** Everyone loves a winner, but everyone also loves a person who can lose with class and dignity. On the other hand, no one loves a bragging winner or a moaning loser. If you are engaged in sports, debate, acting, art shows, or academic competitions, you will encounter winning and losing. Remember, whether you win or lose, **if you're involved and active,** you're already in the top 10 percent of the population. You're already more of a winner than most because you showed up and participated.

■ **Be a giver.** Author, speaker, and teacher Leo Buscaglia states: "You want to make yourself the most brilliant, the most talented, the most fabulous person that you can possibly be so that you can give it all away. The only reason we have anything is to be able to give it away." By giving to other people and sharing your talents and strengths, you begin to live on a level where kindness, selflessness, and others' needs gently collide. Whatever you want in this life, give it away and it will come back to you.

Learning for life

The signs in Key 1.11 point to the need to be a *lifelong learner,* continuing to build knowledge and skills as your career and life demand. This book will help you fulfill that need.

This text gives you tools with which you can learn for life, meeting the changing demands of the modern world. Imagine: You are in class with your *growth mindset,* open to learning. You are ready to use *analytical* and *creative* skills to examine the knowledge you take in and come up with new ideas. You are motivated to use your *practical* skills to move toward your goals. Your *emotional intelligence* has prepared you to adjust to and work with all kinds of people. The bar has been raised. **Get ready to use *Keys to Success* to fly over it and find out just how much you can grow.**

A **CHANGING WORLD** MEANS LEARNING IS FOR LIFE

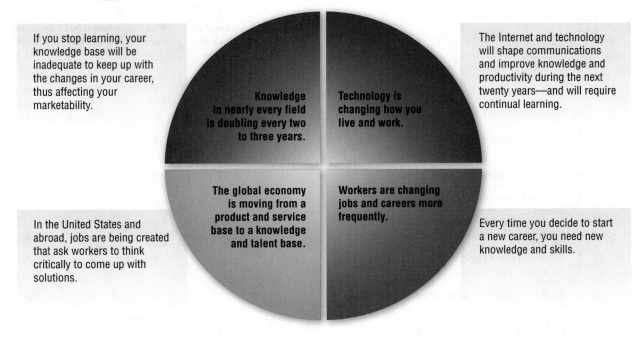

If you stop learning, your knowledge base will be inadequate to keep up with the changes in your career, thus affecting your marketability.

Knowledge in nearly every field is doubling every two to three years.

Technology is changing how you live and work.

The Internet and technology will shape communications and improve knowledge and productivity during the next twenty years—and will require continual learning.

The global economy is moving from a product and service base to a knowledge and talent base.

Workers are changing jobs and careers more frequently.

In the United States and abroad, jobs are being created that ask workers to think critically to come up with solutions.

Every time you decide to start a new career, you need new knowledge and skills.

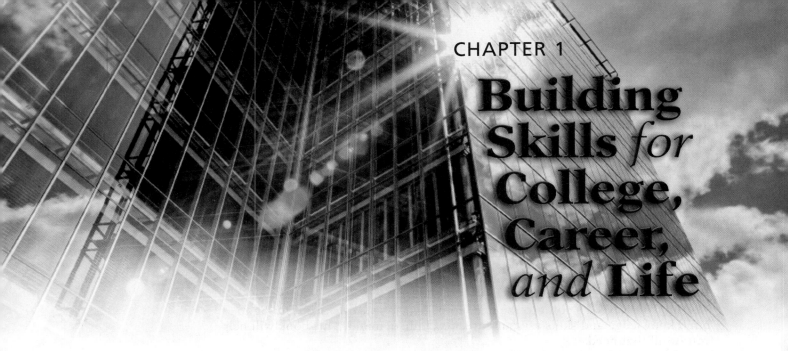

Building Skills *for* College, Career, *and* Life

Steps to Success

Activate Yourself

Robert Sternberg found that people who reach their goals successfully, despite differences in thinking and personal goals, have twenty particular characteristics in common that motivate them to grow.[22] Each of the "I" statements in the following list identifies one of the characteristics.

BUILD BASIC SKILLS. Use this self-assessment to think about how well you can get and stay motivated *right now*.

	1 Not at All Like Me	2 Somewhat Unlike Me	3 Not Sure	4 Somewhat Like Me	5 Definitely Like Me
Please circle the number that best represents your answer.					
1. I motivate myself well.	1	2	3	4	5
2. I can control my impulses.	1	2	3	4	5
3. I know when to persevere and when to change gears.	1	2	3	4	5
4. I make the most of what I do well.	1	2	3	4	5
5. I can successfully translate my ideas into action.	1	2	3	4	5
6. I can focus effectively on my goal.	1	2	3	4	5
7. I complete tasks and have good follow-through.	1	2	3	4	5
8. I initiate action—I move people and projects ahead.	1	2	3	4	5
9. I have the courage to risk failure.	1	2	3	4	5

	1 Not at All Like Me	2 Somewhat Unlike Me	3 Not Sure	4 Somewhat Like Me	5 Definitely Like Me
10. I avoid procrastination.	1	2	3	4	5
11. I accept responsibility when I make a mistake.	1	2	3	4	5
12. I don't waste time feeling sorry for myself.	1	2	3	4	5
13. I independently take responsibility for tasks.	1	2	3	4	5
14. I work hard to overcome personal difficulties.	1	2	3	4	5
15. I create an environment that helps me concentrate on my goals.	1	2	3	4	5
16. I don't take on too much work or too little.	1	2	3	4	5
17. I can delay gratification to receive the benefits.	1	2	3	4	5
18. I can see both the big picture and the details in a situation.	1	2	3	4	5
19. I am able to maintain confidence in myself.	1	2	3	4	5
20. I can balance analytical, creative, and practical thinking skills.	1	2	3	4	5

TAKE IT TO THE NEXT LEVEL. Choose five statements that focus on areas you most want to develop throughout the term. Circle or highlight them on the self-assessment. Then pretend to be an instructor recommending you for a scholarship or a job. Write a short e-mail about how strong you are in those five areas. Save the e-mail as a reminder of what you would like such a person to say about you.

MOVE TOWARD MASTERY. Select one of the five statements chosen in the previous section and take action in the following ways.

1. Find the section in the text that will help you develop this ability. If you wish to procrastinate less, for example, locate the time management information in Chapter 3.
2. Skim the text section and find one concept or strategy that catches your attention. Copy the concept or strategy onto a piece of paper or electronic file. Then, briefly describe how you plan to use it.
3. Take action in the next week based on your plan. You are on the road to growth.

In the last chapter, you will revisit this self-assessment and get more specific about actions you have taken, and plan to take, to promote personal growth.

Writing

Build Intrapersonal and Communication Skills

Record your thoughts on a separate piece of paper, in a journal, or electronically.

EMOTIONAL INTELLIGENCE JOURNAL

How you are feeling now. First, describe what you are feeling right now about college. Then discuss what those feelings tell you about how ready you are for the experience. Last, brainstorm some actions that will help you be as prepared as possible to benefit from the experience of college. (For example, if shyness prevents you from feeling ready to meet new people, one action might be to make a special effort to engage in the discussion board that will help you get to know people more easily.)

Skills you have now. No matter what professional goals you ultimately pursue, the skills that the 21st century workplace demands will be useful in any career area. Look back at Key 1.5 to remind yourself of the four skill areas—and the individual skills within each category—defined as 21st century essentials for success. Identify three skills you have already built and can demonstrate. If you would like to read further, go to www.21stcenturyskills.org/route21 and click on any of the four areas to see details about specific skills.

For each skill, write a short paragraph that contains the following elements:

- A description of your abilities in this skill area
- Specific examples, from school or work, demonstrating these abilities
- Jobs or coursework in which you have built this skill

Keep this information on hand for building your resumé—or if you already have a resumé, use it to update your information and add detail that will keep your resumé current.

Personal Portfolio

Prepare for Career Success

ASSESS YOUR SUCCESSFUL INTELLIGENCE

This is the first of twelve portfolio assignments you will complete, one for each chapter. By the end of the term, you will have compiled a portfolio of documents that can help you achieve career exploration and planning goals.

Type your work and save the documents electronically in one file folder. Use loose paper for assignments that ask you to draw or make collages, and make copies of assignments that ask you to write in the book. For safekeeping, scan and save loose or text pages to include in your portfolio file.

21st Century Learning Building Blocks

- Initiative and Self-Direction
- Critical Thinking and Problem Solving

As you begin this course, use this exercise to get a big picture look at how you perceive yourself as an analytical, creative, and practical thinker. For the statements in each of the three self-assessments, circle the number that best describes how it applies to you.

ASSESS YOUR ANALYTICAL THINKING SKILLS

For each statement, circle the number that feels right to you, from 1 for "not at all true for me" to 5 for "very true for me."

1. I recognize and define problems effectively.	1 2 3 4 5
2. I see myself as a "thinker," "analytical," "studious."	1 2 3 4 5
3. When working on a problem in a group setting, I like to break down the problem into its components and evaluate them.	1 2 3 4 5
4. I need to see convincing evidence before accepting information as fact.	1 2 3 4 5
5. I weigh the pros and cons of plans and ideas before taking action.	1 2 3 4 5
6. I tend to make connections among bits of information by categorizing them.	1 2 3 4 5
7. Impulsive, spontaneous decision making worries me.	1 2 3 4 5
8. I like to analyze causes and effects when making a decision.	1 2 3 4 5
9. I monitor my progress toward goals.	1 2 3 4 5
10. Once I reach a goal, I evaluate the process to see how effective it was.	1 2 3 4 5

Total your answers here: _____

ASSESS YOUR CREATIVE THINKING SKILLS

For each statement, circle the number that feels right to you, from 1 for "not at all true for me" to 5 for "very true for me."

1. I tend to question rules and regulations.   1 2 3 4 5

2. I see myself as "unique," "full of ideas," "innovative."   1 2 3 4 5

3. When working on a problem in a group setting, I generate a lot of ideas.   1 2 3 4 5

4. I am energized when I have a brand-new experience.   1 2 3 4 5

5. If you say something is too risky, I'm ready to give it a shot.   1 2 3 4 5

6. I often wonder if there is a different way to do or see something.   1 2 3 4 5

7. Too much routine in my work or schedule drains my energy.   1 2 3 4 5

8. I tend to see connections among ideas that others do not.   1 2 3 4 5

9. I feel comfortable allowing myself to make mistakes as I test out ideas.   1 2 3 4 5

10. I'm willing to champion an idea even when others disagree with me.   1 2 3 4 5

Total your answers here: _____

ASSESS YOUR PRACTICAL THINKING SKILLS

For each statement, circle the number that feels right to you, from 1 for "not at all true for me" to 5 for "very true for me."

1. I can find a way around any obstacle.   1 2 3 4 5

2. I see myself as a "doer," the "go-to" person; I "make things happen."   1 2 3 4 5

3. When working on a problem in a group setting, I like to figure out who will do what and when it should be done.   1 2 3 4 5

4. I apply what I learn from experience to improve my response to similar situations.   1 2 3 4 5

5. I finish what I start and don't leave loose ends hanging.   1 2 3 4 5

6. I note my emotions about academic and social situations and use what they tell me to move toward a goal.   1 2 3 4 5

7. I can sense how people feel and can use that knowledge to interact with others effectively.   1 2 3 4 5

8. I manage my time effectively.   1 2 3 4 5

9. I adjust to the teaching styles of my instructors and the communication styles of my peers.   1 2 3 4 5

10. When involved in a problem-solving process, I can shift gears as needed.   1 2 3 4 5

Total your answers here: _____

With your scores in hand, use the Wheel of Successful Intelligence to look at all the skills at once. In each of the three areas of the wheel, draw a curved line approximately at the level of your number score and fill in the wedge below that line. Look at what the wheel shows about the level of balance you perceive in your three aspects of successful intelligence. If it were a real wheel, would it roll?

Based on the appearance of the wheel, in which skill do you most need to build strength? Keep this goal in mind as you proceed through the text. In each chapter, pay special attention to the exercise that builds this thinking skill.

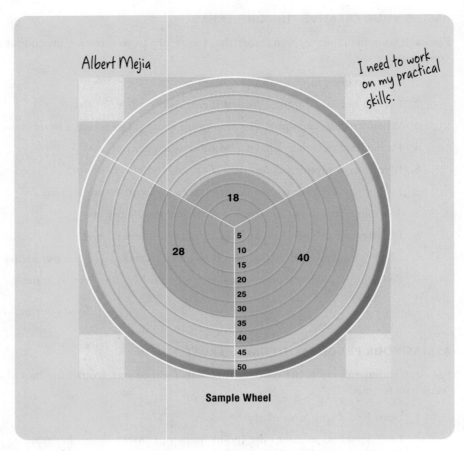

Albert Mejia

I need to work on my practical skills.

18

28   5
           10
           15   40
           20
           25
           30
           35
           40
           45
           50

Sample Wheel

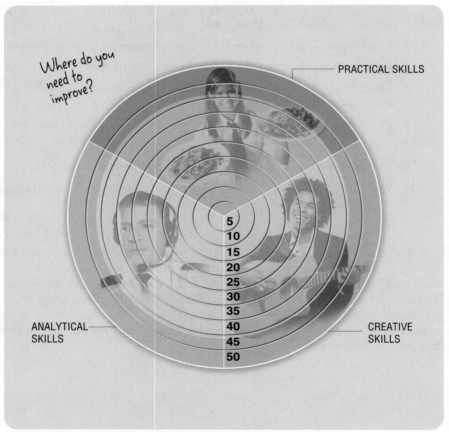

Where do you need to improve?

PRACTICAL SKILLS

5
10
15
20
25
30
35
40
45
50

ANALYTICAL SKILLS

CREATIVE SKILLS

Source: Based on "The Wheel of Life" model developed by the Coaches Training Institute. © Co-Active Space 2000.

Social Networking

CONNECT TO THE WORKING WORLD

One of the most productive uses of online social networking is to help people market themselves and develop networks of professional contacts in the work world. At the end of each Personal Portfolio exercise, this segment will help you build a profile on one of the most widely used tools for this purpose—LinkedIn. The mission of LinkedIn is to help you connect to people you know and trust, and access wider networks of people through them, to become a more successful professional in the career of your choice.

Set up your account on LinkedIn to get started. Do the following:

- Go to www.linkedin.com and click on "What is LinkedIn?" to get an overview.
- Click on "Join Today" and follow the instructions to establish your account name and password.
- Be sure to read the User Agreement and Privacy Policy.

If you already have a LinkedIn account, sign on and make sure your basic information is up to date.

ENDNOTES

1. Thomas Friedman, *The World Is Flat*, New York: Farrar, Straus & Giroux, 2006, p. 8.

2. Daniel Pink, "Revenge of the Right Brain," *Wired Magazine*, February 2005, www.wired.com/wired/archive/13.02/brain.html?pg=1&topic=brain&topic_set=.

3. Robert J. Sternberg, *Successful Intelligence: How Practical and Creative Intelligence Determine Success in Life*, New York: Plume, 1997, pp. 85–90; Carol S. Dweck, *Mindset: The New Psychology of Success*, New York: Random House, 2006, p. 5; and Susanne Jaeggi, Martin Buschkuehl, John Jonides, and Walter J. Perrig, "Improving Fluid Intelligence with Training on Working Memory," 2008, *Proceedings of the National Academy of Sciences USA*, 105, pp. 6829–6833.

4. Sternberg, *Successful Intelligence*, p. 11.

5. Dweck, *Mindset*, pp. 3–4.

6. The Society for Neuroscience, *Brain Facts: A Primer on the Brain and Neurosystem*, Washington, DC: The Society for Neuroscience, 2008, pp. 34–35.

7. Sternberg, *Successful Intelligence*, p. 12.

8. Ibid., p. 127.

9. Ibid., p. 11.

10. Ibid., pp. 127–128.

11. Carol Dweck, "The Mindsets," 2006, www.mindsetonline.com/whatisit/themindsets/index.html.

12. Dweck, *Mindset*, p. 16.

13. Ibid.

14. Rick Pitino, *Success Is a Choice*, New York: Broadway Books, 1997, p. 40.

15. Dweck, *Mindset*, p. 51.

16. Dweck, *Mindset*, p. 35.

17. Ibid., p. 33.

18. John D. Mayer, Peter Salovey, and David R. Caruso, "Emotional Intelligence: New Ability or Eclectic Traits?," September 2008, *American Psychologist*, 63, no. 6, p. 503.

19. David R. Caruso, "Zero In on Knowledge: A Practical Guide to the MSCEIT," Multi-Health Systems, 2008, p. 3.

20. Sandra Blakeslee, "Cells That Read Minds," January 10, 2006, *New York Times*, www.nytimes.com/2006/01/10/science/10mirr.html.

21. Mayer, Salovey, and Caruso, pp. 510–512.

22. List and descriptions based on Sternberg, *Successful Intelligence*, pp. 251–268.

chapter 2

Online Learning

It all started in 1992 while he was volunteering as a firefighter in South Florida.

There was an emergency call to structure fire. A crew of firefighters jump onto the truck and sped to the scene. Curious and eager, he went along with the paid group. They arrived, put out the blaze and all the while, he got a taste of what it meant to really be a firefighter.

And he liked it.

"I knew then that this was the only job for me," said Brock Jester, who years later, is now a battalion chief with the Pensacola (Fla.) Fire Department.

"I think it was the adrenaline, but it was also really getting out and doing something," Jester explained. "We were the ones going in while other people are being shuffled away. As a firefighter, you are always were the action is and you are always there to help."

Jester added that the while firefighting is a true rush, there is another reason he does this job.

"You can see the relief on people's faces when we walk up, it's like they are saying, 'He's going to take care of it.' That's the motivation for me, seeing that relief on people's faces. It kinda makes you fall in love with it," said Jester.

A year into the job, Jester decided to get "training" of his own by seeking a bachelor's degree in fire science with CSU in 2009. "I had already had my two-year degree, but realized I should really have a full bachelor's degree."

"I had a lot of fire science education, but it was here and there. I didn't have anything to kind of pull it altogether and combine what I learned, other than my two-year degree," he explained.

As with many students, CSU took all those classes and certifications in consideration and designed a degree plan for Jester. And with a little prodding from fellow firefighters (or maybe it was the competitiveness) and a CSU learning partner representative, Jester decided to enroll.

"The customer service at CSU is impeccable. I always got returned phone calls and it never took more than a day. And they are always smiling. On the phone, I could hear them smiling," he laughed.

Brock was still learning the ropes of his new administration job when he joined CSU. But he credits the university's flexible course schedule and outstanding faculty with helping him tackle the load. He was able to take classes, handle demands of his new administration job and be there for his family.

"You can do that with online education. You aren't bound by the traditional classroom with CSU. With CSU, I can juggle my responsibilities. That freedom is nice, really nice," Jester added.

"With the flexibility CSU offers and the many opportunities in the fire service industry, I know can go anywhere now."

STATUS *Check*

Taking a self-assessment can help you think more deeply about your own skills and preferences. Consider the questions in this assessment and your responses. What information does this quiz give you about yourself that you can use to develop or improve important skills?

Rate yourself as an online student

For each statement, circle the number that feels right to you, from 1 for "not true for me" to 5 for "very true for me."

▶ I feel prepared to handle online college-level work.	1 2 3 4 5
▶ I understand how online courses differ from offerings in traditional classrooms.	1 2 3 4 5
▶ I feel comfortable communicating in writing.	1 2 3 4 5
▶ I try to find a way to connect new information with what I already know.	1 2 3 4 5
▶ When I learn information or a skill, I consider how it may help me in the future.	1 2 3 4 5
▶ I refer to the syllabus for each of my courses frequently.	1 2 3 4 5
▶ I understand the skills that I will gain from each course in my program and how these will benefit me in my future career.	1 2 3 4 5
▶ I am comfortable using the college's learning management system (LMS).	1 2 3 4 5
▶ When I need help, I find—and reach out to—the resources my college provides.	1 2 3 4 5
▶ I relate effectively to others and can work successfully in a virtual team.	1 2 3 4 5

Now total your scores.

Each of the topics in these statements is covered in this chapter. Note those statements for which you circled a 3 or lower. Skim the chapter to see where those topics appear, and pay special attention to them as you read, learn, and apply new strategies.

REMEMBER: *No matter how prepared you are to succeed in college, you can improve with effort and practice.*

If your total ranges from 38–50, you consider yourself ready to actively engage in your online program. You understand why your course is important to your future success. You are a self-starter who takes responsibility for getting things done, and you feel relatively comfortable writing, which is an often-used skill in online courses.

If your total ranges from 24–37, you consider your online college readiness to be average. A couple of minor adjustments in your expectations, and you should be on your way. When online students understand why a course is important to their future success, it provides motivation during the more difficult times. Make sure you take responsibility for getting things done and learn more about how to motivate yourself, if you need that skill. If you do not feel relatively comfortable writing your thoughts, remember that practice makes perfect. Overcome your fear, and begin. Most of the communication you do in an online course is in writing.

If your total ranges from 10–23, you think you need some additional skills to face the challenges of an online education. Determine why a particular course is important to your future success. Your success is in your hands—and yours alone. Take responsibility for getting work done. You can learn more about how to motivate yourself in this chapter. Because you will be on your own much of the time in an online learning environment, you will need to make yourself take the necessary action. Most of the communication you do in an online course is in writing. If you do not feel comfortable writing, use techniques presented in this course to overcome your fear so you can actively participate.

Analyze: What skills are important for an online course? What skills do you want to develop or improve? How is education online different from that in a traditional classroom? How is it the same?

"Taking online courses has a cost—in time, money, and energy".

By signing up for an online course, you have entered an exciting realm of learning. You are joining a group of over 4.6 million college students who are taking advantage of the convenience and opportunities that online education offers. In fact, online enrollments are growing at a faster rate than traditional course enrollments. Today, more than one in four college students are taking at least one online course.[2]

Benefits of online learning

  ▶ *Flexible scheduling*. Online students can focus on what they need to learn when they choose. You can access the content you need when you need it.

  ▶ *High-quality interaction*. Online students often have *more* interaction and enhanced relationships than in a traditional classroom. You have time to think and process information before responding to others. The virtual collaboration skills you gain by working in groups are highly valued in the workplace.

  ▶ *Interactive and engaging media*. Through new technologies that online courses can offer, including new communication methods, interactivity, animations, videos, and audio podcasts, you can learn complex concepts in a variety of ways.

  ▶ *Technological comfort level*. Graduates from online programs learn to become proactive users of technology.

Though online courses offer a number of resources to enhance your learning experience and help prepare you for a successful career, they can also pose unique challenges. The skills required for successful learning in an online environment are different from those needed in a traditional classroom. For instance, developing virtual peer relationships demands a different approach than building team skills in a face-to-face environment. Reading onscreen differs from reading a textbook. And because writing is the main form of communication in an online course, you will need to be able to communicate effectively in writing both formally, for written assignments, and less formally, for written discussions and e-mails.

The most important skill you can have in an online class is the ability to take charge of your own learning. Instead of receiving the same instruction at the same pace within a planned structure as those in a traditional course, online students often have to make decisions about how and when to access course materials. Will you look at the course resources first, jump to the weblinks

The U.S. Department of Education analyzed research studies undertaken from 1996 to 2008 and has concluded that online education is more effective than face-to-face learning.[1]

You Have Much to Gain from College

Studies by the U.S. Department of Education show the gains that college graduates are likely to make:

- *Increased income.* College graduates earn, on average, around $20,000 more per year than those with only a high school diploma.
- *Increased chances of finding and keeping a job.* The unemployment rate for college graduates is less than half that of high school graduates.
- *Better health.* With the knowledge and increased self-awareness that college often brings, both college graduates and their children are more likely to stay healthy.
- *More money for the future.* College graduates, on average, put away more money in savings.
- *Broader thinking.* College graduates tend to be more open-minded and less prejudiced. They also generally have more understanding of different cultures and more knowledge of what's going on in the world.
- *Better decision making.* As consumers, college graduates tend to think more critically and comprehensively about the pros and cons before making a purchase.

offered, or go to the assignments immediately? The nature of online education can also make you more anonymous. If you never log in, a class could end without anyone calling or e-mailing to find out where your assignments are. **Successful online students tend to be self-starters and highly motivated to complete assignments and do well in these courses.**

Understanding the online learning environment

It is helpful to start your online course or program by knowing as much as you can about what to expect. Though you may have some ideas about how online learning works, there may be aspects that you have not considered. Start by assessing some of the facts and fictions of learning online.

Facts and fictions of online learning

Fact or Fiction?

Online courses can be impersonal, disconnected, and unfulfilling.

■ *Fiction.* Although online courses are set up differently than onsite courses, there is just as much opportunity for interaction once you get used to communicating through cyberspace. Much of the time, in fact, students find that they are more self-revealing and their discussions get deeper than they do in an onsite classroom. In many ways, online courses create a more level playing field where the focus is solely on content and the learning process. You will not need to worry about appearance, age, disability, race, or even your wardrobe. You may be surprised by the rewarding experiences you find in the online classroom environment.

Courtesy of Shutterstock

Fact or Fiction?

Online classes are easier than onsite classes.

■ *Fiction.* Both traditional and online classes will differ in terms of their requirements, the instructor's methods, and your initial level of understanding. However, online courses are *not* easier. In fact, they can be more difficult than an onsite class. For instance, a typical online course is shorter in duration but still requires the same amount of work as its onsite counterpart. In most online courses, there is also a lot of additional writing, which some students find more challenging.

Fact or Fiction?

Online instructors are less attentive than onsite instructors.

■ *Fiction.* Instructors, whether onsite or online, differ in their approach, and their levels of engagement can depend on many factors. However, most online instructors do spend a great deal of time engaging the class. They shoulder a larger burden because they don't have the benefit of nonverbal cues available to an onsite instructor, such as body language or bored yawns. Your instructor's level of engagement, however, is out of your control. **If you find you need additional help to stay engaged, ask your instructor immediately.**

Fact or Fiction?

Online courses are more expensive than onsite courses.

■ *Fiction.* When schools first developed online courses, they were more expensive than they are today. With improvements in technology and the standardization of course development, online courses are competitive and sometimes less expensive than onsite courses. Depending on the school, though, an online course may be more expensive initially. After factoring in transportation, fees, child care, parking, and the time it takes to travel back and forth, you may find that the online course is actually less expensive.

Fact or Fiction?

Online courses fit better into a busier schedule.

■ *Fact.* As an online student, you can often participate in the instruction at times that are convenient for you. You can attend class in the morning before going to work, during your lunch hour, after you have put the kids to bed, or any other time during your day. You will still have a lot of work to do, but it will be at a time that you have selected.

Besides the convenience, this flexibility offers additional benefits. Because you save the time you would have spent traveling to class, you can spend more time on learning. You can also focus on learning what you need to know versus sitting through a lecture that may not address your most significant needs.

Fact or Fiction?

You can participate in an online class from anywhere.

■ *Fiction.* Though distance learning is often called "anywhere, anytime learning," in practice, you may find this not to be the case. Depending on how you best learn and work, you may need to have resources around you and a dedicated amount of time to work on the assignments. There will be times when you need high-speed Internet to get the full advantage of your online courses. There may be videos, audio recordings, and online texts to access and Internet research to conduct. Online courses are demanding, so you will need to have the proper mindset as well to tackle the challenges. You may find that your concentration is best in certain locations or at certain times. To get the most out of your program, approach these courses with intensity and focus and choose the best working environment.

Fact or Fiction?

Education standards are lower for online courses.

■ **Fiction.** Online courses have to be accredited by the same bodies that approve onsite courses. Examined by many authorities, accredited online courses are rigorous and soundly structured, with high standards. They are often developed by the best instructors and use the same curriculum as their onsite counterparts.

Types of online courses

Online courses are not all alike. Classes may be fully online or the online portion may combine with a traditional classroom, or onsite, portion, making what is termed a *blended* course. The online portions of blended courses can vary greatly among different offerings, from large to small percentages or anywhere in between.

Most fully online courses are *asynchronous*, meaning that you can access them at your convenience. Some are *synchronous*, however, with set meeting times when everyone will be online at the same time. Some courses use a combination of synchronous and asynchronous modes.

Online courses can take different approaches to providing content in the methods of presentation, materials used, and types of resources offered.

▶ *Course presentations.* Some online courses will offer textual explanations of the material organized by week or unit, with separately accessed resources. Others might use an integrated course presentation leading the user through the material in a series of screens, with resources such as videos or interactive exercises incorporated into the presentation. Some other courses will simply direct students to access specific information on their own. Pay special attention to material that is within a course presentation—it is usually the most important information.

▶ *Textbooks and other hard copy materials.* Your textbook may be a printed version, an online document accessed through an e-reader program, or a file (such as a .pdf or Microsoft Word document) that can be downloaded and either printed or read onscreen. Your text is usually one of the most important resources for any course.

▶ *Video lectures.* Some online courses include video lectures by an instructor, created specifically for the course or taped from previous presentations.

▶ *Animations and interactive media.* Because of the effort and cost involved in creating animations or interactive media, they are likely centered around the most important concepts in the course. Any interactive media that your course includes is probably worth accessing.

▶ *Podcasts.* Users can subscribe to and automatically download new *podcasts*—audio and video programs published via the Internet. Podcasting in online courses might offer full, unabridged audio recordings of the online presentation. Other courses use podcasts that supplement the online portion with instructional explanations, guest speakers, commentaries on current issues, and integration of news media. If your course uses podcasts to supplement the course material, be sure to access them.

▶ *Weblinks.* Your course might also provide additional weblinks added by the instructor that lead to external websites, videos, and other resources. If you see weblinks listed or any other supplements specifically added by your instructor, these are likely important resources.

Access your online course and find the following resources:

- Announcements
- Discussion boards
- Course content

- Assignments and assessments
- Chat room
- Gradebook

What other resources are available in your course? Skim through one lesson. How is the content presented? Where are the assignments found? Next, skim through another lesson and the assignments. Is it set up in the same way as the first? Find your course objectives and the syllabus and determine how you will be graded. If you cannot find an answer to a question, immediately contact your instructor or a support person at your school to find the information.

Types of assignments

Within any online course, you might find a mix of any or all of the following:

▶ *Graded discussions.* One of the most exciting features of an online course is the discussion forum. An instructor posts a question on the threaded (asynchronous) discussion board. Typically, every student in the class is expected to respond intelligently several times to different people. No one is allowed to sit at the back of the class and refrain from participating. **Discussions are the most "visibility" you will have in the class.**

▶ *Quizzes and exams.* In an online course, quizzes and exams are usually substantially different from traditional tests in that many are open book tests, taken at your convenience within a set time period. Those who experience test anxiety in public will likely be less affected by online tests.

▶ *Ungraded self-assessments.* Some courses offer pre- and post-assessments to help direct your attention to key course concepts. Take the nongraded practice quizzes and assessments that are built into the course to receive valuable feedback and additional motivation to learn the material.

▶ *Short written assignments.* Individual written exercises are generally graded multipart problems or short responses that assess your understanding of the material.

▶ *Longer analysis papers.* These papers are generally several pages long and may require some type of analysis, such as determining cause-and-effect relationships or persuasive writing attempting to convince readers of a particular point of view.

▶ *Group projects.* Online courses often feature group projects, which can vary in several significant ways. They can be large and ongoing throughout the term or small assignments taking only a week or two. You may select your group or the instructor may assign you to one. Communication within the group may be public, for everyone to see, or private, for group members only. Sometimes the group is given one grade, and sometimes your grade will be a combination of the group grade and an individual assessment based on peer reviews.

▶ *Journals.* In some courses journaling is encouraged as a means to reflect on what you are learning and how it relates to your previous knowledge or to some element of your life.

Types of learning management systems

How will you see the content that has been created for an online course? It is usually delivered through what is called a *learning management system* (LMS), which is simply a software program through which a school presents the information and tracks the progress of students. Popular examples include eCollege, Blackboard, Moodle, Joomla, and Desire2Learn. Your school may use one of these or a proprietary LMS designed specifically for your institution.

Focus on the key information in the course content. First, look at the unit or lesson objectives before looking at the material. Take a minute to put yourself in the shoes of the course creator. How would you make sure a student learned important information? As you go through the course material, judge the importance and significance of concepts by comparing them to the lesson objectives.

Learn to use your LMS as soon as you sign up for your first course.
Although differing from each other in some respects, LMSs usually have the
following sections:

- Announcements
- Discussion Boards
- Course Content
- Assignments and Assessments

- Gradebook
- Chat Room
- Resources

Instructions to access and navigate the LMS may be found in an online
user manual that will usually be provided to you. Make sure that you explore
and play around with the course site before your class starts so you know
where to find everything and how to post assignments, discussion responses,
and other course resources.

You may also be required to access software to view multimedia content by
downloading or upgrading to the latest versions of software programs such as the
following:

- Quicktime Player
- Adobe FlashPlayer

- Adobe Reader
- Real Player

If your LMS requires you to use any of these, there should be a link to the
free download page for each.

If your course has an electronic library resource, you can link to it through the
LMS. Make sure you access it and look around at the different resources available.
Electronic libraries provide connections to databases that include full-text online
books, full-text magazines and journals, encyclopedias, dictionaries, and more.
They may also provide traditional library services in the online environment, such
as reference help and curriculum-specific research guides, tutorials, and collections
of frequently asked questions and answers. If your course offers such a resource,
become familiar with it before you begin your course.

Additional strategies to make the most of your LMS can be found in Key 2.1.

Setting yourself up for success: Practices of successful online learners

You can set yourself up for success in your online course by learning habits
that outstanding online students regularly practice (Key 2.2).

1. Prepare for the path ahead
2. Structure your schedule
3. Set priorities
4. Develop discipline and accountability

5. Foster relationships
6. Seek new skills
7. Manage your thoughts and emotions
8. Ask for help

Prepare for the path ahead

The course catalog is one of your most important resources. Not only does it
give you information on school procedures and policies—registration, requirements for majors, transferring, and so on—it also provides a roadmap for your
program. How many courses are included? What order are they in? Your catalog also tells you how the current courses you are taking fit into the big picture.
Every course in your curriculum has been chosen because it is important to your
future career success. Try to determine some of the skills that each course will

ADDITIONAL STRATEGIES
TO MAKE THE MOST OF YOUR LMS

Go through the tutorial offered by the school to introduce your program. Read all materials provided.

If you have any trouble understanding the system, get help NOW! Do not wait to ask questions. Call the academic support number or contact your instructor as soon as possible.

Get your course access instructions the week before the course begins. Go through the elements of the LMS and make sure you know how to access and post assignments and discussion responses.

Access a course presentation and download all required multimedia software. Make sure you can view all multimedia files, like videos or interactive presentations.

Keep your passwords, usernames, and tech support numbers where you can readily find them.

PRACTICES OF SUCCESSFUL
ONLINE LEARNERS

Prepare for the Path Ahead	Structure Your Schedule	Set Priorities	Develop Discipline and Accountability
Good plans shape good decisions. Decide what you want and map out exactly how you're going to get there.	Managing everything you need to do requires a good up-to-date schedule that incorporates due dates for your class, work appointments, and personal commitments.	Keeping your "eye on the prize" can help during the daily grind when multiple demands can seem hard to manage.	The online learning process is normally accelerated and requires commitment. Staying up with the class and completing all work on time is very important.

Foster Relationships	Seek New Skills	Manage Your Thoughts and Emotions	Ask for Help
Being part of a community of learners and establishing a bond or common ground with classmates may mean the difference between a successful, supportive experience and feeling lost and detached.	You may face challenges in developing a new set of skills for a new type of instruction. Determine through this text what is necessary for you and set out to develop those skills.	Your mind can make a huge difference. Trade in negative thoughts for positive ones and become aware of negative emotions.	Surround yourself with motivating and encouraging people. It helps your efforts when you know how to ask for and get the help you need.

help you develop and how the overall skill set you will have at the end of the program will help foster success in your career.

Another important resource is your course syllabus, which tells you everything you need to know about your course—when to read chapters and materials, dates of exams and due dates for assignments, how your final grade is calculated, and more. Refer to the syllabus for each course you take throughout the term.

Understanding where you are going will give you motivation and determination to make it through each of the steps required in a class or program. The following strategies can help you prepare for the path ahead:

▶ Write down your main goal for achieving your education. Keep this in a place where you can see it every day.
▶ Make a list of all the courses in your program. After you read your course catalog identify one or two important skills you will learn from each course.
▶ Map out your program—when you will take each course.

Structure your schedule

Effective goal setting and smart planning are important tools to have for your online journey. Most goals can be broken down into specific "mini" goals that can be incorporated into a daily schedule.

Make use of your syllabus by putting key dates in your calendar program, spotting time crunches, and getting a sense of how much time you need to set aside to study. Keep a "to-do" list near your schedule and get an idea, at least, of when you will do the important items.

Other strategies to help structure your schedule include the following:

▶ *Use a calendar.* Schedule standard times in your calendar for studying. Some students find that scheduling study time daily is helpful whereas others choose specific study days in the week. Pick a schedule that can work for you and stick to it.

▶ *Participate in your course as much as possible.* Check the discussion boards several times throughout the week. If you're required to respond to several posts, you'll get much more out of the course if you do so earlier and then check in later to see what other students have said.

▶ *Take care of yourself.* You will have to devote a lot of time to your online program, especially initially. Though you may not have a lot of extra time now, taking care of yourself is very important. Make time to do things that help you feel replenished.

Logging in to your course every day and checking for new postings or updates can help prevent falling behind.

Set priorities

Establish priorities for your life. Then you can be effective at your studies and take care of everyone and everything else in your life. You've chosen to pursue online education for a reason. Most likely, it fits in with one of your major life goals.

Use the following strategies to help set priorities:

▶ *Understand what you value in life.* How is your education important to your life goals?

▶ *Make the course a priority.* Logging in to your course and making time for schoolwork should take precedence over other activities. Do and say whatever you have to in order to let family and co-workers know that time for your program is not negotiable.

▶ *Read success stories.* Find out about others who have achieved the goals you have set for yourself.

▶ *Think about the effects of your success.* Remind yourself often of what your success will mean to others—those you know and care about already and those current strangers who you are yet to inspire.

Knowing what you want will help you make time for your goals.

Develop discipline and accountability

One of the biggest challenges facing an online student is gaining the self-discipline required to be successful. **There is perhaps no single greater habit for online success than becoming a self-starter and managing yourself.** You have to discipline yourself in maintaining your schedule and not allow any distractions to disrupt your plan.

Use the following strategies to help develop discipline and accountability:

▶ *Keep the pressure down.* Be careful not to put too much pressure on yourself to complete a homework assignment. Leave some time to avoid doing it all at once and to let the concepts "gel" before tackling the project.

▶ *Find someone to help keep you accountable.* If you are supposed to get something done, it helps to have someone to tell after accomplishing your goal. Your support person may be a classmate who can also inspire and help energize you with ideas providing that needed spark to get started on a project or assignment.

Even with the best of schedules and calendars in place, what matters most is whether you get the work done.

▶ *Implement the "10-minute" rule.* If you are really stuck on something and cannot find the motivation to even begin, make yourself do something related to the assignment for only 10 minutes, even if it is simply organizing your materials.

▶ *Remember that this is a marathon and not a sprint.* Long distance runners sometimes find themselves imagining crossing the finish line miles ahead of time. When they come back to reality and realize they aren't anywhere near the end, they can become disheartened. One strategy for runners projecting too far into the future is bringing themselves back to the present with self-talk: "Here I am at mile 8." This gets them back on track emotionally for the run. You can do the same thing. When you find yourself projecting too far ahead, know that the finish line is ahead, but bring yourself back to your present location in the journey.

Foster relationships

To effectively work in a distance learning environment, you need to feel close to your classmates and instructors, despite the miles that may be between you. Not only does learning increase with social interaction, the meaningful connections you make with your online classmates can translate into friendships and career networking opportunities later.

Communicating online is a bit different from communicating in person. Without the benefit of tone, body language, or social cues like proximity or volume, it becomes much more important to stay positive, remain tolerant and polite, and eliminate language that could be easily misinterpreted.

Other strategies to help foster relationships online include the following:

▶ *Interact with the other students as much as possible.* In the discussion forum, add something meaningful by posting a response, question, or comment to several other students' postings. Interact with as many students as possible to build online relationships.

▶ *Value diversity.* You may interact with people from many different backgrounds and cultures in an online course. As you build your knowledge about other cultures and appreciate and accept the differences, you heighten your ability to analyze how people relate to one another. Most important, you develop practical skills that enable you to bridge the gap between yourself and others. Gain as much information as you can by reading about different cultures. Strive to treat others with tolerance and respect, avoiding assumptions and granting them the right to think and believe without being judged.

▶ *Ask questions.* Seek out people you might not ordinarily get a chance to befriend. Ask about their lives and traditions.

▶ *Prioritize personal relationships.* When you devote time and energy to education, work, and activities you enjoy, you get positive results. Do the same for your relationships. If you treat others with the kind of loyalty and support that you appreciate, you are likely to receive the same in return.

▶ *Check in with people based on their past posts.* If someone mentioned a problem earlier, ask about it this week. This is a great way to make your classmates feel valued.

▶ *Be open minded.* Share life, work, and educational experiences as part of the learning process. Telling personal stories makes the material relevant, and revealing something about your life lets classmates know you better.

▶ *Work through tensions, if possible.* Negative feelings can grow and cause problems when left unspoken. Try to resolve the problems if you can. However, know that sometimes relationships fail regardless of what you do. When an important relationship becomes strained or breaks up, analyze the situation and choose practical strategies to move on. Some people need time alone; others need to be with friends and family. Some need a change of scene; others need to let off steam with exercise or other activities. Whatever you do, believe that in time you will emerge from the experience stronger.

Incorporate a plan for regular communication with your classmates into your overall course schedule for greater success in online learning.

online outlook

Rucha
Working professional and online student
Age 35

Challenge
Mother of three and employed full-time

The major benefit of learning online as opposed to a classroom for me is mainly the ability to go to class anytime I want. Having a full-time job, a family, and doing volunteer work requires a lot of time, and I am able to complete most of my schoolwork some evenings and on the weekend without leaving my house and driving to a campus.

The major challenge is just getting my work finished on time. You must have the willpower to sit down and do your work instead of vegging out in front of the TV. It is very easy to procrastinate.

I force myself to sit down and finish a set amount of work or reach a certain point in my reading before I allow myself to do other things.

It helped me to set a desk area up and time slots that are exclusively dedicated to my schoolwork. I am very disciplined about this.

Since most of the reading can be done away from my desk, I usually do that in a comfortable spot, on the bus, or during a break at work.

Prejudice

To be prejudiced means to prejudge others, usually on the basis of gender, race, sexual orientation, disability, religion, and other characteristics. Prejudice may creep up on you without your even knowing it because of factors like the following:

▶ *Influence of family and culture.* Children learn attitudes—including intolerance, superiority, and hate—from their parents, peers, and community.
▶ *Fear of differences.* It is human to fear the unfamiliar and make assumptions about it.
▶ *Experience.* One bad experience with a person of a particular race or religion may lead someone to condemn all people with the same background.

Stereotypes

Prejudice is usually based on **stereotypes**—assumptions made, without proof or critical thinking, about the characteristics of a person or group. Stereotyping comes from factors such as the following:

▶ *Desire for patterns and logic.* People often try to make sense of the world by using the labels, categories, and generalizations that stereotypes provide.
▶ *Media influences.* The more people see stereotypical images, the easier it is to believe that stereotypes are universal.
▶ *Laziness.* Labeling group members according to a characteristic they seem to have in common takes less energy than asking questions that illuminate the qualities of individuals.

Stereotypes derail personal connections and block effective communication, because pasting a label on a person makes it hard for you to see the real person underneath. Even stereotypes that seem "positive" may not be true and may get in the way of perceiving uniqueness.

Seek new skills

Most successful online students tend to have a proficiency in certain study skills. They adapt to reading on a screen, taking notes from online material, collaborating with a diverse group of people, navigating the learning management system used in the course, and embracing new concepts.

Consider how you read online, for instance. Jakob Nielsen, a Web researcher, tested how 232 people read pages on monitors.[3] Using eye-tracking tools to map how vision moves and rests, he found that people read online in a formation that looks like the capital letter "F." At the top, users read all the way across, but as they proceed their descent quickens and horizontal sight contracts, with a slowdown around the middle of the page. Near the bottom, eyes move almost vertically, and the lower-right corner of the page is largely ignored. People read quickly online, too. Though this has advantages for reading a great number of web pages with a lot of content, it might not serve you when reading an online textbook or when needing to understand difficult material. Be aware of your reading patterns and alter them when necessary.

In the online classroom, nearly all communication is written, so it is critical that you feel comfortable expressing yourself in writing.

Collaboration is also a key skill in the online community. You may find yourself learning with people from all over. Being able to communicate and collaborate at a distance is a valuable skill that will help to broaden your horizons.

Find more information about the skills that challenge you and practice them to become a better learner.

Other strategies for seeking out and learning new skills include the following:

▶ *Apply new material to what you already know.* Relate new concepts to a current or past experience.

▶ *Practice with the collaborative technologies available.* "Meet" with your classmates, share documents, or brainstorm on a whiteboard in real time together.

▶ *Put new knowledge to work as soon as possible.* As soon as possible after studying, apply the new knowledge you have learned through collaboration with other classmates, at your place of employment, or in your home.

▶ *If you are having trouble, contact your instructor immediately.* You can also find academic support to help you. Don't wait! Contact them as soon as you don't understand something or have trouble navigating the technology.

Manage your thoughts and emotions

Become aware of any negative thoughts you have. Pay attention to: "should," "ought," "have to," "can't," "always," and "never." Challenge those thoughts—is there a real reason or is it just fear that makes you think them?

Reaching new levels in your life requires changing from the inside out. Successful online students have found ways of preventing burnout or loss of interest by talking themselves through it.

Emotions can be quite high in distance learning, heightened by the lack of face-to-face interaction. Life, in general, has ups and downs too, with commitments, disappointments, and conflict. Find ways to push past the negative thoughts and emotions that may come up. Think of all the advances you have already made, affirm what you will do and how you will do it, and don't try to do too much too quickly. Develop positive thoughts to replace the negative ones and repeat those positive thoughts as often as possible.

Other strategies to manage your thoughts and emotions include the following:

▶ *Take action!* If you have fallen behind in a course, do something simple like finishing the assignment, participating in a discussion, or reading the material. Even small, positive actions can set you back on course.

▶ *Focus on the positives.* Reflect on what you can do, not on what you can't. Think about what you did, not what you didn't, and what you will do instead of what you won't.

▶ *Face your fears by acknowledging them.* Giving fear a name lessens its hold on you. Dig deeper. Is there something else that you are afraid of that you have not seen? Challenge it using positive self-talk. If it persists, feel the fear and do what you need to do anyway.

▶ *Learn the lesson and move on.* If you have made mistakes, learn the lessons from them and then erase the feelings by interrupting your standard thought patterns. Interject funny music in the background of your memories or see people as distorted when you find the scene repeating itself in your memory over and over. See the memory in forward and reverse—thinking about anything silly along with the memory can disrupt how you think about past mistakes so you can move on and not let them hold you back.

▶ *Find the benefits in any situation.* Sometimes you are faced with difficult situations or hard times that you cannot control. First, find the benefit—there is usually something positive in anything. Ask yourself, "What can be good about this?" Perhaps the situation is forcing you to learn a new skill or do something you might not otherwise have had the chance to do. Then ask yourself what is not yet perfect in the situation and what you can do to move it in that direction.

▶ *Spend time with positive people who care about you.* You need and deserve people in your life who support your efforts.

Ask for help

Many students find that they are afraid to ask for help when they don't understand something, whether it is information they learn in a course, general information about their program of study, or specific features of a new technology, such as the learning management system. You are investing significant resources in order to complete your program, and it is your right and your responsibility to find the information you need. Your instructors, lead faculty, program directors, academic counselors, and the entire administration are here to help you. They want to be helpful and are waiting for the opportunity. Even if you feel like you should already know the answer, but don't—ask someone!

You can also ask questions of your fellow classmates. Indeed, asking questions is integral to learning.

In addition to receiving help within your course, you may also find that you need to ask for help from your family and friends to make it through your program. When you do so, you are allowing them to contribute to your efforts and success.

Strategies to ask for help include the following:

▶ *Gather contact information.* Learn how to reach the people who can be resources during your education. Include instructors, administrators, lead faculty, program directors, academic counselors, family members, friends, babysitters, and any other potential resources. Keep their phone numbers handy and make it a habit to ask for and incorporate their help as often as possible.

▶ *Speak clearly.* You deserve the help you need. Identify specifically what you need.

▶ *Understand that not everybody is willing to help.* Have a plan in place for dealing with the people who may try to stop you from doing what you need to do to succeed.

When you do not understand something fully, it is seldom the case that you are alone in your struggle. By asking questions, in fact, you may help other students.

▶ *Lean on your classmates.* They understand what you are going through and can offer suggestions and strategies to get the help you need.

Because everyone must be involved, the online learning environment offers a rich and diverse experience. Unlike on-ground classrooms, one or two people cannot easily dominate an online class. Everyone is expected to respond to every question, and thus participation is much more equitable.

In an online course, you have the opportunity to make connections with other students in various states and time zones, maybe even different countries. Communication in the online environment puts few limits on time and place. The classroom environment is also considered far less intimidating than a face-to-face classroom because almost all communication takes place from your own computer in your own comfortable space.

You can communicate online by using a variety of tools and avenues. Following are the more common ones you will probably be exposed to as you begin and continue your online adventure:

E-mail
Forums/newsgroups
Chat rooms
Wikis and blogs

E-mail

Almost everyone uses electronic mail these days. Proper computer etiquette is essential to communicate well online. Use these strategies when you are communicating by email.

E-mail communication guidelines

Even if you do not consider yourself a writer, as an online student, you will be. And there are certain conventions and considerations to keep in mind to make your writing clear, readable, and inoffensive.

Wallpaper

Avoid background wallpaper or setting your messages up to look like electronic stationery for online messages and e-mails. Although it may look fancy, it can make messages hard to read and actually slows things down between systems because wallpaper takes up more space in the computer's memory.

Fonts

Although you have many options, there are certainly more acceptable fonts when sending messages. Avoid using an offbeat or unusual font, even if you think it is expressive of your personality. It may be difficult for others to read. If all reading is done on screen, stick with sans serif fonts (like this). Serif fonts (like this) are easier to read on a hard-copy page.

Make sure your font size is in the middle and readable range, generally 12 point. Large or small fonts may make reading more difficult for others, depending on their screen size and the keenness of their eyesight.

Color

Although it can be fun and interesting to use different font and background colors, resist the temptation. Some color combinations work better than others: A dark font on a light background is always easier to read and more professional.

Avoid high-contrast colors. For instance, stay away from blue text on an orange background. Colors should have medium tone or brightness so they show up but are not overwhelming on the screen.

As people age, the color red becomes harder to distinguish, so avoid using red for large sections of text.

All caps

Do not use all caps. In an online environment, using capital letters conveys YELLING LOUDLY. In addition, depending on the length of your message, writing in all caps makes your message difficult to read on screen.

Emoticons

Emoticons are emotional graphics used to enhance your message visually. They are best used to be sure you clearly convey your intentions whenever you use humor, anger, or a subtle emotion in a message or posting.

Some people use the winking emoticon to denote humor ;)

Another popular emoticon is the unhappy face to denote something sad in a message: ☹.

Do not overuse emoticons because they can make your messages seem silly or shallow. However, when used sparingly, you can put your point across and express the appropriate tone.

Note: For any of the word-processing functions just discussed, if you do not know how to manipulate fonts, colors, and the rest, ask a classmate or friend, use the tutorials included in the program, or do a search online for information on formatting documents specific to your word-processing program.

Spelling and punctuation

Spelling and punctuation are just as crucial in an online environment as in a hard-copy business letter. You want to come across as an educated person. Poor spelling and grammar skills lead others to lower expectations regarding your intelligence and professionalism. Further, your intended message may be misconstrued, at the very least. Use the tools available in your LMS.

Abbreviations

Any of you who send text messages know there are many common abbreviations. (ttfn = ta-ta for now; ttyl = talk to you later, etc.). But for classroom communication, you need to be more formal and avoid slang abbreviations.

Also, clarity is important, and not everyone is familiar with these abbreviations. It is best to write out terms in the more conventional way. In the end, though, your instructor will set the tone for the class, so pay attention and follow his or her lead about the level of formality of language. In using more traditional abbreviations or acronyms, present the full word or phrase at least once before using the abbreviation or acronym.

In your online communication, be courteous, concise, and positive, but try to express your personality in your writing. You do not want to sound dry or like a robot. It may take you a while to find your voice online, but try to reach a level where your online communication is similar in tone to your voice communication in an on-ground classroom.

Other online communication concerns

■ **Reading between the lines.** Communication is complex, whether written or spoken. When you do not have visual and auditory cues, you can easily misconstrue people's comments. You do not have the same nonverbal cues to reference in an online environment as you do face to face, but you can still gain insight into people's communication.

Different people have different styles. Pay attention to how people express themselves, and you will begin to have a sense of their thoughts beyond just their words as you get to know them. But be cautious in your interpretations. Your own moods and preconceived notions can influence the way you interpret other people's communication. Usually, we can assume all messages are intended in a friendly, professional way, unless strong indicators within the message itself point in another direction.

■ **Learning to listen online.** In a classroom setting, you wouldn't have the TV on or children running around. If you are working in the online classroom, though, there may be numerous distracters in the environment. Try to limit the background noise in the area where you are working and really focus so you can read online content accurately.

For some people, listening to music is not a distracter; for others, any noise disrupts their attention. Do what you need to make your environment work for you so you can focus and process the online content. Consider this: If all you have to add to a discussion is "I agree," maybe you didn't listen or process well enough.

■ **Quality of responses.** Keep in mind that the online communications in your class may be archived for a long time. Any time you misspell a word or say something foolish, your words may live on to haunt you. Take the opportunity to think before you post a message to the class. One good approach is to create all your responses in a separate document and take the time to reread and fine-tune them before you upload them for all of the world to see.

■ **E-mail addresses: keep it professional.** During your program, you will need an e-mail account. Be careful about the names you use because others will see them. Choose your e-mail address name wisely and make it simple and tasteful. We recommend "your first name your last name@gmail.com." It is easy to remember and, most importantly, clear and professional.

■ **Knowing what not to share: personal information.** Surprisingly, in an online environment, people tend to share more, rather than less, information. Sometimes people share too much, disclosing inappropriate details regarding intimate personal subjects in the guise of responding to course questions or assignments. Perhaps this problem relates to the anonymity factor, or perhaps people just get carried away. So keep in mind: Monitor your own communication and try to keep your communication appropriate. Steer away from private disclosure unless personal revelations are the specific focus of an assignment. Your instructor and classmates are wonderful resources, but they are not personal counselors.

Be aware that although you may want to talk about your employer and your job experiences, you should be careful about the information you divulge. Many companies have policies regarding disclosing proprietary information. Lastly, consider what contact information is appropriate. Some students create a signature line and include their phone number. Do you really want your phone number available on every single message you send? Your communication in the online classroom should be professional and courteous rather than soul-baring.

■ **Review of synchronized and asynchronized communication.** Synchronized communication occurs when we are all talking and listening to each other at the same time, whether in a classroom, or over the phone, or through a virtual meeting. Everyone is engaged and participating in the communication at the same time.

Asynchronized communication occurs when we are not all engaged in the conversation at the same time, even though we are all participating. For instance,

▶ The old-fashioned exchange of letters among pen pals
▶ E-mail
▶ Exchanging voice mails
▶ Participating in an online discussion in which one person responds at 8 A.M. and is offline by 9 P.M., and someone else doesn't respond until he comes online from 11 P.M. until 2 A.M.

Whether your course interactions are synchronized or asynchronized depends on the institution and the instructor. Be aware of the nature of any specific communication situation. If it is asynchronized, you probably have more time to review your responses. Consider giving others a chance to respond to your initial postings before you come back for more. The point of online discussions is to hear more than one voice, and the input of others may give you more food for thought.

■ *Threading responses in the term discussion board.* You must deal with a large number of messages every day in the online classroom. You can help others manage the sometimes overwhelming number of messages by creating messages considerately. Here are some examples.

1. **Use an appropriate subject line.** During the course of a conversation, the topic often changes. Therefore, if the subject line reads "Week Two-DQ1" and the conversation has evolved to a discussion on time management, change the subject line. You should be able to maintain the thread with a new subject line without a problem.

2. **Place your message first when replying to someone's message.** The newest addition to the conversation needs to be the first thing read. Then be sure and include the relevant sections of the previous message, or even the entire previous message, so people can follow the conversation. Readers can then elect to read further if they need a reminder about what has gone on before. If the older messages are placed first and the newest at the bottom, readers are forced not only to scroll down to read the latest comment but also they must skim the notes previously read.

3. **Be attentive to the appearance of your notes.** As mentioned earlier, avoid fonts that are difficult to read because of style, color, or size. The format should not be more important than the content. Keep in mind when reading on the computer screen that long paragraphs are difficult to follow. As a general rule, limit each paragraph in an e-mail message to five to seven lines if possible.

4. **Reduce confusion by considering a variety of methods of replying.** Although most often a straightforward reply is appropriate, sometimes you can intersperse comments on each point in the original message, increasing the readability of your response.

5. **Exercise good editing techniques.** In threaded discussions, editing of notes refers to removing those portions of the message to which you are replying that are unnecessary to understand your comments. Although it is important to include enough of the previous message(s) to place the note in context, you will seldom need to include the entire message. It is frustrating to download lengthy messages that include dozens of messages already read, and it is equally annoying to download a message that mentions research but contains no references whatsoever.

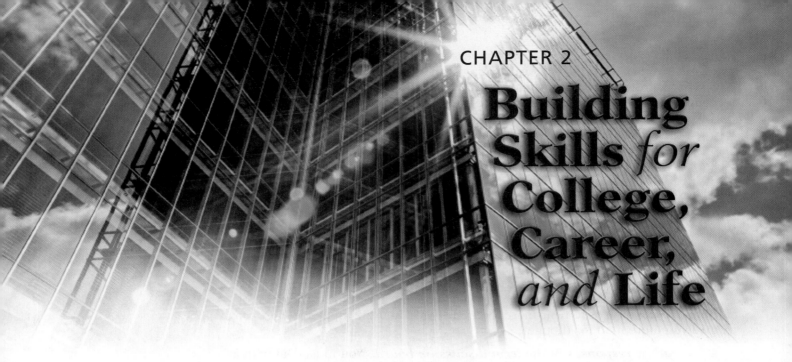

Building Skills *for* College, Career, *and* Life

Steps to Success

Discover Online Learning

BUILD BASIC SKILLS. Successfully adjusting to an online learning environment requires understanding the similarities and differences between traditional face-to-face classes and online classes. How do you think the two types of learning environments are different? How are they the same?

Success in an online learning environment also requires the development of habits specifically for promoting success. What are some things you can do to successfully perform in both face-to-face and online classes? Which habits only work well in an online learning environment?

TAKE IT TO THE NEXT LEVEL. Take a look at your initial observations of the differences and similarities between the two learning environments as well as effective practices common to each.

- What surprised you about the two learning environments?
- What adjustments or changes require you to adapt to the online environment?
- What practices of successful online learners are most important to you and your success?

MOVE TOWARD MASTERY. Select two practices that are most important to your online success. What steps or actions can you take this week to adapt to online learning? Write a short paragraph describing a plan for establishing or improving your success in this class.

Social Networking

IDENTIFY YOURSELF

Sign in to your LinkedIn account and begin to build your profile. Click on "Edit My Profile" and then click on the Edit mark next to your name. Then fill in or edit this basic information:

- First and last name
- Display name (how you want it to appear to others viewing your profile)
- Professional "Headline"—how you identify yourself now (If you are not currently working, you may choose to identify yourself as a student and perhaps include your area of study.)
- Country and zip code
- Industry (if you are working)

60   KEYS TO LEARNING STRATEGIES FOR SUCCESS

ENDNOTES

1. U.S. Department of Education. (2009, May). *Evaluation of Evidence-Based Practices in Online Learning: A Meta-Analysis and Review of Online Learning Studies*. Retrieved March 2, 2010, from www.geteducated.com/images/pdfs/doe_online_education_finalreport.pdf

2. Allen, E., & Seaman, J. (2010). *Learning on Demand: Online Education in the United States, 2009*. Newburyport, MA: The Sloan Consortium and Babson Survey Research Group.

3. Nielsen, J., & Pernice, K. (2009). *Eyetracking Web Usability*. Berkeley, CA: New Riders Press.

Values, Goals, and Time

a veteran in the information technology field, Anthony Terry understands what it means to be flexible and change. After more than 20 years, Terry decided in 2010 to complete a goal that he had set out to do long ago: earn a bachelor's degree.

The busy husband and father of three had taken many courses here and there, but finding the time to go to school, handle a demanding IT job and take care of a family was difficult.

So after learning about Columbia Southern University at an education fair at his wife's job (she is a CSU graduate, too), Terry decided to apply and seek an online bachelor's degree in IT.

"Online education gives you an opportunity to get a college education with the flexibility to complete your courses anytime, anywhere," said Terry. "I feel it gave me a second chance to complete my college education as an adult student. Most of us have started a family and begun a career and just don't have the time to actually go to school. By taking classes online, I had the best of both worlds. I was a full-time college student and a full-time employee."

He added that online education can be challenging. "You still have to be committed to do this. Probably even more so than a student who attends a traditional school. With all the flexibility comes great responsibility."

Terry found CSU courses in IT current and relevant for his career path. "Also, the instructors were great and always helpful. They provided good feedback and communication. The staff at CSU was always helpful when I had a question," he said, particularly in getting his previous coursework transferred.

Another appealing aspect of CSU "was their relationship with some very large corporate organizations. I felt comfortable to know that these organizations were associated with the school."

After completing his degree, Terry later found employment as an IT systems engineer with an Atlanta-based virtualization management and security company. He said his degree played a role in securing the job.

"There are a lot of people out there with experience but having a degree can be a differentiating factor when employers are looking to hire."

STATUS *Check*

▶ *How developed are your self-management skills?*

For each statement, circle the number that feels right to you, from 1 for "not at all true for me" to 5 for "very true for me."

▶ I am aware of my values and beliefs.	**1 2 3 4 5**
▶ I have a system for reminding myself of what my goals are.	**1 2 3 4 5**
▶ I find ways to motivate myself when I am working toward a goal.	**1 2 3 4 5**
▶ When I set a long-term goal, I break it down into a series of short-term goals.	**1 2 3 4 5**
▶ I am aware of my time-related needs and preferences.	**1 2 3 4 5**
▶ I understand my time traps and have ways to avoid them.	**1 2 3 4 5**
▶ I know how to use the SMART approach to plan achievable goals.	**1 2 3 4 5**
▶ When I procrastinate, I know how to get back on track.	**1 2 3 4 5**
▶ I record tasks, events, and responsibilities in a planner of some kind and refer to it regularly.	**1 2 3 4 5**
▶ I understand how managing my time can help reduce my level of stress.	**1 2 3 4 5**

Now total your scores.

Each of the topics in these statements is covered in this chapter. Note those statements for which you circled a 3 or lower. Skim the chapter to see where those topics appear, and pay special attention to them as you read, learn, and apply new strategies.

REMEMBER: *No matter how effectively you set goals and manage time, you can improve with effort and practice.*

Why is it important to know what you value?

You make life choices—what to do, what to believe, what to buy, how to act—based on your personal **values.** The choice to pursue a degree, for example, may reflect how a person values the personal and professional growth that come from a college education. If you like to be on time for classes, you may value punctuality. If you pay bills regularly and on time, you may value financial stability.

Values play a key role in your drive to achieve important goals and use your time wisely, helping you do the following:

▶ *Understand what you want out of life.* Your most meaningful goals will reflect what you value most.
▶ *Choose how to use your valuable time.* When your day-to-day activities align with what you think is most important, you gain greater fulfillment from them.
▶ *Build "rules for life."* Your values form the foundation for your decisions and behavior throughout your life. You will return repeatedly to these rules for guidance, especially in unfamiliar territory.
▶ *Find people who inspire you.* Spending time with people who share similar values will help you clarify how you want to live while finding support for your goals.

> "Successfully intelligent people are well aware of the penalties for procrastination. They schedule their time so that the important things get done—and done well."
>
> —Robert Sternberg

VALUES
Principles or qualities that you consider important.

How values develop and change

Your value system is complex, built piece by piece over time, and coming from many sources—such as family, friends, culture, media, school, work, neighborhood, religious beliefs, and world events. These powerful external influences can so effectively instill values that you don't think about why you believe what you believe. However, you have a *choice* whether or not to adopt any value. Taking advantage of the power to choose requires evaluating values with questions like the following:

Courtesy of Shutterstock

▶ Where did the value come from?
▶ Is this value something from my family or culture that I have accepted without questioning, or have I truly made it my own?
▶ What other different values could I consider?
▶ What might happen as a result of adopting this value?
▶ Have I made a personal commitment to this choice? Have I told others about it?
▶ Do my life goals and day-to-day actions reflect this value?

Values are not set in stone any more than your thinking power is. Your values often shift as you grow. Life changes make it even more important to step back and think about what's truly important to you.

How values affect your life experience

Because what you value often determines the choices you make, it also shapes your life experiences. For example, the fact that you value education may have led you to college, a practical choice that will help you build skills and persistence, choose a major and career direction, find meaningful friends and activities, and achieve learning goals.

Another example is found on today's college campus in the growing diversity of the student body, a diversity also increasingly seen in the working population. If you value human differences, you have taken an important step on the way to working successfully with people of various cultures, stages of life, and value systems both in college and beyond.

Values become goals when you've transformed your beliefs into something tangible and long-lasting. Not every value becomes a goal, but every goal stems from your values.

How do you set and achieve goals?

GOAL
An end toward which you direct your efforts.

When you set a **goal,** you focus on what you want to achieve and create a path that can get you there. Setting goals involves defining your aims in both long-term and short-term time frames. *Long-term* goals are broader objectives you

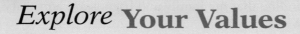

Explore Your Values

Rate each of the listed values on a scale from 1 to 5, 1 being least important to you and 5 being most important.

____ Knowing yourself	____ Being liked by others	____ Reading
____ Self-improvement	____ Taking risks	____ Time to yourself
____ Improving physical/mental health	____ Time for fun/relaxation	____ Lifelong learning
____ Leadership and teamwork skills	____ Staying fit through exercise	____ Competing and winning
____ Pursuing an education	____ Spiritual/religious life	____ Making a lot of money
____ Good relationships with family	____ Community involvement	____ Creative/artistic pursuits
____ Helping others	____ Keeping up with the news	____ Getting a good job
____ Being organized	____ Financial stability	____ Other _____

List your top three values:

1. _____

2. _____

3. _____

Now connect your values to educational goals. Choose one top value that is a factor in an educational choice you have made. Explain the choice and how the value is involved. Example: A student who values helping others chooses to study fire science.

_____

_____

want to achieve over a long period of time, perhaps a year or more. *Short-term* goals move you toward a long-term goal in manageable and achievable steps.

Establish your personal mission

Start with the biggest big picture: Defining your *personal mission* can help you anchor your values and goals in a comprehensive view of what you want out of life. Think of a personal mission as your longest-term goal, within which all other long-term and short-term goals should fit.

Dr. Stephen Covey, author of *The Seven Habits of Highly Effective People*, defines a *mission statement* as a philosophy outlining what you want to be (character), what you want to do (contributions and achievements), and the principles by which you live (your values).[1] Defining your personal mission involves creating a mission statement. The following mission statement was written by Carol Carter, one of the authors of *Keys to Learning Strategies for Success.*

My mission is to use my talents and abilities to help people of all ages, stages, backgrounds, and economic levels achieve their human potential

Goals take effort and planning to reach. This music producer spends days, and even weeks, adjusting equipment and recording tracks on the way to the production of just one song.
©UpperCut Images/Getty Images

through fully developing their minds and their talents. I aim to create opportunities for others through work, service, and family. I also aim to balance work with people in my life, understanding that my family and friends are a priority above all else.

How can you start formulating a mission statement? Try using Covey's three aspects of personal mission as a guide. Think through the following:

▶   *Character.* What aspects of character do you think are most valuable? When you consider the people you admire most, which of their qualities stand out?

▶   *Contributions and achievements.* What do you want to accomplish in your life? Where do you want to make a difference?

▶   *Values.* How do your values inform your life goals? What in your mission could help you live according to what you value most highly?

Because what you want out of life changes as you do, your personal mission should remain flexible and open to revision. Your mission can be the road map for your personal journey, giving meaning to your daily activities, promoting responsibility, and inspiring action. You will have a chance to craft a personal mission at the end of this chapter.

Set long-term goals

What do you want your life to look like in 5 or 10 years? What degree do you want to earn, what job do you want, where do you want to live? How do you want to live your values and activate your personal mission? Answers to questions like these help identify long-term goals.

Long-term goals are objectives that sit out on the horizon, at least 6 months to a year away. They're goals that you can imagine and maybe even visualize, reflecting who you are and what is important to you, but they're too far out for you to touch. The more you know about yourself, the better able you are to set and work toward meaningful long-term goals. One way to make long-term goals real is to put them in writing, as in the following example.

My goal is to build a business in which I, as a family doctor, create opportunities to expose young people in my community to the medical field.

A student 2 years away from college graduation who is pursuing this long-term goal might establish the following supporting set of 1-year long-term goals:

Design courses for the year to make sure I am on track for pre-med course completion. Find medical practices in the area that could serve as a model for my business. Research medical schools.

To determine your long-term goals, think about the values that anchor your personal mission. For someone who values health and fitness, for example, possible long-term goals might involve working for an organic food company or training as a physical therapist. Basing your long-term goals on values increases your motivation to succeed. The stronger the link between your values and your long-term goals, the happier, more motivated, and more successful you are likely to be in setting and achieving those goals.

Set short-term goals

Lasting from an hour or less to as long as several months, *short-term goals* narrow your focus and encourage progress toward long-term goals. If you have a long-term goal of graduating with a degree in nursing, for example, you may set these short-term goals for the next 6 months:

▶ I will learn the name, location, and function of every human bone and muscle.
▶ I will work with a study group to understand the muscular-skeletal system.

These goals can be broken down into even smaller parts, such as the following 1-month goals:

▶ I will work with on-screen tutorials of the muscular-skeletal system until I understand and memorize the material.
▶ I will spend 3 hours a week or more studying.

Set up a SMART goal-achievement plan

At any given time, you are working toward goals of varying importance. First, decide which goals matter most to you and are most deserving of your focus. Then draw up a plan to achieve those goals, using the SMART system to make your goals Specific, Measurable, Achievable, Realistic, and linked to a Time Frame.

▶ *Step 1.* Define an Achievable, Realistic goal. *What do you want?* Is it **achievable**—do you have the skill, ability, and drive to get there? Is it **realistic**—will the external factors (time available, weather, money, other people, and so on) help or hinder you? To develop an achievable, realistic goal, consider your hopes, interests, and abilities. Then, reflect on how realistic it is, given your resources and circumstances. Write out a clear description of your goal.

▶ *Step 2.* Define a Specific path. *How will you get there?* Brainstorm different paths. Choose one; then map out its **specific** steps. Focus on behaviors and events that are under your control.

▶ *Step 3.* Link to a Time Frame. *When do you want to accomplish your goal?* Schedule steps within a realistic **time frame.** Create specific deadlines for each step you defined in Step 1. Charting your progress will help you stay on track.

▶ *Step 4.* Measure your progress. *What safeguards will keep you on track?* Will you record your progress in a weekly journal? Report to a friend? Use an alarm system on your smartphone to remind you to do something? Create a system to **measure** how well you are moving along.

GET CREATIVE!

Find Ways to Get Unstuck

To start, think of a problem on which you tend to get stuck. It could be scheduling homework around extracurricular activities, finding time to hang out with friends, coming up with interesting career paths, or simply figuring out the theme of a literary work.

_____

_____

_____

Now come up with three reasonable ways to get unstuck. For example, if your issue is scheduling homework, one way to get unstuck might be to start your day earlier with a 1-hour work session.

1. _____

2. _____

3. _____

Now that you've determined the most logical solutions, use a visual organizer to think outside of the problem-solving box. First, write your problem in the center bubble. Then, begin filling in the surrounding bubbles with as many ideas as you can think of. Don't question their validity or whether or not they'll work; just keep writing until you've filled in every bubble with a possible solution.

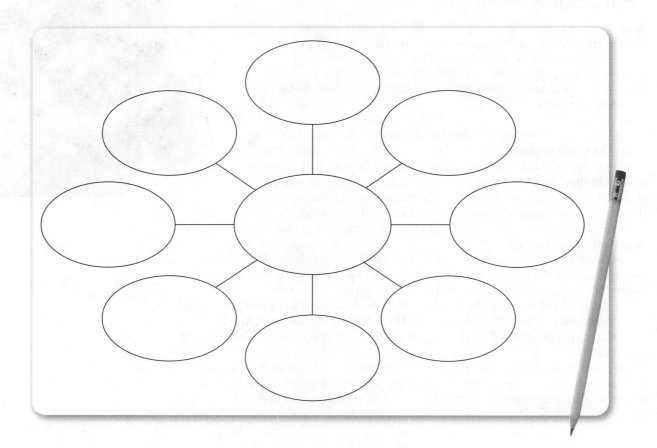

When you're finished, read through all of your creative solutions. Do any of them stick out to you? Find your two favorites and briefly describe how you might be able to use them next time you are faced with a similar situation.

_____

_____

_____

_____

_____

_____

_____

_____

_____

You just got yourself unstuck. Consider using this method when faced with a tough problem. Thinking creatively can be an extremely productive (not to mention fun) way to solve any problem you may encounter.

▶ *Step 5.* Get unstuck: *What will you do if you hit a roadblock?* The path to a goal is often rocky and stressful. Anticipate problems and define **specific** ways to alter your plans if you run into trouble (stress management strategies are presented later in the chapter). Reach out to friends, family, and college personnel who can help you. Remind yourself of the benefits of your goal. Be ready to brainstorm other ideas if your plans don't work. The Get Creative activity will help you think your way past roadblocks.

▶ *Step 6.* Action time. Follow the steps in your plan until you achieve your goal.

See Key 3.1 for a way to apply this goal-setting plan to an important objective that nearly every college student will need to achieve—declaring a **major** or **concentration** (for the sake of simplicity, the term *major* will appear throughout the rest of the text).

MAJOR or CONCENTRATION
An academic subject area chosen as a field of specialization, requiring a specific course of study.

Through the process of working toward your most important goals, you will often be thinking about how well you are using your time. In fact, being able to achieve any significant goal is directly linked to effective time management.

How can you effectively manage your time?

No matter how well you define the steps to your goals, you need to set those steps within a time frame to achieve them. Although the idea of "managing time" may seem impossible, time management can also be thought of as *behavioral*

GOAL: To decide on a major.

SMART KEY	MEANING	EXAMPLE
Specific	Name exactly how you will achieve your goal.	I will read the list of available majors, meet with my academic advisor, talk with instructors, and choose a major by the deadline.
Measurable	Find ways to measure your progress over time.	I will set alarms on my smartphone to remind me of when I should have accomplished steps.
Achievable	Set a goal that your abilities and drive can handle.	I'm driven to declare a major because I want to earn my degree, graduate, and gain work-ready skills.
Realistic	Define a goal that is workable given the resources (time and money) and other circumstances.	Because I'm starting early and already know how the process works, I should have time to think through this carefully.
Time Frame	Set up a time frame for achieving your goal and the steps toward it.	I have a year until the deadline. I will read the catalog in the next month; I will meet with my advisor by the end of the term; I will talk with instructors at the beginning of next term; I will declare a major by the end of next term.

management—adjusting what you do so that you can meet your needs in the time you have available.

Everyone has only 24 hours in a day, and 8 or so of those hours involve sleeping (or should, if you want to remain healthy and alert enough to achieve your goals). You can't manage how time passes, but you *can* manage how you use it. Only by making active choices about your time can you hope to avoid that feeling of being swept along in time's swift tide. The first step in time management is to figure out your time profile and your preferences.

Identify your time profile and preferences

People have unique body rhythms and habits that affect how they deal with time. Some people are night owls who have lots of energy late at night. Others are early birds who do their best work early in the day. Some people are chronically late, whereas others get everything done with time to spare.

The more you're aware of your own time-related behaviors, the better able you'll be to create a schedule that maximizes your strengths and reduces stress. The following steps can help you get in touch with your own inner time clock:

■ *Create a personal time "profile."* Ask yourself these questions: At what time of day do I have the most energy? The least energy? Do I tend to be early, on time, or late? Do I focus well for long stretches or need regular breaks? Your answers will help you determine your profile.

■ *Evaluate the effects of your profile.* Which of your time-related habits and preferences will have a positive impact on your success at school? Which are likely to cause problems? Which can you make adjustments for, and which will just require you to cope?

■ *Establish schedule preferences.* Based on the time profile you have developed, list your preferences—or even map out an ideal schedule as a way of illustrating them. For example, one student's preference list might read, "Study online on Mondays, Wednesdays, and Fridays. Tuesdays and Thursdays free for studying and research. Study time primarily during the day."

Next, build a schedule that takes your profile and preferences into account wherever possible. You will have more control over some things than others. For example, a student who functions best late at night may have more luck scheduling study time when family and children sleep.

Build a schedule

Schedules help you gain control of your life in two ways: They provide segments of time for goal-related tasks and they remind you of tasks, events, due dates, responsibilities, and deadlines.

Use a planner

A planner is a tool for managing your time. Use it to keep track of events and commitments, schedule goal-related tasks, and rank tasks according to priority. Time management expert Paul Timm says that "rule number one in a thoughtful planning process is: Use some form of a planner where you can write things down."[2]

There are two major types of planners. One is a book or notebook, showing either a day or a week at a glance, in which to note commitments. Some planners contain sections for monthly and yearly goals. The other option is an electronic planner or smartphone such as an iPhone or iPod Touch, BlackBerry, or Sidekick. Basic functions allow you to schedule days and weeks, note due dates, make to-do lists, perform mathematical calculations, and create and store an address book. You can also transfer information to and from a computer.

Managing time effectively often means taking advantage of opportunities whenever they arise. This student, also a mother, fits schoolwork in during naptime.
© Michael Newman/PhotoEdit

Though electronic planners are handy and have a large data capacity, they cost more than the paper versions, and they can fail due to software or battery problems. Analyze your preferences and options, and decide which tool you are most likely to use every day. A blank notebook, used conscientiously, may work as well for some people as a top-of-the-line smartphone. You might also consider online calendars, such as Google Calendar, which can "communicate" with your phone or other electronic planning device.

Monday, March 14		
Time	Tasks	Priority
6:00 A.M.		
7:00		
8:00	Up at 8am — finish homewo	
9:00		
10:00	Business Administration	
11:00	Renew driver's license @ DN	
12:00 P.M.		
1:00	Lunch	
2:00	Writing Seminar (peer editin	
3:00	↓	
4:00	check on Ms.Schwartz's off	
5:00	5:30 work out	
6:00	└→6:30	
7:00	Dinner	
8:00	Read two chapters for	
9:00	Business Admin.	
10:00		
11:00		
12:00		

Monday, March 28			
8		Call: Mike Blair	1
9	BIO 212	Financial Aid Office	2
10			3
11	CHEM 203	EMS 262 *Paramedic	4
12		role-play*	5
Evening	6pm yoga class		
Tuesday, March 29			
8	Finish reading assignment!	Work @ library	1
9			2
10	ENG 112	(study for quiz)	3
11	↓		4
12			5
Evening		until 7pm	
Wednesday, March 30			
8		Meet w/advisor	1
9	BIO 212		2
10		EMS 262	3
11	CHEM 203 *Quiz		4
12		Pick up photos	5
Evening	6pm Dinner w/study group		

Keep track of events and commitments

Your planner is designed to help you schedule and remember events and commitments. A quick look at your notations will remind you when items are approaching. Your class syllabus is a crucial tool for keeping track of reading and homework assignments and test dates (see Key 3.2).

When you get your syllabi for the term, enter all relevant dates in your planner right away so you can prepare for crunch times. For example, if you see that you have three tests and a presentation coming up all in one week, you may have to rearrange your schedule during the preceding week to create extra study time.

Among the events and commitments worth noting in your planner are the following:

▶ Test and quiz dates; due dates for papers, projects, and presentations
▶ Details of your academic schedule, including term and holiday breaks

- ▶ Work or professional organization meeting times
- ▶ Personal items—medical appointments, due dates for bills, birthdays, social events
- ▶ Milestones toward a goal, such as due dates for sections of a project

It's important to include class prep time—reading and studying, writing, and working on assignments and projects—in the planner. As you read in Chapter 1, you should schedule at least 2 hours of preparation for every hour of class—that is, if you take six credits, you'll spend twelve hours or more a week on course-related activities. It's tough to get that much studying in, especially if you are a working student, or a parent. Situations like these demand creative time management and attention to your schedule.

Schedule tasks and activities that support your values and goals

Linking day-to-day events in your planner to your values and broader goals will give meaning to your efforts, bring order to your schedule, and keep you motivated. Planning study time for an economics test, for example, will mean more to you if you link the hours you spend to your goal of being accepted into business school and your value of meaningful employment. Here is how a student might translate his goal of entering business school into action steps over a year's time:

- ▶ *This year.* Complete enough courses to meet curriculum requirements for business school and maintain class standing
- ▶ *This term.* Complete my economics class with a B average or higher
- ▶ *This month.* Set up economics study schedule to coincide with quizzes and tests
- ▶ *This week.* Go over material for this week's test
- ▶ *Today.* Go over Chapter 4 in econ text

The student can then arrange his time to move him in the direction of his goal. He schedules activities that support his short-term goal of doing well on the test and writes them in his planner. Achieving his overarching long-term goal of doing well in a course he needs for business school is the source of his motivation.

Before each week begins, remind yourself of your long-term goals and what you can accomplish over the next 7 days to move you closer to them. Additionally, every once in a while, take a hard look at your schedule to see whether you are spending time on what you most value. Key 3.2 shows parts of a daily schedule and a weekly schedule.

Make to-do lists and prioritize

Many people find it useful to create a daily or weekly *to-do list* and check off the items as they are completed. A to-do list can be useful on an especially busy day, during exam week, or at any other time that you anticipate being overloaded.

Making a list, however, is more than doing a "brain dump" of everything you have to do. You need to (prioritize) your list—code it, or organize it, according to how important each item is. Some people use numbers, some use letters (A, B, C), and some use different-colored pens or, for electronic planners, highlighting and font color tools. Prioritizing helps you focus the bulk of your energy and time on the most important tasks. Because many top-priority items (classes, work) occur at designated times, prioritizing helps you lock in these activities and schedule less urgent items around them.

Prioritizing isn't just for time management. You should also prioritize your long-term and short-term goals and the steps leading up to each. Keep these priorities alongside your daily lists so you can see how they influence one another.

Whether it's a task or goal you're scheduling, set basic priority levels according to the following guidelines.

PRIORITIZE
To arrange or deal with in order of importance.

■ *Priority 1.* The most crucial items—you must do them. They may include attending class, working at a job, picking up a child from day care, and paying bills. Enter Priority 1 items in your planner first, before scheduling anything else.

■ *Priority 2.* Important items but with flexibility in scheduling. Examples include library study time and working out. Schedule these around the Priority 1 items.

■ *Priority 3.* Least important items—the "nice to do" activities. Examples include phoning a friend or upgrading software for your iPod.

Plan and track

As you work on the tasks in your to-do lists and planner, follow these guidelines to stay focused on your goals:

▶ *Plan regularly.* Set aside a regular time each day to plan your schedule (right before bed, with your morning coffee, on your commute to or from school, or whatever time and situation works best for you). This reduces stress and saves the hassle of forgetting something important.

▶ *Actively manage your schedule.* The most detailed planner won't do you a bit of good unless you look at it. Check your schedule at regular intervals throughout the day or week.

▶ *Use monthly and yearly calendars at home.* A standard monthly or yearly wall calendar is a great place to keep track of your major commitments. A wall calendar like the monthly calendar in Key 3.3 gives you the "big picture" overview you need.

▶ *Work to stay motivated.* If you can get a task done ahead of time, get it done; it will help you avoid pressure later. Focus on your growth mindset, reminding yourself that achievement requires persistent effort.

▶ *Avoid time traps.* Stay away from situations that eat up time. Learn to say no when you just can't fit in an extra responsibility. Reduce time spent with anything that distracts you, such as your cell phone, social networking sites, or Twitter account.

▶ *Schedule downtime.* It's easy to get so caught up in completing tasks that you forget to relax and breathe. Even a half hour of downtime a day will refresh you and improve your productivity when you get back on task.

KEEP TRACK OF YOUR TIME WITH A **MONTHLY CALENDAR**

MARCH

SUNDAY	MONDAY	TUESDAY	WEDNESDAY	THURSDAY	FRIDAY	SATURDAY
	1 WORK	2 Turn in English paper topic	3 Dentist 2 pm	4 WORK	5	6
7 Frank's birthday	8 Psych Test 9 am WORK	9	10 6:30 pm Meeting @ Acad Ctr	11 WORK	12	13 Dinner @ Ryan's
14	15 English paper due WORK	16 Western Civ paper	17	18 Library 6 pm WORK	19 Western Civ makeup class	20
21	22 WORK	23 2 pm meeting, psych group	24 Start running: 2 miles	25 WORK	26 Run 2 miles	27
28 Run 3 miles	29 WORK	30 Western Civ paper due	31 Run 2 miles			

Confront procrastination

It's human, and common for busy students, to leave difficult or undesirable tasks until later. If taken to the extreme, however, procrastination can develop into a habit that causes serious problems. For example, procrastinators who don't get things done in the workplace may prevent others from doing their work, possibly losing a promotion or even a job because of it.

This excerpt from the Study Skills Library at California Polytechnic State University at San Luis Obispo illustrates how procrastination can quickly turn into a destructive pattern.

> The procrastinator is often remarkably optimistic about his ability to complete a task on a tight deadline. . . . For example, he may estimate that a paper will take only five days to write; he has fifteen days; there is plenty of time, no need to start. Lulled by a false sense of security, time passes. At some point, he crosses over an imaginary starting time and suddenly realizes, "Oh no! I am not in control! There isn't enough time!"
>
> At this point, considerable effort is directed toward completing the task, and work progresses. This sudden spurt of energy is the source of the erroneous feeling that "I work well only under pressure." Actually, at this point you are making progress only because you haven't any choice. . . . Progress is being made, but you have lost your freedom.

PROCRASTINATION
The act of putting off a task until another time.

Conquer Your Time Traps

Different people get bogged down by different time traps. What are yours? They could be productive activities, like working out, or less productive activities, like checking your e-mail. Think of two common time traps that you encounter. For each, come up with two ways to say no graciously—to someone else, or even to yourself, as in the following example.

Time Trap: Text Messaging

Response 1: "I'll call you in an hour. I need to finish this paper."

Response 2: "I will respond to my text messages after I've read five pages."

Your turn:

Time Trap: _____

Response 1: _____

_____

Response 2: _____

_____

Time Trap: _____

Response 1: _____

_____

Response 2: _____

_____

Choose one of the situations you just named and use one or both of your responses the next time the trap threatens your time. Afterward, answer these questions:

How did the response affect your ability to take control of the situation? Did it help? Hurt? How?

_____

_____

_____

_____

What did the response teach you about your personal time traps? Do you find yourself needing to be stricter with your time? Why?

_____

_____

_____

_____

Barely completed in time, the paper may actually earn a fairly good grade; whereupon the student experiences mixed feelings: pride of accomplishment (sort of), scorn for the professor who cannot recognize substandard work, and guilt for getting an undeserved grade. But the net result is *reinforcement:* The procrastinator is rewarded positively for his poor behavior ("Look what a decent grade I got after all!"). As a result, the counterproductive behavior is repeated time and time again.[3]

People procrastinate for various reasons.

■ ***Perfectionism.*** According to Jane B. Burka and Lenora M. Yuen, authors of *Procrastination: Why You Do It and What to Do About It,* habitual procrastinators often gauge their self-worth solely by their ability to achieve. In other words, "an outstanding performance means an outstanding person; a mediocre performance means a mediocre person."[4] To the perfectionist procrastinator, not trying at all is better than an attempt that falls short of perfection.

■ ***Fear of limitations.*** Some people procrastinate in order to avoid the truth about what they can achieve. "As long as you procrastinate, you never have to confront the real limits of your ability, whatever those limits are," say Burka and Yuen.[5] A fixed mindset naturally leads to procrastination. "I can't do it," the person with the fixed mindset thinks, "so what's the point of trying?"

■ ***Being unsure of the next step.*** If you get stuck and don't know what to do, sometimes it seems easier to procrastinate than to make the leap to the next level of your goal.

■ ***Facing an overwhelming task.*** Some big projects create fear. If a person facing such a task fears failure, she may procrastinate in order to avoid confronting the fear. Get into your growth mindset and use the strategies from Chapter 1 to work through this or any other kind of fear, taking steps forward and knowing that you stand to learn something valuable.

Although it can bring relief in the short term, avoiding tasks almost always causes problems, such as a buildup of responsibilities and less time to complete them, work that is not up to par, the disappointment of others who depend on your work, and stress brought on by unfinished tasks. Particular strategies can help you avoid procrastination and its associated problems.

▶ *Analyze the effects.* What may happen if you continue to put off a task? Chances are you will benefit more in the long term facing the task head-on.

▶ *Set reasonable goals.* Unreasonable goals intimidate and immobilize you. If you concentrate on achieving one small step at a time, the task becomes less burdensome.

▶ *Get started whether you "feel like it" or not.* Take the first step. Once you start, you may find it easier to continue.

▶ *Ask for help.* Once you identify what's holding you up, find someone to help you face the task. Another person may come up with an innovative method to get you moving again.

▶ *Don't expect perfection.* People learn by starting at the beginning, making mistakes, and learning from them. If you avoid mistakes, you deprive yourself of learning and growth.

▶ *Reward yourself.* Boost your confidence when you accomplish a task. Celebrate progress with a reward—a break, a movie, whatever feels like a treat to you.

Take a look at Key 3.4 to explore five major reasons that people waste time and procrastinate—and how to take control of each.

Be flexible

Change is a part of life. No matter how well you think ahead and plan your time, sudden changes—ranging from a schedule change to a medical emergency—can upend your plans. However, you have some control over how you handle circumstances. Your ability to evaluate situations, come up with creative options, and put practical plans to work will help you manage changes.

Small changes—the need to work an hour overtime at your job, a meeting that runs late—can result in priority shifts that jumble your schedule. For changes that occur frequently, think through a backup plan ahead of time. For surprises, the best you can do is to keep an open mind about possibilities and rely on your internal and external resources.

Key 3.4

TAKE CONTROL OF
TIME WASTERS

	1. **Television** It's easy to just keep flipping the channels when you know you've got something due. *Take Control:* Record favorite shows using a digital video recorder (DVR) or watch a movie instead. When your program of choice is over, turn the TV off.
	2. **Commute** Though not often something you can control, the time spent commuting from one place to another can be staggering. *Take Control:* Use your time on a bus or train to do homework, study, read assignments, or work on your monthly budget.
	3. **Internet Browsing** Currently, Internet misuse in the American workplace costs companies more than $178 billion per year in lost productivity. *Take Control:* If you use the Internet for research, consider subscribing to RSS feeds that can alert you when relevant information becomes available. When using the Internet for social or personal reasons, stick to a time limit.
	4. **Fatigue** Being tired can lead to below-quality work that may have to be redone and can make you feel ready to quit altogether. *Take Control:* Determine a stop time for yourself. When your stop time comes, put down the book, turn off the computer, and *go to bed.* During the day when you can, take naps to recharge your battery.
	5. **Confusion** When you don't fully understand an assignment or problem, you may spend unintended time trying to figure it out. *Take Control:* The number one way to fight confusion is to *ask.* As the saying goes, ask early and ask often. Students who seek help show that they want to learn.

Manage your time
in online courses

Managing time on a daily basis can be hard enough, but doing so while taking online courses can be even more challenging. Some of the most time-challenging areas for most online students include e-mail, discussions, and course material.

Manage E-mail

In your online course, you will most likely have to e-mail other students and your instructor from time to time. You may receive important e-mails with tasks you need to accomplish, and these e-mails may come directly into your

Instant Message:
Look at me! I'm here to distract you from your course and all your other goals!

Write down key due dates from your syllabus in one or more additional places that you will refer to regularly. Check these dates before you agree to any work, social, or personal commitments that could conflict with your school demands.

Identify your goals for an online course. What grade do you want to receive? How does this grade fit into your long-term goals? With your goal in mind, and the idea that typical courses take at least 10 to 15 hours of your time per week to successfully complete, review the amount of time you will devote to the course. How and when will you fit the necessary studying into your schedule?

online outlook

Tim

Full-time accountant and father of two
Age 38

Challenge

Not enough time in the day

I wanted to go back to school to get my B.S. in business administration in finance and decided the best way for me to do that was in an online program. I'm in my last term with just a few more assignments to go. The main thing that surprised me was the time my courses required. I used to think that online learning would take less time, but I have found that it actually sometimes takes me more time.

Almost everything seems to take longer online.

Even asking an instructor a question can take 2 days instead of 2 minutes; participating in discussions can be days, depending on the subject. You also can't rely on technology working whenever you want it to . . . something that should take 10 minutes might take 2 hours if the Internet is down or you run into some glitch.

It ultimately worked out best for me anyway because I saved a lot of time not driving back and forth and have been able to spend more time with my family than I would have been able to do otherwise.

inbox or through your learning management system (LMS). Key 3.5 highlights important tips for managing e-mail.

Manage discussion forums

Participating in required online discussions requires discipline. During a typical week, you might need to post an initial response to a question and then follow up by responding to what others have posted.

Check the course at the beginning of the week and read the discussion questions. Plan out an approach, such as the following:

► Writing your initial response and posting by Wednesday
► Responding to another's post by Friday
► Finishing any required responses by Sunday

Review Key 3.6 to learn practical ways to manage course discussions.

Manage course resources

Most online courses provide several resources, such as learning objectives, overviews, videos, audio podcasts, interactive learning objects, and lesson presentations. Familiarize yourself with all the standard features of the course. Then tailor the tools to your needs. For instance, if you like to listen to presentations on podcasts that you can download to your iPod or MP3 player, keep doing that, but if it becomes repetitive or you begin tuning out, you might want to use your time differently. If you are struggling with learning a complex concept and the course offers interactive activities or videos, use those to help decrease the time you spend trying to learn new material on your own.

Manage your noneducational computer time

Being online means having instant access to almost everything and everyone. You could have the best system in place to manage your time and be doing everything right, and then . . . you get an e-mail that someone has posted something to your social networking site, and you feel that you just have to respond. Before you know it, you're all caught up with everyone you know,

Bookmarks are Internet shortcuts for your favorite websites. Once you set them up, you can click on the bookmark instead of entering the Web address. Each Web browser has different steps to set these up. You may go to Favorites > Add Favorites (Internet Explorer) or click on the + sign (Safari). Search the Help feature of your browser to find its steps for bookmarking.

If you are stumped by a concept and the course materials are not helping, communicate that immediately to the instructor.

TIPS FOR
MANAGING E-MAIL

Check your e-mails every day. At a set time or times every day, check your e-mail in your inbox and in the LMS. You may have to check even more often if you are working on a group project.

Flag e-mails with reminders. Most e-mail programs allow you to flag a message and remind you to do something at a later time or date. Learn about this feature from the Help menu of your e-mail program and use it to your advantage.

Clean out your inbox daily. Most e-mail programs also allow you to create new folders. You can archive old messages in one generic archive folder or create specific folders to organize your messages.

Keep a copy of all messages sent and received. Keep all e-mail messages until the end of each course, at least. Organize your messages by folders in case you need to access them later.

STRATEGIES TO MANAGE COURSE DISCUSSIONS

Check the online class web page every day to keep up with discussions. Consider bookmarking the class web page. Some web browsers allow you to create a list of websites that automatically load every day. If yours has this capability, put your course web page on this list.

Be sure not to use the discussion area as a social networking system. Manage your time in the discussions so you make sure to participate but also don't go overboard. You don't want to be online so much that it affects your ability to manage your time effectively.

Be considerate. Think carefully before you post a message. Correcting misunderstandings can take a lot of time and effort. When responding to a post, restate the message in your own words, say something positive first before giving any critique, and then give your thought-out opinion.

Seek to understand. As much as possible, let go of the need to convince someone you are right. Instead, try to fully understand why someone may have a differing opinion than you do. Understanding does not imply agreement; it offers mental challenge, and it can also save you time in the long run.

but hours have gone by and you're not at *all* caught up with your assignments that are due tomorrow. Interacting on social networking sites can take a lot of time, so you will want to be careful about when you access these sites. Consider creating a new e-mail account specifically for social network site notifications. While you are online, you can also set your status to "offline" or to "Do Not Disturb." Use these sites as a reward when you complete your assignments. Set a specific amount of time you will allow yourself to correspond with people, and determine when and under what circumstances you will use it. For example, you can tell yourself, "After I read and take notes on each of the three sections of this chapter, I'll check Facebook for five minutes."

Courtesy of Shutterstock

Gaming, instant messaging, watching television shows or movies online, or talking on Internet video conferencing programs such as Skype can take a chunk of your time that you might not have planned on spending. Although a certain amount of downtime is needed, online distractions can become a problem when the time spent engaging in these activities grows too much. Close the programs when you need to concentrate on your schoolwork.

Put off procrastination

Even the most motivated person occasionally puts things off. It's only human to leave difficult or undesirable tasks until later. However, if taken to the extreme, **procrastination,** the act of putting off a task until another time, can develop into a habit that causes serious problems. For example, procrastinators who don't get things done in the workplace, besides preventing others from doing their work, may lose a promotion or even a job because of it.

Develop good habits

Establish a routine

As much as possible, try to establish a routine in which you work at the same times during the day or week. Start by identifying your most productive times of the day and plan to do most of your important work then. Most people know whether they're an afternoon or a morning person, but what a lot of

Begin each school week on Monday, even if you only have time to glance at the materials and print out the schedule.

people don't know is that it's a physical phenomenon, and there are real reasons for it.

If you find yourself staring at the screen during certain times of the day, recognize that you may not be productive at these times and schedule something else. Likewise, recognize when you do get the most done.

Be organized

Computer folders and subfolders can help you manage your files. Some of the Microsoft Windows operating systems use Start > Documents whereas Mac uses Finder to keep folders organized.

Even a brilliant time management plan will run aground if you find yourself constantly looking for necessary items. Set aside a workspace and keep it organized so you can sit down at any time and focus on the work you need to do.

Create an organization system on your computer. If you do not know how to do this, there are many resources appropriate for your operating system.

Windows and Mac each have websites that offer free tutorials. Do an Internet search for "managing documents in Windows" or "managing documents in Mac."

Back up your system often (Famous last words)

You have probably heard this advice before, perhaps by someone who lost all their work because they did not take a few minutes to back it up. Save your data in another place (an external hard drive, CD, flash drive).

An easy way to do this is to keep all your working files in folders in one main directory folder (such as Documents). On a set day of the week, you can simply copy that directory folder. If you copy it to the same place every time, the computer will scan for changes to files and only save those files, taking only seconds to back up your work.

Prioritize

Use a planner to list each task you hope to accomplish. Set the priority of each task and check them off as you accomplish them. Your goal is not to do everything in one day but to keep aware of your obligations and priorities. In this way you will do everything in a timely fashion.

If you find that you have problems saying no to requests, get over that hesitation now. No one benefits when you cannot fulfill an obligation you agreed to do or let your priorities suffer because of it. Say no confidently without being apologetic or listing all of your reasons. You have a right to manage your life.

Vilfredo Pareto, a 19th century Italian economist and sociologist, developed a principle that has been used frequently. Pareto's 80/20 Principle implies that about 20 percent of what we do in any given area delivers 80 percent of the results. Going after the "right" 20 percent will get you 80 percent of the results.

Pace yourself

When you spend a lot of time at the computer, it becomes more difficult, but more important, to take care of yourself. When working hard, take frequent breaks to eat and stay hydrated. This will help you process information faster and will save time in the long run. Get the appropriate amount of sleep that you need. You will be more productive if you do. Also make sure that you are eating well and getting the nutrition your body and mind need to function most effectively. Though you will likely not have the perfect life balance while in an intense educational program, strive to find some outlets that are important to you: physical exercise, spiritual practice, or anything that gives you a sense of vitality. Schedule periods of structured as well as unstructured time for rejuvenation, relaxation, and reflection.

Take advantage of downtime

If you watch television while you are eating dinner, consider watching a course video or listening to the course podcast during this time instead.

You will literally spend years of your life waiting—in line, for appointments and meetings, for web pages to load, and so on. You can take advantage of these pockets of time. Keep a notebook handy to jot down quick thoughts that you might not have time to get into right away. Keep note cards and outlines

ADDITIONAL HABITS FOR BECOMING AN EFFECTIVE TIME MANAGER

Associate a new habit with an old one. If you drink coffee, make that first cup the time to write out and prioritize your tasks.

Embrace your inner elementary school student. For larger projects, post a chart of deadlines on your bulletin board or a calendar in your study area. Check each task off as you accomplish it and give yourself a reward.

Only handle things once. When you sort through papers, such as your mail, put the pieces into three piles: items that need action (put these on your to-do list), items to file for future reference, and recycling. Do this for your e-mail and voicemail, as well.

Practice the 5-minute principle. If there's anything you absolutely must do that you can do in 5 minutes or less, do it now.

Working toward goals and managing time are lifelong tasks. Your ability to successfully perform these tasks rises and falls according to your circumstances. Remember that you are not in this alone. When you seek help from the numerous resources available and especially from the people who are in place for support as you move ahead, you give yourself the best chance for success.

---

around for review, continue with a reading assignment, or work on a problem set. Make incremental progress whenever possible.

If you have downtime in an airport, coffee shop, library, or other locale with wireless access, log in to your course and see what you can accomplish. See Key 3.7 for more tips.

How can you manage stress?

Going to school, working full- or part-time, raising children, participating in activities, doing an internship, volunteering—it can add up to a lot of time and stress. If you're feeling high levels of *stress*—the physical or mental strain that occurs when your body reacts to pressure—you're not alone. Stress levels tend to be high among college students.

Dealing with stress can be an everyday challenge. The greater your stress, the greater the toll it may take on your health and on your ability to achieve your goals. However, this doesn't mean that you should try to get rid of *all* stress. Moderate stress can actually be helpful, motivating you to do well on tests, finish assignments on time, and prepare for presentations. Key 3.8, based on research conducted by Drs. Robert M. Yerkes and John E. Dodson, shows that stress can be helpful or harmful, depending on how much you experience.

Psychologists T. H. Holmes and R. H. Rahe found that stress is linked to both positive *and* negative changes. Key 3.9 is an adaptation of their stress-rating scale, designed for college students. Based on events you've encountered within the last year, it delivers a "stress score" that indicates your likelihood of having or developing a stress-related health problem. Knowing the factors that create stress can help you learn to handle demands and ongoing pressures.

"Successfully intelligent people are flexible in adapting to the roles they need to fulfill. They recognize that they will have to change the way they work to fit the task and situation at hand, and then they analyze what these changes will have to be an make them."

—Robert Sternberg

STRESS LEVELS CAN HELP OR HINDER PERFORMANCE

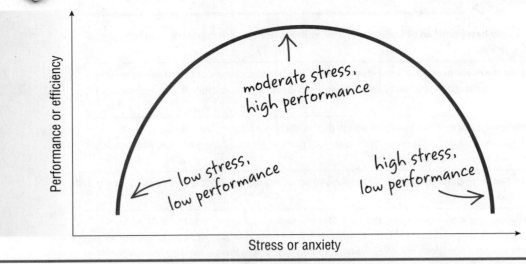

Source: From *Your Maximum Mind* by Herbert Benson M.D., copyright © 1987 by Random House, Inc. Used by permission of Crown Publishers, a division of Random House, Inc.

USE THIS ASSESSMENT TO DETERMINE YOUR "STRESS SCORE"

Add up the number of points corresponding to the events you have experienced in the past 12 months.

1.	Death of a close family member	100	16.	Increase in work load at school	37
2.	Death of a close friend	73	17.	Outstanding personal achievement	36
3.	Divorce between parents	65	18.	First quarter/semester in college	36
4.	Jail term	63	19.	Change in living conditions	31
5.	Major personal injury or illness	63	20.	Serious argument with an instructor	30
6.	Marriage	58	21.	Lower grades than expected	29
7.	Firing from a job	50	22.	Change in sleeping habits	29
8.	Failing an important course	47	23.	Change in social activities	29
9.	Change in health of a family member	45	24.	Change in eating habits	28
10.	Sex problem	44	25.	Chronic car trouble	26
11.	Serious argument with close friend	40	26.	Change in the number of family gatherings	26
12.	Change in financial status	39	27.	Too many missed classes	25
13.	Change in major	39	28.	Change of college	24
14.	Trouble with parents	39	29.	Dropping more than one class	23
15.	New girlfriend or boyfriend	37	30.	Minor traffic violations	20

Total: _____

If your score is 300 or higher, you are at high risk for developing a health problem. If your score is between 150 and 300, you have a 50 percent chance of experiencing a serious health change within 2 years. If you score is below 150, you have a 30 percent chance of a serious health change.

Source: Paul Insel and Walton Roth, *Core Concepts in Health* (4th ed.). Palo Alto, CA: Mayfield Publishing Company, 1985, p. 29.

Being as physically and mentally healthy as possible is a crucial stress management tool. You are making a difference in your health, recent studies say, by simply being in school. Scientists and researchers who study aging report that statistically, more education is linked to longer life. Some potential causes for this link may be that education teaches cause-and-effect thinking, helping people to plan ahead and make better choices for their health, and that educated people tend to be better equipped to delay gratification, reducing risky behavior.[6]

No one is able to make healthy choices and delay gratification all the time. However, you can pledge to do your best to maintain your physical and mental health.

DELAY GRATIFICATION
To forgo an immediate pleasure or reward in order to gain a more substantial one later.

Key 3.10 THREE TYPES OF MAJOR STRESSORS IN LIFE

TYPE	CAUSE	WHAT YOU CAN DO REDUCE STRESS
Situational		
	Change in physical environment.	• If at all possible, change your residence or physical environment to better suit your needs. If you can't change it, talk to the people involved and explain your feelings.
	Change in social environment	• Work hard to meet new friends who support you and on whom you can rely in times of need. • Get involved in some type of social or work activity.
	Daily hassles	• Try to keep things in perspective, and work to reduce the things that you allow to stress you out. • Allow time in your schedule for unexpected events. • Find a quiet place to relax and study.
	Poor time management	• Work out a time management plan that allows time to get your projects complete while allowing time for rest and joy, too. • Create to do lists.
	Conflicts at work, home, and school	• Read about conflict management and realize that conflict can be managed. • Avoid "hot" topics such as religion or politics if you feel this causes you to engage in conflicts. • Be assertive, not aggressive or rude.
	People	• Try to avoid people who stress you out. • Put people into perspective and realize that we're all different, with different needs, wants, and desires. • Realize that everyone is not going to be like you.
	Relationships	• Work hard to develop healthy, positive relationships. • Move away from toxic, unhealthy relationships and people who bring you down. • Understand that you can never change the way another person feels, acts, or thinks.

TYPE	CAUSE	WHAT YOU CAN DO REDUCE STRESS
	Death of a loved one	• Try to focus on the good times you shared and what they meant to your life. • Remember that death is as much a part of life as living. • Talk about the person with your friends and family—share your memories. • Consider what the deceased person would have wanted you to do.
	Financial problems	• Cut back on your spending. • Seek the help of a financial planner. • Determine why your financial planning or spending patterns are causing you problems. • Apply for financial assistance.
Psychological		
	Unrealistic expectations	• Surround yourself with positive people, and work hard to set realistic goals with doable timelines and results. • Expect and anticipate less.
	Homesickness	• Surround yourself with people who support you. • Call or visit home as often as you can until you get more comfortable.
	Fear	• Talk to professors, counselors, family, and friends about your fears. Put them into perspective. • Visualize success and not failure. • Do one thing every day that scares you to expand your comfort zone.
	Anxiety over your future and what is going to happen	• Put things into perspective and work hard to plan and prepare, but accept that life is about constant change. • Talk to a counselor or advisor about your future plans, and develop a strategy to meet your goals. • Don't try to control the uncontrollable. • Try to see the "big picture" and how "the puzzle" is going to come together.
	Anxiety over your past	• Work hard to overcome past challenges, and remember that your past does not have to dictate your future. • Learn to forgive. • Focus on your future and what you really want to accomplish.
Biological		
	Insomnia	• Watch your caffeine intake. • Avoid naps. • Do not exercise two hours prior to your normal bedtime. • Complete all of your activities before going to bed (studying, watching TV, e-mailing, texting, etc.). Your bed is for sleeping.

Key 3.10 CONTINUED

TYPE	CAUSE	WHAT YOU CAN DO REDUCE STRESS
	Anxiety	• Laugh more. Share a joke. • Enjoy your friends and family. • Practice breathing exercises. • Talk it out with friends. • Learn to say "no" and then do it. • Turn off the TV if the news makes you anxious or nervous.
	Weight loss/gain	• Develop an exercise and healthy eating plan. • Meet with a nutrition specialist in the community. • Join a health-related club or group.
	Reduced physical activities	• Increase your daily activity. • Take the stairs instead of the elevator.
	Sexual difficulties/ dysfunction	• Seek medical help in case something is physically wrong. • Determine if your actions are in contradiction with your value system.

Manage stress by managing time

If you are feeling more (stress) in your everyday life as a student, you are not alone. Stress levels among college students have increased dramatically.[7] Stress factors for college students include adjusting to a new environment with increased work and difficult decisions as well as juggling school, work, and personal responsibilities.

STRESS Physical or mental strain or tension produced in reaction to pressure.

Dealing with the stress of college life is, and will continue to be, one of your biggest challenges. But here's some good news: *Every time management strategy in this chapter contributes to your ability to cope with stress.* Remember that stress refers to how you react to pressure. When you create and follow a schedule that gets you places on time and helps you take care of tasks and responsibilities, you reduce pressure. Less pressure, less stress.

Analyze, and adjust if necessary, the relationship between stress and your time management habits.

The following practical strategies can help you cope with stress through time management.

■ *Be realistic about time commitments.* For example, many students attempting to combine work and school find that they have to trim one or the other to reduce stress and promote success. Overloaded students often fall behind and experience high stress levels that can lead to dropping out. Determine what is reasonable for you; you may find that taking longer to graduate is a viable option if you need to work while in school.

■ *Put sleep into your schedule.* Sleep-deprived bodies and minds have a hard time functioning, and research reports that one-quarter of all college students are chronically sleep deprived.[8] Figure out how much sleep you need and do your best to get it. When you pull an all-nighter, make sure you play catch-up

over the days that follow. With time for relaxation, your mind is better able to manage stress, and your schoolwork improves.

■ ***Actively manage your schedule.*** The most detailed datebook page can't help you unless you look at it. Get in the habit of checking at regular intervals throughout the day. Also, try not to put off tasks. If you can get it done ahead of time, get it done.

■ ***Focus on one assignment at a time.*** Stress is at its worst when you have pressing assignments in two different classes all due in the next week. Focus on one at a time, completing it to the best of your ability as quickly as you can before moving to the next until you're through.

■ ***Check things off.*** Each time you complete a task, check it off your to-do list, delete it from your electronic scheduler, or crumple up the sticky note. This physical action promotes the feeling of confidence that comes from getting something done.

Sometimes stress freezes you in place and blocks you from finding answers. At those times, remember that taking even a small step is a stress management strategy because it begins to move you ahead.

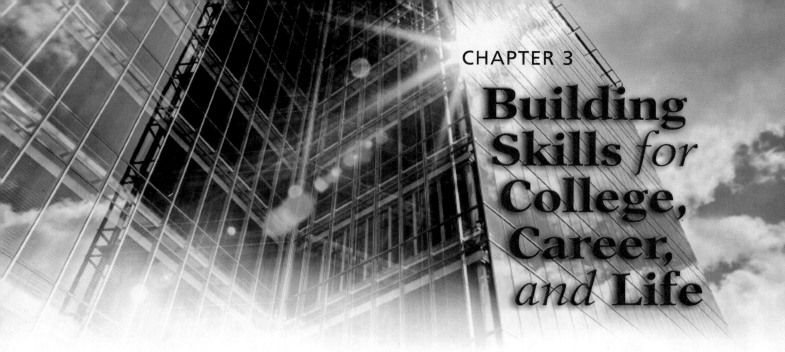

Building Skills *for* College, Career, *and* Life

Steps to Success

Discover How You Spend Your Time

BUILD BASIC SKILLS. Everyone has exactly 168 hours in a week. How do you spend yours? Start by making a guess, or estimate, about three particular activities. In a week, how much time do you spend on the following?

_____ hours   Working

_____ hours   Studying

_____ hours   Sleeping

_____ hours   Interacting with media and technology (computer, online services, cell phone, texting, video games, television) for nonstudy purposes

Now, to find out the real story, record how you spend your time for 7 days. The chart on the next pages has blocks showing half hour increments. As you go through the week, write down what you do each hour, indicating starting and stopping times. Include sleep and leisure time. Record your *actual* activities instead of the activities you think you should be doing. There are no wrong answers.

After a week, add up how many hours you spent on each activity (round off to half hours—that is, mark 15 to 44 minutes of activity as a half hour and 45 to 75 minutes as one hour). Log the hours in the boxes of the table on page 92 using tally marks, with a full mark representing one hour and a half-size mark representing a half hour. In the third column, total the hours for each activity, and then add the totals in that column to make sure that your grand total is approximately 168 hours (if it isn't, go back and check your grid and calculations and fix any errors you find). Leave the "Ideal Time in Hours" column blank for now.

TAKE IT TO THE NEXT LEVEL. Take a look at your results, paying special attention to how your estimates of sleep, study, work and technology time compare to your actual logged activity hours for the week. Use a separate sheet of paper or electronic file to answer the following questions:

- What surprises you about how you spend your time?
- Do you spend the most time on the activities representing your most important values—or not?
- Where do you waste the most time? What do you think that is costing you?
- On which activities do you think you should spend *more* time? On which should you spend *less* time?

TIME	MONDAY activity	TUESDAY activity	WEDNESDAY activity	THURSDAY activity
6:00 A.M.				
6:30 A.M.				
7:00 A.M.				
7:30 A.M.				
8:00 A.M.				
8:30 A.M.				
9:00 A.M.				
9:30 A.M.				
10:00 A.M.				
10:30 A.M.				
11:00 A.M.				
11:30 A.M.				
12:00 P.M.				
12:30 P.M.				
1:00 P.M.				
1:30 P.M.				
2:00 P.M.				
2:30 P.M.				
3:00 P.M.				
3:30 P.M.				
4:00 P.M.				
4:30 P.M.				
5:00 P.M.				
5:30 P.M.				
6:00 P.M.				
6:30 P.M.				
7:00 P.M.				
7:30 P.M.				
8:00 P.M.				
8:30 P.M.				
9:00 P.M.				
9:30 P.M.				
10:00 P.M.				
10:30 P.M.				
11:00 P.M.				
11:30 P.M.				
12:00 A.M.				
12:30 A.M.				
1:00 A.M.				
1:30 A.M.				
2:00 A.M.				

TIME	FRIDAY activity	SATURDAY activity	SUNDAY activity
6:00 A.M.			
6:30 A.M.			
7:00 A.M.			
7:30 A.M.			
8:00 A.M.			
8:30 A.M.			
9:00 A.M.			
9:30 A.M.			
10:00 A.M.			
10:30 A.M.			
11:00 A.M.			
11:30 A.M.			
12:00 P.M.			
12:30 P.M.			
1:00 P.M.			
1:30 P.M.			
2:00 P.M.			
2:30 P.M.			
3:00 P.M.			
3:30 P.M.			
4:00 P.M.			
4:30 P.M.			
5:00 P.M.			
5:30 P.M.			
6:00 P.M.			
6:30 P.M.			
7:00 P.M.			
7:30 P.M.			
8:00 P.M.			
8:30 P.M.			
9:00 P.M.			
9:30 P.M.			
10:00 P.M.			
10:30 P.M.			
11:00 P.M.			
11:30 P.M.			
12:00 A.M.			
12:30 A.M.			
1:00 A.M.			
1:30 A.M.			
2:00 A.M.			

Activity	Time Tallied Over One-Week Period	Total Time in Hours	Ideal Time in Hours
Example: Class	ⅲⅲ ⅲⅲ ⅲⅲ ⅲⅲ ⅱ	16.5	
Class			
Work			
Studying			
Sleeping			
Eating			
Family time/child care			
Commuting/traveling			
Chores and personal business			
Friends and important relationships			
Telephone time			
Leisure/entertainment			
Spiritual life			
Other			

MOVE TOWARD MASTERY. Go back to the chart above and fill in the "Ideal Time in Hours" column. Consider the difference between actual hours and ideal hours. What changes are you willing to make to get closer to how you want to be spending your time? Write a short paragraph describing, in detail, two time management changes you plan to make this term so that you are focusing your time more effectively on your most important goals and values.

Writing

Build Intrapersonal and Communication Skills

Record your thoughts on a separate piece of paper, in a journal, or electronically.

EMOTIONAL INTELLIGENCE JOURNAL

How you feel about your time management. Paying attention to your feelings about how you spend time can be a key step toward making time management choices that are more in line with your values. Think, and then write, about how your most time-demanding activities make you feel. What makes you happiest, most fulfilled, or most satisfied? What makes you most anxious, frustrated, or drained? What do these feelings tell you about your day-to-day choices? Describe how you could adjust your mindset, or make different choices, to feel better about how you spend your time.

Examine two areas of academic specialty. Use your course catalog to identify two academic areas that look interesting. Write a short report comparing and contrasting the majors or concentrations in these areas, being sure to note GPA requirements, number of courses, relevance to career areas, campus locations, "feel" of the department offices, other requirements, and any other relevant characteristics. Conclude your report with observations about how this comparison and evaluation process has refined your thinking.

Personal Portfolio

Prepare for Career Success

EXPLORE CAREER GOALS THROUGH PERSONAL MISSION

21st Century Learning Building Blocks
- Initiative and Self-Direction
- Creativity and Innovation
- Productivity and Accountability

Complete the following in your electronic portfolio or separately on paper.

No matter what employment goals you ultimately pursue, a successful career will be grounded in your personal mission in one or more ways.

First, write a draft of your personal mission. Refer to the list on page 33 to remind yourself of the elements of a personal mission statement. Use these questions to get you thinking:

1. You are at your retirement dinner. You have had an esteemed career in your chosen field. Your best friend stands up and talks about the five aspects of your character that have taken you to the top. What do you think they are?
2. You are preparing for a late-in-life job change. Updating your resumé, you need to list your contributions and achievements. What would you like them to be?
3. You have been told that you have 1 year to live. With family or close friends, you talk about the values that mean the most to you. Based on that discussion, how do you want to spend your time in this last year? Which choices will reflect what is most important to you?

After you have a personal mission statement to provide vision and motivation, take some time to think more specifically about your working life. Spend 15 minutes brainstorming everything that you wish you could be, do, have, or experience in your career 10 years from now—the skills you want to have, money you want to earn, benefits, experiences, travel, anything you can think of. List your wishes, draw them, depict them using cutouts from magazines, or combine ideas—whatever you like best.

Now, group your wishes in order of priority. On paper or computer pages labeled Priority 1, Priority 2, and Priority 3, write each wish where it fits, with Priority 1 being the most important, Priority 2 the second most important, and Priority 3 the third.

Look at your priority lists. What do they tell you about what is most important to you? What fits into your personal mission, and what doesn't? Circle or highlight three high-priority wishes that mesh with your personal mission. For each, write down one action step you may have to take soon to make it come true.

You may want to look back at these materials at the end of the term to see what changes may have taken place in your priorities.

Social Networking

HELP OTHERS GET TO KNOW YOU

As you are building your self-knowledge, help viewers of your LinkedIn profile get to know you as well. Sign in to your LinkedIn account and click on "Edit My Profile." Look for "Summary" and click on the Edit mark next to it. Then, fill in the two areas there:

- Professional Experience & Goals (If you don't have any professional experience, you can fill in Goals only. Remember, too, that you can include experience from internships, work study, apprenticeships, etc.)
- Specialties (In conjunction with talking about what you do well, you may want to consider including information related to learning styles—that you are highly visual, for example, or a strong organizer.)

In addition, scroll down to the "Personal Information" section and fill in any of the following that you choose to have visible on your profile:

- Phone
- Address
- IM
- Birthday
- Marital status

Finally, you may choose to post a photo. Only use a respectable-looking one. Click on "Edit My Profile," then on "Add Photo" underneath the photo icon. It will then direct you to upload a photo.

ENDNOTES

1. Stephen Covey, *The Seven Habits of Highly Effective People*, New York: Simon & Schuster, 1989, pp. 70–144, 309–318.

2. Paul Timm, *Successful Self-Management: A Psychologically Sound Approach to Personal Effectiveness*, Los Altos, CA: Crisp Publications, 1987, pp. 22–41.

3. William E. Sydnor, "Procrastination," from the California Polytechnic State University Study Skills Library, www.sas.calpoly.edu/asc/ssl/procrastination.html. Based on *Overcoming Procrastination* by Albert Ellis. Used with permission.

4. Jane B. Burka and Lenora M. Yuen, *Procrastination: Why You Do It, What to Do About It*, Reading, MA: Perseus Books, 1983, pp. 21–22.

5. Ibid.

6. Rudd Center for Food Policy and Obesity, "Employment," 2005, www.yaleruddcenter.org/default.aspx?id=77.

7. mtvU and Associated Press College Stress and Mental Health Poll Executive Summary, Spring 2008, www.halfofus.com/_media/_pr/mtvU_AP_College_Stress_and_Mental_Health_Poll_Executive_Summary.pdf.

8. Jane E. Brody, "At Every Age, Feeling the Effects of Too Little Sleep," *New York Times*, October 23, 2007, www.nytimes.com/2007/10/23/health/23brod.html.

Learning How You Learn

a self-described "career student," Mike Moreno knows the importance of getting an education to further your career goals.

While working as a code compliance officer in Hallandale, Fla., in early 2009, Moreno decided to alter his career path toward one of his passions: the environment. Moreno started scouring various colleges in South Florida.

"I started looking, but because of scheduling conflicts, I started looking online for a degree in environmental management. I found CSU and it covered everything I was looking for," Moreno said. Soon, the Coast Guard Reservist began working toward his master's degree in occupational safety and health/environmental management with CSU.

After finishing his coursework, Moreno learned about an environmental inspector job opening with the Public Works Department in Fort Lauderdale, Fla., his hometown. Fate smiled.

"You needed a four-year degree and I exceeded that with the master's degree and my military background," he said.

In fact, the degree helped him achieve a more desirable job in the Coast Guard. He moved out of his job as a port security specialist to a marine science technician in May 2009, which he had been working toward for about five years. "The degree was a win-win. Not only did it help my civilian career, but it helped my military career as well," added Moreno, a former U.S. Army staff sergeant.

"My experience with CSU has been excellent," he said. "One of first things I noticed when I found the university was the structured system and easy access. It is far superior to anything out there."

Moreno also says the online education experience "is not that much different than being in a brick-and-mortar classroom."

However, "You get more attention in the online classes, especially compared to class with 50-plus students," he commented.

Another high point for Moreno about CSU was the textbooks policy, which he referred to often when telling friends about CSU. "What impressed me was that the books are included in the price of tuition. No other college offered that. That's why I came back to pursue another online degree."

The degree he's speaking of was a master's degree in business administration with emphasis on human resources management. Moreno, who maintains his environmental inspector job, secured the degree in 2011 "in case, later on, I want to go into management."

In 2010, Moreno's love and respect of the environment was evident when he worked with the Coast Guard in the Orange Beach-Gulf Shores, Ala., area as part of an effort to respond to and monitor pollution calls related to the oil spill in the Gulf of Mexico. "Hopefully, we'll never have another one of this magnitude. My experiences and education can help me educate other Coast Guard members in responding to other oil hazards."

STATUS *Check*

▶ *How aware are you of how you learn?*

For each statement, circle the number that feels right to you,
from 1 for "not at all true for me" to 5 for "very true for me."

▶ I believe I can develop my skills and abilities through self-knowledge and hard work.	1 2 3 4 5
▶ I have a pretty clear idea of my strengths and abilities.	1 2 3 4 5
▶ I understand which subjects and situations make it more difficult for me to succeed.	1 2 3 4 5
▶ In my work in the classroom and out, I try to maximize what I do well.	1 2 3 4 5
▶ I recognize that being comfortable with the subject matter isn't necessarily enough to succeed in a course.	1 2 3 4 5
▶ I assess an instructor's teaching style and make adjustments so that I can learn effectively.	1 2 3 4 5
▶ I choose study techniques that tap into how I learn best.	1 2 3 4 5
▶ I try to use technology that works well with how I learn.	1 2 3 4 5
▶ I've taken a skills and/or interests inventory to help find a major or career area that suits me.	1 2 3 4 5
▶ I understand what a learning disability is and am aware of several different types of disabilities.	1 2 3 4 5

Now total your scores.

Each of the topics in these statements is covered in this chapter. Note those statements for which you circled a 3 or lower. Skim the chapter to see where those topics appear, and pay special attention to them as you read, learn, and apply new strategies.

REMEMBER: *No matter how well know yourself as a learner, you can improve with effort and practice.*

"Successfully intelligent people figure out their strengths and their weaknesses, and then find ways to capitalize on their strengths—make the most of what they do well—and to correct for or remedy their weaknesses—find ways around what they don't do well, or make themselves good enough to get by."

—Robert Sternberg

LEARNING STYLE
A particular way in which the mind receives and processes information.

Why explore who you are as a learner?

Have you thought about how you learn? Now, as you begin college, is the perfect time for thinking about how you learn, think, and function in the world. Thinking about thinking is known as *metacognition* (something you are building with each chapter-opening self-assessment). Building metacognition and self-knowledge will help you become a better student and decision maker because the more you know about yourself, the more effectively you can analyze courses, study environments, and study partners; self-knowledge can also help you come up with ideas as well as make practical choices about what, how, and where to study.

Use assessments to learn about yourself

Every person is born with a unique learning style and particular levels of ability and potential in different areas. This combines with effort and environment to create a "recipe" for what you can achieve. Part of that recipe is the way you perceive your strengths and challenges, which comes from many different sources and starts in childhood. Maybe your mother thinks you are "the funny one" or "the quiet one." A grade school teacher may have called you a "thinker" or "slacker," "go-getter" or "shy." These labels—from yourself and others—influence your ability to set and achieve goals.

The danger in accepting a label as truth, as Sternberg did as a child (see Chapter 1), is that it can put you in a fixed mindset and limit your potential. You are not simply stuck with what you've been given. As you read in the first chapter, brain studies show that humans of any age are able to build new neuropathways and thereby learn new ideas and skills, supporting theories that intelligence can grow over time if you work to keep learning.

Picture a bag of rubber bands of different sizes. Some are thick, and some are thin; some are long, and some are short—*but all of them can stretch*. A small rubber band, stretched out, can reach the length of a larger one that lies unstretched. In other words, with effort and focus, you can grow whatever raw material you have at the start, perhaps beyond the natural gifts of someone not making any effort.

Ask yourself: Who am I right now? Where could I be, and where would I like to be, in 5 years? Assessments focused on how you learn and interact with others can help you start to answer these big questions. Assessments have a different goal than tests. Whereas a test seeks to identify a level of performance, an assessment, as professor and psychologist Howard Gardner puts it, is "the obtaining of information about a person's skills and (potentials) . . . providing useful feedback to the person." You can think of an assessment as an exploration that, if honest, will reliably produce interesting and helpful information.

> POTENTIALS
> Abilities that may be developed.

The assessments you will take in this chapter provide the questions that get you thinking actively about your strengths and challenges. As you search for answers, you will be gathering important information about yourself. With this information, you will be able to define your rubber band and get ready to stretch it to its limit.

Use assessments to make choices and to grow

There is much about yourself, your surroundings, and your experiences that you cannot control. However, self-knowledge gives you tools to choose how you respond to circumstances. Although you cannot control the courses you are required to take or how your instructors teach, for example, you can manage how you respond in each situation.

The two assessments in this chapter will give you greater insight into your strengths and weaknesses. The material after the assessments will help you think practically about how to maximize what you do well and compensate for challenging areas by making specific choices about what you do in class, during study time, and in the workplace.

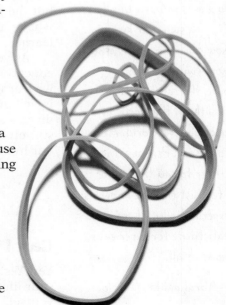

Understanding yourself as a learner will also help you choose how to respond to others in a group situation. In a study group, classroom, or workplace, each person takes in material in a unique way. You can use what you know about how others learn to improve communication and teamwork.

Remember: An assessment is simply a snapshot of where you are at a given moment. There are no "right" answers, no "best" scores. And because many educators are aware of research that shows the benefit from learning in a variety of ways—kind of li-ke cross-training for the brain—they will often challenge you to learn in ways that aren't as comfortable for you.

As you complete this chapter's assessments, compare the experience to trying on new glasses to correct blurred vision. The glasses will not create new paths and possibilities, but they will enable you to see more clearly the ones in front of you. Furthermore, as you gain experience, build skills, and learn more, your learning patterns are apt to change over time. You may want to take the assessments again in the future to see whether your results are different.

Have you encountered people with learning styles different from yours? How?
Courtesy of Shutterstock

We hope you learned your lesson!

What is this thing called learning, anyway?

In its purest and simplest form, learning is a ***cognitive mental action*** in which new information is acquired or old information is used in a new way. Learning can be ***conscious*** or ***unconscious***. Do you remember the very day you learned how to walk or talk? Probably not. This learning was more of an unconscious nature. However, you probably do remember studying the 50 states or subtraction or reading an Edgar Allan Poe poem for the first time. This learning was more conscious in nature. Learning can also be ***formal*** (schooling) or ***informal*** ("street knowledge"). Learning can happen in many ways, such as through play, trial and error, mistakes, successes, repetition, environmental conditioning, parental discipline, social interactions, media, observation, and yes, through formal study methods.

Learning is what you do ***for*** yourself; it is not done ***to*** you. Try as they might, parents may discipline you time and time again, but until you learn the lesson trying to be taught, it will not be learned. Teachers can talk until they are blue in the face about the 13 original colonies, but until you commit them to memory, they will not be learned. That is what this chapter is all about—helping you discover how and why you learn, and assisting you in finding the best way to learn so that you can do the learning for yourself on a more effective level.

What do the experts say?

The question still begs, ***how do we really learn?*** By studying a textbook? By reading a newspaper? By looking at pictures? By interviewing someone about a topic? By watching a movie? By trying something to see if it works? Yes, but the process is much more complex than this. Study Key 4.1 and consider what some of the leading experts throughout history have said about how we learn.

As you can see from these historical experts in the fields of learning, educational psychology, and philosophy, there are many theories on just how we learn best. Perhaps the most important thing to take from these examples is tied into Jean Piaget's theory of holistic learning—that as individuals with diverse and varied needs, backgrounds, and experiences, we require a variety of stimuli to help us learn, and that we all learn differently at different stages in our lives from a variety of things.

Give your brain a workout

Can I really learn all this stuff?

Yes! Yes! Yes! You can learn! Think about all that you have already learned in your lifetime. You learned how to eat, walk, talk, play, make decisions, dress yourself, have a conversation, tie your shoes, make your bed, ride a bicycle, play

"Many things in life cannot be transmitted well by words, concepts, or books. Colors that we see cannot be described to a person born blind. Only a swimmer knows how swimming feels; the non-swimmer can get only the faintest idea of it with all the words and books in the world. And so it goes. Perhaps it is better to say that all of life must first be known experientially. There is no substitute for experience, none at all."

—Abraham H. Maslow

a sport, drive a car, protect yourself, make associations based on observations, use a cell phone, play a video game, ask questions, and countless other simple and highly complex skills. There is proof that you can learn because you have learned in the past. The old excuse of "I can't learn this stuff" is simply hogwash! You have the capacity to know more, do more, experience more, and acquire more knowledge. Your brain is a natural learning machine, just as your heart is a natural pumping machine. It is in our nature to learn every single day. You just have to understand how this process works in order to make the most of your brain's natural learning power. And you have to devote the time necessary to learn the basics of something new and then build on that knowledge base. Time and effort are very important aspects of the learning process.

You also have to give your brain a "workout" to make sure it stays in shape. Just as your body needs exercise and activities to stay in shape, your brain does, too. When you work out your brain and use it to learn new material, your brain

"The mind is not a vessel to be filled, but rather a fire to be kindled."

—Plutarch

LEARNING THROUGH **THE AGES**

Socrates	Around 300 b.c., the great Greek philosopher Socrates introduced his theory of learning. He believed that we learn by asking questions. This is called the *Socratic Method.*
Plato	Socrates' student Plato expanded on this theory and believed that we learn best by dialogue, or the *Dialectic Method*, which involved "the searcher" beginning a conversation on a topic and having a dialogue with "an expert." Plato believed that through this back-and-forth conversation, knowledge could be acquired.
Lao_Tse	In the fifth century b.c., the Chinese philosopher Lao-Tse wrote, "If you tell me, I will listen. If you show me, I will see. But if you let me experience, I will learn." He was one of the first to proclaim that active, involved learning was a viable form of acquiring information.
Kung Fu-tse (Confucius)	Confucius first introduced the case study, which included telling stories or parables and then having people discuss the issues in the case to learn and acquire knowledge.
John Locke	In 1690, the English philosopher John Locke introduced the theory of "the blank slate." He believed that all humans are born with empty minds and that we learn information about the world through what our senses bring to us (sensory learning). He believed that learning is like a pyramid—we learn the basics and then build on those simple principles until we can master complex ideas.
Jean-Jacques Rousseau	In the 1760s, the French philosopher Jean-Jacques Rousseau expanded on a theory that suggests that people learn best by experiencing rather than by listening. In other words, we learn best by doing something rather than being told how someone else did it. He was the first to thoroughly introduce individual learning styles, believing that learning should be natural to us and follow our basic instincts and feelings.
J. B. Watson	In the early 1900s, an American psychologist, J. B. Watson, developed the theory of behaviorism, believing that we learn best by conditioning or training. His theory was based on that of Pavlov (and his dog) and held the tenet that we act and learn in certain ways because we have been conditioned or trained to do so. If a dog (or a person) is fed when it rings a bell, the dog (or the person) quickly learns to ring the bell when it wants to be fed.
Jean Piaget	In the mid-1900s, Swiss psychologist Jean Piaget introduced the groundbreaking theory of holistic learning. This theory is widely held today as one of the most important breakthroughs in educational psychology. He believed that we learn best by experiencing a wide variety of stimuli, such as reading, listening, experimenting, exploring, and questioning.
Benjamin Bloom	In 1956, Benjamin Bloom introduced his Taxonomy of Learning. Bloom believed in a mastery approach to learning. This theory suggests that we learn simple information and then transform that information into more complex ideas, solutions, and creations. His was an idea of learning how to process and actually use information in a meaningful way.

did you know?

Pablo Picasso

Pablo Picasso, the world renowned, trend-setting artist, was born in Spain. He had a hard time in school and is said to have had a very difficult time with reading. He was diag-nosed with a learning disability and his for-mal education never really benefited him. He left his college-level courses at the Academy of Arts in Madrid after less than a year of study. However, because of his immense artistic talent, he changed the way the world looks at art through his cubist interpretation of the universe. He is listed in the *Guinness Book of World Records* as the most prolific painter in history, having completed nearly 14,000 paintings.

PHOTO: Dalmas/Sipa Press/ Newscom

releases a chemical called *cypin* (sigh-pin). Cypin is found throughout the body, but in the brain, it helps build new branches, like a tree sprouting new growth. In a nutshell, when you exercise your brain, your brain rewards you with new learning patterns and new learning receptors. This is sometimes referred to as *neuroplastic-ity* (new-ro-plas-tis-i-ty), or the brain's ability to change with new knowledge.

The learning process

What are the steps to active, authentic learning?

"Human beings have an innate learning process, which includes a motivation to learn" (Smilkstein, 2003). You may be saying to yourself, "If I have a natural, innate ability to learn, then why is chemistry so difficult for me to master? Why is English such a crazy language with so many rules?" The answer could rest in the notion that you are going against your natural, neurological learning pattern—that you are being taught, or trying to learn by yourself, in a way that is unnatural to you, and your brain simply is having trouble adapting to this unnatural process.

If you learn best by doing and touching, *you need to do and touch.* If you learn best by listening and questioning, you need to *listen and question.* If you learn best by reading and studying in a quiet place, you need to **find a quiet place to read and study.** Basically, you must figure out your natural inclination for learning and build on it. You will also need to understand that learning takes time and people need different amounts of time to master material. Janet may learn Concept X in a few hours, but it may take William three days of constant practice to learn the same concept. One thing is true: The more involved you are with the information you are trying to learn, the more you retain.

In the chart in Key 4.2, we have tried to simplify thousands of years of educational study on the topic of learning. Basically, learning something new can happen in the six steps outlined there.

As a practice activity, research one of the following topics (all of which we purposefully chose because of their uniqueness or esotericism) using the six steps in the Key 4.2 to discover something new. You can do this in your notebook or online journal. Remember, however, you will need to devote some time to this activity. Learning new information does not happen instantaneously. You will also need to use a variety of sources. Yes, there are other sources out there!

THE **LEARNING PROCESS**

1   Motivation to learn the material is the first step in the learning process. You have to possess the internal motivation and passion to want to learn what is being presented or what you are studying. You must also be motivated enough to devote the time to learning something new. Deep, purposeful learning does not happen in an instant; it takes work, patience, and yes, motivation.

2   Understand the material through ambitious curiosity, keen observations, purposeful questioning, intense studying, eager determination, robust effort, and time devoted to task. You must be able to answer such questions as: Who is involved? What happened? When did it happen? Where did it happen? How did it happen? How could it have happened? What does it all mean? Why is it important? What is the relationship between x and y? You should be able to describe it, discuss it, give examples, put the information into your own words, and tell others about it clearly.

3   Internalize the material by asking, How can this information affect my life, my career, my studies, and my future? Why does this information matter? How can I control my emotions regarding the value of this information? If I think this information is useless, how can I change this perception?

4   Apply the material by asking, How can I use this information to improve? How can I use this information to work with others, to develop new ideas, or to build meaningful conclusions? Can I demonstrate it? Can I share this information with or teach this information to others intelligently? It is possible to practice what I have learned?

5   Evaluate the material by determining the value of what you just learned. Ask yourself, Do I trust my research and sources? Have I consulted others about their findings and knowledge? What did they learn? What can I learn from them? Have I asked for feedback? Can I debate this information with others?

6   Use the material to grow and change. Ask yourself, How could I take this information (or the process of learning this information) and change my life, attitudes, or emotions? How could this information help me grow? What can I create out of this new information? How can I expand on this knowledge to learn more?

Possible topics

▶ What was Kristallnacht?

▶ Why and how long can a cockroach live without a head? Why?

▶ Who invented the electric chair and why?

▶ What is Sanskrit?

▶ How is paper made?

▶ Who was Vlad the Impaler? What famous character did his life inspire?

Understanding your strengths

What are the advantages of discovering and polishing your talents?

Here you will have the opportunity to complete three inventories: one to identify your **learning style,** one to identify your **personality type,** and one to identify your **dominant intelligence.** Later, you will have the opportunity to pull all of this information together to help you understand your learning patterns and to formulate a learning plan for the future.

These assessments are in no way intended to "label you." They are not a measure of how smart you are. They do not measure your worth or your capacities as a student or citizen. The three assessments are included so that you might gain a better understanding of your dominant intelligence, identify your learning style, and discover your strongest personality type.

There are no right or wrong answers, and there is no one best way to learn. We hope that you will experience a "wow" or "aha!" moment as you explore and discover new and exciting components of your education. We also hope that you will learn the skills needed to more effectively use your dominant traits and improve your less dominant characteristics.

Understanding multiple intelligences

Why is it important to discover new ways of looking at yourself?

In 1983, Howard Gardner, a Harvard University professor, developed a theory called *multiple intelligences* (MI). In his book *Frames of Mind,* he outlines seven intelligences that he feels are possessed by everyone: visual/spatial, verbal/linguistic, musical/rhythmic, logical/mathematical, bodily/kinesthetic, interpersonal, and intrapersonal. In 1996, he added an eighth intelligence: naturalistic. For more information about the intelligences, see Key 4.4.

In short, if you have ever done things that came easily for you, you were probably drawing on one of your well-developed intelligences. On the other hand, if you have tried to do things that are very difficult to master or understand, you may be dealing with material that calls on one of your less developed intelligences. If playing the piano by ear comes easily to you, your musical/rhythmic intelligence may be very strong. If you have trouble writing an English paper, your verbal/linguistic intelligence may not be as well developed. This does not mean that you will never be able to write a paper; it simply means that this is not your dominant intelligence, and you may need to spend more time on this activity.

TAKE THE
MIS (MULTIPLE INTELLIGENCES SURVEY)

Directions: Read each statement carefully and thoroughly. After reading the statement, rate your response using the scale below. There are no right or wrong answers. This is not a timed survey. The MIS is based, in part, on Howard Gardner's 1983 book, *Frames of Mind.*

3 = Often Applies   2 = Sometimes Applies   1 = Never or Almost Never Applies

_____ 1. When someone gives me directions, I have to visualize them in my mind in order to understand them.

_____ 2. I enjoy crossword puzzles and word games like Scrabble.

_____ 3. I enjoy dancing and can keep up with the beat of music.

_____ 4. I have little or no trouble conceptualizing information or facts.

_____ 5. I like to repair things that are broken, such as toasters, small engines, bicycles, and cars.

_____ 6. I enjoy leadership activities on campus and in the community.

_____ 7. I have the ability to get others to listen to me.

_____ 8. I enjoy working with nature, animals, and plants.

_____ 9. I know where everything is in my home, such as supplies, gloves, flashlights, camera, and compact discs.

_____ 10. I am a good speller.

_____ 11. I often sing or hum to myself in the shower or car or while walking or just sitting.

_____ 12. I am a very logical, orderly thinker.

_____ 13. I use a lot of gestures when I talk to people.

_____ 14. I can recognize and empathize with people's attitudes and emotions.

_____ 15. I prefer to study alone.

_____ 16. I can name many different things in the environment, such as clouds, rocks, and plant types.

_____ 17. I like to draw pictures, graphs, and charts to better understand information.

_____ 18. I have a good memory for names and dates.

_____ 19. When I hear music, I "get into it" by moving, humming, tapping, or even singing.

_____ 20. I learn better by asking a lot of questions.

_____ 21. I enjoy playing competitive sports.

_____ 22. I communicate very well with other people.

_____ 23. I know what I want and I set goals to accomplish it.

_____ 24. I have some interest in herbal remedies and natural medicine.

_____ 25. I enjoy working puzzles and mazes.

_____ 26. I am a good storyteller.

_____ 27. I can easily remember the words and melodies of songs.

_____ 28. I enjoy solving problems in math and chemistry and working with computer programming problems.

_____ 29. I usually touch people or pat them on the back when I talk to them.

_____ 30. I understand my family and friends better than most other people do.

_____ 31. I don't always talk about my accomplishments with others.

_____ 32. I would rather work outside around nature than inside around people and equipment.

_____ 33. I enjoy and learn more when seeing movies, slides, or videos in class.

_____ 34. I am a very good listener, and I enjoy listening to others' stories.

_____ 35. I need to study with music.

_____ 36. I enjoy games like Clue, Battleship, chess, and Rubik's Cube.

_____ 37. I enjoy physical activities, such as bicycling, jogging, dancing, snowboarding, skateboarding, and swimming.

_____ 38. I am good at solving people's problems and conflicts.

_____ 39. I have to have time alone to think about new information in order to remember it.

_____ 40. I enjoy sorting and organizing information, objects, and collectibles.

CONTINUED

Refer to your score on each individual question. Place that score beside the appropriate question number below. Then, tally each line across and put the total at the side.

SCORE					TOTAL ACROSS	CODE
1 ___	9 ___	17 ___	25 ___	33 ___	_____	Visual/Spatial
2 ___	10 ___	18 ___	26 ___	34 ___	_____	Verbal/Linguistic
3 ___	11 ___	19 ___	27 ___	35 ___	_____	Musical/Rhythmic
4 ___	12 ___	20 ___	28 ___	36 ___	_____	Logical/Mathematical
5 ___	13 ___	21 ___	29 ___	37 ___	_____	Bodily/Kinesthetic
6 ___	14 ___	22 ___	30 ___	38 ___	_____	Interpersonal
7 ___	15 ___	23 ___	31 ___	39 ___	_____	Intrapersonal
8 ___	16 ___	24 ___	32 ___	40 ___	_____	Naturalistic

MIS Tally

Look at the scores on the MIS. What are your top three scores? Write them in the spaces below.

Top Score _____   Code _____

Second Score _____   Code _____

Third Score _____   Code _____

This tally can help you understand where some of your strengths may be. Again, this is not a measure of your worth or capacities, nor is it an indicator of your future successes. Read the following section to better understand multiple intelligences.

© Robert M. Sherfield

UNDERSTANDING AND USING THE **EIGHT INTELLIGENCES**

INTELLIGENCE	HOW TO USE IT
Visual/Spatial (picture smart) Thinks in pictures, knows where things are in the house, loves to create images and work with graphs, charts, pictures, and maps.	• Use visuals in your notes, such as timelines, charts, graphs, and geometric shapes. • Work to create a mental or visual picture of the information at hand. • Use colored markers to make associations or to group items together. • Use mapping or webbing so that your main points are easily recognized. • Re-type your notes on the computer; consider using a spreadsheet. • When taking notes, draw pictures in the margins to illustrate the main points. • Visualize the information in your mind.
Verbal/Linguistic (word smart) Communicates well through language, likes to write, is good at spelling, is great at telling stories, loves to read books.	• Establish study groups so that you will have the opportunity to talk about the information. • Using the information you studied, create a story or a skit. • Read as much information about related areas as possible. • As you read chapters, outline them in your own words. • Summarize and recite your notes aloud.

Musical/Rhythmic (music smart) Loves to sing, hum, and whistle; comprehends music; responds to music immediately; performs music.	• Listen to music while studying (if it does not distract you). • Write a song, jingle, or rap about the chapter or information. • Take short breaks from studying to listen to music, especially classical music. • Commit the information being studied to the music from your favorite song.
Logical/Mathematical (number smart) Can easily conceptualize and reason, uses logic, has good problem-solving skills, enjoys math and science.	• Strive to make logical connections between subjects. • Don't just memorize the facts; apply them to real-life situations. • As you study the information, think of problems in society and how this information could solve those problems. • Organize the material in a logical sequence. • Create analyzing charts. Draw a line down the center of the page, put the information at hand in the left column, and analyze, discuss, relate, and synthesize it in the right column. • Allow yourself some time to reflect after studying.
Bodily/Kinesthetic (body smart) Learns through body sensation, moves around a lot, enjoys work involving the hands, is graced with some athletic ability.	• Don't confine your study area to a desk or chair—move around, explore, go outside. • Act out the information. • Study with a group of people, and change groups often. • Use charts, posters, flash cards, and chalkboards to study. • When appropriate or possible, build models using the information studied. • Verbalize the information to others. • Use games such as chess, Monopoly, Twister, or Clue when studying. • Trace words as you study them. • Use repetition to learn facts; write them many times. • Make study sheets.
Interpersonal (people smart) Loves to communicate with other people, possesses great leadership skills, has lots of friends, is involved in extracurricular activities.	• Study in groups. • Share the information with other people. • Teach the information to others. • Interview outside sources to learn more about the material at hand. • Have a debate with others about the information.
Intrapersonal (self smart) Has a deep awareness of own feelings, is very reflective, requires time to be alone, does not get involved with group activities.	• Study in a quiet area. • Study by yourself. • Allow time for reflection and meditation about the subject matter. • Study in short time blocks, and then spend some time absorbing the information. • Work at your own pace.
Naturalistic (environment smart) Has interest in the environment and in nature; can easily recognize plants, animals, rocks, and cloud formations; may like hiking, camping, and fishing.	• Study outside whenever possible. • Categorize information. • Relate the information to the effect on the environment whenever possible. • When given the opportunity to choose your own topic or research project, choose something related to nature. • Collect your own study data and resources. • Organize and label your information. • Keep separate notebooks on individual topics so that you can add new information to each topic as it becomes available to you.

In Key 4.4, you will find each intelligence described and some helpful tips to assist you in creating a study environment and study habits using the eight intelligences. Read each category, because you may need to improve your less dominant intelligence in some of the classes you take. This list can help you build on your strengths and develop your less dominant areas.

Understanding learning styles theory

Why is it important to know how I learn?

A learning style (LS) is "the way in which each learner begins to concentrate on, process, and retain new and difficult information" (Dunn and Griggs, 2000). There is a difference between a *learning style* and a *learning strategy.* A learning style is innate and involves your five senses. It is how you best process information that comes to you. A learning strategy is how you might choose to learn or study, such as by using note cards, flip charts, or color slides. Learning strategies also involve where you study (such as at a desk, in bed, in the library, in a quiet place, with music, etc.), how long you study, and what techniques you use to help you study (such as mnemonics, cooperative learning teams, or SQ3R).

If you learn best by *seeing* information, you have a more dominant *visual learning style.* If you learn best by *hearing* information, you have a more dominant *auditory learning style.* If you learn best by *touching or doing,* you have a more dominant *tactile learning style.* You may also hear the tactile learning style referred to as *kinesthetic* or *hands-on.*

Some of the most successful students master information and techniques by using all three styles. If you were learning how to use a computer, you might learn best by *hearing someone* talk about the different styles or techniques. Others might learn best by *watching a video* where someone demonstrates the techniques. Still others would learn best by actually getting on the computer and *trying it.* Those who engage all of their senses gain the most.

After taking the LEAD in Key 4.5 and reading more about learning styles, list at least three concrete strategies that you can employ to enhance your learning strategies for each of the three areas.

Wanted: A visual learner with tactile skills

Do you know the differences between your primary learning style and your dominant intelligence?

As discussed earlier, a *learning style* and a *learning strategy* are different. A learning style and a *dominant intelligence* are also quite different. When you read over the descriptions of MI theory and LS theory, you probably noticed several common elements. Both theories deal with the visual, auditory, and tactile (or kinesthetic). There are also similarities between the two theories, but the differences are great and important.

Simply stated, you can have a visual learning style and yet *not have* visual/spatial as your dominant intelligence. "How can this be possible?" you may be asking. It may be that you *learn best* by watching someone paint a picture—

TAKE THE **LEAD (LEARNING EVALUATION AND ASSESSMENT DIRECTORY)**

Directions: Read each statement carefully and thoroughly. After reading the statement, rate your response using the scale below. There are no right or wrong answers. This is not a timed survey. The LEAD is based, in part, on research conducted by Rita Dunn.

3 = Often Applies   2 = Sometimes Applies   1 = Never or Almost Never Applies

_____ 1. I remember information better if I write it down or draw a picture of it.

_____ 2. I remember things better when I hear them instead of just reading or seeing them.

_____ 3. When I get something that has to be assembled, I just start doing it. I don't read the directions.

_____ 4. If I am taking a test, I can "see" the page of the text or lecture notes where the answer is located.

_____ 5. I would rather the professor explain a graph, chart, or diagram than just show it to me.

_____ 6. When learning new things, I want to "do it" rather than hear about it.

_____ 7. I would rather the instructor write the information on the board or overhead instead of just lecturing.

_____ 8. I would rather listen to a book on tape than read it.

_____ 9. I enjoy making things, putting things together, and working with my hands.

_____ 10. I am able to quickly conceptualize and visualize information.

_____ 11. I learn best by hearing words.

_____ 12. I have been called "hyperactive" by my parents, spouse, partner, or professor.

_____ 13. I have no trouble reading maps, charts, and diagrams.

_____ 14. I can usually pick up on small sounds like bells, crickets, and frogs, and distant sounds like train whistles.

_____ 15. I use my hands and gesture a lot when I speak to others.

Refer to your score on each individual question. Place that score beside the appropriate question number below. Then, tally the total for each line at the side.

SCORE					TOTAL ACROSS	CODE
1 ___	4 ___	7 ___	10 ___	13 ___	_____	Visual
2 ___	5 ___	8 ___	11 ___	14 ___	_____	Auditory
3 ___	6 ___	9 ___	12 ___	15 ___	_____	Tactile

© Robert M. Sherfield

LEAD Score

Look at the scores on the LEAD. What is your top score?

Top Score _____   **Code** _____

watching his or her brush stokes, method of mixing paints, and spatial layout. (This is your dominant *visual learning* style.) However, you may not be as engaged or as talented at actually painting as the person you watched. Your painting may lack feeling, depth, and expression. You may find it hard to paint anything that is not copied from something else. You can't visualize a landscape in your mind because your visual/spatial intelligence is not very strong. In other words, you are not an innate artist at heart. This is an example of how your visual learning style can be a strong way for you to learn, but your visual/spatial intelligence may not be your dominant intelligence.

An Activity for Critical Reflection

Kristin knew that her most powerful learning style was visual. She knew that she had always learned best when she could "see" the information in pictures, charts, graphs, PowerPoints, videos, or other powerful visuals. Kristin also knew that when she was able to get involved with the information, she seemed to retain it better. She did not know what this was called, but later learned that she was also a tactile or "hands-on" learner.

When she discovered that different people have different ways of learning and instructors have different ways of teaching, things began to make more sense to her. She wondered why she had also done poorly in classes that were all lecture—like her history class. This semester, she was becoming increasingly worried about her literature class. It, too, was all lecture about poems, plays, and sonnets. She decided to go to the Tutoring Center to find out what she could do to retain the information more effectively. Her tutor showed her how to make the terms and ideas more "visual" by drawing pictures beside each one, using colors in her notes, creating small story-boards, and creating a visual image of what was being discussed.

In your own words, what would you suggest that a classmate do if he or she was having trouble understanding, interpreting, or remembering information from a class in drawing where there was very little discussion or lecture and he or she is a very strong auditory learner? List at least three things that could be done to strengthen his or her less dominant intelligence, learning style, and/or personality type. Think about what services are offered on your campus and what people might be of assistance to him or her.

1. _____
_____

2. _____
_____

3. _____
_____

In your own words, compare and contrast your primary learning style with your dominant intelligence. Give one example.

_____

_____

_____

Understanding **personality type**

Are you ENFJ, ISTP or ENTJ, and why does it matter?

In 1921, Swiss psychologist Carl Jung published his work *Psychological Types*. In this book, Jung suggested that human behavior is not random. He felt that behavior follows patterns, and these patterns are caused by differences in the

In the space below, use the information from the LEAD and the information on learning styles to create a study plan for each learning style.

VISUAL LEARNING STYLE
(Eye Smart)

Thinks in pictures. Enjoys visual instructions, demonstrations,and descriptions; would rather read a text than listen to a lecture; an avid note-taker; needs visual references; enjoys using charts, graphs, and pictures.

I can improve my visual learning style by...

1. _____
_____
2. _____
_____
3. _____
_____

AUDITORY LEARNING STYLE
(Ear Smart)

Prefers verbal instructions; would rather listen than read; often tapes lectures and listens to them in the car or at home; recites information out loud; enjoys talking, discussing issues, and verbal stimuli; talks out problems.

I can improve my auditory learning style by...

1. _____
_____
2. _____
_____
3. _____
_____

TACTILE LEARNING STYLE
(Action Smart)

Prefers hands-on approaches to learning; likes to take notes and uses a great deal of scratch paper; learns best by doing something, by touching it, or manipulating it; learns best while moving or while in action; often does not concentrate well when sitting and reading.

I can improve my tactile learning style by...

1. _____
_____
2. _____
_____
3. _____
_____

way people use their minds. In 1942, Isabel Briggs-Myers and her mother, Katharine Briggs, began to put Jung's theory into practice. They developed the Myers-Briggs Type Indicator, which after more than 50 years of research and refinement has become the most widely used instrument for identifying and studying personality.

Personality typing can "help us discover what best motivates and energizes each of us as individuals" (Tieger and Barron-Tieger, 2007). The questions on the PAP in Key 4.7 will help you discover whether you are an **E or I** (**E**xtroverted or **I**ntroverted), **S or N** (**S**ensing or i**N**tuitive), **T or F** (**T**hinking or **F**eeling), and **J or P** (**J**udging or **P**erceiving). When all of the combinations of E/I,

TAKE THE PAP
(PERSONALITY ASSESSMENT PROFILE)

Directions: Read each statement carefully and thoroughly. After reading the statement, rate your response using the scale below. There are no right or wrong answers. This is not a timed survey. The PAP is based, in part, on the Myers-Briggs Type Indicator (MBTI) by Katharine Briggs and Isabel Briggs-Myers.

3 = Often Applies   2 = Sometimes Applies   1 = Never or Almost Never Applies

_____ 1a. I am a very talkative person.

_____ 1b. I am a more reflective person than a verbal person.

_____ 2a. I am a very factual and literal person.

_____ 2b. I look to the future and I can see possibilities.

_____ 3a. I value truth and justice over tact and emotion.

_____ 3b. I find it easy to empathize with other people.

_____ 4a. I am very ordered and efficient.

_____ 4b. I enjoy having freedom from control.

_____ 5a. I am a very friendly and social person.

_____ 5b. I enjoy listening to others more than talking.

_____ 6a. I enjoy being around and working with people who have a great deal of common sense.

_____ 6b. I enjoy being around and working with people who are dreamers and have a great deal of imagination.

_____ 7a. One of my motivating forces is to do a job very well.

_____ 7b. I like to be recognized. I am motivated by my accomplishments and awards.

_____ 8a. I like to plan out my day before I go to bed.

_____ 8b. When I get up on a non-school or non-work day, I just like to let the day "plan itself."

_____ 9a.   I like to express my feelings and thoughts.

_____ 9b.   I enjoy a great deal of tranquility and quiet time to myself.

_____ 10a. I am a very pragmatic and realistic person.

_____ 10b. I like to create new ideas, methods, or ways of doing things.

_____ 11a. I make decisions with my brain.

_____ 11b. I make decisions with my heart.

_____ 12a. I am a very disciplined and orderly person.

_____ 12b. I don't make a lot of plans.

_____ 13a. I like to work with a group of people.

_____ 13b. I would rather work independently.

_____ 14a. I learn best if I can see it, touch it, smell it, taste it, or hear it.

_____ 14b. I learn best by relying on my gut feelings or intuition.

_____ 15a. I am quick to criticize others.

_____ 15b. I compliment others very easily and quickly.

_____ 16a. My life is systematic and organized.

_____ 16b. I don't really pay attention to deadlines.

_____ 17a. I can be myself when I am around others.

_____ 17b. I can be myself when I am alone.

_____ 18a. I live in the here and now, in the present.

_____ 18b. I live in the future, planning and dreaming.

_____ 19a. I think that if someone breaks the rules, the person should be punished.

_____ 19b. I think that if someone breaks the rules, we should look at the person who broke the rules, examine the rules, and look at the situation at hand before a decision is made.

_____ 20a. I do my work, then I play.

_____ 20b. I play, then do my work.

Refer to your score on each individual question. Place that score beside the appropriate question number below. Then, tally the total for each line at the side.

SCORE					TOTAL ACROSS	CODE
1a ____	5a ____	9a ____	13a ____	17a ____	_____	E Extrovert
1b ____	5b ____	9b ____	13b ____	17b ____	_____	I Introvert
2a ____	6a ____	10a ____	14a ____	18a ____	_____	S Sensing
2b ____	6b ____	10b ____	14b ____	18b ____	_____	N iNtuition
3a ____	7a ____	11a ____	15a ____	19a ____	_____	T Thinking
3b ____	7b ____	11b ____	15b ____	19b ____	_____	F Feeling
4a ____	8a ____	12a ____	16a ____	20a ____	_____	J Judging
4b ____	8b ____	12b ____	16b ____	20b ____	_____	P Perceiving

Pap Scores

Look at the scores on your PAP. Is your score higher in the E or I line? Is your score higher in the S or N line? Is your score higher in the T or F line? Is your score higher in the J or P line? Write the code to the side of each section below.

Is your higher score   E or I   Code ____

Is your higher score   S or N   Code ____

Is your higher score   T or F   Code ____

Is your higher score   J or P   Code ____

© Robert M. Sherfield

S/N, T/F, and J/P are combined, there are 16 personality types. Everyone will fit into *one* of the following categories:

ISTJ	ISFJ	INFJ	INTJ
ISTP	ISFP	INFP	INTP
ESTP	ESFP	ENFP	ENTP
ESTJ	ESFJ	ENFJ	ENTJ

Let's take a look at the four major categories of typing. Notice that the higher your score in one area, the stronger your personality type is for that area. For instance, if you scored 15 on the E (extroversion) questions, this means that you are a strong extrovert. If you scored 15 on the I (introversion) questions, this means that you are a strong introvert. However, if you scored 7 on the E questions and 8 on the I questions, your score indicates that you possess almost the same amount of extroverted and introverted qualities. The same is true for every category on the PAP.

E Versus I (Extroversion/Introversion)

This category deals with the way we *interact with others and the world around us—how we draw our energy.*

   Extroverts prefer to live in the outside world, drawing their strength from other people. They are outgoing and love interaction. They usually make decisions with others in mind. They enjoy being the center of attention. There are usually few secrets about extroverts.

   Introverts draw their strength from the inner world. They need to spend time alone to think and ponder. They are usually quiet and reflective. They usually make decisions by themselves. They do not like being the center of attention. They are private.

S Versus N (Sensing/Intuition)

This category deals with the way we *learn and deal with information.*

   Sensing types gather information through their five senses. They have a hard time believing something if it cannot be seen, touched, smelled, tasted, or heard. They like concrete facts and details. They do not rely on intuition or gut feelings. They usually have a great deal of common sense.

   Intuitive types are not very detail-oriented. They can see possibilities, and they rely on their gut feelings. Usually, they are very innovative people. They tend to live in the future and often get bored once they have mastered a task.

T Versus F (Thinking/Feeling)

This category deals with the way we *make decisions.*

   Thinkers are very logical people. They do not make decisions based on feelings or emotions. They are analytical and sometimes do not take others' values into consideration when making decisions. They can easily identify the flaws of others. They can sometimes be seen as insensitive and lacking compassion.

   Feelers make decisions based on what they feel is right and just. They like to have harmony, and they value others' opinions and feelings. They are usually very tactful people who like to please others. They are very warm people.

J Versus P (Judging/Perceiving)

This category deals with the way we *live and our overall lifestyle.*

   Judgers are very orderly people. They must have a great deal of structure in their lives. They are good at setting goals and sticking to their goals. They are the type of people who would seldom, if ever, play before their work was completed.

   Perceivers are just the opposite. They are less structured and more spontaneous. They do not like timelines. Unlike judgers, they will play before their work is done. They will take every chance to delay a decision or judgment. Sometimes, they can become involved in too many things at one time.

   After you have studied Key 4.8 and other information regarding your personality type, you can make some decisions about your study habits and even your career choices. For instance, if you scored very strong in the extroversion section, it may not serve you well to pursue a career where you would be forced to work alone. It would probably be unwise to try to spend all of your time studying alone. If you are a strong extrovert, you would want to work and study around people.

A CLOSER LOOK AT
YOUR PERSONALITY TYPE

ISTJ: THE DUTIFUL (7–10% OF AMERICANS)

Have great power of concentration; very serious; dependable; logical and realistic; take responsibility for their own actions; not easily distracted

Possible Careers:

Accountant, purchasing agent, real estate agent, IRS agent, corrections officer, investment counselor, law researcher, technical writer, judge, mechanic

ISFJ: THE NURTURER (7–10% OF AMERICANS)

Hard workers; detail-oriented; considerate of others' feelings; friendly and warm to others; very conscientious; down-to-earth and like to be around the same

Possible Careers:

Dentist, physician, biologist, surgical technician, teacher, speech pathologist, historian, clerical worker, bookkeeper, electrician, retail owner, counselor

INFJ: THE PROTECTOR (2–3% OF AMERICANS)

Enjoy an atmosphere where all get along; do what is needed of them; have strong beliefs and principles; enjoy helping others achieve their goals

Possible Careers:

Career counselor, psychologist, teacher, social worker, clergy, artist, novelist, filmmaker, health care provider, human resource manager, coach, crisis manager, mediator

INTJ: THE SCIENTIST (2–3% OF AMERICANS)

Very independent; enjoy challenges; inventors; can be skeptical; perfectionists; believe in their own work, sometimes to a fault

Possible Careers:

Economist, financial planner, banker, budget analyst, scientist, astronomer, network specialist, computer programmer, engineer, curriculum designer, coroner, pathologist, attorney, manager

ISTP: THE MECHANIC (4–7% OF AMERICANS)

Very reserved; good at making things clear to others; interested in how and why things work; like to work with their hands; can sometimes be misunderstood as idle

Possible Careers:

Police officer, intelligence officer, firefighter, athletic coach, engineer, technical trainer, logistic manager, EMT, surgical technician, banker, office manager, carpenter, landscape architect

ISFP: THE ARTIST (5–7% OF AMERICANS)

Very sensitive and modest; adapt easily to change; respectful of others' feelings and values; take criticism personally; don't enjoy leadership roles

Possible Careers:

Artist, chef, musician, nurse, medical assistant, surgeon, botanist, zoologist, science teacher, travel agent, game warden, coach, bookkeeper, clerical worker, insurance examiner

INFP: THE IDEALIST (3–4% OF AMERICANS)

Work well alone; must know others well to interact; faithful to others and their jobs; excellent at communication; open-minded; dreamers; tend to do too much

Possible Careers:

Entertainer, artist, editor, musician, professor, researcher, counselor, consultant, clergy, dietitian, massage therapist, human resources manager, events manager, corporate leader

INTP: THE THINKER (3–4% OF AMERICANS)

Extremely logical; very analytical; good at planning; love to learn; excellent problem solvers; don't enjoy needless conversation; hard to understand at times

Possible Careers:

Software designer, programmer, systems analyst, network administrator, surgeon, veterinarian, lawyer, economist, architect, physicist, mathematician, college professor, writer, agent, producer

ESTP: THE DOER (6–8% OF AMERICANS)

Usually very happy; don't let trivial things upset them; have very good memories; very good at working with things and taking them apart

Possible Careers:

Police officer, firefighter, detective, military, investigator, paramedic, banker, investor, promoter, carpenter, chef, real estate broker, retail sales, insurance claims agent

ESFP: THE PERFORMER (8–10% OF AMERICANS)

Very good at sports and active exercises; good common sense; easygoing; good at communication; can be impulsive; do not enjoy working alone; have fun and enjoy living and life

Possible Careers:

Nurse, social worker, physician assistant, nutritionist, therapist, photographer, musician, film producer, social events coordinator, news anchor, fund raiser, host, retail sales

ENFP: THE INSPIRER (6–7% OF AMERICANS)

Creative and industrious; can easily find success in activities and projects that interest them; good at motivating others; organized; do not like routine

Possible Careers:

Journalist, writer, actor, newscaster, artist, director, public relations, teacher, clergy, psychologist, guidance counselor, trainer, project manager, human resources manager

ENTP: THE VISIONARY (4–6% OF AMERICANS)

Great problem solvers; love to argue either side; can do almost anything; good at speaking/motivating; love challenges; very creative; do not like routine; overconfident

Possible Careers:

Entrepreneur, manager, agent, journalist, attorney, urban planner, analyst, creative director, public relations, marketing, broadcaster, network solutions, politician, detective

ESTJ: THE GUARDIAN (12–15% OF AMERICANS)	ESFJ: THE CAREGIVER (11–14% OF AMERICANS)	ENFJ: THE GIVER (3–5% OF AMERICANS)	ENTJ: THE EXECUTIVE (3–5% OF AMERICANS)
"Take charge" people; like to get things done; focus on results; very good at organizing; good at seeing what will not work; responsible; realists	Enjoy many friendly relationships; popular; love to help others; do not take criticism very well; need praise; need to work with people; organized; talkative; active	Very concerned about others' feelings; respect others; good leaders; usually popular; good at public speaking; can make decisions too quickly; trust easily	Excellent leaders; speak very well; hard working; may be workaholics; may not give enough praise; like to learn; great planners; enjoy helping others reach their goals
Possible Careers:	**Possible Careers:**	**Possible Careers:**	**Possible Careers:**
Insurance agent, military, security, coach, credit analyst, project manager, auditor, general contractor, paralegal, stockbroker, executive, information officer, lawyer, controller, accounts manager	Medical assistant, physician, nurse, teacher, coach, principal, social worker, counselor, clergy, court reporter, office manager, loan officer, public relations, customer service, caterer, office manager	Journalist, entertainer, TV producer, politician, counselor, clergy, psychologist, teacher, social worker, health care provider, customer service manager	Executive, senior manager, administrator, consultant, editor, producer, financial planner, stockbroker, program designer, attorney, psychologist, engineer, network administrator

Source: Adapted from Tieger and Barron-Tieger, 2007; and Personality Type Portraits, 2008.

Reflections on learning
how to learn

Unlike an **IQ** test, learning styles, multiple intelligence, and personality type assessments do not pretend to determine if you are "smart" or not. These assessments simply allow you to look more closely at how you learn, what innate strengths you possess, and what your dominant intelligence may be.

Discovering your learning style can greatly enhance your classroom performance. For example, finally understanding that your learning style is visual and that your professor's teaching style is totally verbal (oral) can answer many questions about why you may have performed poorly in the past in a strictly "lecture class." Now that you have discovered that you are a feeling extrovert, you can better understand why you love associating with others and learn a great deal by working in groups. And now that you have discovered that your primary intelligence is logical/mathematical, you know why math and science are easier for you than history or literature.

Possessing this knowledge and developing the tools to make your learning style, dominant intelligence, and personality type work for you, not against you, will be paramount to your success. As you continue to use your learning style, dominant intelligence, and personality type to enhance learning, consider the following:

▶ Get involved in a variety of learning and social situations.

- Use your less dominant areas more often to strengthen them.

- Read more about personality typing and learning styles.

- Surround yourself with people who learn differently from you.

- Try different ways of learning and studying.

- Remember that inventories do not measure your worth.

By understanding how you process information, learning can become an entirely new and exciting venture for you. Good luck to you on this new journey.

"Education is learning what you did not know you did not know."

—Daniel Boorstin

Building Skills *for* College, Career, *and* Life

Steps to Success

Link How You Learn to Coursework and Careers

Apply what you know about yourself to some future academic planning.

BUILD BASIC SKILLS. On paper or on a computer, summarize yourself as a learner in a paragraph or two. Focus on what you have learned about yourself from the chapter assessments.

Done? Check here. _____

TAKE IT TO THE NEXT LEVEL. Schedule a meeting with your academic advisor.

Name of advisor: _____

Contact information: _____

Time/date of meeting: _____

Give the advisor an overview of your learning strengths and challenges, based on your summary. Ask for advice about courses that might interest you and fit into your degree program. Take notes. Based on your discussion, name two courses to consider next:

1. _____

2. _____

Finally, create a separate to-do list of how you plan to explore one course offering and one major. Set a deadline for each task. And keep in mind that if you are having trouble choosing a major because of uncertainty about a career direction, see an advisor in the career center for guidance.

Writing

Build Intrapersonal and Communication Skills

Record your thoughts on a separate piece of paper, in a journal, or electronically.

EMOTIONAL INTELLIGENCE JOURNAL

Your interactions with others. With your Personality Assessment profile in mind, think about how you generally relate to people. Describe the type(s) of people that you tend to get along well with. How do you feel around these people? Then describe the types that tend to irk you. How do those people make you feel? Use your emotional intelligence to discuss what those feelings tell you and how you can adjust your mindset or take action to create the best possible outcome in interactions with people with whom you just don't get along.

REAL-LIFE WRITING

Ask an instructor for support. Reach out to an instructor for a course that clashes with your learning style—in terms of the material itself, the style in which it is presented, or the way the classroom is run. Draft a friendly and respectful e-mail requesting help that describes how you perceive yourself as a learner and details the issue you are having with the material or coverage. Include any ideas you have about how the instructor might be able to help you.

When you are done, make something happen: Send it and follow through on the response you receive.

Personal Portfolio

Prepare for Career Success

SELF-PORTRAIT

21st Century Learning Building Blocks
- Creativity and Innovation
- Initiative and Self-Direction

Complete the following on separate sheets of paper or electronically (if you can use a graphics program).

Because self-knowledge helps you to make the best choices about your future, a self-portrait can be an important tool in your career exploration. Use this exercise to synthesize everything you have been exploring about yourself into one comprehensive "self-portrait." Design your portrait in think link (mind map) style, using words and visual shapes to describe your dominant multiple intelligences, Personality Spectrum dimensions, values, abilities and interests, personal characteristics, and anything else that you have discovered through self-exploration.

A think link is a visual construction of related ideas, similar to a map or web, representing your thought process. Ideas are written inside geometric shapes, often boxes or circles, and related ideas and facts are attached to those ideas by lines that connect the shapes (see the note-taking section in Chapter 6 for more about think links).

If you want to use the style shown in Key 4.9, create a "wheel" of ideas coming off your central shape. Then, spreading out from each of those ideas (interests, values, and so forth), draw lines connecting the thoughts that go along with that idea. Connected to "Interests," for example, might be "singing," "stock market," and "history."

You don't have to use the wheel image, however. You might instead want to design a treelike think link, a line of boxes with connecting thoughts, or anything else you like. Let your design reflect who you are, just as your writing does. You may want to look back at it at the end of the term to see how you have changed and grown from the self-image you have today.

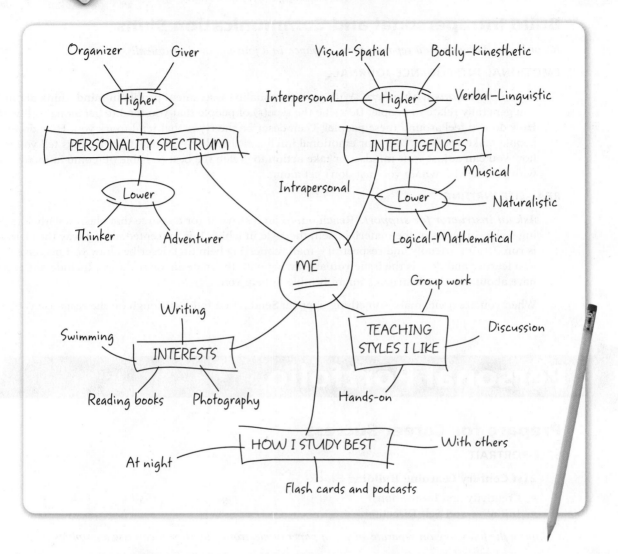

Social Networking

ESTABLISH YOUR HISTORY

Broaden your profile with information about any work history you have. Sign in to your LinkedIn account and click on "Edit My Profile." Then, fill in work information on the following (as applicable):

- Current (Click on "Current" and add information about your current employment: company name, job title, when you started working there, and description.)
- Past (Click on "Past" and add information about one or more past jobs: company name, job title, time period you worked, and description.)

If you have a lean or nonexistent work history, start thinking now about how to build that history while you are in school. Besides paid jobs in the workforce, other possibilities include internships, volunteering, and working with faculty. Be sure to update your resumé and LinkedIn profile with work history as you build it.

Learning Strategies

*a*s a daughter in a military family, it seemed logical that Tifani Hightower would pursue a career in the armed forces.

However, instead of one career as a human resource specialist in the U.S. Army Reserves, Hightower decided to pair her duty with her other job.

"I chose Army Reserve because I had just begun working with UPS in 2008, and the idea of pursuing two careers at once was too enticing for me to turn down. I figured if I didn't like one, I had the other to fall back on," she explained.

While things were good, Hightower desired more and in December 2010, she decided to pursue a master's degree in business administration with a focus on human resource management.

"To join the ranks as an officer in the United States Army, one must possess a college degree," Hightower said, adding that the degree would make her "a more marketable contender, from within, for the regional human resource position that I want with UPS."

While attending CSU, she said the staff was very helpful and made her feel like more than a number. "CSU has the best customer service ever! Anytime I called, or had a question the reply was always prompt."

She offers this advice to any "freshman" online students, "If you find that you aren't able to do a little something every day, set up a schedule for yourself when you designate time during the week that you'll devote only to your online studies. Deciding to get a college degree is a huge feat within itself, seeing it through is the other challenge, but I tell you from experience, it's not impossible!"

After graduation in 2012, Hightower feels her MBA in human resource management has made selection into an officer program with the military is within reach and greatly improved her chances for promotion in UPS.

"I like to set examples for others. I'm the first among my siblings to earn an undergraduate degree, and now I'm the first grandchild for both sets of grandparents to earn a master's degree," she added. "I used to think to myself, if that person can do it, I'm sure I can! Now others can look at me and say, 'If Tifani can do it, I know I can do it!,' and they can!"

For each statement, circle the number that feels right to you, from 1 for "not at all true for me" to 5 for "very true for me."

▶ I make choices in when and how I read that help me boost focus and comprehension.	1 2 3 4 5
▶ I preview a text before studying it by skimming and scanning front matter, chapter elements, and back matter for clues about content and organization.	1 2 3 4 5
▶ I develop questions to guide me before I begin to read.	1 2 3 4 5
▶ I practice reciting what I've learned from the reading by working with a study partner, taking notes, using flash cards, or some other study technique.	1 2 3 4 5
▶ I use text note taking and highlighting to turn my texts into study tools.	1 2 3 4 5
▶ I have a process for reading on-screen assignments and articles.	1 2 3 4 5
▶ I prioritize my reading assignments so that I focus on what is most important.	1 2 3 4 5
▶ When I get a research or writing assignment, I go first to general references for an overview.	1 2 3 4 5
▶ I don't just rely on the Internet for research—I also consult library materials.	1 2 3 4 5
▶ I evaluate every Internet source for signs of bias, validity, credibility, and reliability.	1 2 3 4 5

Now total your scores.

Each of the topics in these statements is covered in this chapter. Note those statements for which you circled a 3 or lower. Skim the chapter to see where those topics appear, and pay special attention to them as you read, learn, and apply new strategies.

REMEMBER: *No matter how developed your reading and information literacy skills are, you can improve with effort and practice.*

If IQ rules, it is only because we let it. And when we let it rule, we choose a bad master. We got ourselves into the test mess; we can get ourselves out of it. It's a mess from which I personally had to extricate myself.

—Robert Sternberg

Is reading fundamental or just pure torture?

Getting ready to read college-level material

Quick question: What are the top two academic problems among students today? According to faculty members, assessments, national tests, and yes, even your peers around the nation, the two greatest problems students face today are math classes and reading comprehension—and some math problems can even be attributed to poor reading skills.

How many times have you read to the bottom of a page or completed a section in a textbook and said to yourself, "I don't remember a thing I just read"? In actuality, all of us have done this at one time or another. The strategies outlined here will help you eliminate this common occurrence from your study time. By applying these strategies, you will be able to read a page, a section, or an entire chapter so that when you reach the end, you will comprehend and remember what you just read.

As you begin to explore the methods in this chapter, you may say to yourself, "How much time do they think I have?" Although our methods do take some time, if properly used, you will never get to the bottom of a page again and not know what you've read. Think of it this way: Would you rather read

---

the material four or five times and *not* remember what you read or read it one time and have it? That is the beauty knowing how to effectively read college-level material. Key 5.1 details the "six-pack" you will need to effectively read and comprehend material.

Discovering your reading style

Are you active or passive?

Active reading is really nothing more than a mindset (see Key 5.2). It is the attitude you have as you begin the reading process. For the next few days, try approaching your reading assignments with a positive and open mind and notice the difference in your own satisfaction, understanding, and overall comprehension. Instead of saying things like, "I hate reading" or "This stuff is worthless," reframe your self-talk into statements such as "I'm going to learn from this" and "I think I can apply this to my life now."

I feel the need . . . the need for speed!

Have you ever timed yourself to determine how long it takes you to read a complete chapter?
Courtesy of Shutterstock

Do you know your personal reading rate?

You've heard the advertisements: "Breeze through a novel on your lunch hour," "Read an entire computer instruction book over dinner," or "Read *The New York Times* in 10 minutes." Sure, there are people who have an incredible gift for speed reading and a photographic memory, but those people are not the norm.

In Key 5.3, you will find a passage on binge drinking. Read the section at your normal pace. Use a stopwatch or a watch with a second hand to accurately record your time, and then calculate your rate and comprehension level using the scales provided.

This section is included to give you some idea about how long it will take to read a chapter so that you can *plan your reading time* more effectively. There is an average of 450 words on a college textbook page. If you read at 150 words per minute, each page may take you an average of three minutes to read.

WHAT ARE THE INGREDIENTS FOR
SUCCESSFUL READING?

- The material you are reading
- Pens or pencils and a highlighter
- Paper for taking notes
- A dictionary (traditional or online)
- Time devoted exclusively to reading
- An open mind

DISCOVERING YOUR
READING STYLE

Key 5.2

Take a few moments and circle TRUE or FALSE for each of the statements below to determine if you are more of an active or passive reader.

1.	I enjoy reading for pleasure.	TRUE	FALSE
2.	College textbooks have little connection to my real life.	TRUE	FALSE
3.	I look for the deeper meaning in words and phrases.	TRUE	FALSE
4.	I seldom visualize what I am reading.	TRUE	FALSE
5.	I look up words that I do not understand.	TRUE	FALSE
6.	I read only what I have to read, and that is a stretch for me.	TRUE	FALSE
7.	I stop reading to ponder what something means.	TRUE	FALSE
8.	I never take notes when reading.	TRUE	FALSE
9.	Reading brings me great joy.	TRUE	FALSE
10.	My mind wanders constantly when I read.	TRUE	FALSE
11.	I make time for reading even when I am not required to read.	TRUE	FALSE
12.	Words are just words—they add no real meaning to my life or work.	TRUE	FALSE
13.	I get excited about reading something new because I know I will learn something new and useful.	TRUE	FALSE
14.	When reading, I just want to get it over with.	TRUE	FALSE
15.	I usually have no trouble concentrating when reading.	TRUE	FALSE
16.	I never look up words; I just read on.	TRUE	FALSE

Total of even-numbered TRUE responses _____
Total of odd-numbered TRUE responses _____

If you answered TRUE to more even numbers, you tend to be a more passive reader.
If you answered TRUE to more odd numbers, you tend to be a more active reader.

CALCULATING YOUR
READING RATE

Key 5.3

Start Time _____ : _____ : _____
          Hour   Min.   Sec.

BINGE DRINKING

Binge drinking is classified as having more than five drinks at one time. Many people say, "I only drink once a week." However, if that one drinking spell includes drink after drink after drink, it can be extremely detrimental to your liver, your memory, your digestive system, and your overall health.

Most college students report that they do not mean to binge drink, but it is caused by the situation, such as a ballgame, a party, a campus event, or special occasion. Researchers at Michigan State University found that only 5 percent of students surveyed say they party to "get drunk" (Warner, 2002).

In their breakthrough work, *Dying to Drink*, Harvard researcher Henry Wechsler and science writer Bernice Wuethrich explore the problem of binge drinking. They suggest that "two out of every five college students regularly binge drink, resulting in approximately 1,400 student deaths, a distressing number of assaults and rapes, a shameful amount of vandalism, and countless cases of academic suicide" (Wechsler and Wuethrich, 2002).

It is a situation reminiscent of the old saying "Letting the fox guard the henhouse." After a few drinks, it is hard to "self-police," meaning that you may not be able to control your actions once the drinking starts.

Perhaps the greatest tragedy of drug and alcohol abuse is the residual damage of pregnancy, sexually transmitted diseases, traffic fatalities, verbal/physical abuse, and accidental death. You know that drugs and alcohol lower your resistance and can cause you to do things that you would not normally do, such as drive drunk or have unprotected sex. Surveys and research results suggest that students who participate in heavy episodic (HE) or binge drinking are more likely to participate in unprotected sex with multiple sex partners. One survey found that 61 percent of men who do binge drink participated in unprotected sex, as compared to 23 percent of men who do not binge drink. The survey also found that 48 percent

of women who do binge drink participated in unprotected sex, as compared to only 8 percent of women who do not binge drink (Cooper, 2002).

These staggering statistics suggest one thing: alcohol consumption can cause people to act in ways in which they may never have acted without alcohol—and those actions can result in personal damage from which recovery may be impossible. (386 words)

Finishing Time _____ : _____ : _____
              Hour   Min.   Sec.

Reading time in seconds = _____

Words per minute (use the following chart) = _____

Example: If you read this passage in 2 minutes and 38 seconds, your reading time in seconds would be 158. Using the Rate Calculator Chart, your reading rate would be about 146 words per minute.

RATE CALCULATOR FOR "BINGE DRINKING" PASSAGE	
TIME IN SECONDS	**WORDS PER MINUTE**
40	581
50	464
60 (1 minute)	387
120 (2 minutes)	194
130	179
140	165
150	155
160	145
170	137
180 (3 minutes)	129
190	122
200	116
210	110
220	106
230	101

Test Your Comprehension Skills

Answer the following questions with T (true) or F (false) without looking back over the material.

_____ 1. Binge drinking has resulted in the deaths of students.

_____ 2. Men who binge drink have unprotected sex more often than men who do not binge drink.

_____ 3. Women who binge drink have unprotected sex no more often than women who do not binge drink.

_____ 4. "Self-policing" means that you are able to look out for yourself.

_____ 5. Binge drinking is classified as having more than three drinks at one time.

Each question is worth 20%. Comprehension = _____ %

Example: If you answered two correctly, your comprehension rate would be 40% (2 × 20%). If you answered four correctly, your comprehension rate would be 80% (4 × 20%).

Test Your Comprehension Skills Answers: 1 = T, 2 = T, 3 = F, 4 = T, 5 = F

This is a *raw number* for just reading. It does not allow for marking, high-lighting, taking notes, looking up unfamiliar words, reflecting, or comprehension. When these necessary skills are coupled with basic reading, they can sometimes triple the amount of reading time required. So, that page that you estimated would take you three minutes to read may actually take you nine to ten minutes. This matters greatly when you have a 40-page chapter to read for homework.

Developing a powerful vocabulary

Do you have to be a logodaedalian to enjoy words?

Thankfully, it is not every day you run across words like *logodaedalian*. (A logodaedalian is a person who has a great passion for unique, sly, and clever words and phrases.) Perhaps the best way to develop a dynamic vocabulary is through reading. By reading, you come across words that you may have never seen before. You are exposed to aspects of language that you may not have experienced in your family, neighborhood, or geographic location.

Of course, unfamiliar words in a passage, section, or chapter will not become a part of your vernacular unless you stop and look them up. This is the way to begin building a masterful vocabulary.

Let's start by looking up the noun *vernacular*. Using a dictionary (in print, online, or from a free smartphone app), take a moment and jot down the definition.

Vernacular means: _____

_____

_____

See how simple that was? Now you have a new word in your vocabulary. Actually, you have two new words in just a few paragraphs: *vernacular* and *logodaedalian*. You have taken a step toward becoming a logophile!

Here are some more tips to develop a strong vocabulary:

▶ Look up words that you do not know (you can download a free dictionary on your smartphone).
▶ Read often and widely—including difficult material.
▶ Ask for clarifications.
▶ Try to remember a word's usage, whether in a phrase, sentence, or explanation.
▶ Keep a running list of words you do not know (put them in your memo section of your smartphone).
▶ Make connections by rhyming the new word with familiar words.
▶ Draw pictures of the word's definition on a index card.
▶ Work crossword puzzles and word games such as Scrabble.

Expand your vocabulary

As reading materials become more complex, your vocabulary influences how much you comprehend—and how readily you do so. When reading a text-book, the first "dictionary" to search is the end-of-book glossary that explains technical words and concepts. The definitions there are usually limited to the meanings used in the text. Standard dictionaries provide broader information such as word origin, pronunciation, part of speech, synonyms, antonyms, and multiple meanings. Buy a standard dictionary and investigate websites like dictionary.com. The suggestions in Key 5.4 will help you make the most of your dictionary.

Key 5.4

MAKE THE MOST
OF YOUR DICTIONARY

Use the word in the next 24 hours.

Not only does this demonstrate that you know how the word is used, but it also aids memorization.

Analyze word parts.

Many English words combine prefixes, roots, and suffixes. *Prefixes* are word parts added to the beginning of a root. *Suffixes* are added to the end of the root. The *root* is the central part or basis of a word around which prefixes and/or suffixes are added to produce different words. Recognizing these word parts can boost comprehesion.

Read beyond the first definition.

Then think critically about which meaning suits the context of the word in question and choose the one that makes the most sense.

dic·tio·nary

Pronunciation; \ˈdik-shə-ˌner-ē, -ˌne-rē\

Function: *noun*

Inflected Form(s): *plural* **dic·tio·nar·ies**

Etymology: Medieval Latin *dictionarium*, from Late Latin *diction-*, *dictio* word, from Latin, speaking

Date: 1526

1. A reference source in print or electronic form containing words usually alphabetically arranged along with information about their forms, pronunciations, functions, etymologies, meanings, and syntactical and idiomatic uses.

2. A book giving information on particular subjects or on a particular class of words, names, or facts, usually arranged alphabetically: *a biographical dictionary; a dictionary of mathematics.*

3. (*computing*) An associative array, a data structure where each value is referenced by a particular key, analogous to words and definitions in a physical dictionary.

Say and spell new words to boost recall.

Listen to the pronunciation on a hand-held electronic or online dictionary. Then practice writing the word to verify that you know the spelling.

Restate the definition in your own words.

When you can do this with ease, you know that you understand the meaning and are not merely parroting a dictionary definition.

Learning *to* read faster and smarter

Can you improve speed and comprehension?

As you begin to practice reading for comprehension, review the following tips to help you read the material more quickly and understand it more clearly. Whenever you are faced with having to choose between *comprehension* or *speed*, choose comprehension! The following steps will help as you begin to master reading college-level material.

Learn to concentrate

Speed and comprehension both require deep, **mindful concentration**. Neither can be achieved without it. In order to comprehend information, your body needs to be ready to concentrate. You need sleep, rest, and proper nutrition. Most importantly, you need a quiet, peaceful place to concentrate on your reading. To increase your concentration and comprehension, consider the following:

► Reduce outside distractions such as people talking, rooms that are too hot or cold, cell phones ringing, and so on.
► Reduce internal distractions such as fatigue, self-talk, daydreaming, hunger, and emotions that cause you to think of other things.
► Set a goal for reading a certain amount of material in an allotted time. This goal can help you focus.

did you know

Jay Leno

Jay Leno has always been a hard worker. Having mild dyslexia, he did not do very well in high school, getting mainly C's and D's. Jay, however, was determined to accomplish his goals. Despite his poor grades, he was resolute about attending Emerson College in Boston.

The admissions office decided that Jay was not a good candidate for the college and refused him admission. However, he had his heart set on attending Emerson, so he sat outside the admission officer's office 12 hours a day, five days a week until he was accepted into the university.

He credits his dyslexia with helping him develop the drive and perseverance needed to succeed in comedy, and life in general.

(*Source:* Levinson Medical Center for Learning Disabilities. "Dyslexic? You're Not Alone." Retrieved from www.dyslexiaonline.com.)

PHOTO: Kathy Hutchins/Newscom

- Take a short break every 20 minutes. Don't get distracted and do something else; come back to your reading in three to five minutes.
- Take notes as you read. This helps reading become an active process.
- When reading online material, don't become distracted by e-mails, Facebook posts, and so on.

Overcome fixation

Fixation is another important step in learning to read for speed and comprehension. Fixation is when your eyes stop on a single word to read it. Your eyes stop for only a fraction of a second, but those fractions add up over the course of a section or chapter. Your mind sees the words something like this:

Nutrition   is   important   to   good   health.

As you read this, you probably had six fixations because the words are spaced out. However, if they were not spaced, many people would still have six fixations. To increase your speed, try to see two words with one fixation; this will cut your reading time nearly in half. Try to see the sentence like this:

Nutrition is important   to good health.

Smith (2007) states that "research has shown that the average reader can see approximately 2.5 words per fixation." To reduce your fixation time for active reading, practice seeing two or more words with one fixation. As you practice, try to read in phrases like the example below:

Nutrition is important   to good health. Therefore,   you should work hard   to eat proper meals   every day.   By doing this you can maintain   good health.

How can SQ3R improve your reading?

Reading may look like a one-way street in which you, the reader, take in words the author has written. However, it is intended as an interactive communication. The author communicates ideas to you and invites your response. How can you respond? One answer is provided in the SQ3R reading strategy, which stands for *Survey, Question, Read, Recite,* and *Review*.[1] This straightforward technique helps readers take in, understand, and remember what they read. It encourages you to fulfill your side of interactive communication by asking questions, marking key ideas, introducing your own connections, and more.

As you move through the stages of SQ3R, you will skim and scan your text. **Skimming** refers to the rapid reading of such chapter elements as section introductions and conclusions, boldface or italicized terms, pictures and charts, and summaries. The goal of skimming is a quick construction of the main ideas. In contrast, **scanning** involves a careful search for specific information. You might use scanning during the SQ3R review phase to locate particular facts.

Just like many strategies presented to you throughout your college career, SQ3R works best if you adapt it to your own needs. Explore techniques, evaluate what works, and then make the system your own. As you become familiar with the system, keep in mind that SQ3R works best with textbook-based courses like science, math, social sciences, and humanities. SQ3R is not recommended for literature courses.

SKIMMING
Rapid, superficial reading of material to determine central ideas and main elements.

SCANNING
Reading material in an investigative way to search for specific information.

Step 1: Survey

Surveying, the first stage in SQ3R, is the process of previewing, or prereading, a book before you study it. Compare it to looking at a map before starting a road trip; determining the route and stops along the way in advance will save time and trouble while you travel. Gary made extensive use of the survey tools that most textbooks provide, including elements like the following that provide a big picture overview of the main ideas and themes.

■ ***Front matter.*** Skim the *table of contents* for the chapter titles, the main topics in each chapter and the order in which they will be covered, as well as special features. Then skim the *preface,* which is a personal note from the author that tells you what the book will cover and its point of view. For example, the preface for the American history text *Out of Many* states that it highlights "the experiences of diverse communities of Americans in the unfolding story of our country."[2] This tells you that cultural diversity is a central theme.

■ ***Chapter elements.*** Text chapters use various devices to structure the material and highlight content.

- ▶ *Chapter titles* establish the topic and often the author's perspective.
- ▶ *Chapter introductions or outlines* generally list objectives or key topics.
- ▶ *Level headings* (first, second, third), including those in question form, break down material into bite-size chunks.
- ▶ *Margin materials* can include definitions, quotes, questions, and exercises.
- ▶ *Tables, charts, photographs, and captions* illustrate important concepts in a visual manner.
- ▶ *Sidebars or boxed features* are connected to text themes and introduce extra tidbits of information that supplement the text.
- ▶ *Different styles or arrangements of type* (**boldface**, *italics*, <u>underlining</u>, larger fonts, bullet points, boxed text) can flag vocabulary or important ideas.
- ▶ *End-of-chapter summaries* review chapter content and main ideas.
- ▶ *Review questions and exercises* help you understand and apply content in creative and practical ways.

In Key 5.5, a typical page from the college textbook *Psychology: An Introduction,* by Charles G. Morris and Albert A. Maisto, how many elements do you recognize? How do these elements help you grasp the subject even before reading it?

■ ***Back matter.*** Some texts include a *glossary* that defines text terms, an *index* to help you locate topics, and a *bibliography* that lists additional readings.

Step 2: Question

The next step is to ask questions about your assignment. Using the *questioning* process that follows leads you to discover knowledge on your own, making an investment in the material and in your own memory.

Ask yourself what you know

Before you begin reading, think about—and summarize in writing if you can—what you already know about the topic, if anything. This step prepares you to apply what you know to new material. Building on current knowledge is especially important in your major, where the concepts you learn from intro courses prepare you for the higher-level material in classes to come later on.

Write questions linked to chapter headings

Next, examine the chapter headings and, on a separate page or in the text margins, write questions linked to them. When you encounter an assignment without headings, divide the material into logical sections and then develop

186   **Chapter 5** • Learning

Classical (or Pavlovian) conditioning The type of learning in which a response naturally elicited by one stimulus comes to be elicited by a different, formerly neutral stimulus.

Unconditioned stimulus (US) A stimulus that invariably causes an organism to respond in a specific way.

Unconditioned response (UR) A response that takes place in an organism whenever an unconditioned stimulus occurs.

Conditioned stimulus (CS) An originally neutral stimulus that is paired with an unconditioned stimulus and eventually produces the desired response in an organism when presented alone.

Conditioned response (CR) After conditioning, the response an organism produces when only a conditioned stimulus is presented.

you are experiencing insight. When you imitate the steps of professional dancers you saw last night on television, you are demonstrating observational learning. Like conditioning, cognitive learning is one of our survival strategies. Through cognitive processes, we learn which events are safe and which are dangerous without having to experience those events directly. Cognitive learning also gives us access to the wisdom of people who lived hundreds of years ago, and it will give people living hundreds of years from now some insight into our experiences and way of life.

Our discussion begins with *classical conditioning*. This simple kind of learning serves as a convenient starting point for examining what learning is and how it can be observed.

Classical Conditioning

How did Pavlov's discovery of classical conditioning help to shed light on learning?

Ivan Pavlov (1849–1936), a Russian physiologist who was studying digestive processes, discovered classical conditioning almost by accident. Because animals salivate when food is placed in their mouths, Pavlov inserted tubes into the salivary glands of dogs to measure how much saliva they produced when they were given food. He noticed, however, that the dogs salivated before the food was in their mouths: The mere sight of food made them drool. In fact, they even drooled at the sound of the experimenter's footsteps. This aroused Pavlov's curiosity. What was making the dogs salivate even before they had the food in their mouths? How had they learned to salivate in response to the sound of the experimenter's approach?

To answer these questions, Pavlov set out to teach the dogs to salivate when food was not present. He devised an experiment in which he sounded a bell just before the food was brought into the room. A ringing bell does not usually make a dog's mouth water but, after hearing the bell many times just before getting fed, Pavlov's dogs began to salivate as soon as the bell rang. It was as if they had learned that the bell signaled the appearance of food, and their mouths watered on cue even if no food followed. The dogs had been conditioned to salivate in response to a new stimulus—the bell—that would not normally have prompted that response (Pavlov, 1927). Figure 5–1, shows one of Pavlov's procedures in which the bell has been replaced by a touch to the dog's leg just before food is given.

Elements of Classical Conditioning

Generally speaking, **classical (or Pavlovian) conditioning** involves pairing an *involuntary* response (for example, salivation) that is usually evoked by one stimulus with a different, formerly neutral stimulus (such as a bell or a touch on the leg). Pavlov's experiment illustrates the four basic elements of classical conditioning. The first is an **unconditioned stimulus (US)**, such as food, which invariably prompts a certain reaction—salivation, in this case. That reaction—the **unconditioned response (UR)**—is the second element and always results from the unconditioned stimulus: Whenever the dog is given food (US), its mouth waters (UR). The third element is the neutral stimulus—the ringing bell—which is called the **conditioned stimulus (CS)**. At first, the conditioned stimulus is said to be "neutral" with respect to the desired response (salivation), because dogs do not salivate at the sound of a bell unless they have been conditioned to react in this way by repeatedly presenting the CS and US together. Frequent pairing of the CS and US produces the fourth element in the classical conditioning process: the **conditioned response (CR)**. The conditioned response is the behavior that the animal has learned in response to the conditioned stimulus. Usually, the unconditioned response and the conditioned

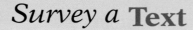

Survey a Text

Practice will improve your surveying skills. Start now with this text or another you are currently using.

Skim the front matter, including the table of contents and preface. What does this material tell you about the theme? About the book's approach and point of view?

_____

_____

_____

Are there unexpected topics listed in the table of contents? Are there topics you expected to see that are missing?

_____

_____

Now look at a typical chapter. List the devices that organize the structure and content of the material.

_____

_____

After skimming the chapter, what do you know about the material? What elements helped you skim quickly?

_____

_____

Finally, skim the back matter. What elements can you identify?

_____

_____

How do you plan to use each of the elements you identified in your text survey when you begin studying?

_____

_____

questions based on what you think is the main idea of each section. There are no "correct" questions. Given the same headings, two students could create two different sets of questions. Your goal in questioning is to begin to think critically about the material.

Key 5.6 shows how this works. The column on the left contains primary and secondary headings from a section of *Out of Many*. The column on the right rephrases these headings in question form.

Use Bloom's Taxonomy to formulate questions

Questions can seek different types of answers and may require different levels of analytical thinking to solve. To help you understand and use different types of questions, consider the system educational psychologist Benjamin Bloom developed based on the idea that deeper learning occurs when the effort to understand is more rigorous.[3] Although some questions ask for a simple recall, said Bloom, others ask for higher thinking levels.

CREATE QUESTIONS
FROM HEADINGS

HEADINGS	QUESTIONS
The Meaning of Freedom	What did freedom mean for both slaves and citizens in the United States?
Moving About	Where did African Americans go after they were freed from slavery?
The African American Family	How did freedom change the structure of the African American family?
African American Churches and Schools	What effect did freedom have on the formation of African American churches and schools?
Land and Labor After Slavery	How was land farmed and maintained after slaves were freed?
The Origins of African American Politics	How did the end of slavery bring about the beginning of African American political life?

Key 5.7 shows the six levels of questions identified by Bloom: knowledge, understanding, application, analysis, synthesis, and evaluation. It also identifies verbs associated with each level. As you read, use these verbs to create specific questions that will help you learn. For instance, if you were to continue Key 5.6's process of creating questions based on the headings from *Out of Many*, the questions would change based on the level specified by Bloom's Taxonomy. See Key 5.8 for an example.

Step 3: Read

Your text survey and questions give you a starting point for *reading*, the first R in SQ3R. Retaining what you read requires an active approach.

▶ *Focus on the key points of your survey.* Pay special attention to points raised in headings, in boldface type, in the chapter objectives and summary, and in other emphasized text.

▶ *Focus on your Q-stage questions.* Read the material with the purpose of answering each question. Write down or highlight ideas and examples that relate to your questions.

▶ *Create text tabs.* Place plastic index tabs or adhesive notes at the start of each chapter so you can flip back and forth with ease.

▶ *Mark up your text.* Write notes in the margins, circle main ideas, or underline supporting details to focus on what's important. For an e-book, use the "Insert comments" feature. These cues will boost memory and help you study for exams. Here are some tips for *annotating*—taking marginal notes on the pages of your text:

- Use pencil so you can erase comments or questions that are answered later.
- Write your Q questions in the margins next to text headings.
- Mark critical sections with marginal notations such as "Def." for definition, "e.g." for helpful example, "Concept" for an important concept, and so on.
- Write notes at the bottom of the page connecting the text to what you learned in class or in research. You can also attach adhesive notes with your comments.

▶ *Highlight your text.* *Highlighting* involves the use of special markers or regular pens or pencils to flag important passages. When working with e-books, make note of the highlighting function, which allows you to overlay a color on important text. When used correctly, highlighting is an essential learning technique. However,

USE BLOOM'S TAXONOMY TO
FORMULATE QUESTIONS
AT DIFFERENT COGNITIVE LEVELS

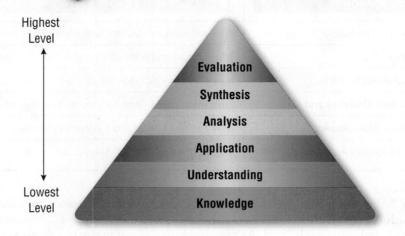

Highest Level

Lowest Level

Verbs That Indicate Each Level

1. **Knowledge:** average, define, duplicate, label, list, memorize, name, order, recognize, relate, recall, repeat, reproduce, state.

2. **Understanding:** classify, describe, discuss, explain, express, identify, indicate, locate, recognize, report, restate, review, select, translate.

3. **Application:** apply, choose, demonstrate, dramatize, employ, illustrate, interpret, operate, practice, schedule, sketch, solve, use, write.

4. **Analysis:** analyze, appraise, calculate, categorize, compare, contrast, criticize, differentiate, discriminate, distinguish, examine, experiment, question, test.

5. **Synthesis:** arrange, assemble, collect, compose, construct, create, design, develop, formulate, manage, organize, plan, prepare, propose, set up, write.

6. **Evaluation:** appraise, argue, assess, attach, choose, compare, defend, estimate, judge, predict, rate, score, select, support, value, evaluate.

experts agree that you will not learn what to highlight unless you *interact* with the material through surveying, questioning, reciting, and reviewing. Use the following tips to make highlighting a true learning tool:

- *Develop a system and stick to it.* Decide whether you will use different colors to highlight different elements, brackets for long passages, or pencil underlining.
- *Consider using a regular pencil or pen instead of a highlighter pen.* The copy will be cleaner and may look less like a coloring book.
- *Mark text carefully if you are using a rented book or a book to be resold.* Use pencil as often as possible and erase your marks at the end of the class. Write on sticky notes that you can remove. Make copies of important chapters or sections for marking.
- *Read an entire paragraph before you begin to highlight, and don't start until you have a sense of what is important.* Only then put pencil or highlighter to paper as you pick out the main idea, key terms, and crucial supporting details and examples.

FOLLOW A QUESTION THROUGH
THE STAGES OF BLOOM'S TAXONOMY

The Origins of African American Politics

Knowledge
- *List* three main characters of the early African American political scene.

Understanding
- *Explain* the struggles faced by African American politicians.

Application
- *Interpret* the impact of slavery on the early African American politicians.

Analysis
- *Compare* and *contrast* the Caucasian political environment of the time with the emerging African American politicians.

Synthesis
- *Arrange* the major events of the era as they corresponded with the emerging political movement.

Evaluation
- *Rate* the effectiveness of the first African American political campaign and note any changes since.

- *Avoid overmarking.* Too much color can be overwhelming. Try enclosing long passages with brackets and avoid underlining entire sentences, when possible.

Key 5.9, from an introduction to business textbook describing the concepts of target marketing and market segmentation, shows how to underline and take marginal notes.

Find the main idea

Understanding what you read depends on your ability to recognize *main ideas* and link other ideas to them. The main idea may appear in a (topic sentence) at the beginning of the paragraph followed by supporting details, or at the end of the paragraph with supporting details leading up to it. Sometimes, though, it is harder to figure out. When the main idea of a passage is unclear, use a three-step approach to decide what it is:[4]

    1. *Search for the topic of the paragraph.* The topic of the paragraph is not the same as the main idea. Rather, it is the broad subject being discussed—for example, Apple CEO Steve Jobs, hate crimes on campus, or binge drinking on campus.
    2. *Identify the aspect of the topic that is the paragraph's focus.* If the general topic is Steve Jobs, the author may focus on any of thousands of aspects of that

> TOPIC SENTENCE
> A one- to two-sentence statement describing the main idea of a paragraph.

How does target marketing and market segmentation help companies sell product?

TARGET MARKETING AND MARKET SEGMENTATION

Marketers have long known that products cannot be all things to all people. Buyers have different tastes, goals, lifestyles, and so on. The emergence of the marketing concept and the recognition of consumer needs and wants led marketers to think in terms of **target markets**—groups of people with similar wants and needs. Selecting target markets is usually the first step in the marketing strategy.

Target marketing requires **market segmentation**—dividing a market into categories of customer types or "segments." Once they have identified segments, companies may adopt a variety of strategies. Some firms market products to more than one segment. General Motors *(www.gm.com)*, for example, offers compact cars, vans, trucks, luxury cars, and sports cars with various features and at various price levels. GM's strategy is to provide an automobile for nearly every segment of the market.

In contrast, some businesses offer a narrower range of products, each aimed toward a specific segment. Note that segmentation is a strategy for analyzing consumers, not products. The process of fixing, adapting, and communicating the nature of the product itself is called *product positioning.*

Definitions

↓

target market
Group of people that has similar wants and needs and that can be expected to show interest in the same products

← *GM eg*

market segmentation
Process of dividing a market into categories of customer types

GM makes cars for diff. market segments

How do companies identify market segments?

Identifying Market Segments

By definition, members of a market segment must share some common traits that affect their purchasing decisions. In identifying segments, researchers look at several different influences on consumer behavior. Three of the most important are *geographic, demographic,* and *psychographic variables.*

What effect does geography have on segmentation strategies?

Geographic Variables Many buying decisions are affected by the places people call home. The heavy rainfall in Washington State, for instance, means that people there buy more umbrellas than people in the Sun Belt. Urban residents don't need agricultural equipment, and sailboats sell better along the coasts than on the Great Plains. **Geographic variables** are the geographical units, from countries to neighborhoods, that may be considered in a segmentation strategy.

These patterns affect decisions about marketing mixes for a huge range of products. For example, consider a plan to market down-filled parkas in rural Minnesota. Demand will be high and price competition intense. Local newspaper ads may be

Buying decisions influenced by where people live

geographic variables
Geographical units that may be considered in developing a segmentation strategy

*— good eg —
selling parkas in Minnesota*

*Thought
Geographical variables change with the seasons*

Source: Ronald J. Ebert and Ricky W. Griffin, *Business Essentials,* 5th ed., © 2005. Printed and electronically reproduced by permission of Pearson Education, Inc., Upper Saddle River, NJ.

topic, such as his cofounding of Apple Computer in 1976; his role in Pixar, a computer animation company; or his involvement in the development of the iPod portable music player.

3. *Find what the author wants you to know about that specific aspect.* This is the main idea or topic sentence. Whereas the topic establishes the subject, a topic sentence narrows down the purpose of the paragraph into one or two focused statements. Thus, although the topic of the paragraph might be Apple CEO Steve Jobs, the main idea, or topic sentence, might be, "In his role as CEO of Apple, Steve Jobs oversaw the creation of the iPod portable music player, which changed the way the world listens to and purchases music."

Step 4: Recite

Once you finish reading a topic, stop and answer the questions you raised in the Q stage of SQ3R. Even if you have already done this during the reading phase, do it again now—with the purpose of learning and committing the material to memory by *reciting* the answers.

You can say each answer aloud, silently speak the answers to yourself, "teach" the answers to another person, or write your ideas and answers in note form. Whatever recitation method you choose, make sure you know how ideas connect to one another and to the general concept being discussed.

Writing is often the most effective way to learn new material. Write responses to your Q-stage questions and use your own words to explain new concepts; save your writing as a study tool for review. Writing gives you immediate feedback: When it agrees with the material you are studying, you know the information. When it doesn't, you still need work with the text or a study partner.

Keep your learning styles in mind while exploring different strategies. For example, an intrapersonal learner may prefer writing, whereas an interpersonal learner may choose to recite answers aloud to a classmate. A logical-mathematical learner may benefit from organizing material into detailed outlines or charts, as opposed to a musical learner, who might chant information aloud to a rhythm.

When do you stop to recite? Waiting for the end of a chapter is too late; stopping at the end of one paragraph is too soon. The best plan is to recite at the end of each text section, right before a new heading. Repeat the question–read–recite cycle until you complete the chapter. If you fumble for thoughts, reread the section until you are on solid ground.

Step 5: Review

Reviewing, both immediately and periodically in the days and weeks after you read, will help you memorize, understand, and learn material. If you close the book after reading it once, chances are that you will forget almost everything, which is why students who read material for the first time right before a test don't tend to do too well. *Reviewing is your key to learning.*

Reviewing the same material in several sessions over time will also help you identify knowledge gaps. It's natural to forget material between study sessions, especially if it's complex. When you come back after a break, you can focus on where you need the most help.

Examine the following reviewing techniques (more on these in Chapter 7). Try them all, and use the ones that work best for you. Try using more than one strategy when you study—switching among several different strategies tends to strengthen learning and memory.

▶ Reread your notes. Then summarize them from memory.
▶ Review and summarize in writing the text sections you highlighted or bracketed.

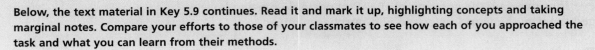

GET PRACTICAL!

Mark Up a Page to Learn a Page

Below, the text material in Key 5.9 continues. Read it and mark it up, highlighting concepts and taking marginal notes. Compare your efforts to those of your classmates to see how each of you approached the task and what you can learn from their methods.

298

Part IV: Understanding Principles of Marketing

effective, and the best retail location may be one that is easily reached from several small towns.

Although the marketability of some products is geographically sensitive, others enjoy nearly universal acceptance. Coke, for example, gets more than 70 percent of its sales from international markets. It is the market leader in Great Britain, China, Germany, Japan, Brazil, and Spain. Pepsi's international sales are about 15 percent of Coke's. In fact, Coke's chief competitor in most countries is some local soft drink, not Pepsi, which earns 78 percent of its income at home.

demographic variables
Characteristics of populations that may be considered in developing a segmentation strategy

Demographic Variables Demographic **variables** describe populations by identifying such traits as age, income, gender, ethnic background, marital status, race, religion, and social class. For example, several general consumption characteristics can be attributed to certain age groups (18–25, 26–35, 36–45, and so on). A marketer can, thus, divide markets into age groups. Table 10.1 lists some possible demographic breakdowns. Depending on the marketer's purpose, a segment can be a single classification (*aged 20–34*) or a combination of categories (*aged 20–34, married with children, earning* $25,000–$34,999). Foreign competitors, for example, are gaining market share in U.S. auto sales by appealing to young buyers (under age 30) with limited incomes (under $30,000). Whereas companies such as Hyundai *(www.hyundai.net)*, Kia *(www.kia.com)*, and Daewoo *(www.daewoous.com)* are winning entry-level customers with high quality and generous warranties, Volkswagen *(www.vw.com)* targets under-35 buyers with its entertainment-styled VW Jetta.[4]

psychographic variables
Consumer characteristics, such as lifestyles, opinions, interests, and attitudes, that may be considered in developing a segmentation strategy

Psychographic Variables Markets can also be segmented according to such **psychographic variables** as lifestyles, interests, and attitudes. Take, for example, Burberry *(www.burberry.com)*, whose raincoats have been a symbol of British tradition since 1856. Burberry has repositioned itself as a global luxury brand, like Gucci *(www.gucci.com)* and Louis Vuitton *(www.vuitton.com)*. The strategy, which recently resulted in a 31-percent sales increase, calls for attracting a different type of customer—the top-of-the-line, fashion-conscious individual—who shops at such stores as Neiman Marcus and Bergdorf Goodman.[5]

Psychographics are particularly important to marketers because, unlike demographics and geographics, they can be changed by marketing efforts. For example, Polish companies have overcome consumer resistance by promoting the safety and desirability of using credit rather than depending solely on cash. One product of changing attitudes is a booming economy and the emergence of a robust middle class.

TABLE 10.1

Demographic Variables

Age	Under 5, 5–11, 12–19, 20–34, 35–49, 50–64, 65+
Education	Grade school or less, some high school, graduated high school, some college, college degree, advanced degree
Family life cycle	Young single, young married without children, young married with children, older married with children under 18, older married without children under 18, older single, other
Family size	1, 2–3, 4–5, 6+
Income	Under $9,000, $9,000–$14,999, $15,000–$24,999, $25,000–$34,999, $35,000–$45,000, over $45,000
Nationality	African, American, Asian, British, Eastern European, French, German, Irish, Italian, Latin American, Middle Eastern, Scandinavian
Race	Native American, Asian, Black, White
Religion	Buddhist, Catholic, Hindu, Jewish, Muslim, Protestant
Sex	Male, female

- ► Rewrite key points and main concepts in your own words. Create written examples that will help solidify the content in your mind.
- ► Answer the end-of-chapter review, discussion, and application questions.
- ► Reread the preface, headings, tables, and summary.
- ► Recite important concepts to yourself, or record and play them back on a tape player.
- ► Listen to MP3 audio recordings of your text and other reading materials on your iPod.
- ► Make flash cards with a word or concept on one side and a definition, examples, or other related information on the other. Test yourself.
- ► Quiz yourself, using the questions you raised in the Q stage.
- ► Discuss the concepts with a classmate or in a study group. Answer one another's Q-stage questions.
- ► Ask your instructor for help with difficult material.

Refreshing your knowledge is easier and faster than learning it the first time. Make a weekly review schedule and stick to it until you're sure you know everything.

What strategies help with specific subjects and formats?

If your college has **general education requirements**, you may have to take a wide variety of courses to graduate. Knowing how to approach reading materials in different academic areas will help you learn.

→ GENERAL EDUCATION REQUIREMENTS
Courses required for graduation in a variety of academic fields, including the humanities, social sciences, math, and science.

Math and science

Math and science courses relate closely to one another, and almost all science courses require a base of math knowledge. Mathematical and scientific strategies help you develop thinking and problem-solving skills. In a world that is being transformed by new discoveries and technologies, a strong math and science background prepares you for tomorrow's jobs and can also help you create monthly budgets, choose auto insurance, understand illnesses, and more.

Math and science textbooks move *sequentially*. That is, your understanding of later material depends on how well you learned material in earlier chapters. Try the following strategies to get the most from your textbooks, and get extra help right away when you are confused.

■ *Interact with math material actively through writing.* Math textbooks are made up of problems and solutions. As you read, highlight important information and take notes on examples. Work out any missing problem steps on your pad or in the book. Draw sketches to help visualize the material. Try not to move on until you understand example problems and how they relate to the central ideas. Write down questions for your instructor or fellow students.

■ *Pay attention to formulas.* Math and science texts are filled with **formulas**. Focus on learning the main ideas behind each formula, and do problems to make sure your understanding sticks.

→ FORMULAS
General facts, rules, or principles usually expressed in mathematical symbols.

■ *Use memory strategies to learn science.* Science textbooks are packed with vocabulary specific to the field (for example, an environmental science text may refer to the *greenhouse effect, integrated waste management,* and the *law of limiting factors*). To remember what you read, use mnemonic devices, test yourself with flash cards, and rehearse aloud or silently.

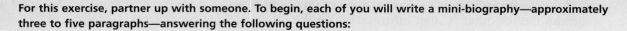

GET CREATIVE!

Use SQ3R to Make a Connection

For this exercise, partner up with someone. To begin, each of you will write a mini-biography—approximately three to five paragraphs—answering the following questions:

▶ Where are you from?

▶ How would you describe your family?

▶ How have they influenced the student you are today?

▶ What three facts or ideas about yourself would you like someone else to know?

Include a title that reflects your biography as a whole. Also, for each paragraph in the middle (not the first or last), provide a title "header" that tells the reader what to expect in the paragraph (for example, "My Childhood in Malaysia," "Daytime Student, Nighttime Employee," and so on).

Once you're finished, read over what you've written for spelling, punctuation, and clarity. Switch papers with your partner and read his or her biography. Using SQ3R:

1. *Survey:* Scan your partner's paper for any words that stand out or phrases that seem important. Circle or highlight anything you notice right away.

2. *Question:* Thinking about what you learned from your survey, write questions in the margins. Your questions should reflect what you expect to learn as you read.

3. *Read:* Read through the biography. Make notes in the margins when you find answers to your Q-stage questions. Use your pen to circle or underline main ideas.

4. *Recite:* Discuss what you learned from the paper with your partner. How accurate was your comprehension of the biography? Were there any areas that were not clear or that you misunderstood? If so, what might help in those cases?

5. *Review:* Summarize the biography of your partner in writing for yourself. Be sure to note any important information that relates to getting to know your partner. If there is time, solidify your review by reciting the summary aloud in front of the class. Introduce your partner to the class as if he or she had just joined, focusing on the most interesting and unique information from the biography.

Finally, discuss the impact of using SQ3R with your partner. How did it affect your comprehension of the biography? What might you try differently next time?

Social sciences and humanities

Courses in the social sciences and humanities prepare you to be a well-rounded person, able and ready to fulfill your responsibilities to yourself, your family, and a free democracy. They also prepare you for 21st century jobs by focusing on critical thinking, civic and historic knowledge, and ethical reasoning. As you study these disciplines, look for themes with critical thinking as the foundation for your work. Build knowledge by using what you know to learn new material.

Themes

The National Council for the Social Studies (www.socialstudies.org) organizes the study of the social sciences and humanities under ten themes, providing "umbrellas" under which you can group ideas that you encounter in different classes and reading materials:

- ▶ Culture
- ▶ Time, continuity, and change
- ▶ People, places, and environment
- ▶ Individual development and identity
- ▶ Individuals, groups, and institutions
- ▶ Power, authority, and governance
- ▶ Production, distribution, and consumption
- ▶ Science, technology, and society
- ▶ Global connections
- ▶ Ideals and practices of citizenship

Look for these themes as you read, even if they are not spelled out. For example, as you read a chapter in a political science text on presidential politics, you might think of the history of presidential elections or how the Internet is changing electoral politics.

Think critically

Courses in the social sciences ask hard questions about ethics, human rights and freedoms, personal and community responsibility, looking at these topics over time and in different cultures. Critical thinking will help you maximize learning and understanding as you ask questions about what you read, think of material in terms of problems and solutions, look for evidence in arguments, consider possible bias of the writers, and examine big picture statements for solid cause-and-effect logic.

Literature

Even if you're not an English major, you will probably take one or more literature courses, exposing you to books that allow you to experience other times and cultures and understand how others react to the problems of daily life. Additionally, the thoughts and emotions you experience in reaction to what you read give you the opportunity to learn more about yourself.

Literature courses ask you to look at different literary elements to find meaning on various levels. As you read, use critical reading skills to consider the various aspects.

- ▶ *Character*. How do characters reveal who they are? How are the main characters similar or different? How do a character's actions change the course of the story?
- ▶ *Plot*. How would you evaluate the power of the story? Did it hold your interest?
- ▶ *Setting*. How does the setting relate to the actions of the major and minor characters?
- ▶ *Point of view*. How are the author's views expressed through characters' actions?
- ▶ *Style*. How would you describe the writing style?
- ▶ *Imagery*. How does the author use imagery as part of the theme?
- ▶ *Theme*. What is the goal of the work? What is it trying to communicate?

Apply Different Intelligences to Concepts in Sociology

INTELLIGENCE	USE MI STRATEGIES TO BECOME A BETTER READER	APPLY MI READING STRATEGIES TO LEARN ABOUT SOCIAL GROUPS FOR YOUR INTRODUCTION TO SOCIOLOGY COURSE
Verbal-Linguistic	• Use the steps in SQ3R, focusing especially on writing Q-stage questions, summaries, and so on. • Make marginal text notes as you read.	• Summarize in writing the technical differences among social groups, categories, and crowds.*
Logical-Mathematical	• Logically connect what you are reading with what you already know. Consider similarities, differences, and cause-and-effect relationships. • Draw charts showing relationships and analyze trends.	• Create a table comparing and contrasting the characteristics of primary and secondary social groups.
Bodily-Kinesthetic	• Use text highlighting to take a hands-on approach to reading. • Take a hands-on approach to learning experiments by trying to recreate them yourself.	• Create an experiment that might turn a crowd of strangers into a social group joined together by a common problem.
Visual-Spatial	• Make charts, diagrams, or think links illustrating difficult ideas you encounter as you read. • Take note of photos, tables, and other visual aids in the text.	• Create a visual aid showing four primary mechanisms through which people with shared experiences, loyalties, and interests meet—for example, through school and business—and how initial contacts may lead to deep social group relationships.
Interpersonal	• Discuss reading material and clarify concepts in a study group. • Talk to people who know about the topic you are studying.	• Interview people who shared a difficult experience with a crowd of strangers—for example, people stuck in an elevator or train for an extended period—about how relationships changed as focus turned to a common problem.
Intrapersonal	• Apply concepts to your own life; think about how you would manage. • Try to understand your personal strengths and weaknesses to lead a study group on the reading material.	• After reading about the nature of primary groups, think about the nature of your personal family relationships and the degree to which family members are your key support system.
Musical	• Recite text concepts to rhythms or write a song to depict them. • Explore relevant musical links to the material.	• Listen to a rock concert that was performed in front of a live crowd. Then listen to the same music recorded in a studio. Think about performance differences that might link to the presence or absence of a crowd.
Naturalistic	• Tap into your ability to notice similarities and differences in objects and concepts by organizing reading materials into relevant groupings.	• Over the next few weeks, ask some close friends if you can have dinner with them and their families. After the visits, try to identify characteristics that all the families share. Create a chart to report your findings.

*For information on social groups, see John J. Macionis, *Sociology*, 11th ed., Upper Saddle River, NJ: Prentice Hall, 2007.

Visual aids

Many textbooks use tables, charts, drawings, maps, and photographs—all types of visual aids—to show, clarify, or summarize information in a form that is easy to read and understand. Pay attention to these elements as you are reading—often they contain important information not found elsewhere. Visual learners especially may benefit from information delivered in a format other than chapter text.

Certain types of visual aids—word and data tables as well as charts/graphs (pie, bar, or line)—are designed to compare information and statistics that show the following types of information:

- ▶ *Trends over time.* For example, the number of computers with Internet connections per household in 2010 compared to 2002
- ▶ *Relative rankings.* For example, the sizes of the advertising budgets of four major companies
- ▶ *Distributions.* For example, student performance on standardized tests by geographic area
- ▶ *Cycles.* For example, the regular upward and downward movement of the nation's economy as defined by periods of prosperity and recession

Reading online material

Do I need a new set of reading skills?

You may be asking, "Is reading online really different from reading the printed word?" The answer is yes, especially with today's online, interactive, multimedia environment. Not too long ago, college students purchased their books or reading packets from the college bookstore and read the printed word. Today, this is not always the case. You may be required to download entire books or chapters, you will be assigned websites by your instructors, and you will sometimes decide to explore topics further through online research. Reading online requires an adjusted set of skills. You will still need to use the reading tips in this chapter, especially SQ3R, but you will also need to familiarize yourself with the strategies for successfully reading online (nontextual) material. Consider the tips offered in Key 5.10.

Online reading challenges

Complex material

Understanding sentence structure is quite important, especially when reading challenging college-level material online. Better readers understand the basic rules of grammar and sentence structure. Primarily, they are able to separate a subject phrase from a predicate, or verb, phrase in a sentence. This "phrase-

If you need more help with understanding the elements of grammar and sentence structure, there are many free sources online. You can also check out a grammar book from any library and review it. Understanding grammar can help improve your comprehension more than anything else. After you have the rules down, it is just a matter of practice—reading as much as you can.

TIPS FOR
READING ONLINE MATERIAL

- ▶ Before you even open the site, plan some undisturbed time to survey, explore, and read the site. Make it a point to avoid distractions or multitasking such as downloading songs on iTunes, reading your Facebook page, or checking e-mail. Devote this time to reading the material.
- ▶ Know why you are reading the online material.
- ▶ As you open the site, browse through (survey) it first to determine the length, view the main headings, and find out if you'll need to download plug-ins or any additional programs on your computer to access the material. Get a "feel" for the site and the matter.
- ▶ Click on any menus or tabs to determine what additional information is available.
- ▶ Work to avoid eye strain. You can do this several ways:
  - Read in periods of 20 minutes. After 20 minutes, take a short break.
  - Increase the size of your view screen to make the site larger.
  - Copy the material, paste it into a Word document, and enlarge the font so that you can read it more clearly.
- ▶ While reading, use virtual sticky notes to mark important material. You can download several free sticky notes programs by going online and searching "Free Online Sticky Notes."
- ▶ While reading, use an online highlighter to mark important material. To access an online highlighter, download one of the free online highlighting programs such as www.awesomehighlighter.com.
- ▶ While reading online, just as reading from printed material, take notes! This is one of the most important tools for memory and comprehension. As you read online material, take notes the traditional way or take virtual online notes. To do this, open a word-processing program, reduce it into the bottom menu bar, and as you read, click on it and add notes to your online page. Double space between each sentence to make it easier to read during your review period. You can also download several free online note-taking systems by searching "Free Online Note-Taking Software." You may want to consider investing in a dual monitor set-up for your computer.
- ▶ Use free text-to-speech programs to convert your online material to verbal material. If you're on the run, download any free text-to-speech program and then copy and paste the written work into the program. Next, download the file to your mp3 player or burn it to a CD. You now have "reading on the run."

cutting" strategy was observed in print material as early as A.D. 400, when Saint Jerome first noticed that some scribes had placed phrases on separate lines as a way to help poor readers read the text aloud.

For complicated material, you can follow this same strategy if you can cut and paste the material into a word processing program. From there, you can manipulate the text and break large, complex material down into shorter chunks. Divide the text into phrases or thematic segments like paragraphs or subheadings to better enable you to sift through it.

Eyestrain

Online reading has unique challenges. Not only do you have to locate information quickly and accurately, but you have to do this while looking at a computer

Find a website with one or two pages of higher-level material that you are able to copy and paste into a Word document. Copy the same material into two documents. In one of the documents, insert extra spaces and divisions between paragraphs. In the other document, do not make any changes. First, read the unchanged document. Note the time it takes you to get through the page and any reading challenges you face. Next, read the document with extra spaces. As you read using the READERS strategy, insert additional spaces when you find a division between ideas or phrases. Which reading experience is more effective and enjoyable? What other strategies can you implement to make reading complex material easier?

screen for hours at a time. The reading material is very visually intensive, and you may experience eyestrain. The stationary screens of desktop and laptop computers lend themselves to static and tiring reading positions. In addition, most applications and text formats are designed for the word processors and Web browsers, so their resolution is lower than desired for minimizing eye strain.

When you spend a lot of time at the computer, be sure to take frequent short breaks, look away from the screen, close your eyes, or focus on something else across the room.

Expand or maximize the window so it fills the entire screen. This will make reading easier. Also, make the print larger so you are not hunched over the computer or straining to see what's on the screen.

Extensive practice is an essential part of learning any skill, including reading. No one can learn to read complicated material by trying once or twice. Effective practice requires active, focused, repeated effort over time. Practice being an active reader whenever you get the opportunity.

Reading strategies for different learning styles

Use your strengths to improve your reading comprehension. Recall your learning style. Can you apply any additional suggestions from previous discussions of these factors here? See Key 5.11 for more ideas.

At this point in the term you undoubtedly have some reading to do. Put what you have learned in this chapter to use in becoming a more strategic and critical reader. Practice these skills whenever you get a chance. As you have learned, reading skills are *very* important for your future career success.

The number one reason patients visit eye doctors is because of computer strain. The U.S. Occupational Safety and Health Administration has issued guidelines to reduce eyestrain from computer display use in the workplace. For more information on the guidelines, go to www.osha.gov/SLTC/etools/computerworkstations/components_monitors.html

Look to continually challenge yourself. Stretch beyond your current reading level and make yourself work at understanding.

online outlook

Peter
Online reader
Age 40

Challenge
Reading online

I am one of those people who like to read on the computer. For some reason, I have always found the light that comes off the computer screen stimulating. I like to read from the computer when I can. Although I do occasionally suffer from eyestrain, it seems to have lessened the more time I spend at my computer.

For months after I first began working on computers every day, all day, I found sunlight too strong. I would scrunch my eyelids and my eyes would water every lunchtime.

I do print out many documents still and when I can, I copy and paste poorly designed website material into Word. Then, I can change the color and fonts to make it easier to read.

READING STRATEGIES FOR
DIFFERENT LEARNING STYLES

INTELLIGENCE	STRATEGIES
Verbal-Linguistic	▶ Use text-to-speech software to have the text selection read aloud to you as you read it. ▶ Sound out difficult words, and read difficult passages aloud. ▶ Try guessing word meanings based on what you read before and after difficult vocabulary. Then, look the words up in a dictionary. ▶ Take advantage of online dictionaries, audio guides to word pronunciation, and the ability to modify the presentation of online text to one which you can easily read. ▶ Using a word processor, turn digital text into an outline or cut and paste examples that support the main points of the reading. ▶ Use highlight features of any e-books to highlight important sections. ▶ Use other software programs, such as PowerPoint or website design programs, to summarize readings.
Logical-Mathematical	▶ Logically connect what you are reading with what you already know. ▶ Draw charts and graphs showing relationships. ▶ Take notes in a spreadsheet program that can help you identify similarities and differences and causes and effects. ▶ Use a word processing, website design, or drawing program to cut and paste the main ideas and supporting information, and make connections between them. Rearrange or add other ideas to make additional connections.
Bodily-Kinesthetic	▶ Print out text and highlight important parts of the reading. ▶ After reading, go on a walk while you are summarizing the material aloud.
Visual-Spatial	▶ Make use of any visuals, such as pictures, charts, and diagrams provided, to help you assess your prior knowledge, inspire questions, and determine the main ideas of the reading. ▶ Consider other visuals you could add that could help explain the concepts. ▶ Create a simple video by drawing pictures representing the main points of the reading on small pieces of paper and then flipping through them while recording. ▶ Take pictures of charts and diagrams and assemble the images in a PowerPoint type presentation or animation program. ▶ Visualize or imagine a "word picture" that will help you relate your experience with the reading. ▶ Draw a word-map to understand the relationships of concepts to a key word. ▶ Make use of site maps to help tell you where particular sections or pages are found within the site.
Interpersonal	▶ Consult with the professor, a tutor, an academic advisor, a classmate, a study group, or other resource if you have difficulty comprehending what you are reading. ▶ Collaborate with others, sharing outlines and understandings of the meaning, brainstorming relationships to other ideas, etc. ▶ Set up wikis for collaborative reading, where each person can share their background knowledge before reading, their summaries, and their opinions after reading.
Intrapersonal	▶ Keep your mind on the connected thought as you read. ▶ Apply the concepts to your own life. ▶ Browse the online library collection for related ideas. ▶ As you read, consider different outcomes. Predict what the author will say. ▶ Practice reading aloud for continuity and smoothness.
Musical	▶ Read aloud, creating a rhythm, pace and cadence that includes pauses. ▶ Use expressive tones that represent the action or emotion. ▶ Consider what musical score would go along with the text presentation. ▶ Write songs that summarize the material.
Naturalistic	▶ Cut and paste parts of the text in a word processing program, grouping common elements together. ▶ Organize your reading materials and notes into relevant groupings. ▶ Some web pages are also now being encoded with information to categorize and structure their information, with the goal of creating a "semantic web" that can give readers new power to access, organize, and analyze digital information. Research more about this as it becomes further developed.

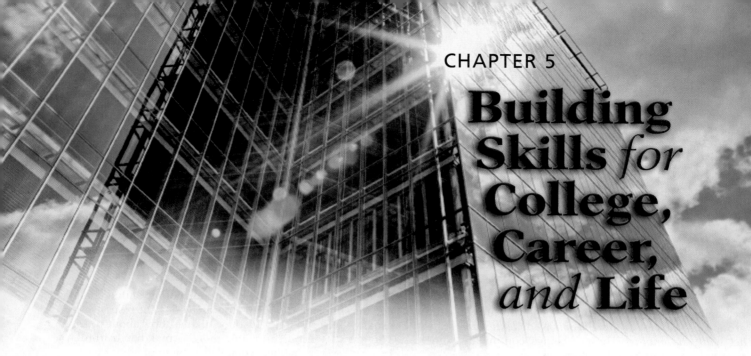

CHAPTER 5

Building Skills *for* College, Career, *and* Life

Steps to Success

Study a Text Page

BUILD BASIC SKILLS. The facing page is from the chapter "Groups and Organizations" in the sixth edition of John J. Macionis's *Sociology*.[5] Skim the excerpt. Identify the headings on the page and the relationships among them. Mark primary-level headings with a numeral 1, secondary headings with a 2, and tertiary (third-level) headings with a 3.

TAKE IT TO THE NEXT LEVEL. Analyze the headings and text.

Which heading serves as an umbrella for the rest?

_____

What do the headings tell you about the content of the page?

_____

_____

_____

_____

Name three concepts that seem important to remember.

1. _____

2. _____

3. _____

Based on the three concepts you pulled out, write three study questions that you can review with an instructor, a teaching assistant, or a fellow student.

1. _____

2. _____

3. _____

Courtesy of Stockbroker/Alamy

SOCIAL GROUPS

Virtually everyone moves through life with a sense of belonging; this is the experience of group life. A social group refers to *two or more people who identify and interact with one another.* Human beings continually come together to form couples, families, circles of friends, neighborhoods, churches, businesses, clubs, and numerous large organizations. Whatever the form, groups encompass people with shared experiences, loyalties, and interests. In short, while maintaining their individuality, the members of social groups also think of themselves as a special "we."

Groups, Categories, and Crowds

People often use the term "group" imprecisely. We now distinguish the group from the similar concepts of category and crowd.

■ **Category.** A *category* refers to people who have some status in common. Women, single fathers, military recruits, homeowners, and Roman Catholics are all examples of categories.

Why are categories not considered groups? Simply because, while the individuals involved are aware that they are not the only ones to hold that particular status, the vast majority are strangers to one another.

■ **Crowd.** A *crowd* refers to a temporary cluster of individuals who may or may not interact at all. Students sitting in a lecture hall do engage one another and share

some common identity as college classmates; thus, such a crowd might be called a loosely formed group. By contrast, riders hurtling along on a subway train or bathers enjoying a summer day at the beach pay little attention to one another and amount to an anonymous aggregate of people. In general, then, crowds are too transitory and impersonal to qualify as social groups.

The right circumstances, however, could turn a crowd into a group. People riding in a subway train that crashes under the city streets generally become keenly aware of their common plight and begin to help one another. Sometimes such extraordinary experiences become the basis for lasting relationships.

Primary and Secondary Groups

Acquaintances commonly greet one another with a smile and the simple phrase, "Hi! How are you?" The response is usually a well scripted, "Just fine, thanks, how about you?" This answer, of course, is often more formal than truthful. In most cases, providing a detailed account of how you are *really* doing would prompt the other person to beat a hasty and awkward exit.

Sociologists classify social groups by measuring them against two ideal types based on members' genuine level of personal concern. This variation is the key to distinguishing *primary* from *secondary* groups.

According to Charles Horton Cooley (1864–1929), a **primary group** is a *small social group whose members share personal and enduring relationships.* Bound together by primary relationships, individuals in primary groups typically spend a great deal of time together, engage in a wide range of common activities, and feel that they know one another well. Although not without periodic conflict, members of primary groups display sincere concern for each other's welfare. The family is every society's most important primary group.

Cooley characterized these personal and tightly integrated groups as *primary* because they are among the first groups we experience in life. In addition, the family and early play groups also hold primary importance in the socialization process, shaping attitudes, behavior, and social identity.

Source: John J. Macionis, *Sociology,* 6th ed., p. 145, © 1997 Prentice-Hall, Inc. Reproduced by permission of Pearson Education, Inc., Upper Saddle River, NJ.

MOVE TOWARD MASTERY. Read the excerpt, putting SQ3R to work. Using a marker pen, highlight key phrases and sentences. Write short marginal notes to help you review the material later. After reading this page thoroughly, write a short summary paragraph.

_____

_____

_____

_____

Writing

Build Intrapersonal and Communication Skills

Record your thoughts on a separate piece of paper, in a journal, or electronically.

EMOTIONAL INTELLIGENCE JOURNAL

Reading challenges. Which current course presents your most difficult reading challenge? Describe what makes the reading tough—type of material, length of assignments, level of difficulty, or something else. What feelings come up for you when you read, and what effect do they have on your reading? Describe techniques you learned in this chapter that can help you get into a growth mindset to read productively.

REAL-LIFE WRITING

Ask for help. Self-help plans often involve reaching out to others. Draft an e-mail to your instructor describing the difficulties in your challenging course as well as the specific help you need to move to the next step. Make sure that your message is clear and accurate, your grammar, spelling, and punctuation correct, and your tone appropriate. *Whether you send the e-mail or not is up to you.* In either case, writing it will help you move forward in your reading improvement plan.

Personal Portfolio

Prepare for Career Success

READING SKILLS ON THE JOB

21st Century Learning Building Blocks

- Information Literacy
- Media Literacy
- ICT Literacy

Complete the following in your electronic portfolio or separately on paper.

Excellent reading skills are a requirement for almost every 21st century job. Employers expect that you will read independently to master new skills and keep up with change. Whether in print or electronic form, on-the-job reading will challenge you as does college reading. For example, sociology courses may involve reading textbooks, journals, and case studies, but actually working in the field requires that you keep on top of case reports, government regulations, court documents, and an unending stream of work-related e-mails.

Prepare yourself by honestly assessing your practical skills *right now*. Use the following list to rate your ability on a scale of 1 to 10, with 10 being the highest:

- Ability to concentrate, no matter the distractions
- Ability to use emotional triggers to learn and remember material
- Ability to define your reading purpose and use it to guide your focus and pace
- Ability to use specific vocabulary-building techniques to improve comprehension
- Ability to use every aspect of SQ3R to master content
- Ability to skim and scan
- Ability to use analytical thinking skills when reading
- Ability to use highlighting and notes to help you master content

For the two skill areas in which you rated yourself lowest, think about how you can improve. Make a problem-solving plan for each. Check your progress in one month and at the end of the term. Finally, write down how you anticipate using the reading skills you learned in this chapter in your chosen career.

Social Networking

INCLUDE YOUR EDUCATION

Information about your education is often important when networking for jobs. Sign in to your LinkedIn account and click on "Edit My Profile." Then, click on "Education" and fill in the following:

- Country
- State
- Degree (either attained or working toward)
- Field(s) of study
- Dates attended (Current students enter their graduation year.)
- Activities and societies
- Additional notes (Give any other information about your education that you think would be valuable to a contact or potential employer—awards, honors, details about your major, study abroad, and so on.)

If you have a previously earned degree at another institution, don't forget to fill in a separate Education field about that as well.

ENDNOTES

1. Francis P. Robinson, Effective Behavior, New York: Harper & Row, 1941.

2. John Mack Faragher, Mari Jo Buhle, Daniel Czitrom, and Susan H. Armitage, *Out of Many: A History of the American People*, 5th ed., Upper Saddle River, NJ: Prentice Hall, 2005, p. xxxvii.

3. Benjamin S. Bloom, *Taxonomy of Educational Objectives, Handbook I:* *The Cognitive Domain*, New York: McKay, 1956.

4. Ophelia H. Hancock, *Reading Skills for College Students*, 5th ed., Upper Saddle River, NJ: Prentice Hall, 2001, pp. 54–59.

5. John J. Macionis, *Sociology*, 6th ed., Upper Saddle River, NJ: Prentice Hall, 1997, p. 174.

Note Taking for Online Courses

*A*fter seven years with the Navy, William Payne decided to put his skills in communications technology to use to launch a career in 1995. He decided to go into information technology and started a company. After many years of business, Payne decided to seek an online bachelor's degree in his profession in 2009 with Columbia Southern University.

"Education in the technology arena is extremely important. We are competing at an international level. And there are people walking around you that have high credentials," he explained. As a CEO of a company, Payne thought it was also important to strengthen his education and appeal in today's marketplace considering the dynamics of the economy.

He chose CSU for its reputation, credibility and affordability. "CSU rates are extremely cost effective. The rates reduced my expected spending to about half," Payne said.

During his educational journey, Payne faced a few obstacles. "The greatest challenge for me was looking at all of the classes that I had to take when I initially enrolled," he said. "It was somewhat overwhelming and I had a sense of not being able to complete the program because of situations or circumstances that may arise."

However, Payne said CSU faculty and staff provided a strong network of support to help him reach his goals. In addition, "I changed my views of what was ahead and looked more to what was accomplished, in terms of class completion. My accomplishments gave me the confidence and energy to tackle the next term of courses until I successfully completed the program," Payne explained.

After proudly graduating from CSU summa cum laude, Payne felt "receiving a degree from CSU validated my years of technology experience."

STATUS *Check*

► *How developed are your listening and note-taking skills?*

"Successfully intelligent people find their path and then pursue it, realizing that there will be obstacles along the way and that surmounting these obstacles is part of their challenge."

—Robert Sternberg

LISTENING
A process that involves sensing, interpreting, evaluating, and reacting to spoken messages.

"You cannot truly listen to anyone and do anything else at the same time."

—M. Scott Peck

How can you become a better listener?

The act of *hearing* is not the same as the act of listening. *Hearing* refers to sensing spoken messages and sounds from their source. You can hear all kinds of things and not understand or remember any of them. Listening, however, is a communication process that starts with hearing but also includes focused thinking about what you hear. Listening is a learnable skill that engages your analytical, creative, and practical thinking abilities and extends far beyond the classroom, enhancing your ability to relate with work and school colleagues, friends, and family.

The importance of listening

Why does listening really matter in classes and relationships?

Listening is a survival skill. Period! It is that simple! "I know listening is important," you might say, but few ever think of the paramount significance listening has on our everyday lives. It is necessary for:

- ▶ Establishing and improving relationships
- ▶ Personal growth
- ▶ Showing respect to others
- ▶ Professional rapport
- ▶ Showing empathy and compassion
- ▶ Learning new information
- ▶ Understanding others' opinions and views
- ▶ Basic survival
- ▶ Entertainment
- ▶ Health

How much time do you think you spend listening every day? Research suggests that we spend almost 70 percent of our waking time communicating, and **53 percent of that time is spent in listening situations** (Adler, Rosenfeld, and Proctor, 2010). Effective listening skills can mean the difference between success or failure, A's or F's, relationships or loneliness, and in some cases and careers, life or death.

For students, good listening skills are critical. Over the next two to four years, you will be given a lot of information through lectures. Cultivating and improving your active listening skills will help you to understand the material, take accurate notes, participate in class discussions, communicate with your peers more effectively, and become more actively engaged in your learning process.

I think I heard you listening

Is there really a difference between listening and hearing?

No doubt you've been in a communication situation in which a misunderstanding took place. Perhaps you heard something incorrectly, or someone heard you incorrectly, or it could be that someone heard your message but misinterpreted it. These communication blunders arise because we tend to view listening (and communication in general) as an automatic response when in fact it is not.

Listening is a learned, voluntary activity. You must choose to do it. It is a skill, just like driving a car, painting a picture, or playing the piano. Becoming an active listener requires practice, time, mistakes, guidance, and active participation.

Hearing, however, is not learned; it is automatic and involuntary. If you are within range of a sound, you will probably hear it, although you may not be listening to it. Hearing a sound does not guarantee that you know what it is or from where it came. Listening actively, though, means making a conscious effort to focus on the sound and determine what it is.

Listening defined

According to Adler, Rosenfeld, and Towne (2006), the drawing of the Chinese verb "to listen" (shown in Key 6.1) provides a comprehensive and practical definition of listening.

Listening to other students can be as important as listening to instructors. These students may learn something useful from their fellow student's presentation.
© iStockPhoto

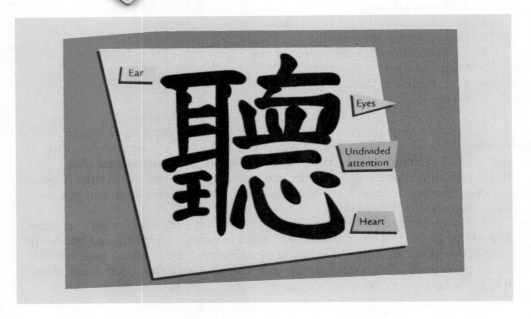

To the Chinese, listening involves your *ears,* your *eyes,* your ***undivided attention,*** and your *heart.* Do you make it a habit to listen with more than your ears? The Chinese view listening as a whole-body experience. People from Western cultures seem to have lost the ability to involve their whole body in the listening process. We tend to use only our ears, and sometimes we don't even use them very well.

At its core, listening is "the ability to hear, understand, analyze, respect, and appropriately respond to the meaning of another person's spoken and nonverbal messages" (Daly and Engleberg, 2006). Although this definition involves the word *hear,* listening goes far beyond just the physical ability to catch sound waves.

The first step in listening is hearing, but true listening involves one's full attention and the ability to filter out distractions, emotional barriers, cultural differences, and religious biases. Listening means that you are making a conscious decision to understand and show reverence for the other person's communication efforts.

Listening needs to be personalized and internalized. To understand listening as a whole-body experience, we can define it on three levels:

1. Listening with a **purpose**
2. Listening **objectively**
3. Listening **constructively**

Listening with a purpose suggests a need to recognize different types of listening situations—for example, class, worship, entertainment, and relationships. People do not listen the same way in every situation.

Listening objectively means listening with an open mind. You will give yourself few greater gifts than the gift of knowing how to listen without bias and prejudice. This is perhaps the most difficult aspect of listening. If you have been cut off in mid-conversation or mid-sentence by someone who disagreed with you, or if someone has left the room while you were giving your opinion of a situation, you have had the experience of talking to people who do not know how to listen objectively.

Listening constructively means listening with the attitude: "How can this be helpful to my life, my education, my career, or my finances?" This type of listening involves evaluating the information you hear and determining whether it has meaning to your life. Sound easy? It is more difficult than it sounds because, again, we all tend to shut out information that we do not view as immediately helpful or useful. To listen constructively, you need to know how to listen and store information for later.

Four listening styles defined

What is your orientation?

According to interpersonal communication expert, author, and educator Steven McCornack (2007), there are *four different listening styles*. They are action-oriented, time-oriented, people-oriented, and content-oriented. Study Key 6.2 to determine which best describes you as a listener.

Which style best describes you?_____

_____

FOUR
LISTENING STYLES

Action-Oriented Listeners:

► Want to get their messages quickly and to-the-point
► Do not like fluff and grow impatient when they perceive people to be wasting their time
► Become frustrated when information is not orderly
► Are quick to dismiss people who ramble and falter when they speak.

Time-Oriented Listeners:

► Want their information in brief, concise messages
► Are consumed with how much time is taken to convey a message
► Set time limits for listening (and communicating in general)
► Will ask people to "move the message along" if they feel it is taking too long

People-Oriented Listeners:

► Are in contrast to time- and action-oriented listeners
► View listening as a chance to connect with other people
► Enjoy listening to people so that relationships can be built
► Become emotionally involved with the person communicating

Content-Oriented Listeners:

► Enjoy an intellectual challenge
► Like to listen to technical information, facts, and evidence
► Enjoy complex information that must be deciphered and filtered
► Carefully evaluate information and facts before forming an opinion
► Enjoy asking questions

What are the pros of being this type of listener_____

_____

_____

What are the cons of being this type of listener? _____

_____

_____

Listening **can be so hard**

Can you really overcome the obstacles to listening?

Several major obstacles stand in the way of becoming an effective listener. To begin building active listening skills, you first have to remove some barriers.

Obstacle 1: Prejudging

Prejudging, one of the biggest obstacles to active listening, means that you automatically shut out what is being said. You may prejudge because you don't like or agree with the information or the person communicating. You may also have prejudging problems because of your environment, culture, social status, or attitude.

Do you prejudge information or its source?

Answer yes or no to each of the following questions:

1.	I tune out when something is boring.	**Yes**	**No**
2.	I tune out when I do not agree with the information.	**Yes**	**No**
3.	I argue mentally with the speaker about information.	**Yes**	**No**
4.	I do not listen to people I do not like.	**Yes**	**No**
5.	I make decisions about information before I understand all of its implications or consequences.	**Yes**	**No**

If you answered yes to two or more of these questions, you tend to prejudge in a listening situation.

Tips for overcoming prejudging

► Listen for information that may be valuable to you as a student. Some material may not be pleasant to hear but may be useful to you later on.

► Listen to the message, not the messenger. If you do not like the speaker, try to go beyond personality and listen to what is being said, without regard to the person saying it. Conversely, you may like the speaker so much that you automatically accept the material or answers without listening objectively to what is being said.

► Try to remove cultural, racial, gender, social, and environmental barriers. Just because a person is different from you or holds a different point of view does not make that person wrong; and just because a person is like you and holds a similar point of view does not make that person right. Sometimes, you have to cross cultural and environmental barriers to learn new material and see with brighter eyes.

Obstacle 2: Talking

Not even the best listener in the world can listen while he or she is talking. The next time you are in a conversation with a friend, try speaking while your friend is speaking—then see if you know what your friend said. To become an effective listener, you need to learn the power of silence. Silence gives you the opportunity to think about what is being said before you respond. The first rule of listening is to stop talking. The second rule of listening is to stop talking. And, you guessed it—the third rule of listening is to stop talking.

Are you a talker rather than a listener?

Answer yes or no to the following questions:

1. I often interrupt the speaker so that I can say what I want.   **Yes   No**
2. I am thinking of my next statement while others are talking.   **Yes   No**
3. My mind wanders when others talk.   **Yes   No**
4. I answer my own questions.   **Yes   No**
5. I answer questions that are asked of other people.   **Yes   No**

If you answered yes to two or more questions, you tend to talk too much in a listening situation.

Tips for overcoming the urge to talk too much

▶ Avoid interrupting the speaker. Force yourself to be silent at parties, family gatherings, and friendly get-togethers. You should not be unsociable, but force yourself to be silent for 10 minutes. You'll be surprised at what you hear. You may also be surprised how hard it is to do this. Test yourself.

▶ Ask someone a question, and then allow that person to answer the question. Too often we ask questions and answer them ourselves. Force yourself to wait until the person has formulated a response. If you ask questions and wait for answers, you will force yourself to listen.

▶ Concentrate on what is being said at the moment, not what you want to say next.

Obstacle 3: Becoming too emotional

Emotions can form a strong barrier to active listening. Worries, problems, fears, and anger can keep you from listening to the greatest advantage. Have you ever sat in a lecture, and before you knew what was happening, your mind was a million miles away because you were angry or worried about something? If you have, you know what it's like to bring your emotions to the table.

Do you bring your emotions to the listening situation?

Answer yes or no to the following questions:

1. I get angry before I hear the whole story.   **Yes   No**
2. I look for underlying or hidden messages in information.   **Yes   No**
3. Sometimes, I begin listening on a negative note.   **Yes   No**
4. I base my opinions of information on what others are saying or doing.   **Yes   No**
5. I readily accept information as correct from people whom I like or respect.   **Yes   No**

If you answered yes to two or more of these questions, you tend to bring your emotions to a listening situation.

Discover Yourself as a Listener

Complete the following as you focus on your personal listening habits:

Analyze how present you are as a listener. Are you easily distracted, or can you focus well? Do you prefer to listen, or do you tend to talk?

_____

_____

When you are listening, what tends to distract you?

_____

_____

What happens to your listening skills when you become confused?

_____

_____

How do you react when you strongly disagree with something your instructor says—when you are convinced that you are right and your instructor is wrong?

_____

_____

Thinking about your answers, list two strategies from the chapter that will help you improve listening skills.

1. _____

2. _____

Tips for overcoming emotions

▶ Know how you feel before you begin the listening experience. Take stock of your emotions and feelings ahead of time.
▶ Focus on the message; determine how to use the information.
▶ Create a positive image about the message you are hearing.
▶ Avoid overreacting and jumping to conclusions.

TAKING EFFECTIVE NOTES

How can you improve your note-taking skills?

Taking notes makes you an active class participant—even when you don't say a word—and provides you with study materials. What's on the line is nothing short of your academic success.

Notes have two primary purposes: to serve as a record of what happened and to use for studying, alone and in combination with your text notes.

Because it is virtually impossible to take notes on everything, note taking encourages you to use your analytical intelligence to critically evaluate what is worth remembering. Exploring the strategies outlined in this chapter can help you prepare to take notes, review notes, and take notes on reading materials.

Examples of various note-taking systems, and a more thorough discussion, appear later in the chapter.

Good listening powers note taking. When taking notes in class, stop to listen to the information before deciding what to write down.
© iStockPhoto

Record information effectively

The following practical suggestions will help you record what is important in a format that you can review later:

▶ *Start a new page or section for each new topic*.
▶ *Write down all key terms and definitions* so that you can refer back to them easily.
▶ *Note relevant examples, applications, and links to other material* when you encounter difficult concepts.
▶ *Be organized, but not fussy*. Remember that you can always improve your notes later.
▶ *Leave blank spaces between points* to make it easy see where one topic ends and another begins. (This suggestion does not apply if you are using a think link.)
▶ *Draw pictures and diagrams* to illustrate ideas.
▶ *Be consistent*. Use the same system to show importance—such as indenting, spacing, or underlining—on each page.
▶ *Record as much as you can if you have trouble understanding a concept*. Then leave space for an explanation and flag the margin with a large question mark. Try to clarify your questions by reading the text or ask your instructor for help.
▶ *Consider that your notes are only part of the picture*. You will learn best when you combine your notes and other instructional materials.

Review and revise

By their very nature, notes require revision. They may be incomplete in some places, confusing in others, and illegible in others. That is why it is critical to review and revise your notes as soon as possible. This will enable you to fill in gaps while the material is fresh, to clarify sloppy handwriting, or to raise questions.

If you can review your notes within 24 hours of taking them down, you are likely to reactivate and strengthen the new neural pathways you created when you learned the material. Waiting longer than 24 hours can result in losing the information you worked so hard to record. Reviewing and revising your notes prepares you for the vital step of moving the information to short term memory.

What note-taking systems can you use?

Now that you have gathered some useful note-taking strategies, take a look at different approaches to note taking. As you read, keep some questions in mind:

▶ What class or type of instruction would this system be best suited for? Why?
▶ How could I make use of this system?

GET PRACTICAL!

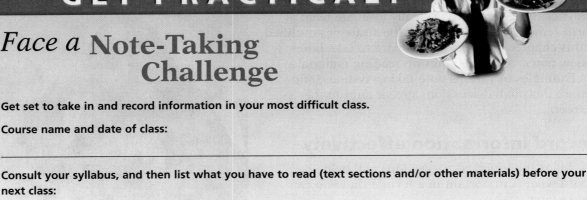

Face a Note-Taking Challenge

Get set to take in and record information in your most difficult class.

Course name and date of class:

_____

Consult your syllabus, and then list what you have to read (text sections and/or other materials) before your next class:

_____

_____

Where will you sit in class to focus your attention and minimize distractions?

_____

Which note-taking system is best suited for the class and why?

_____

_____

Write the phone numbers and e-mail addresses of two classmates whose notes you can borrow if you are confused about material:

_____

_____

▶ Which system seems most comfortable to me?
▶ What system might be most compatible with my learning style strengths? Why?

Outlines

Outlines use a standard structure to show how ideas interrelate. *Formal outlines* indicate idea dominance and subordination with Roman numerals, uppercase and lowercase letters, and numbers. In contrast, *informal outlines* show the same associations but replace the formality with a system of consistent indenting and dashes.

An informal outline can show how ideas and supporting details relate while also indicating levels of importance. Key 6.3 shows how the structure of an informal outline helps a student take notes on the topic of tropical rain forests. The multiple intelligences table in this chapter (see page 160) is designed to help harness different learning approaches for an earth science course. Specifically, the table will suggest different note-taking strategies you can use to study the topic of tropical rain forests.

When an instructor's presentation is disorganized, it may be difficult to use an outline. Focus instead on taking down whatever information you can as you try to connect key topics. The Cornell system and other note-taking methods discussed next can be beneficial in such situations.

Tropical Rain Forests

What are tropical rain forests?

— Areas in South America and Africa, along the equator

— Average temperatures between 25° and 30° C (77°–86° F)

— Average annual rainfalls range between 250 to 400 centimeters (100 to 160 inches)

— Conditions combine to create the Earth's richest, most biodiverse ecosystem.

  – A biodiverse ecosystem has a great number of organisms coexisting within a defined area.

  – Examples of rain forest biodiversity

   – 2½ acres in the Amazon rain forest has 283 species of trees

   – a 3-square-mile section of a Peruvian rain forest has more than 1,300 butterfly species and 600 bird species.

   – Compare this biodiversity to what is found in the entire U.S.—only 400 butterfly species and 700 bird species

How are humans changing the rain forest?

— Humans have already destroyed about 40% of all rain forests.

  – They are cutting down trees for lumber or clearing the land for ranching or agriculture.

— Biologist Edwin O. Wilson estimates that this destruction may lead to the extinction of 27,000 species.

— Rain forest removal is also linked to the increase in atmospheric carbon dioxide, which worsens the greenhouse effect.

  – The greenhouse effect refers to process in which gases such as carbon dioxide trap the sun's energy in the Earth's atmosphere as heat resulting in global warning.

— Recognition of the crisis is growing as are conservation efforts.

Source: Teresa Audesirk, Gerald Audesirk, and Bruce E. Byers. *Life on Earth,* 2nd ed. Upper Saddle River, NJ: Prentice Hall, 2000, pp. 660–662.

From time to time, an instructor may give you a guide, usually in outline form, to help you take notes. This outline, known as *guided notes,* may be on the board, projected onto a screen, or in a handout that you receive at the beginning of class. Because guided notes are usually general and sketchy, they require that you fill in the details.

Cornell T-note system

The *Cornell note-taking system,* also known as the *T-note system,* consists of three sections on ordinary notepaper.[1]

▶ *Notes,* the largest section, is on the right. Record your notes here in whatever form you choose. Skip lines between topics so you can clearly see where a section begins and ends.

▶ The *cue column* goes to the left of your notes. Leave it blank while you read or listen, and then fill it in later as you review. You might insert keywords or comments that highlight ideas, clarify meaning, add examples, link ideas, or draw diagrams. Many students use this column to raise questions, which they answer when they study.

▶ The *summary* goes at the bottom of the page. Here you reduce your notes to critical points, a process that will help you learn the material. Use this section to provide an overview of what the notes say.

Create this note-taking structure before taking notes. Picture an upside-down letter *T* as you follow these directions:

▶ Start with a sheet of 8½-by-11-inch lined paper. Label it with the date and text title.

Apply Different Intelligences to Concepts to Taking Notes in Earth Science

INTELLIGENCE	USE MI STRATEGIES TO IMPROVE YOUR NOTES	APPLY MI NOTE-TAKING STRATEGIES TO THE TOPIC OF TROPICAL RAIN FORESTS FOR AN EARTH SCIENCE COURSE
Verbal-Linguistic	• Rewrite your class notes in an alternate note-taking style to see connections more clearly. • Combine class and text notes to get a complete picture.	• Rewrite and summarize your reading and lecture notes to understand the characteristics of tropical rain forests.*
Logical-Mathematical	• When reviewing or rewriting notes, put information into a logical sequence. • Create tables that show relationships.	• Create a table comparing and contrasting the different species found in a typical rain forest.
Bodily-Kinesthetic	• Think of your notes as a crafts project that enables you to see "knowledge layers." Use colored pens to texture your notes. • Study with your notes spread in sequence around you so that you can see knowledge building from left to right.	• Fill a tube with 160 inches of water (that's 13⅓ feet!) to give you a physical sense of the annual rainfall in a rain forest. Or fill a bathtub with 10 inches of water and multiply by 16 to imagine rainfall totals. How would you react to living with so much rain? Take notes on your reaction.
Visual-Spatial	• Take notes using colored markers or pens. • Rewrite lecture notes in think link format, focusing on the most important points.	• As part of your notes, create a chart that covers the types of vegetation that grow in a rain forest. Use a different colored marker for each plant species.
Interpersonal	• Try to schedule a study group right after a lecture to discuss class notes. • Review class notes with a study buddy. Compare notes to see what the other missed.	• Interview someone you know who has visited a rain forest about what she saw, or interview a natural scientist at a museum about this environment. Use a different note-taking system for each person.
Intrapersonal	• Schedule some quiet time soon after a lecture to review and think about your notes. • As you review your notes, decide whether you grasp the material or need help.	• Think about the conflict between economic modernization and the preservation of rain forests in underdeveloped areas. Include your thoughts in your notes.
Musical	• To improve recall, recite concepts in your notes to rhythms. • Write a song that includes material from your class and text notes. Use the refrain to emphasize what is important.	• Use the Internet to find songs about the biodiversity of rain forests written by indigenous peoples who live in or near them. Then, use the song to remember key concepts. Take notes on what you find.
Naturalistic	• Notice similarities and differences in concepts by organizing material into natural groupings.	• If possible, visit a museum of natural history with exhibits of rain forests. Try to see common characteristics that make vegetation and species thrive in this environment. Take notes on your observations.

*For information on tropical rain forests, see Frederick Lutgens, Edward Tarbuck, and Dennis Tasa, *Foundations of Earth Science*, 5th ed., Upper Saddle River, NJ: Prentice Hall, 2008.

▶ To create the cue column, draw a vertical line about 2½ inches from the left side of the paper. End the line about two inches from the bottom of the sheet.

▶ To create the summary area, start at the point where the vertical line ends (about two inches from the bottom of the page) and draw a horizontal line that spans the entire paper.

Key 6.4 shows how the Cornell system is used in a business course.

THE **CORNELL SYSTEM** HAS SPACE
FOR NOTES, COMMENTS, AND A SUMMARY

October 3, 2010, p. 1

Label a sheet of paper with the date and title of the lecture.

Understanding Employee Motivation

Why do some workers have a better attitude toward their work than others?

Some managers view workers as lazy; others view them as motivated and productive.

Maslow's Hierarchy

self-actualization needs (challenging job)
esteem needs (job title)
social needs (friends at work)
security needs (health plan)
physiological needs (pay)

Purpose of motivational theories
— To explain role of human relations in motivating employee performance
— Theories translate into how managers actually treat workers

2 specific theories
— Human resources model, developed by Douglas McGregor, shows that managers have radically different beliefs about motivation.
— Theory X holds that people are naturally irresponsible and uncooperative
— Theory Y holds that people are naturally responsible and self-motivated
— Maslow's Hierarchy of Needs says that people have needs in 5 different areas, which they attempt to satisfy in their work.
— Physiological need: need for survival, including food and shelter
— Security need: need for stability and protection
— Social need: need for friendship and companionship
— Esteem need: need for status and recognition
— Self-actualization need: need for self-fulfillment
Needs at lower levels must be met before a person tries to satisfy needs at higher levels.
— Developed by psychologist Abraham Maslow

Create the cue column by drawing a vertical line about 2½ inches from the left side of the paper. End the line about 2 inches from the bottom of the sheet.

Two motivational theories try to explain worker motivation. The human resources model includes Theory X and Theory Y. Maslow's Hierarchy of Needs suggests that people have needs in 5 different areas: physiological, security, social, esteem, and self-actualization.

Create the summary area by starting where the vertical line ends (about 2 inches from the bottom of the page) and drawing a horizontal line across the paper.

Think links

A *think link*, also known as a *mind map* or *word web*, is a visual form of note taking that encourages flexible thinking. When you draw a think link, you use shapes and lines to link ideas with supporting details and examples. The visual design makes the connections easy to see, and shapes and pictures extend the material beyond words.

To create a think link, start by circling or boxing your topic in the middle of the paper. Next, draw a line from the topic and write the name of one major idea at the end of the line. Circle that idea. Then jot down specific facts related to the idea, linking them to the idea with lines. Continue the process, connecting thoughts to one another with circles, lines, and words. Key 6.5, a think link on the sociological concept "stratification," follows this structure.

Examples of think link designs include stair steps showing connected ideas that build toward a conclusion and a tree with trunk and roots as central concepts and branches as examples.

Other visual strategies

Other strategies that help organize information are especially useful to visual learners. Use them when taking text notes or for review.

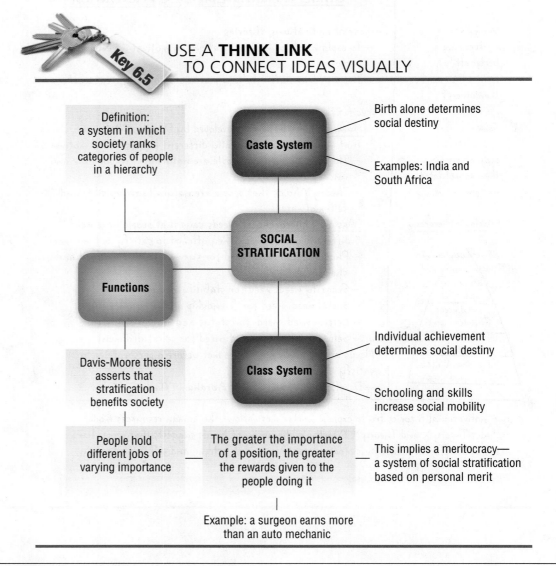

Key 6.5

USE A **THINK LINK** TO CONNECT IDEAS VISUALLY

Definition: a system in which society ranks categories of people in a hierarchy

Caste System

Birth alone determines social destiny

Examples: India and South Africa

SOCIAL STRATIFICATION

Functions

Davis-Moore thesis asserts that stratification benefits society

People hold different jobs of varying importance

Class System

Individual achievement determines social destiny

Schooling and skills increase social mobility

The greater the importance of a position, the greater the rewards given to the people doing it

This implies a meritocracy— a system of social stratification based on personal merit

Example: a surgeon earns more than an auto mechanic

► *Pictures and diagrams.* Copy any and all diagrams and feel free to adapt your own. Make complex concepts into images or cartoons. The act of converting material into a visual display will activate both your bodily-kinesthetic attributes as well as your visual intelligence.

► *Timelines.* Use a timeline to organize information into chronological order. Draw a vertical or horizontal line on the page and connect each item to the line, in order, noting the dates and basic event descriptions.

► *Tables.* Use the columns and rows of a table to organize information as you condense and summarize your class and text notes.

► *Hierarchy charts.* Charts showing an information hierarchy can help you visualize how pieces fit together. For example, you can use a hierarchy chart to show ranks within a government bureaucracy or levels of scientific classification of animals and plants.

Note-taking for multimedia presentations

Watching a video lecture or Web conference, whether live or prerecorded, can make it possible to see and hear an instructor or expert source as though you were attending a lecture in real life.

When taking notes from a live Web conference, lecture, news event, or other presentation, it is very helpful to be comfortable with the technology before it begins. Log in a few minutes early so that if you encounter any technical problems, you have time to troubleshoot or ask for help.

Consider the following strategies when taking notes from multimedia sources:

► *Review any previous notes and readings.* Looking over earlier material can provide context for new information.

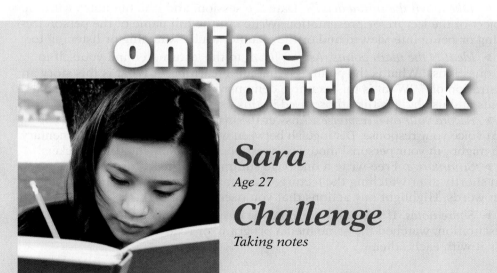

online outlook

Sara
Age 27

Challenge
Taking notes

One of the things that helped me the most with taking notes was to look at how my friends did it. One friend, in particular, was a master at taking notes from the text.

He marked up every page without fear! He circled words; he wrote his own headings in the margins; he used arrows to connect paragraphs or ideas; he underlined key passages.

It was a marvel to me! I learned a lot from looking at how he did it.

Active Listening

You may not get many opportunities in an online course to practice valuable listening skills, but watching video lectures provides a chance to improve. Listening isn't always easy and it isn't always comfortable. Take the words of Robert Frost for instance: "Education is the ability to listen to almost anything without losing your temper or your self-confidence." Keeping an open, awake, and engaged mind takes practice, but when excellent listening becomes second nature, you'll thank yourself for the work it took.

Strategies for listening actively to speakers include the following:

- Get enough sleep to stay alert and eat enough so you're not hungry—or have small snacks nearby.

- Put your worries aside. If you can't, take a break if possible and come back to the lecture refocused.

- Start with a productive mindset. If the material is difficult, that's all the more reason to pay attention.

- Concentrate. Work to take in the whole message so you will be able to read over your notes later and think critically about what is important. Making connections between ideas can alleviate the difficulty of the material in some cases—or boredom if you're familiar with the concepts.

- If you experience a listening lapse, get back into the lecture quickly instead of worrying about what you missed. Ask your professor for clarification and check with your classmates to fill in the gaps.

- Be aware. Pay attention to verbal signposts—words or phrases that call attention to what comes next, help organize information, connect ideas, or indicate what is important and what is not.

- Be careful not to rush to judgment. Know that you can't hear others—and therefore can't learn anything—if you are filled with preconceived notions about them and their ideas.

▶ *Anticipate what is coming.* Before the lecture, write down a predicted outline of the topic.

▶ *Take down the initial details.* Date the session, and title the notes with the subject of the lecture or presentation. Write out the full name of the person lecturing or being interviewed and/or the channel you're watching or listening to.

▶ *Identify the main points.* As you listen to the lecture, remind yourself to ask questions. "What is the point?" "What am I learning?" "What is this story an illustration of?" "What is this example demonstrating?" Skip lines after crucial points and use bullets (like those used in this list) for supporting information.

▶ *Record your own responses.* Answer the instructor's questions, even if you don't voice your response. Distinguish between what is said and your commentary. You might put your personal thoughts, questions, and commentary in brackets.

▶ *Summarize.* Free-write a one page summary of the lecture or presentation shortly after watching the lecture. Summarize important points in your own words. Highlight any actions that you need to take.

▶ *Share notes.* If you can find someone else who attended the lecture or presentation, watched the same media program, or read the same material, discuss it with each other.

SHORTHAND
A system of rapid handwriting that employs symbols, abbreviations, and shortened words to represent words and phrases.

How can you take notes faster?

Personal shorthand is a practical intelligence strategy that enables you to write faster. Because you are the only intended reader, you can misspell and abbreviate words in ways that only you understand. A risk of using shorthand is that you might forget what your writing means. To avoid this problem, review your notes and spell out words that are confusing.

The suggestions that follow will help you master shorthand. Many will be familiar and, in fact, you may already use many of them to speed up your e-mail and text messaging.

1. Use standard abbreviations in place of complete words.

w/, w/o	with, without	Cf	compare, in comparison to
ur	you are	Ff	following
→	means; resulting in	Q	question
←	as a result of	gr8	great
↑	increasing	Pov	point of view
↓	decreasing	<	less than
∴	therefore	>	more than
b/c	because	=	equals
≈	approximately	b&f	back and forth
+ or &	and	Δ	change
Y	why	2	to; two; too
no. or #	number	Afap	as far as possible
i.e.	that is,	e.g.	for example
cos	change of subject	c/o	care of
Ng	no good	lb	pound
POTUS	President of the United States	hx	history

2. Shorten words by removing middle vowels.

prps = purpose
lwyr = lawyer
cmptr = computer

3. Substitute word beginnings for entire words.

assoc = associate; association
info   = information
subj   = subject

4. Form plurals by adding *s* to shortened words.

prblms = problems
envlps = envelopes
prntrs = printers

5. Make up your own symbols and use them consistently.

b/4   = before
4tn   = fortune
2thake = toothache

6. Use standard or informal abbreviations for proper nouns such as places, people, companies, scientific substances, events, and so on.

DC   = Washington, D.C.
H_2O = water
Moz.   = Wolfgang Amadeus Mozart

7. If you know that a word or phrase will be repeated, write it once and then establish an abbreviation for the rest of your notes. For example, the first

GET CREATIVE!

Craft Your Own Shorthand

Now that you've read through some suggestions for shorthand, it's time to customize it to your needs.

Identify a class in which you take a lot of notes or one in which you would like to begin taking better notes.

_____

Next, write ten terms that are used often in this class. For instance, if you were creating a list for your psychology class, you might include terms like *Sigmund Freud, child development,* or *neuropsychology.*

_____

_____

_____

_____

_____

Finally, create a list of shorthand terms for the items you chose. Be creative but remember that they should be easy for you to remember and use. Thus, your shorthand should not be longer or more complex than the word itself. Use numbers, symbols, or even small images (like a heart or smiley face). For the list of psychology terms, the shorthand might look like the following:

Sigmund Freud	=	SigFrd
Child development	=	ChDev
Neuropsychology	=	nro-psych

time the text mentions the Iraq Study Group, the 2006 bipartisan commission that issued recommendations to the president on the Iraq War, write the name in full. After that, use the initials ISG.

8. Write only what is essential. Include only the information nuggets you want to remember. Do this by paring down your writing. Say, for example, the text had the following to say on the subject of hate crimes.[2]

> After the terrorist attacks on September 11, 2001, law enforcement officials noted a dramatic shift in the nature of hate crimes. For the first time, replacing crimes motivated by race as the leading type of hate crime were crimes that targeted religious and ethnic groups and particularly Muslims.

Your shorthand notes might look something like this:

—After 9/11 HCs ▲ focus & targeted religious and ethnic groups, esp. Muslims.
—Reduction of HC based on race.

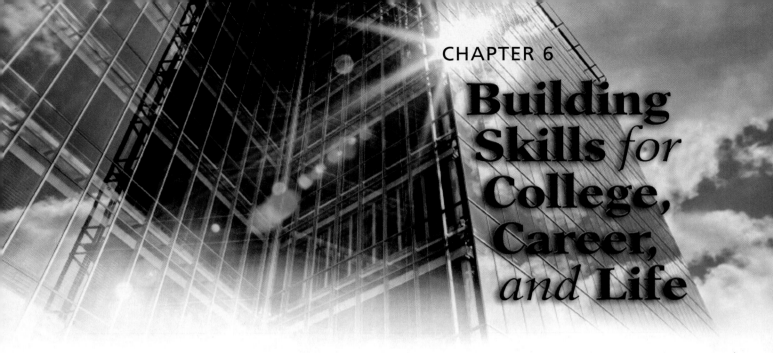

Building Skills for College, Career, and Life

Steps to Success

Your Best Listening and Note-Taking Conditions

BUILD BASIC SKILLS. Think of a recent class in which you were *able to listen and take notes effectively.*

Describe the environment (course title, classroom setting, and so on):

_____
_____
_____
_____

Describe the instructor's style (lecture, group discussion, Q and A):

_____
_____
_____
_____

Describe your level of preparation and attitude toward the class:

_____
_____
_____
_____

Describe the note-taking style you generally use in the class and how effective it is for you:

_____
_____
_____
_____

Describe any barriers to effective listening that were present:

_____

_____

_____

_____

Now think of a recent class in which you found it *hard to listen and take notes.*

Describe the environment (course title, classroom setting, and so on):

_____

_____

_____

_____

Describe the instructor's style (lecture, group discussion, Q and A):

_____

_____

_____

Describe your level of preparation and attitude toward the class:

_____

_____

_____

_____

Describe the note-taking style you generally use in the class and how effective it is for you:

_____

_____

_____

_____

Describe any barriers to effective listening that were present:

_____

_____

_____

_____

TAKE IT TO THE NEXT LEVEL. Examine the two situations. From what you notice, identify three conditions that seem, for you, to be crucial for effective listening and note taking:

1. _____

2. _____

3. _____

MOVE TOWARD MASTERY. Think about the more difficult listening and note-taking situation. For each of the three conditions you named, describe either how you can make sure that condition occurs or how you can compensate for it if it is out of your control.

1. _____

2. _____

3. _____

Writing

Build Intrapersonal and Communication Skills

Record your thoughts on a separate piece of paper, in a journal, or electronically.

EMOTIONAL INTELLIGENCE JOURNAL

Understanding your needs and making changes. Think about a situation when you've had trouble taking effective notes. Was it the teacher's pace? The subject matter of the class? How did you feel about the situation, and what did you do? After you describe the situation, find and write three note-taking strategies discussed in this chapter that could help you in the future. How might they help you create a more positive outcome?

REAL-LIFE WRITING

Determining the best method for you. Over the next week, commit to trying at least two different types of note-taking systems in your classes. If possible, choose a different method for each subject. Prepare for your method before entering the class by readying your notebook with the correct formatting. Try to complete your classes using the new method. When the week is over, reflect on which style worked best for you and which would be the most beneficial going forward.

Personal Portfolio

Prepare for Career Success

LEARN MORE ABOUT CAREER SUCCESS

21st Century Learning Building Blocks

- Financial, Economic, Business, and Entrepreneurial Literacy
- Information Literacy
- Media Literacy

Complete the following in your electronic portfolio or on separate paper.

Put your listening and note-taking skills to work as you investigate what brings success in the workplace. Write down a few potential career areas that interest you.

1. _____

2. _____

3. _____

Next, visit an Internet website that hosts user-loaded videos like YouTube.com. Perform a search for a career interview of your choice. You might try search terms like "marketing interview," "what's it like to be a dental technician?" or "what does a movie producer do?" When you've found a usable video (keep in mind that you're looking for credible, realistic information), practice one of the note-taking techniques discussed in this chapter.

Watch the video once all the way through, concentrating on main points and overall themes. Then, watch it again focusing on filling in gaps, understanding key terms and concepts, and gathering interesting extras. Remember to use shorthand when necessary.

After you've watched the video twice and taken thorough notes, write a one-page summary of the career for your portfolio. Include important information discussed in the video, such as the training required, salary expectations, daily duties, and so on. Keep the summary in your portfolio for future career searches.

 ## Social Networking

BUILD CONTACTS

Begin to build, or continue to build, your network on LinkedIn. Sign in to your account and click on "Add Connections." Find and contact 10 people in one of the following ways:

- Enter the name of someone you know in the "People" field at the top of the screen to see whether that person has a LinkedIn account. If they do, click on "Add to network" to invite them to join your network.
- Use the "See Who You Already Know on LinkedIn" feature to search your e-mail contacts for people who have LinkedIn accounts.
- In the "Enter E-mail Addresses" box, enter the e-mail addresses of people you want to invite to your network. Each will receive an invitation, regardless of whether they are already LinkedIn members.

Think carefully about who you want as part of your network. Consider family, friends, and coworkers. Choose people who you believe will help you move forward toward your goals, and who you think may have interesting and useful networks themselves.

ENDNOTES

1. System developed by Cornell professor Walter Pauk. See Walter Pauk, *How to Study in College*, 10th ed. Boston: Houghton Mifflin, 2011, pp. 236–241.

2. Information from Frank Schmalleger, *Criminal Justice Today*, 8th ed., Upper Saddle River, NJ: 2005, p. 71.

Memory and Studying

For most police officers, chasing criminals is a lot easier than chasing down free time. So when Pensacola (Fla.) police officer Greg Gordon decided to pursue a bachelor's degree, he wanted to make sure time would not be too much of an issue.

"Schedule was a big factor for me in pursuing a degree from Columbia Southern University," the 11-year veteran officer said. "The ease that I had to access all my materials and my professors was the No. 1 factor in my decision."

Gordon, who graduated in 2009 with a business administration degree, added that his educational journey with CSU was great because he was able to work on his own timeline. "And the staff has been great. They have always been there to answer my questions," he said.

The 36-year-old chose to focus on tourism and hospitality within the business administration degree program. "I was looking into the aspects of asset protection and threat assessment. In today's world, we have seen attacks at hotels, shopping malls and businesses," Gordon explained. "I felt with my law enforcement background and training I would be able to use my experience after retirement or if I change careers."

He credits his CSU bachelor's degree with opening doors and providing opportunities in his career field. "I have been able to apply for jobs on the federal level since I received my degree," Gordon explained. "At the Pensacola Police Department, I also qualified to take promotional exams for sergeant, lieutenant and captain positions. My degree has opened many doors that I would still be knocking on if I had not pursued higher education at CSU."

An Ann Arbor, Mich., native, Gordon came aknockin' on Pensacola's door in 1995 to be closer to family. He was hired as a cadet by the police department in April 1996 and was promoted to police officer in July 1999. He has earned several citations including Officer of Month in 2007 and a very special honor in 2010—the Gold Medal of Valor, the police department's highest award for heroism. He also received an official copy of the United States Congressional Record from Florida congressman Jeff Miller in recognition of his bravery.

Gordon, who enjoys the outdoors and running and competing in triathlons, hopes to return to CSU obtain a master's degree. He said he would advise others to do so, too.

"CSU is a great school and I would tell others don't let the traditional brick and mortar university overshadow your search for a university that will allow you to reach your dreams."

STATUS *Check*

For each statement, circle the number that feels right to you,
from 1 for "not at all true for me" to 5 for "very true for me."

▶ I know that not everything that I hear and read will necessarily stay in my memory for long—or at all.	1 2 3 4 5
▶ When I am studying, I try to choose what is most important to remember.	1 2 3 4 5
▶ Through trial and error, I have figured out study locations and times that work best for me.	1 2 3 4 5
▶ After a test or presentation is over, I retain much of what I had to know.	1 2 3 4 5
▶ I write, rewrite, and summarize information to remember it.	1 2 3 4 5
▶ I use flash cards and other active memory strategies to remember what I study.	1 2 3 4 5
▶ I create mnemonic devices with images and associations as memory hooks.	1 2 3 4 5
▶ I try to review material in several sessions over time rather than cram the night before a test.	1 2 3 4 5
▶ If I find myself looking up something over and over again, I make an effort to memorize it.	1 2 3 4 5
▶ I know how to study class and text notes effectively to prepare for tests.	1 2 3 4 5

Now total your scores. _____

Each of the topics in these statements is covered in this chapter. Note those statements for which you circled a 3 or lower. Skim the chapter to see where those topics appear, and pay special attention to them as you read, learn, and apply new strategies.

REMEMBER: *No matter how developed your memory and studying skills are, you can improve with effort and practice.*

"Successfully intelligent people are aware of the circumstances under which they are able to function at their best. They create those circumstances and then use them to their maximum advantage."

—Robert Sternberg

How does memory work?

Memory anchors all learning and performance—on tests as well as at work. The information you remember—concepts, facts, processes, formulas, and more—is the raw material with which you think, write, create, build, and perform day-to-day in school and out. Tasks ranging from high-level chemistry experiments to running a load of laundry through the washing machine all require you to retain and use information in your memory.

Memorization also gives you the tools to tackle higher-level thinking. You need to recall and understand information before you can apply, analyze, synthesize, or evaluate it.

Through studying, you build your memory and use it to move toward your goals. This chapter provides a host of memory improvement techniques that you can make your own with a positive attitude and active involvement. The first step is exploring how memory works.

The information processing model of memory

Memory refers to the way the brain stores and recalls information or experiences that are acquired through the five senses. Although you take in thousands of pieces of information every second—everything from the shape and

UNDERSTAND THE **INFORMATION PROCESSING** MODEL OF MEMORY

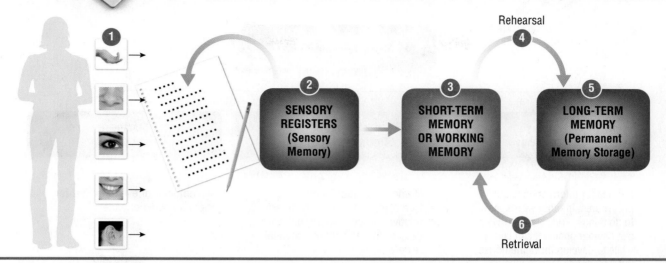

color of your chair to how your history text describes Abraham Lincoln's presidency—you remember few. Unconsciously, your brain sorts through stimuli and stores only what it considers important.

Key 7.1 illustrates how the brain forms lasting memories.

1. Raw information, gathered through the five senses, reaches the brain (for example, the tune of a song you're learning in your jazz ensemble class).

2. This information enters **sensory registers**, where it stays for only seconds. (As you play the notes for the first time, the sounds stop first in your auditory register.)

3. You then choose whether to pay attention to information in the sensory register. When you selectively look, listen, smell, taste, or feel the information, you move it into **short-term memory**, also known as *working memory*, which contains what you are thinking at any moment and from where information can be made available for further processing. (The part of the song that is your responsibility, for example, the clarinet solo, will likely take up residence in your working memory.) You can temporarily keep information in short-term memory through *rote rehearsal*—the process of repeating information to yourself or even out loud.

4. Information moves to **long-term memory** through focused, active rehearsal repeated over time. (As you practice the song in class and at home, your brain stores the tone, rhythm, and pace in your long-term memory, where you will be able to draw on it again.) Long-term memory stores everything you know from Civil War battle dates to the location of your grade school. As shown in Key 7.2, long-term memory has three separate storage houses. There are no limits to how much information long-term memory can hold or how long it is held, but most people retain memories of personal experiences and procedures longer than concepts, facts, formulas, and dates.

When you need a piece of information from long-term memory, the brain retrieves it and places it in short-term memory. On test day, this enables you to choose the right answer on a multiple-choice question or lay out a fact-based argument for an essay question.

> SENSORY REGISTER
> Brain filters through which sensory information enters the brain and is sent to short-term memory.

> SHORT-TERM MEMORY
> The brain's temporary information storehouse, in which information remains for a limited time (from a few seconds to half a minute).

> LONG-TERM MEMORY
> The brain's permanent information storehouse, from which information can be retrieved.

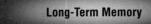
Long-Term Memory

Storage of Procedural Memory	**Storage of Declarative Memory**	**Storage of Episodic Memory**
Storage for information about procedures, in other words, how to do things—ride a bike, drive a car, tie your shoes. It can take a while to develop these memories, but they are difficult to lose.	Memories of facts, concepts, formulas, and so on. These are relatively easy to learn, but are easy to forget without continual review.	Memories of events linked to personal experiences.

$$x = \frac{-b \pm \sqrt{b^2 - 4ac}}{2a}$$

The movement of information in your brain, from short-term to long-term memory and then back again, strengthens the connections among neurons (brain cells). As you read in Chapter 3, learning happens and memories are built when neurons grow new dendrites and form new synapses. When you learn an algebra formula, for example, your brain creates new connections. Every time you review it, the connections get stronger.

Why you forget

Health issues and poor nutrition can cause memory problems. Stress is also a factor; research shows that even short-term stress can interfere with cell communication in the learning and memory regions of the brain.[1] However, *the most common reason that information fails to stay in long-term memory is ineffective studying*—not doing what you should to retain what you learn.

As Key 7.3 shows, retaining information requires continual review. You are still learning information 10 minutes after you hear it the first time. If you review the material over time—after 24 hours, a week, a month, 6 months, and more—you will retain the knowledge. If you do not review, the neural connections will weaken, and eventually you will forget.

In a classic study conducted in 1885, researcher Herman Ebbinghaus memorized a list of meaningless three-letter words such as CEF and LAZ. He then examined how quickly he forgot them. Within 1 hour, he had forgotten more than 50 percent of

REVIEWING IS ESSENTIAL FOR
MAINTAINING MEMORIES

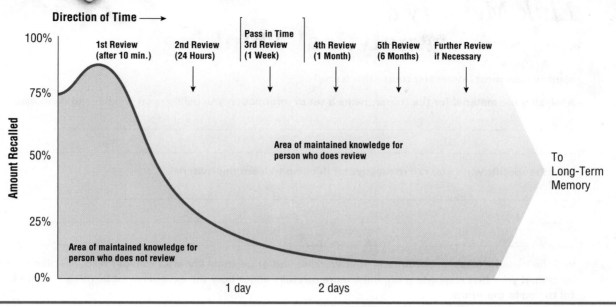

Direction of Time ⟶

| | 1st Review (after 10 min.) | 2nd Review (24 Hours) | Pass in Time 3rd Review (1 Week) | 4th Review (1 Month) | 5th Review (6 Months) | Further Review if Necessary | |

Amount Recalled: 100%, 75%, 50%, 25%, 0%

Area of maintained knowledge for person who does review

To Long-Term Memory

Area of maintained knowledge for person who does not review

1 day   2 days

Source: From Tony Buzan, *Use Both Sides of Your Brain,* copyright © 1974, 1983, 1991 by Tony Buzan. Used by permission of Dutton, a division of Penguin Group (USA) Inc., and by kind permission of Tony Buzan, www.thinkbuzan.com.

what he had learned; after 2 days, he knew fewer than 30 percent of the memorized words. Although Ebbinghaus's recall of the nonsense syllables remained fairly stable after that, his experiment shows how fragile memory can be—even when you take the time and expend the energy to memorize information.[2]

Now that you know more about how memory works, get down to the business of how to retain the information you think is important—and provide that information when you need it.

How can you remember what you study?

Whatever you study—textbooks, course materials, notes, primary sources— your goal is to anchor important information in long-term memory so that you can use it, for both short-term goals like tests and long-term goals like being an information technology specialist. To remember what you study, you need to carefully figure out and use what works best for you. One great way to do this is with *journalists' questions*— the six questions journalists need to answer to write an effective newspaper story.

1. **When, Where, Who**—determine the times, places, and company (or none) that suit you.
2. **What, Why**—choose what is important to study, and set the rest aside.
3. **How**—find the specific tips and techniques that work best for you.

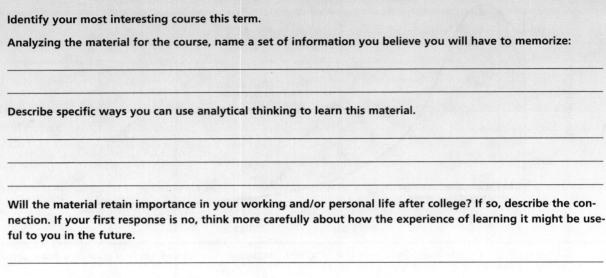

GET ANALYTICAL!

Link Memory and Analytical Thinking

Identify your most interesting course this term.

Analyzing the material for the course, name a set of information you believe you will have to memorize:

_____

_____

Describe specific ways you can use analytical thinking to learn this material.

_____

_____

_____

Will the material retain importance in your working and/or personal life after college? If so, describe the connection. If your first response is no, think more carefully about how the experience of learning it might be useful to you in the future.

_____

_____

When, where, and who: Choosing your best setting

Figuring out the when, where, and who of studying is all about self-management. You analyze what works best for you, create ideas about how to put that self-knowledge to work, and use practical thinking to implement those ideas as you study.

When

The first part of *When* is "How Much." Having the right amount of time for the job is crucial. One formula for success is the simple calculation you have read about earlier in this book: *For every hour you spend in the classroom each week, spend at least 2 to 3 hours preparing for the class.* For example, if you are carrying a course load of six credit hours, you should spend twelve hours a week studying outside of class. Check your syllabus for the dates reading assignments are due, and give yourself enough time to complete them.

The second part of *When* is "What Time." If two students go over their biology notes from 8 to 9 A.M., but one is a morning person who went to bed at 11 P.M. and the other is a night owl who hit the sack around 2 A.M., you can guess who has a greater chance of remembering the information. First, determine the time available to you in between classes, work, and other commitments. Then, thinking about when you function best, choose your study times carefully. You may not always have the luxury of being free during your peak energy times—but do the best you can.

The third part of *When* is "How Close to Original Learning." Because most forgetting happens right after learning, as you saw in Key 7.3, the review that helps you retain information most effectively happens close to when you first learn the material. If you can, review notes the same day you took them, make an organizer of important information from a text chapter shortly after you read it, or write a summary within 24 hours.

The final part of *When* is "When to Stop." Take a break, or go to sleep, when your body is no longer responding. Forcing yourself to study when you're not focused doesn't work.

Where

Where you study matters. As with time, consider your restrictions first—there may be only so many places available to you, within a reasonable travel distance, and open when you have study time free. Also, analyze previous study sessions. If you spent over 20 percent of your time blocking out distractions at a particular location, try someplace different.

The study location that works for you depends on your individual needs. This student has found he can concentrate best on his physical geology material if he reads it at a table in the library.
© Davis Barber/PhotoEdit

Who

Some students prefer to study alone, and some in pairs or groups. Many mix it up, doing some kinds of studying— first reading, close reading, creating note sets—alone, and others—test review, problem sets—with one or more people. Some find that they prefer to study certain subjects alone and others with a group.

Even students who study primarily alone can benefit by working with others from time to time. Besides the obvious benefit of greater communication and teamwork skills, group study enhances your ability to remember information in several ways:[3]

▶ Gets you to say what you know out loud, which solidifies your understanding
▶ Exposes you to the ideas of others and gets you thinking in different ways
▶ Increases the chance that all of the important information will be covered
▶ Motivates you to study in preparation for discussing the topic with others
▶ Subjects you to questions about your knowledge, and maybe even some challenges, that make you clarify and build on your thinking

One final part of *Who* is dealing with "Who Might Be Distracting." You may have friends who want you to go out. You may have young children or other family members who need you. Think carefully about your choices. Do you want to head out with a group of friends you can see anytime, even if it compromises your ability to do well in an important course? Can you schedule your study time when your kids are occupied for an hour or so?

Tell your friends why studying is important to you. Friends who truly care about you are likely to support your goals. Tell your kids (if they are old enough to understand) what your education and eventual degree will mean to you—and to them. Children may be more able to cope if they see what lies at the end of the road. Key 7.4 shows some ways that parents or others caring for children can maximize their efforts.

Answer Your
Journalists' Questions

Think about a past study session that did not prepare you well for a test, and recall which strategies—if any—you used.

Now, plan a study session that will take place within the next 7 days—one that will help you learn something important to know for one of your current courses. Answer the following questions to create your session:

When will you study, and for how long?

_____

Where will you study?

_____

Who will you study with, if anyone?

_____

What will you study?

_____

Why is this material important to know?

_____

How will you study it—what strategy (or strategies) do you plan to use?

_____

_____

How do you think the journalists' questions in this structure would have helped you get more from your previous study session?

_____

_____

The final step is putting this plan to work. Date you will use it: _____

What and why:
Evaluating study materials

Even if you had hours of study time and boundless energy, you would be likely to go on overload if you studied every word and bit of information. Before you get ready to dive into your books and materials, engage your analytical thinking skills for a critical task: Decide *what* to study by examining *why* you need to know it. Here's how to accomplish this:

▶ *Choose materials to study.* Put away materials or notes you know you do not need to review. Then examine what's left. Within textbooks or other materials, which chapters or sections are important to know for your immediate goal (for example, to study for an upcoming test) and why? Thinking about the *Why* highlights your purpose and can increase your focus.

MANAGE CHILDREN
WHILE STUDYING

STUDYING WITH CHILDREN	STUDYING WITH INFANTS

- **Keep them up-to-date on your schedule.** Kids appreciate being involved, even though they may not understand entirely. Let them know when you have a big test or project due and what they can expect of you.
- **Find help.** Know your schedule and arrange for child care if necessary. Consider offering to help another parent in exchange for babysitting, hiring a sitter, or using a day care center.
- **Utilize techonology.** You may be able to have a study session over the phone, through instant messaging, by e-mail, or over social networking sites. Additionally, some sites offer tools that allow multiple users to work on a document or project remotely.
- **Be prepared and keep them active.** Consider keeping some toys, activities, or books that only come out during study time. This will make the time special for children.
- **Plan for family time.** Offset your time away from your children with plans to do something together such as a movie or ice cream. Children may be more apt to let you study when they have something to look forward to.

- **Utilize your baby's sleeping schedule.** Study at night if your baby goes to sleep early or in the morning if your baby sleeps late.
- **Make time in the middle.** Study during nap times if you aren't too tired yourself.
- **Talk to your baby.** Recite your notes to the baby. The baby will appreciate the attention, and you will get work done.
- **Keep them close.** Put your baby in a safe and fun place while you study, such as a playpen, motorized swing, or jumping seat.

▶ *Prioritize materials.* First of all, there's no point in spending the bulk of your study time reviewing material you already know well. Determine what you need the most work on, and study that first. Almost every student has more steam at the beginning of a study session than at the end; plus, fatigue or an interruption may prevent you from covering everything.

▶ *Set specific goals.* Looking at what you need to cover and the time available, decide what you will accomplish—for example, reading a specific section in a certain textbook, reviewing three sets of class notes, and creating a study sheet from both the book and your notes. Make a list for reference and check things off as you go.

▶ *Within the sections you study, separate main points from unimportant details.* Ask yourself, "What is the most important information?" Highlight only the key points in your texts, and write notes in the margins about main ideas.

How: Using study strategies

After figuring out the *When, Where, Who, What,* and *Why* of studying, focus on the *How*—the strategies that will anchor the information you need in your brain (Key 7.5). You may already use several of them. Try as many as you can, and keep what works.

Have purpose, intention, and emotional connection

If you can remember the lyrics to dozens of popular songs but not the functions of the pancreas, perhaps emotion is involved. When you care about something, your brain responds differently, and you learn and remember more easily.

Key 7.5

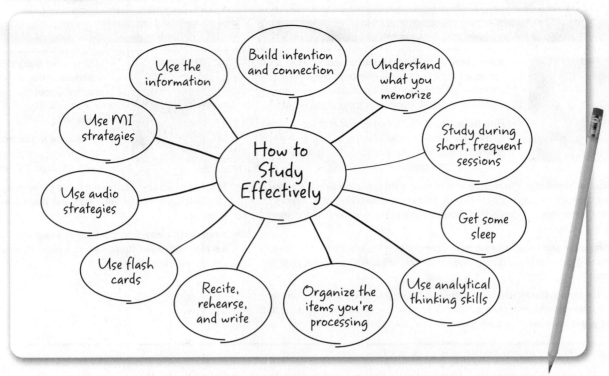

- Use the information
- Build intention and connection
- Understand what you memorize
- Use MI strategies
- Study during short, frequent sessions
- Use audio strategies
- **How to Study Effectively**
- Get some sleep
- Use flash cards
- Recite, rehearse, and write
- Organize the items you're processing
- Use analytical thinking skills

To achieve the same results in college, try to create a purpose and will to remember by a kind of emotional involvement with what you study. For example, an accounting student might think of a friend who is running a small business and needs to keep his records in order—to pay bills on time, to record income, to meet tax payments. Putting himself in the position of his friend's accountant, the student connects learning accounting principles with making a difference in a friend's life.

Put your notes to work

It is common to let notes sit in a notebook unread until just before midterms or finals. Even the most comprehensive, brilliant notes won't do you any good if you don't refer back to them. Regularly reread your notes in batches (for example, every one or two weeks) to build your recall of information. As you reread, do the following:

Courtesy of Shutterstock

- ▶ Fill in any gaps or get help with trouble spots.
- ▶ Mark up your notes by highlighting main ideas and key supporting points.
- ▶ Add recall or practice test questions in the margins.
- ▶ Add relevant points from homework, text, and labwork into your notes.

Apply Different Intelligences to Remembering Material for Psychology

INTELLIGENCE	USE MI STRATEGIES TO REMEMBER MORE EFFECTIVELY	APPLY MI MEMORY STRATEGIES TO THE TOPIC OF MOTIVATION AND EMOTION FOR A PSYCHOLOGY COURSE
Verbal-Linguistic	• Develop a story line for a mnemonic first; then work on the visual images. • Write out answers to practice essay questions.	• Answer learning objectives as though they were essay questions: "What are three types of needs?" "What are instinct approaches to motivation?"*
Logical-Mathematical	• Create logical groupings that help you memorize knowledge chunks. • When you study material in the middle, link it to what comes before and after.	• Group and compare the theories of emotion—the James-Lange theory, the Cannon-Bard theory, the Schachter-Singer and cognitive arousal theory, the facial feedback hypothesis, and Lazarus's cognitive-mediational theory.
Bodily-Kinesthetic	• Reenact concepts physically if you can to solidify them in memory. • Record information onto a digital recorder and listen as you walk between classes.	• Model facial expressions with another student and take turns guessing the emotion behind the expression.
Visual-Spatial	• Focus on visual mnemonics such as mental walks. • Use markers to add color to the images you use in your mnemonics.	• Create a colorful mnemonic to remember maladaptive eating problems such as obesity, anorexia nervosa, and bulimia.
Interpersonal	• Do flash card drills with a study partner. • Recite important material to a study partner.	• Working with a study partner, recite and explain Maslow's hierarchy of needs to each other.
Intrapersonal	• Listen to an audio podcast that reviews test material. • Create vocabulary cartoons and test yourself on the material.	• Understand incentive approaches by considering what kind of external stimuli create incentive for you.
Musical	• Play music while you brainstorm ideas. • Create a mnemonic in the form of a musical rhyme.	• Write a rap that lists and explains the different approaches to understanding motivation.
Naturalistic	• Organize what you have to learn so you see how everything fits together. • Sit outside and go through your flash cards.	• Make a chart organizing explanatory details of the three elements of emotion—physiology, behavior, and subjective experience.

*For information on motivation and emotion, see Saundra K. Ciccarelli and Glenn E. Meyer, *Psychology*. Upper Saddle River, NJ: Prentice Hall, 2006.

Understand what you memorize

It sounds kind of obvious—but something that has meaning is easier to recall than something that makes little sense. This basic principle applies to everything you study. Figure out logical connections, and use these connections to help you learn. For example, in a plant biology course, memorize plants in family groups; in a history course, link events in a cause-and-effect chain.

When you are have trouble remembering something new, think about how the new idea fits into what you already know. A simple example: If you can't remember what a word means, look at the word's root, prefix, or suffix. Knowing that the root *bellum* means "war" and the prefix *ante* means "before" will help you recognize that *antebellum* means "before the war."

Study during short, frequent sessions

You can improve your chances of remembering material by learning it more than once. A pattern of short sessions—say, three 20-minute study sessions—followed by brief periods of rest is more effective than continual studying with little or no rest.

In addition, scheduling regular, frequent review sessions over time will help you retain information more effectively. If you have 2 weeks before a test, set up study sessions three times per week instead of putting the final 2 days aside for hours-long study marathons.[4]

Get your body ready

Even though sleep may take a back seat with all you have to do in crunch times, research indicates that shortchanging your sleep during the week impairs your ability to remember and learn, even if you try to make up for it by sleeping all weekend.[5] Sleep improves your ability to remember what you studied before you went to bed. So does having a good breakfast. Even if you're running late, grab enough food to fill your stomach.

Use analytical thinking skills

Analytical, or critical, thinking encourages you to associate new information with what you already know. Imagine you have to remember information about the signing of the Treaty of Versailles, which ended World War I. How can critical thinking help?

▶ Recall everything that you know about the topic.
▶ Think about how this event is similar to other events in history.
▶ Consider what is different and unique about this treaty in comparison to other treaties.
▶ Explore the causes that led up to this event, and look at the event's effects.
▶ Evaluate how successful you think the treaty was.

This critical exploration makes it easier to remember the material you are studying.

Organize the items you are processing

▶ *Divide material into manageable sections.* Master each section, put all the sections together, and then test your memory of all the material.

► *Use the chunking strategy.* (Chunking) increases the capacity of short-term and long-term memory. For example, though it is hard to remember these ten digits—4808371557—it is easier to remember them in three chunks—480 837 1557. In general, try to limit groups to ten items or fewer. The 8-day study plan in Key 7.6 relies on chunking.

CHUNKING
Placing disconnected information into smaller units that are easier to remember.

STUDY PLAN SUCCESS
DEPENDS ON A GOOD MEMORY

Key 7.6

DAY 8 (IN EIGHT DAYS, YOU'LL BE TAKING A TEST)

PLANNING DAY
- List everything that may be on the exam. (Check your syllabus and class notes; talk with your instructor.)
- Divide the material into four learning chunks.
- Decide on a study schedule for the next 7 days—when you will study, with whom you will study, the materials you need, and so on.

DAY 7 (COUNTDOWN: SEVEN DAYS TO GO)
- Use the techniques described in Chapters 7 and 8 to study chunk A.
- Memorize key concepts, facts, formulas, and so on that may be on the test.
- Take an active approach to learning: take practice tests, summarize what you read in your own words, use critical thinking to connect ideas.

DAY 6 (COUNTDOWN: SIX DAYS TO GO)
- Use the same techniques to study chunk B.

DAY 5 (COUNTDOWN: FIVE DAYS TO GO)
- Use the same techniques to study chunk C.

DAY 4 (COUNTDOWN: FOUR DAYS TO GO)
- Use the same techniques to study chunk D.

DAY 3 (COUNTDOWN: THREE DAYS TO GO)
- Combine and review chunks A and B.

DAY 2 (COUNTDOWN: TWO DAYS TO GO)
- Combine and review chunks C and D.

DAY 1 (COUNTDOWN: ONE DAY TO GO)

PUT IT ALL TOGETHER: REVIEW CHUNKS A, B, C, AND D
- Take an active approach to review all four chunks.
- Make sure you have committed every concept, fact, formula, process, and so on to memory.
- Take a timed practice test. Write out complete answers so that concepts and words stick in your memory.
- Create a sheet with important information to memorize (again) on test day.

TEST DAY—DO YOUR BEST WORK
- Look at your last-minute study sheet right before you enter the test so that difficult information sticks.
- As soon as you open your test, write down critical facts.

Source: Adapted from the University of Arizona. "The Eight-Day Study Plan." (http://ulc.arizona.edu/documents/8day_074.pdf)

▶ *Use organizational tools.* Rely on an outline, a think link, or another organizational tool to record material with logical connections among the elements.

▶ *Be mindful when studying more than one subject.* When studying for several tests at once, avoid studying two similar subjects back-to-back. Your memory may be more accurate when you study history after biology rather than chemistry after biology.

▶ *Notice what ends up in the middle—and practice it.* When studying, you tend to remember what you study first and last. The weak link is likely to be what you study midway. Knowing this, try to give this material special attention.

Recite, rehearse, and write

Repetition is a helpful memory tool. The more you can repeat, and the more ways you can repeat, the more likely you are to remember. Reciting, rehearsing, and writing help you diversify your repetition and maximize memory.

When you *recite* material, you repeat key concepts aloud, summarizing them in your own words, to aid memorization. *Rehearsing* is similar to reciting but is done silently. *Writing* is reciting on paper. The following steps represent one way to benefit from these strategies:

▶ Focus as you read on *main ideas*, which are usually found in the topic sentences of paragraphs. Then recite, rehearse, or write the ideas down.

▶ Convert each main idea into a keyword, phrase, or visual image—something easy to recall that will set off a chain of memories bringing you back to the original material. Write each keyword or phrase on an index card.

▶ One by one, look at the keywords on your cards and recite, rehearse, or write all the associated information you can recall. Check your recall against the original material.

These steps are part of the process of consolidating and summarizing lecture and text notes as you study—a key study strategy explored later in this chapter.

Reciting, rehearsing, and writing involve more than rereading material and then parroting words out loud, in your head, or on paper. Because rereading does not necessarily require involvement, you can reread without learning. However, you cannot help but think and learn when you convert text concepts into key points, rewrite main ideas as keywords and phrases, and assess what you know and what you still need to learn.

Use flash cards

Flash cards give you short, repeated review sessions that provide immediate feedback. Either find an online site on which you can create electronic flash cards or use the front of a 3-by-5-inch index card to write a word, idea, or phrase you want to remember. Use the back for a definition, explanation, example, or other key facts. Key 7.7 shows two flash cards used to study for a psychology exam.

The following suggestions can help you make the most of your flash cards:

▶ *Use the cards as a self-test.* As you go through them, create two piles—the material you know and the material you are learning.

▶ *Carry the cards with you and review frequently.* You'll learn the most if you start using cards early in the course, well ahead of exam time.

FLASH CARDS HELP YOU MEMORIZE IMPORTANT FACTS

Theory

- Definition: Explanation for a phenomenon based on careful and precise observations

- Part of the scientific method

- Leads to hypotheses

Hypothesis

- Prediction about future behavior that is derived from observations and theories

- Methods for testing hypotheses: case studies, naturalistic observations, and experiments

▶ *Shuffle the cards and learn the information in various orders.* This will help you avoid putting too much focus on some items and not enough on others.

▶ *Test yourself in both directions.* First, look at the terms and provide the definitions or explanations. Then turn the cards over and reverse the process.

▶ *Reduce the stack as you learn.* Eliminate cards when you know them well. As the pile shrinks, your motivation may grow. Do a final review of all the cards before the test.

Use audio strategies

Although audio strategies can benefit all students, they are especially useful if you learn best through hearing.

▶ *Create audio flash cards.* Record short-answer study questions by leaving 10 to 15 seconds blank after questions, so you can answer out loud. Record the correct answer after the pause to give yourself immediate feedback. For example, part of a recording for a writing class might say, "Three elements that require analysis before writing are . . . [10–15 second pause] . . . topic, audience, and purpose."

▶ *Use podcasts.* An increasing amount of information is presented in podcasts—knowledge segments that are downloadable to your computer or MP3 player. Ask your instructors if they intend to make any lectures available in podcast format.

Use learning styles strategies

Look back to your MI and Personality Assessment profile assessments. Identify your strongest areas and locate study techniques applicable for each. For example, if you scored high in bodily-kinesthetic, try reciting material aloud while standing or walking. Be open to trying something new—even if it sounds a little odd to begin with. Effective studying is about finding what works, often by any means necessary.

Use the information

In the days after you learn something new, try to use the information in every way you can. Apply it to new situations and link it to problems. Explain the material to a classmate. Test your knowledge to make sure the material is in long-term memory. "Don't confuse recognizing information with being able to recall it," says learning expert Adam Robinson. "Be sure you can recall the information without looking at your notes for clues. And don't move on until you have created some sort of sense-memory hook for calling it back up when you need it."[6]

What will help you remember math and science material?

The strategies you've just explored apply to all sorts of academic areas. However, recalling what you learn in math and science courses can demand particular attention and some specific techniques.

■ *Review processes and procedures.* Much of math and science work involves knowing how to work through each step of a proof, a problem-solving process, or a lab experiment. Review your notes as soon as possible. Look at your notes with the textbook alongside and compare the lecture information to the book. Fill in missing steps in the instructor's examples before you forget them. You may want to write the instructor's examples in the book next to the corresponding topics.

■ *Do problems, problems, and more problems.* Working through problems provides examples that will help you understand concepts and formulas. Plus, becoming familiar with a group of problems and related formulas will help you apply what you know to similar problems on other assignments and tests.

■ *Fight frustration with action.* If you are stuck on a problem, go on to another one. If you repeatedly get a wrong answer, look at the steps you've taken and see whether anything doesn't make sense. If you hit a wall, take a break to clear your head. If you have done the assigned homework but still don't feel secure, do additional problems or ask for help.

■ *Focus on learning styles.* Use strategies that activate your strengths. A visual learner might draw pictures to illustrate problems, and an interpersonal learner might organize a study group. Musical learners might create songs describing math concepts. Barbara Aaker wrote 40 songs for her students at the Community College of Denver to help musical learners retain difficult concepts. Key 7.8 presents one of her algebra songs.

■ *Strive for accuracy.* Complete a step of an algebra problem or biology lab project inaccurately, and your answer will be incorrect. In class, the consequences of inaccuracy are reflected in low grades. In life, the consequences could show in a patient's health or in the strength of a bridge. Check over the details of your work and always try to get it exactly right.

"HOW MUCH IS THAT *X* IN THE EQUATION?"

(to the tune of "How Much Is That Doggie in the Window?")

How much is that **x** in the equation?
What value will make it be true?
To find the **x** and get the solution
The numbers attached we **undo.**

The **connector** is plus or minus seven,
To find **x** we have to **undo.**
Just write below both sides—make it even.
We **undo** to find the **x** value.

If multiply or divide is showing,
The **connector** tells what has been done.
To **undo** is where we still are going—
We're trying to get **x** alone.

Source: Reprinted with permission. Barbara Aaker, *Mathematics: The Musical,* Denver: Crazy Broad Publishing, 1999.

Because many math and science courses require you to memorize sets and lists of information, one key tool is the *mnemonic device.* As you will see next, mnemonic devices create sense-memory hooks that are difficult to forget.

How can mnemonic devices **boost recall?**

Certain performers entertain audiences by remembering the names of 100 strangers or flawlessly repeating 30 ten-digit numbers. Although these performers probably have superior memories, they also rely on memory techniques, known as mnemonic devices (pronounced neh-MAHN-ick), for assistance. Mnemonics include visual images and associations and acronyms.

> MNEMONIC DEVICES
> Memory techniques that use vivid associations and acronyms to link new information to what you already know.

Mnemonics depend on vivid associations (relating new information to other information) that engage your emotions. Instead of learning new facts by *rote* (repetitive practice), associations give you a "hook" on which to hang these facts and retrieve them later. Mnemonics make information unforgettable through unusual mental associations and visual pictures.

Mnemonics take time and effort to create, and you'll have to be motivated to remember them. Because of this, use them only when necessary—for instance, to distinguish confusing concepts that consistently trip you up. Also know that no matter how clever they are and how easy they are to remember, *mnemonics* usually do not contribute to understanding. Their objective is to help you memorize.

GET CREATIVE!

Craft Your Own Mnemonic

Create a mnemonic to help you remember some facts.

Identify a group of facts that you have to memorize—for example, the names of all the world's major religions or a series of elements in the periodic table.

_____

_____

Now create your own mnemonic to remember the grouping, using any of the devices in this chapter. Write the mnemonic here (or, if you need more space, use separate paper).

_____

_____

_____

Describe your mnemonic. Is it focused on images or sounds—or both? Is it humorous, ridiculous, or colorful?

_____

_____

Considering your learning style preferences, describe why you think this particular device will help you retain the information.

_____

_____

_____

Create visual images and associations

Turning information into mental pictures helps improve memory, especially for visual learners. To remember that the Spanish artist Picasso painted *The Three Women,* you might imagine the women in a circle dancing to a Spanish song with a pig and a donkey (*pig-asso*). The best images involve bright colors, three dimensions, action scenes, inanimate objects with human traits, and humor.

As another example, say you are trying to learn some Spanish vocabulary, including the words *carta, libro,* and *dinero.* Instead of relying on rote learning, you might come up with mental images such as those in Key 7.9.

Use visual images to remember items in a list

With the *mental walk* strategy, you imagine storing new ideas in familiar locations. Say, for example, that on your next biology test you have to remember the body's major endocrine glands. To do this, think of your route to the library.

VISUAL IMAGES AID **RECALL**

Key 7.9

SPANISH WORD	DEFINITION	MENTAL IMAGE
carta	letter	A person pushing a shopping cart filled with letters into a post office.
dinero	money	A man eating lasagna at a diner. The lasagna is made of layers of money.
libro	book	A pile of books on a table at a library.

You pass the college theater, the science center, the bookstore, the cafeteria, the athletic center, and the social science building before reaching the library. At each spot along the way, you "place" a concept you want to learn. You then link the concept with a similar-sounding word that brings to mind a vivid image (see Key 7.10):

▶ At the campus theater, you imagine bumping into the actor Brad *Pitt* (pituitary gland).
▶ At the science center, you visualize a body builder with bulging *thighs* (thyroid gland).
▶ At the campus bookstore, you envision a second body builder with his *thighs* covered in *mus*tard (thymus gland).
▶ In the cafeteria, you bump into *Dean Al* (adrenal gland).
▶ At the athletic center, you think of the school team, the Panthers—nicknamed the Pans—and remember the sound of the cheer *"Pans-R-Us"* (pancreas).
▶ At the social science building, you imagine receiving a standing *ovation* (ovaries).
▶ And at the library, you visualize sitting at a table taking a *test* that is *easy* (testes).

Make acronyms

Another helpful association method involves (acronyms.) In history class, you can remember the Allies during World War II—Britain, America, and Russia—with the acronym BAR. This is an example of a *word acronym*, because the first letters of the items you want to remember spell a word. The word (or words) spelled don't necessarily have to be real words. See Key 7.11 for an acronym—the name Roy G. Biv—that will help you remember the colors of the spectrum.

> ACRONYM
> A word formed from the first letters of a series of words created to help you remember the series.

Other acronyms take the form of an entire sentence, in which the first letters of the words in the sentence stand for the first letters of the memorized terms. This is called a *list order acronym*. When astronomy students want to remember the list of planets in order of distance from the sun (Mercury, Venus, Earth, Mars, Jupiter, Saturn, Uranus, and Neptune), they might learn the sentence *My very elegant mother just served us nectarines.*

Suppose you want to remember the names of the first six U.S. presidents. You notice that the first letters of their last names—Washington, Adams, Jefferson, Madison, Monroe, and Adams—together read W A J M M A. To remember

A **MENTAL WALK** HELPS YOU REMEMBER ITEMS IN A LIST

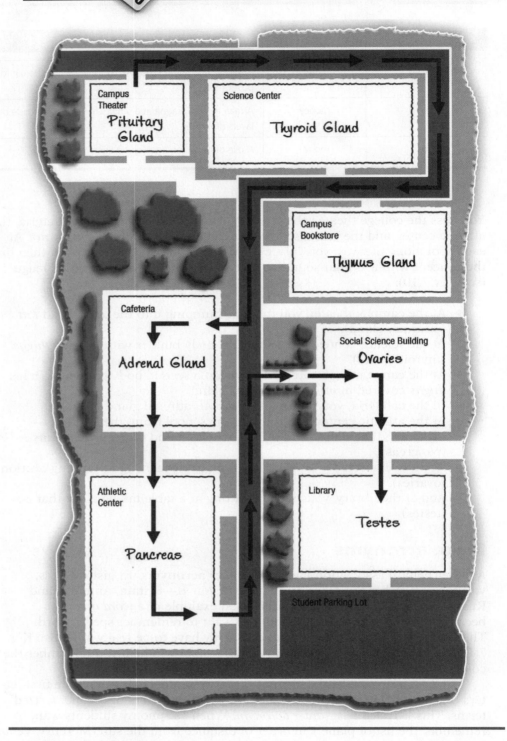

them, first you might insert an *e* after the *j* and create a short nonsense word—*wajemma*. Then to make sure you don't forget the nonsense word, visualize the six presidents sitting in a row and wearing pajamas.

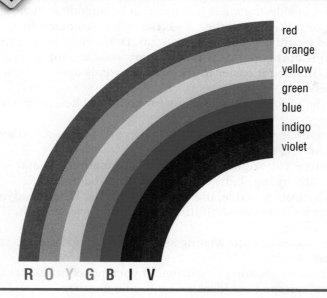

USE THIS **ACRONYM** TO REMEMBER
THE COLORS OF THE SPECTRUM

red
orange
yellow
green
blue
indigo
violet

R O Y G B I V

Use songs or rhymes

Some of the classic mnemonic devices are rhyming poems that stick in your mind. One you may have heard is the rule about the order of *i* and *e* in spelling:

> Spell *i* before *e*, except after *c*, or when sounded like *a* as in *neighbor* and *weigh*. Four exceptions if you please: *either, neither, seizure, seize*.

Make up your own poems or songs, linking familiar tunes or rhymes with information you want to remember. Thinking back to the *wajemma* example, imagine that you want to remember the presidents' first names as well. You might set those first names—George, John, Thomas, James, James, and John—to the tune of "Happy Birthday." Or to extend the history theme, you might use the first musical phrase of the national anthem.

Improving your memory requires energy, time, and work. It also helps to master SQ3R, the textbook study technique introduced in Chapter 5. By going through the steps in SQ3R and using the specific memory techniques described in this chapter, you will be able to learn more in less time—and remember what you learn long after exams are over. These techniques will be equally valuable when you start a career.

What study strategies help you put it all together?

Especially in the later stages of review, strategies that help you combine and condense information are crucial. Such strategies help you relate information to what you know, connect information in new ways, and boost your ability to use it to think analytically and creatively—especially important for essay exams.

Create a summary of reading material

When you summarize main ideas in your own words, you engage analytical thinking, considering what is important to include as well as how to organize and link it together. To construct a summary, focus on the main ideas and examples that support them. Don't include your own ideas or evaluations at this point. Your summary should simply condense the material, making it easier to focus on concepts and interrelationships when you review.

Use the following suggestions for creating effective summaries:

▶ Organize your summary by subject or topic—a textbook chapter, for example, or an article.

▶ Before you summarize, identify the main ideas and key supporting details by highlighting or annotating the material.

▶ Wherever possible, use your own words. When studying a technical subject with precise definitions, you may have little choice but to use text wording.

▶ Try to make your writing simple, clear, and brief. Eliminate less important details.

▶ Consider creating an outline of your notes or the portion of the text so you can see how ideas relate to one another.

▶ Include information from tables, charts, photographs, and captions in your summary; these visual presentations may contain important information not written in the text.

▶ Combine word-based and visual note-taking forms that effectively condense the information, such as a concept map, timeline, chart, or outline.

▶ Use visual strategies such as a color-coding system to indicate different ideas or different-colored pens to indicate levels of importance for information.

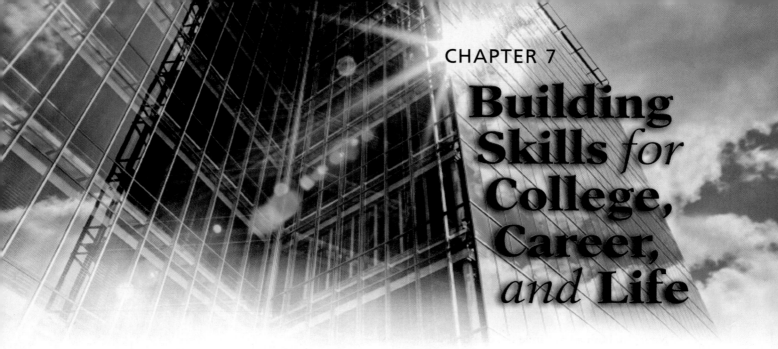

Building Skills *for* College, Career, *and* Life

Steps to Success

Evaluate Your Memory

BUILD BASIC SKILLS. Under each of these classifications of information in long-term memory, write down an example from your personal experience:

Episodic memory (events). Example: I remember the first time I conducted an experiment in chemistry class.

_____

_____

Declarative memory (facts). Example: I know that the electoral college must vote before a new U.S. president is officially elected.

_____

_____

Procedural memory (motion). Example: I know how to type without looking at the keyboard.

_____

_____

TAKE IT TO THE NEXT LEVEL.

Which type of information (events, facts, motion) is easiest for you to remember? Why?

_____

_____

_____

Which type of information is hardest for you to remember? Why?

_____

_____

MOVE TOWARD MASTERY. Address the type of information you find *most difficult* to remember.

Name an example from your life of some information in this category that you need to be able to recall and use.

_____

_____

_____

Name two approaches from the chapter that you believe will help you strengthen it.

1. _____

2. _____

Now give both a try. Circle the one that worked best.

Writing

Build Intrapersonal and Communication Skills

Record your thoughts on a separate piece of paper, in a journal, or electronically.

EMOTIONAL INTELLIGENCE JOURNAL

How feelings connect study success. Think about how you were feeling when you were most able to recall and use information in a high-stress situation—a test, a workplace challenge, a group presentation. What thought, action, or situation put you in this productive mindset that helped you succeed? Did you go for a run? talk to your best friend? take 30 minutes for yourself? Create a list of thoughts or actions you can call on when you will be faced with a challenge to your memory and want the best possible outcome.

REAL-LIFE WRITING

Combining class and text notes. Choose a course for which you have a test coming up in the next 4 weeks. Create a master set of notes for that course combining one week's classes and reading assignments (make sure it is material you need to know for your test). Your goal is to summarize and connect all the important information covered during the period.

Personal Portfolio

Prepare for Career Success

MEMORY AND NETWORKING

21st Century Learning Building Blocks

- Communication and Collaboration
- Social and Cross-Cultural Skills

Complete the following in your electronic portfolio or separately on paper.

Your ability to remember people you meet or interact with in the workplace—their names, what they do, other relevant information about them—is an enormous factor in your career success.

Consider this scenario: You are introduced to your supervisor's new boss, someone who is in a position to help you advance in the company, and you both exchange small talk for a few minutes. A week later you run into him outside the building. If you greet him by name and ask whether his son is over the case of the flu he had, you have made a good impression that is likely to help you in the future. If you call him by the wrong name, realize your mistake, and slink off to work, you may have set up a bit of a hurdle for yourself as you try to get ahead.

Using what you know about memory strategies and what works for you, set up a system to record and retain information about people you meet whom you want to remember. For your system, decide on a tool (address book, set of notecards, electronic organizer, computer file), what to record (name, phone, e-mail, title, how you met, important details), and how you will update. Choose a tool that you are most likely to use and that will be easy for you to refer to and update.

Tool of choice: _____

Information to record:

_____

When to record and how often to check or update:

_____

Get started by putting in information for all the people you consider to be important networking contacts at this point—family, friends, instructors and advisors, or work colleagues and supervisors. Make this the start of a database that will serve you throughout your career.

Social Networking

REMEMBER INFORMATION ABOUT YOUR CONTACTS

Use LinkedIn to connect with the list of important contacts you just developed—sign in to your account and invite them to join your network using any of the methods from the Chapter 6 exercise.

When at least three of these contacts have responded by joining your network, use the LinkedIn "My Connections" area to fill in helpful information about them that you want to remember.

- Click on "My Connections."
- Choose a name from your connections list and click on "view and edit details" beneath that person's name.
- Fill in any relevant information—phone, address, website, birthday, and notes about your contact with this person.

ENDNOTES

1. University of California–Irvine, "Short-Term Stress Can Affect Learning and Memory," *ScienceDaily*, March 13, 2008, www.sciencedaily.com/releases/2008/03/080311182434.htm.

2. Herman Ebbinghaus, *Memory: A Contribution to Experimental Psychology*, trans. H. A. Ruger and C. E. Bussenius, New York: Teachers College, Columbia University, 1885.

3. Bulletpoints from Kenneth C. Petress, "The Benefits of Group Study," 2004, *Education*, 124, www.questia.com/googleScholar.qst;jsessionid=L4TDXZJvQmb4whQFL7v1mjGfBgp4YGzjJyg0mL3g1SJKyjvXK4hN!-747430471!743789914?docId=5006987606.

4. Dartmouth College Academic Skills Center, "How to Avoid Cramming for Tests," 2001, www.dartmouth.edu/~acskills/handouts.html.

5. "Study Shows How Sleep Improves Memory," *Science Daily*, June 29, 2005, www.sciencedaily.com/releases/2005/06/050629070337.htm.

6. Adam Robinson, *What Smart Students Know: Maximum Grades, Optimum Learning, Minimum Time*, New York: Three Rivers Press, 1993, p. 118.

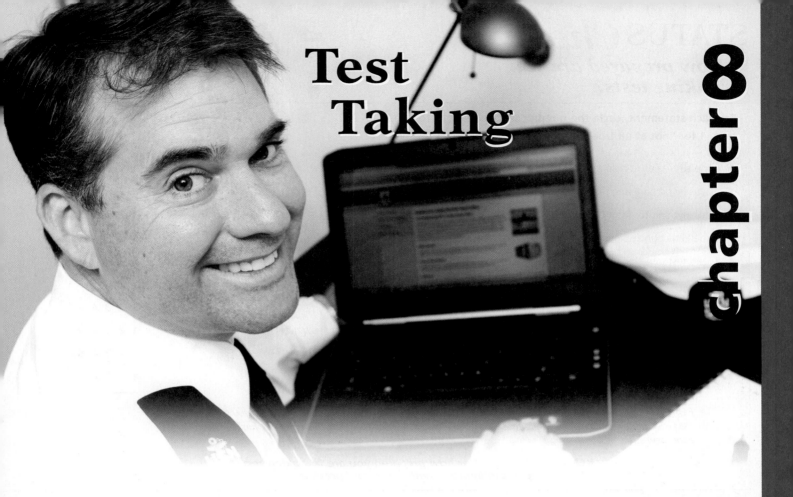

Test Taking

*P*erhaps there is truth to the saying: The journey of a thousand steps begins with one... Tem Frierson saw this when he conversed with a Columbia Southern University representative about enrolling in the online school. "The conversation about the college helped me see the feasibility of actually earning my degree through little steps instead of only seeing the entire journey."

And what a journey it has been for Frierson, who has served in the Navy for the past 23 years and completed his service with the rank of chief and a job as an advertising/marketing director for recruiting in Atlanta.

Upon enrolling with CSU in January 2007, he decided to pursue a bachelor's degree in business. Frierson chose this degree plan because "I like business and the unique opportunities of this career field."

As he moved through his studies, Frierson said he found it "rewarding as I progressed from the AAS to the BSBA."

"I appreciated the communication of the staff and the concern of those who became my friends and mentors throughout

my journey," Frierson added. "What an exciting accomplishment to fulfill a goal that at one time seemed out of reach!"

And at times, the journey was a little rough for Frierson who admits he is aggressive towards achieving goals. "I enjoyed setting my own schedules and timelines," says Frierson. "But, I knew I was in control of my accomplishments!"

And he accomplished much with what he learned during his CSU education. "I had the opportunity to put into practice many of the business lessons that I learned through my studies," he explained. "As the marketing director, I built a plan around the foundations that I learned in 'Strategic Management,' 'Business Ethics' and 'Business Policy and Strategy.' The same year I completed my education, I was also selected as the Marketing Director of the Year (nationally). I feel this is no coincidence."

The retired Navy chief is excelling in the corporate world with his new position as a strategic marketing manager with a firm in Atlanta.

STATUS *Check*

▶ *How prepared are you for taking tests?*

For each statement, circle the number that feels right to you, from 1 for "not at all true for me" to 5 for "very true for me."

▶ I use strategies to help me predict what will be on tests.	1 2 3 4 5
▶ I actively prepare and review before taking exams.	1 2 3 4 5
▶ I do anything to avoid cramming.	1 2 3 4 5
▶ When I recognize signs of test anxiety, I use relaxation methods to calm down.	1 2 3 4 5
▶ I read test directions before beginning.	1 2 3 4 5
▶ I use certain strategies to answer questions I'm unsure of.	1 2 3 4 5
▶ I don't think cheating is worth the price.	1 2 3 4 5
▶ I know the difference between objective and subjective questions and how to answer each.	1 2 3 4 5
▶ I look for action verbs when answering essay questions.	1 2 3 4 5
▶ I learn from my testing mistakes and actively grow from them.	1 2 3 4 5

Now total your scores.

Each of the topics in these statements is covered in this chapter. Note those statements for which you circled a 3 or lower. Skim the chapter to see where those topics appear, and pay special attention to them as you read, learn, and apply new strategies.

REMEMBER: *No matter how prepared you are for taking tests, you can improve with effort and practice.*

"Successfully intelligent people seek to perform in ways that not only are competent but distinguish them from ordinary performers. They realize that the gap between competence and excellence may be small but the greatest rewards, both internal and external, are for excellence."

—Robert Sternberg

How can preparation improve test performance?

Although you may dread taking tests and exams, consider this: *The goal of a test is to see what you have learned.* Every day that you are learning—by attending class, staying on top of assignments, completing readings and projects, and participating in class discussions—you are preparing for tests. The following strategies, specific to tests, put your analytical, creative, and practical thinking skills into action to help you be as prepared as possible.

Identify test type and what you will be expected to know

Before you begin studying, take practical steps to find out as much as you can about the test, including the following:

▶ *Topics that will be covered.* Will the test cover everything since the term began or will it be more limited?
▶ *Material you will be tested on.* Will the test cover only what you learned in class and in the text or will it also include outside readings?

▶ *Types of questions.* Will the questions be objective (multiple choice with only one correct answer, multiple choice with more than one correct answer, true/false, sentence completion), subjective (essay), or a combination?

▶ *Supplemental information you may be able to have.* Is the test open book (meaning you can use your class text)? Open note (meaning you can use any notes you've taken)? Both? Or neither? Are you able to work with a partner on any part of it? Will you be expected to complete part or all of it online?

Instructors routinely answer questions like these. If you are unsure, ask for clarification. Chances are, some other students are wondering the same thing.

As you begin thinking about the test, remember that not all tests are created equal—a quiz is not as important as a midterm or final, although accumulated grades on small quizzes add up and can make a difference in your final grade. Plan and prioritize your study time and energy according to the value of the quiz or test. Consult your syllabus for test and quiz dates and times.

Here are other practical strategies for predicting what may be on a test.

▶ *Use your textbook.* Check features such as summaries, vocabulary terms, and study questions for clues about what's important to remember.

▶ *Contact your instructor.* Spending a few minutes talking about the test may clarify misunderstandings and help you focus on what to study.

▶ *Get information from people who already took the course.* Try to get a sense of test difficulty, whether tests focus primarily on assigned readings or class notes, what materials are usually covered, and the types of questions that are asked.

Part of successful test preparation is knowing when to stop. To avoid overload, study in shorter segments over a period of time, and get the sleep you need before test day.
© Alvis Upitis/Image Bank/Getty Images

After taking the first exam in a course, you will have a better idea of what to expect.

Determine where and how the test will be given

Where you take a test can affect your performance. For instance, an open-book exam may sound like an easy A, but distractions like children and TV can threaten your focus. Being prepared for the stresses of your environment will help you manage test time.

Online tests, like open book tests, may seem easier than tests in the classroom. In reality, due to the wide amount of information available at your fingertips, online tests are generally more challenging and require strong critical thinking skills. You may be able to Google factual information about a topic, but test questions will probably ask you to analyze and evaluate situations related to that information.

Create a study schedule and checklist

If you establish a plan ahead of time and write it down, you are more likely to follow it. Use journalists' questions to map out a study plan.

▶ Ask *what* and *why* to decide what you will study. Go through your notes, texts, related primary sources, and handouts, and set aside materials you don't need. Then prioritize the remaining materials to focus on the information most likely to be on the exam.

▶ Ask *when, where,* and *who*—and use the time management and goal-setting skills—to prepare a schedule. Consider all of the relevant factors—your study materials, who you will study with, the number of days until the test, and the time and place you can study each day. Note study sessions in your planner ahead of time.

▶ Ask *how* to figure out what strategies you will use.

A comprehensive *checklist* will help you organize and stay on track as you prepare. Use the checklist to assign specific tasks to particular study times and sessions. Try out the checklist in Key 8.1 or create your own.

Use reading and studying strategies

Put what you have learned about thinking, reading, memory, and studying in Chapters 4, 5, 6, and 7 into action to give yourself the best shot at remembering material.

▶ *Think analytically.* College exams often ask you to analyze and apply material in more depth than you experienced in high school. For example, your history instructor may ask you to place a primary source in its historical context. Prepare for these challenges as you study by continually asking analytical thinking questions and using the higher levels of Bloom's taxonomy.

▶ *Use SQ3R.* This reading method provides an excellent structure for reviewing your reading materials.

▶ *Employ strategies from* how *questions.* Use flash cards, audio strategies, chunking, or anything else that suits you and the material you are studying.

▶ *Create mnemonic devices.* Memory strategies help make what you review stick.

▶ *Actively review your combined class and text notes.* Summaries and master sets of combined text and class notes provide comprehensive study tools.

Courtesy of Shutterstock

Make and take a pretest

Use end-of-chapter text questions to create your own pretest. If your course doesn't have an assigned text, develop questions from notes and assigned readings. Old homework problems will also help target areas that need work. Some texts also provide a website with online activities and pretests designed to help you review material. Keep in mind that the same test-preparation skills you learn in college will help you do well on standardized tests for graduate school.

Answer your questions under test-like conditions—in a quiet place where you can see a clock to tell you when to quit, with no books or notes (unless the exam is open book). This type of low-pressure test experience may help people calm test-taking fears.

Prepare physically

Most tests ask you to work at your best under pressure, so try to get a good night's sleep before the exam. Sleep improves your ability to remember what you studied before you went to bed.

Key 8.1 PREPARE FOR A TEST

Complete the following checklist for each exam to define your study goals, get organized, and stay on track:

Course: _____   Instructor: _____

Date, time, and place of test: _____

Type of test (Is it a midterm or a minor quiz?): _____

What instructor said about the test, including types of test questions, test length, and how much the test counts toward your final grade:

_____

_____

Topics to be covered on the test, in order of importance (information should also come from your instructor):

1. _____

2. _____

3. _____

4. _____

5. _____

Study schedule, including materials you plan to study (texts, class notes, homework problems, and so forth) and dates you plan to complete each:

Material   **Completion Date**

1. _____   _____

2. _____   _____

3. _____   _____

4. _____   _____

5. _____   _____

Materials you are expected to bring to the test (textbook, sourcebook, calculator, etc.):

_____

_____

_____

Special study arrangements (such as planning study group meeting, asking the instructor for special help, getting outside tutoring):

_____

_____

_____

Life-management issues (such as rearranging work hours):

_____

_____

_____

Source: Adapted from Ron Fry, *"Ace" Any Test,* 3rd ed., Franklin Lakes, NJ: Career Press, 1996, pp. 123–124.

GET CREATIVE!

Write Your Own Test

Use the tips in this chapter to predict the material that will be covered, the types of questions that will be asked (multiple choice, essay, etc.), and the nature of the questions (a broad overview of the material or specific details).

Then be creative. Your goal is to write questions that your instructor is likely to ask—interesting questions that tap what you have learned and make you think about the material in different ways. Go through the following steps:

1. Write the questions you come up with on a separate sheet of paper.

2. Use what you have created as a pretest. Set up test-like conditions—a quiet, timed environment—and see how you do.

3. Evaluate your pretest answers against your notes and the text. How did you do?

    _____

    _____

4. Finally, after you take the actual exam, evaluate whether you think this exercise improved your performance. Would you use this technique again? Why or why not?

    _____

    _____

Eating a light, well-balanced meal including protein (eggs, milk, yogurt, meat and fish, nuts, or peanut butter) will keep you full longer than carbohydrates alone (breads, candy, or pastries). When time is short, don't skip breakfast—grab a quick meal such as a few tablespoons of peanut butter, a banana, or a high-protein granola bar.

Make the most of last-minute cramming

Cramming—studying intensively and around the clock right before an exam—often results in information going into your head and popping right back out when the exam is over. *If learning is your goal, cramming will not help you reach it.* The reality, however, is that you are likely to cram for tests, especially midterms and finals, from time to time in your college career. You may also cram if anxiety leads you to avoid studying. Use these hints to make the most of this study time:

> ▶ *Focus on crucial concepts.* Summarize the most important points and try to resist reviewing notes or texts page by page.

▶ *Create a last-minute study sheet to review right before the test.* Write down key facts, definitions, and formulas on a single sheet of paper or on flash cards.

▶ *Arrive early.* Review your study aids until you are asked to clear your desk.

After the exam, evaluate how cramming affected your performance. Did it help, or did it load your mind with disconnected details? Did it increase or decrease anxiety at test time? Then evaluate how cramming affected your recall. Within a few days, you will probably remember very little—a reality that will work against you in advanced courses that build on the knowledge being tested and in careers that require it. Think ahead about how you can start studying earlier next time.

How can you work
through test anxiety?

A certain amount of stress can be a good thing. You are alert, ready to act, and geared up to do your best. Some students, however, experience incapacitating stress before and during exams, especially midterms and finals. Test anxiety can cause sweating, nausea, dizziness, headaches, and fatigue. It can reduce concentration and cause you to forget everything you learned. Sufferers may get lower grades because their performance does not reflect what they know or because their fear has affected their ability to prepare effectively.

Prepare well and have a positive attitude

Being prepared—both by reviewing material and following a detailed study plan—is the most essential way to ready yourself for an academic showdown. Only by knowing the material as best you can will you have reason to believe in your ability to pass the test. The other key tool is a positive attitude that says, "I know this material and I'm ready to show it."

Anxiety is defined as an emotional disturbance, meaning that it tends to be based on an imagined risk rather than an actual one, and often leads you away from your goals rather than toward them.[1] With this in mind, think metacognitively about your anxiety over a test:

▶ Look at the risk you *think* you are facing—and compare it with the *actual* risk. Consider the possibility that you may be more prepared than you realize.

▶ Look at your goal for this test. Identify the physical and mental responses caused by your anxiety, and note how they are affecting your ability to reach that goal.

Use the strategies in Key 8.2 to be both prepared and positive.

Math anxiety

For some students, math exams cause more anxiety than other academic challenges. A form of test anxiety, *math anxiety* is often based on common misconceptions about math, such as the notion that an ability to think quantitatively

Key 8.2

USE STRATEGIES TO **BUILD A POSITIVE ATTITUDE** AND GET PREPARED

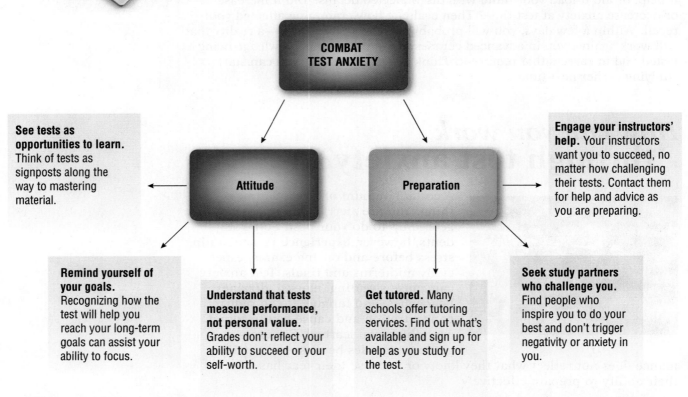

COMBAT TEST ANXIETY

Attitude

Preparation

See tests as opportunities to learn. Think of tests as signposts along the way to mastering material.

Engage your instructors' help. Your instructors want you to succeed, no matter how challenging their tests. Contact them for help and advice as you are preparing.

Remind yourself of your goals. Recognizing how the test will help you reach your long-term goals can assist your ability to focus.

Understand that tests measure performance, not personal value. Grades don't reflect your ability to succeed or your self-worth.

Get tutored. Many schools offer tutoring services. Find out what's available and sign up for help as you study for the test.

Seek study partners who challenge you. Find people who inspire you to do your best and don't trigger negativity or anxiety in you.

is an inborn talent some people have and others don't or that men are better at math than women. Students who feel that they can't do math may give up without asking for help. At exam time, they may experience test anxiety symptoms that reduce their ability to concentrate and leave them feeling defeated.

The test anxiety strategies just discussed will also help combat math anxiety. In addition, math anxiety sufferers should focus heavily on problem-solving techniques, as in the math and science study strategies, and should also seek help from instructors and tutors early and often.

Test time strategies

When test time comes, several strategies may help you manage and calm test anxiety.

▶ *Manage your environment.* Make a conscious effort to sit away from students who might distract you. If it helps, listen to relaxing music on an MP3 player while waiting for class to begin.

▶ *Use positive self-talk.* Tell yourself that you can do well and that it is normal to feel anxious, particularly before an important exam.

▶ *Practice relaxation.* Close your eyes, breathe deeply and slowly, and visualize positive mental images like getting a good grade. Or try a more physical tensing-and-relaxing method:[2]

1. Put your feet flat on the floor.
2. With your hands, grab underneath the chair.
3. Push down with your feet and pull up on your chair at the same time for about 5 seconds.
4. Relax for 5 to 10 seconds.
5. Repeat the procedure two or three times.
6. Relax all your muscles except those actually used to take the test.

▶ *Bring a special object.* You may have an object that has special meaning for you—a photograph, a stone or crystal, a wristband, a piece of jewelry, a hat. Bring it along and see if it provides comfort or inspiration at test time. Use it to get focused and to calm yourself during the test.

Test anxiety and the returning student

If you're returning to school after years away, you may wonder how well you will handle exams. To deal with these feelings, focus on what you have learned through life experience, including the ability to handle work and family pressures. Without even thinking about it, you may have developed many time management, planning, organizational, and communication skills needed for college success.

In addition, your life experiences will give real meaning to abstract classroom ideas. For example, workplace relationships may help you understand social psychology concepts, and refinancing your home mortgage may help you grasp a key concept in economics—how the actions of the Federal Reserve Bank influence interest rate swings.

What general strategies can help you succeed on tests?

Even though every test is different, certain general strategies will help you handle almost all tests, from short-answer to essay exams.

Test day strategies

▶ *Choose the right test taking environment.* Find a test taking environment that will put you in the right frame of mind and minimize distractions. Choose a place near a window, next to a wall, or in the front row so you can look into the distance.

▶ *Write down key facts.* Before you even look at the test, write down key information, including formulas, rules, and definitions, that you don't want to forget.

▶ *Start with the big picture.* Spend a few minutes at the start gathering information about the questions—how many of which types are in each section, along with their point values. Use this information to schedule your time. Take level of difficulty into account as you parcel out your time. For example, if you think you can do the short-answer questions in 45 minutes and sense that

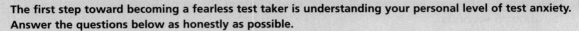

Assess Test Anxiety with the Westside Test Anxiety Scale

The first step toward becoming a fearless test taker is understanding your personal level of test anxiety. Answer the questions below as honestly as possible.

Rate how true each of the following is of you, from "Always true" to "Never true." Use the following 5 point scale. Circle your answers.

5 = Always true; 4 = Usually true; 3 = Sometimes true; 2 = Seldom true; 1 = Never true

1. The closer I am to a major exam, the harder it is for me to concentrate on the material.	5 4 3 2 1
2. When I study for my exams, I worry that I will not remember the material on the exam.	5 4 3 2 1
3. During important exams, I think that I am doing awful or that I may fail.	5 4 3 2 1
4. I lose focus on important exams, and I cannot remember material that I knew before the exam.	5 4 3 2 1
5. I remember answers to exam questions only after the exam is already over.	5 4 3 2 1
6. I worry so much before a major exam that I am too worn out to do my best on the exam.	5 4 3 2 1
7. I feel out of sorts or not really myself when I take important exams.	5 4 3 2 1
8. I find that my mind sometimes wanders when I am taking important exams.	5 4 3 2 1
9. After an exam, I worry about whether I did well enough.	5 4 3 2 1
10. I struggle with written assignments, or avoid doing them, because I want them to be perfect.	5 4 3 2 1

Sum of the 10 questions: _____

Now divide the sum by 10. Write it here. _____ This is your test anxiety score.

Compare your score against the following scale. How does your level of test anxiety rate? In general, students that score a 3.0 or higher on the scale tend to have more test anxiety than normal and may benefit from seeking additional assistance.

1.0–1.9   Comfortably low test anxiety

2.0–2.4   Normal or average test anxiety

2.5–2.9   High normal test anxiety

3.0–3.4   Moderately high (some items rated 4—high)

3.5–3.9   High test anxiety (half or more of the items rated 4—high)

4.0–5.0   Extremely high anxiety (items rated 4—high and 5—extreme)

Reflect on your results. Do they show a high level of test anxiety? A normal level? Based on what you've learned about yourself, select anxiety-reducing strategies that you will use when studying for or taking your next test. Record your plan on a sheet of paper or computer file.

Source: Used by permission of Richard Driscoll.

Apply Different Intelligences to Preparing for a Geometry Exam

INTELLIGENCE	USE MI STRATEGIES TO IMPROVE TEST PREPARATION	APPLY MI TEST-PREP STRATEGIES TO STUDY FOR A TEST ON GEOMETRIC SHAPES AND MEASUREMENT*
Verbal-Linguistic	• Write test questions your instructor might ask. Answer the questions and then try rewriting them in a different format (essay, true/false, and so on). • Underline important words in review or practice questions.	• Underline important vocabulary words in the chapter. Then make a set of flash cards, with the word on one side and the definition on the other. Test yourself.
Logical-Mathematical	• Logically connect what you are studying with what you know. Consider similarities, differences, and cause-and-effect relationships. • Draw charts that show relationships and analyze trends.	• Create a table that highlights the similarities and differences among polygons, circles, and three-dimensional shapes. Use columns to note qualities such as number of sides, number of angles, measurement of angles, formulas that apply consistently, and special features (for example, in a rectangle, all angles are right angles).
Bodily-Kinesthetic	• Use text highlighting to take a hands-on approach to studying. • Create a sculpture, model, or skit to depict a tough concept that will be on the test.	• Use pencils, Popsicle sticks, pipe cleaners, containers, or other materials to create the shapes on which you will be tested.
Visual-Spatial	• Make charts, diagrams, or think links illustrating concepts. • Make drawings related to possible test topics.	• Draw illustrations that represent all of the postulates (statements assumed to be true) in the chapter.
Interpersonal	• Form a study group to prepare for your test. • In your group, come up with possible test questions. Then use the questions to test each other's knowledge.	• With a study partner, work through the exercise set on polygons and circles. Try either working through problems together or having partners "teach" problems to each other.
Intrapersonal	• Apply concepts to your own life; think about how you would manage. • Brainstorm test questions and then take the sample "test" you developed.	• Reread the "Geometry Around Us" material in your text to reinforce your understanding of how geometry functions in the real world. Write two additional ideas about how geometry relates to your world.
Musical	• Recite text concepts to rhythms or write a song to depict them. • Explore relevant musical links to reading material.	• Write a song that helps you remember the types of triangles and their definitions.
Naturalistic	• Try to notice similarities and differences in objects and concepts by organizing your study materials into relevant groupings.	• Create a table or visual organizer that arranges all of the types of two- and three-dimensional shapes into logical groupings.

*For information on geometric shapes and measurement, see Gary L. Musser, Lynn E. Trimpe, and Vikki R. Maurer, *College Geometry: A Problem-Solving Approach with Applications,* 2nd ed., Upper Saddle River, NJ: Pearson/Prentice Hall, 2008.

the writing section will take longer, you can budget 1 hour and 15 minutes for the essay.

▶ *Directions count, so read them.* Reading test directions carefully can save you trouble. For example, you may be required to answer only one of three essay questions, or you may be penalized for incorrect responses to short-answer questions.

▶ *Mark up the questions.* Mark up instructions and keywords to avoid careless errors. Circle (qualifiers) such as *always, never, all, none, sometimes,* and *every;* verbs that communicate specific instructions; and concepts that are tricky or need special attention.

QUALIFIERS
Words and phrases that can alter the meaning of a test question and thus require careful attention.

▶ *Be precise when taking a machine-scored test.* Use the right pencil (usually a no. 2) on machine-scored tests, and mark your answer in the correct space, filling it completely. Periodically check answer numbers against question numbers to make sure they match.

▶ *Work from easy to hard.* Begin with the easiest questions and answer them quickly without sacrificing accuracy. This will boost your confidence and leave more time for harder questions. Mark tough questions as you reach them, and return to them after answering the questions you know.

▶ *Watch the clock.* If you are worried about time, you may rush through the test and have time left over. When this happens, check over your work instead of leaving early. If, on the other hand, you are falling behind, be flexible about the best use of the remaining time.

▶ *Take a strategic approach to questions you cannot answer.* Key 8.3 has ideas to consider when you face questions that stump you.

▶ *Use special techniques for math tests.* Use the general test-taking strategies presented in this chapter as well as the techniques in Key 8.4 to achieve better results on math exams.

How can you master different **types of test questions?**

Every type of test question is a different way of finding out how much you know. Questions fall into two general categories.

■ *Objective questions.* You generally choose or write a short answer, often selecting from a limited number of choices, for objective questions. They can include multiple-choice, fill-in-the-blank, matching, and true/false questions.

■ *Subjective questions.* Demanding the same information recall as objective responses, subjective questions also require you to plan, organize, draft, and refine a response. All essay questions are subjective.

Key 8.3 shows samples of real test questions from Western civilization, macroeconomics, Spanish, and biology college texts published by Pearson Education. Included are exercises and multiple-choice, true/false, fill-in-the-blank, matching, and essay questions. Analyzing the types, formats, and complexities of these questions will help you gauge what to expect when you take your exams.

Look also at the Multiple Intelligence Strategies for Test Preparation on page 207. Harness the strategies that fit your learning strengths to prepare for geometry exams.

Note that some suggestions are repeated in the following sections, in order to reinforce the importance of these suggestions and their application to different types of test questions.

ANALYZE REAL **TEST QUESTIONS**
FROM REAL COLLEGE TEXTS

**FROM CHAPTER 29, "THE END OF IMPERIALISM,"
IN WESTERN CIVILIZATION: A SOCIAL AND CULTURAL HISTORY, 2ND EDITION**

- **MULTIPLE-CHOICE QUESTION**

  India's first leader after independence was:

  A. Gandhi   B. Bose   C. Nehru   D. Sukharno

  (answer: C)

- **FILL-IN-THE-BLANK QUESTION**

  East Pakistan became the country of _____ in 1971.

  A. Burma   B. East India   C. Sukharno   D. Bangladesh

  (answer: D)

- **TRUE/FALSE QUESTION**

  The United States initially supported Vietnamese independence.

         T   F

  (answer: false)

- **ESSAY QUESTION**

  Answer one of the following:

  1. What led to Irish independence? What conflicts continued to exist after independence?

  2. How did Gandhi work to rid India of British control? What methods did he use?

**FROM CHAPTER 6, "UNEMPLOYMENT AND INFLATION,"
IN MACROECONOMICS: PRINCIPLES AND TOOLS, 3RD EDITION**

- **MULTIPLE-CHOICE QUESTION**

  If the labor force is 250,000 and the total population 16 years of age or older is 300,000, the labor-force participation rate is

  A. 79.5%   B. 83.3%   C. 75.6%   D. 80.9%

  (answer: B)

- **FILL-IN-THE-BLANK QUESTION**

  Mike has just graduated from college and is now looking for a job, but has not yet found one. This causes the employment rate to _____ and the labor-force participation rate to _____.

  A. increase; decrease   C. stay the same; stay the same
  B. increase; increase   D. increase; stay the same

  (answer: C)

- **TRUE/FALSE QUESTION**

  The Consumer Price Index somewhat overstates changes in the cost of living because it does not allow for substitutions that consumers might make in response to price changes.   T   F   *(answer: true)*

- **ESSAY QUESTION**

  During a press conference, the Secretary of Employment notes that the unemployment rate is 7.0%. As a political opponent, how might you criticize this figure as an underestimate? In rebuttal, how might the secretary argue that the reported rate is an overestimate of unemployment?

  (Possible answer: The unemployment rate given by the secretary might be considered an underestimate because discouraged workers, who have given up the job search in frustration, are not counted as unemployed. In addition, full-time workers may have been forced to work part-time. In rebuttal, the secretary might note that a portion of the unemployed have voluntarily left their jobs. Most workers are unemployed only briefly and leave the ranks of the unemployed by gaining better jobs than they had previously held.)

FROM MOSAICOS: SPANISH AS A WORLD LANGUAGE, 3RD EDITION

- **MATCHING QUESTION**

  You are learning new words and your teacher asks you to think of an object similar to or related to the words he says. His words are listed below. Next to each word, write a related word from the list below.

  el reloj   el cuaderno   el pupitre   una computadora
  el televisor   la tiza   el lápiz   la mochila

  1. el escritorio _____   2. el bolígrafo _____

- **ESSAY QUESTION**

  Your mother always worries about you and wants to know what you are doing with your time in Granada. Write a short letter to her describing your experience in Spain. In your letter, you should address the following points:

  1. What classes you take

  2. When and where you study

  3. How long you study every day

FROM MOSAICOS: SPANISH AS A WORLD LANGUAGE, 3RD EDITION

• **MATCHING QUESTION**

3. la videocasetera _____   5. el libro _____

4. la pizarra _____

(answers: 1. el pupitre; 2. el lápiz; 3. el televisor; 4. la tiza; 5. el cuaderno)

• **ESSAY QUESTION**

4. What you do with your time (mention three activities)

5. Where you go during your free time (mention two places)

FROM CHAPTER 13, "DNA STRUCTURE AND REPLICATION," IN BIOLOGY: A GUIDE TO THE NATURAL WORLD, 2ND EDITION

• **MULTIPLE-CHOICE QUESTION**

What units are bonded together to make a strand of DNA?

A. chromatids   B. cells   C. enzymes   D. nucleotides
E. proteins   (answer: D)

• **FILL-IN-THE-BLANK QUESTION**

In a normal DNA molecule, adenine always pairs with _____ and cytosine always pairs with _____.

(answers: thymine, guanine)

• **TRUE/FALSE QUESTION**

Errors never occur in DNA replication, because the DNA polymerases edit out mistakes.   T   F

(answer: false)

• **MATCHING QUESTIONS**

Match the scientists and the approximate time frames (decades of their work) with their achievements.

Column 1

_____ 1. Modeled the molecular structure of DNA

_____ 2. Generated X-ray crystallography images of DNA

_____ 3. Correlated the production of one enzyme with one gene

Column 2

_____ A. George Beadle and Edward Tatum, 1930s and 1940s

_____ B. James Watson and Francis Crick, 1950s

_____ C. Rosalind Franklin and Maurice Wilkins, 1950s

(answers 1–B; 2–C; 3–A)

Sources: [*Western Civilization* test items] Margaret L. King, *Western Civilization: A Social and Cultural History,* 2nd ed., Upper Saddle River, NJ: Pearson Education, Inc., 2003. Questions from *Instructor's Manual and Test Item File* by Dolores Davison Peterson. Used with permission. [*Macroeconomics* test items] Arthur O'Sullivan and Steven M. Sheffrin, *Macroeconomics: Principles and Tools,* 3rd ed., Upper Saddle River, NJ: Pearson Education, Inc., 2003. Questions from *Test Item File 2* by Linda Ghent. Used with permission. [*Mosaicos* test items] Matilde Olivella de Castells, Elizabeth Guzmán, Paloma Lupuerta, and Carmen García, *Mosaicos: Spanish as a World Language,* 3rd ed., Upper Saddle River, NJ: Pearson Education, Inc., 2002. Questions from *Testing Program* by Mark Harpring. Used with permission. [*Biology* test items] David Krogh, *Biology: A Guide to the Natural World,* 2nd ed., Upper Saddle River, NJ: Pearson Education, Inc., 2002. Questions from *Test Item File* edited by Dan Wivagg. Used with permission.

Multiple-choice questions

Multiple-choice questions are the most popular type of question on standardized tests. The following analytical and practical strategies will help you answer them:

▶ *Read the directions carefully and try to think of the answer before looking at the choices.* Then read the choices and make your selection.

▶ *Underline keywords and significant phrases.* If the question is complicated, try to break it down into small sections that are easy to understand.

▶ *Make sure you read every word of every answer.* Focus especially on qualifying words such as *always, never, tend to, most, often,* and *frequently.* Look also for negatives in a question ("Which of the following is *not* . . .").

▶ *When questions are linked to a reading passage, read the questions first.* This will help you focus on the information you need to answer the questions.

Source: Gary W. Piggrem and Charles G. Morris, *Test Item File for Understanding Psychology,* 3rd ed., © 1996 Prentice-Hall, Inc. Reprinted by permission of Pearson Education, Inc., Upper Saddle River, NJ.

True/false questions

Read true/false questions carefully to evaluate what they are asking. Look for absolute qualifiers (such as *all, only,* or *always,* which often make an otherwise true statement false) and conservative qualifiers (*generally, often, usually,* or *sometimes,* which often make an otherwise false statement true). For example, "The grammar rule '*i* before *e* except after *c*' is *always* true" is false, whereas "The grammar rule '*i* before *e* except after *c*' is *usually* true" is true.

Be sure to read *every* word of a true/false question to avoid jumping to an incorrect conclusion. Common problems in reading too quickly include missing negatives (*not, no*) that would change your response and deciding on an answer before reading the complete statement.

Source: Gary W. Piggrem and Charles G. Morris, *Test Item File for Understanding Psychology,* 3rd ed., © 1996 Prentice-Hall, Inc. Reprinted by permission of Pearson Education, Inc., Upper Saddle River, NJ.

Matching questions

Matching questions ask you to match the terms in one list with the entries in another list. For example, the directions may tell you to match a communicable disease with the microorganism that usually causes it. The following strategies will help you handle these questions.

▶ *Make sure you understand the directions.* The directions tell you whether each answer can be used only once (common practice) or more than once.

▶ *Work from the column with the longest entries.* The column on the left usually contains terms to be defined or questions to be answered, with the column on the right for definitions or answers. As a result, entries on the right are usually longer than those on the left. Reading those items only once will save time.

▶ *Start with the matches you know.* On your first run-through, type or write down these matches. When you can use an answer only once, you may have to adjust if you rethink a choice.

▶ *Finally, tackle the matches you're not sure of.* Think back to your class lectures, text notes, and study sessions as you try to visualize the correct response. If one or more phrases seem to have no correct answer and you can use answers only once, consider the possibility that one of your sure-thing answers is wrong.

Fill-in-the-blank questions

Fill-in-the-blank questions, also known as *sentence completion questions,* ask you to supply one or more words or phrases to complete the sentence. These strategies will help you make successful choices.

▶ *Be logical.* Insert your answer; then reread the *sentence from beginning* to end to be sure it makes sense and is factually and grammatically correct.

▶ *Note the lengths and number of the blanks.* If two blanks appear right after one another, the instructor is probably looking for a two-word answer. If a blank is longer than usual, the correct response may require additional space.

▶ *If there is more than one blank and the blanks are widely separated, treat each one separately.* Answering each as if it were a separate sentence-completion question increases the likelihood that you will get at least one answer correct.

▶ *If you are uncertain, guess.* Have faith that after hours of studying, the correct answer is somewhere in your subconscious mind and that your guess is not completely random.

The following examples show fill-in-the-blank questions you might encounter in an introductory astronomy course (correct answers follow questions):

1. A _____ is a collection of hundreds of billions of stars. *(galaxy)*

2. Rotation is the term used to describe the motion of a body around some _____. *(axis)*

3. The solar day is measured relative to the sun; the sidereal day is measured relative to the _____. *(stars)*

4. On December 21, known as the _____ _____, the sun is at its _____ _____. *(winter solstice; southernmost point)*

Source: Eric Chaisson and Steve McMillan, *Astronomy Today,* 3rd ed., 1999. Reprinted by permission of Pearson Education, Inc., Upper Saddle River, NJ.

Essay questions

Essay questions ask you to express your knowledge and views in a less structured way than short-answer questions. With freedom of thought and expression comes the challenge to organize your ideas and write well under time pressure. The following steps—basically a shortened version of the writing process (see Appendix A)—will help you plan, draft, revise, and edit your responses.

1. *Read every question.* Decide which to tackle (if there's a choice). Use critical thinking to identify exactly what the question is asking.

2. *Map out your time.* Schedule how long to allot for each answer, remembering that things don't always go as planned. Above all, be flexible.

3. *Focus on action verbs.* Key 8.4 shows verbs that tell you what to do to answer the question. Underline action verbs and use them to guide your writing.

4. *Plan.* Think about what the question is asking and what you know. On scrap paper, outline or map your ideas and supporting evidence. Then develop a thesis statement that defines your content and point of view. Don't skimp on planning. Not only does planning result in a better essay, but it also reduces stress because it helps you get in control.

Courtesy of Shutterstock

5. *Draft.* Note the test directions before drafting your answer. Your essay may need to be of a certain length, for example, or may need to take a certain format. Use the following guidelines as you work:

- State your thesis, and then get right to the evidence that backs it up.
- Structure your essay so that each paragraph presents an idea that supports the thesis.
- Use clear language and tight logic to link ideas to your thesis and to create transitions between paragraphs.
- Look back at your planning notes periodically to make sure you cover everything.
- Wrap it up with a short, to-the-point conclusion.

6. *Revise.* Although you may not have the time to rewrite your entire answer, you can improve it with minor changes. Check word choice, paragraph structure, and style. If you notice anything missing, use editing marks to neatly insert it into the text. When you're done, make sure your response is the best possible representation of your ideas.

As you check over your essay, ask yourself questions about it:

- Have I answered the question?
- Does my essay begin with a clear thesis statement, and does each paragraph start with a strong topic sentence that supports the thesis?
- Have I provided the support necessary in the form of examples, statistics, and relevant facts to prove my argument, organized with tight logic?
- Have I covered all the points in my original outline or map?
- Is my conclusion an effective wrap-up?

7. *Edit.* Check for mistakes in grammar, spelling, punctuation, and usage. Correct language leaves a positive impression and helps your grade.

FOCUS ON **ACTION VERBS**
IN ESSAY TESTS

ANALYZE—Break into parts and discuss each part separately.

COMPARE—Explain similarities and differences.

CONTRAST—Distinguish between items being compared by focusing on differences.

CRITICIZE—Evaluate the issue, focusing on its problems or deficiencies.

DEFINE—State the essential quality or meaning.

DESCRIBE—Paint a complete picture; provide the details of a story or the main characteristics of a situation.

DIAGRAM—Present a drawing, chart, or other visual.

DISCUSS—Examine completely, using evidence and often presenting both sides of an issue.

ELABORATE ON—Start with information presented in the question, and then add new material.

ENUMERATE/LIST/IDENTIFY—Specify items in the form of a list.

EVALUATE—Give your opinion about the value or worth of a topic and justify your conclusion.

EXPLAIN—Make meaning clear, often by discussing causes and consequences.

ILLUSTRATE—Supply examples.

INTERPRET—Explain your personal views and judgments.

JUSTIFY—Discuss the reasons for your conclusions or for the question's premise.

OUTLINE—Organize and present main and subordinate points.

PROVE—Use evidence and logic to show that a statement is true.

REFUTE—Use evidence and logic to show that a statement is not true or tell how you disagree with it.

RELATE—Connect items mentioned in the question, showing, for example, how one item influenced another.

REVIEW—Provide an overview of ideas and establish their merits and features.

STATE—Explain clearly, simply, and concisely.

SUMMARIZE—Give the important ideas in brief, without comments.

TRACE—Present a history of a situation's development, often by showing cause and effect.

Courtesy of Shutterstock

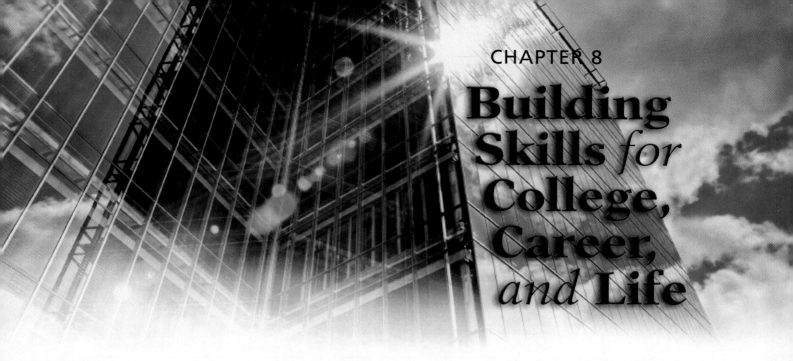

CHAPTER 8

Building Skills *for* College, Career, *and* Life

Steps to Success

Prepare Effectively for Tests

Take a careful look at your performance on and preparation for a recent test.

BUILD BASIC SKILLS. Think about how you did on the test.

Were you pleased or disappointed with your performance and grade? Why?

_____

_____

Circle any of the listed problems that you experienced on this exam. If you experienced one or more problems not listed here, write them in the blank spaces provided.

- Incomplete preparation
- Fatigue
- Feeling rushed during the test
- Shaky understanding of concepts
- Poor guessing techniques
- Feeling confused about directions
- Test anxiety
- Poor essay organization or writing

_____

_____

_____

Now for each problem you identified, think about why you made mistakes.

TAKE IT TO THE NEXT LEVEL. Be creative about test-preparation strategies.

If you had all the time and materials you needed, how would you have prepared for this test? Describe briefly what your plan would be and how it would address your problem(s).

_____

_____

Now think back to your actual test preparation—the techniques you used and the amount of time you spent. Describe the difference between your ideal study plan and what you actually did.

_____

_____

_____

MOVE TOWARD MASTERY. Improve your chances for success on the next exam by coming up with specific changes in your preparation.

What I did this time but do not intend to do next time:

_____

_____

What I did not do this time but intend to do next time:

_____

_____

Writing

Build Intrapersonal and Communication Skills

Record your thoughts on paper, in a journal, or electronically.

EMOTIONAL INTELLIGENCE JOURNAL

Test types. What type of test do you feel most comfortable with, and what type brings up more negative feelings? Thinking of a particular situation involving the test type that challenges you, describe how it made you feel and how that feeling affected your performance. Discuss ways in which you might be able to shift your mindset in order to feel more confident about this type of test.

REAL-LIFE WRITING

Ask your instructor for feedback on a test. Nearly every student has been in the position of believing that a response on an essay exam was graded unfairly. The next time this happens to you—when you have no idea why you lost points or disagree with the instructor's assessment of your work—draft a respectful e-mail to your instructor explaining your position and asking for a meeting to discuss the essay. Use clear logic to defend your work and refer back to what you learned in class and in the text. It is important to address specifically any comments or criticisms the instructor made on the test paper. Before sending the e-mail, analyze your argument: Did you make your case effectively or was the instructor correct? When you have the meeting, the work you did on the e-mail will prepare you to defend your position.

Personal Portfolio

Prepare for Career Success

ON-THE-JOB TESTING

21st Century Learning Building Blocks

- Information Literacy
- Initiative and Self-Direction
- Productivity and Accountability

Complete the following in your electronic portfolio or separately on paper.

You will probably encounter different tests throughout your career. For example, if you are studying to be a nurse you are tested on subjects like anatomy and pharmacology. After you graduate you will be required to take certification and recertification exams that gauge your mastery of the latest information in different aspects of nursing.

Some postgraduate tests are for entry into the field; some test proficiency on particular equipment; some move you to the next level of employment. Choose one career you are thinking about and investigate what tests are involved as you advance through different career stages.

Use the accompanying grid to organize what you find. You'll be searching for the following information:

- The name of the test
- When the test is taken and if it needs to be retaken
- What it covers
- How you can prepare
- Web resources like pretests, websites, or review materials

TEST NAME	WHEN TAKEN	WHAT IT COVERS	PREPARATION	WEB RESOURCES

Social Networking

ESTABLISH YOUR PRIVACY

Informed users of technology take advantage of tools that help them control it. You are in charge of what you allow people to view and send you on LinkedIn. Sign in to your account, click on "Settings" at the top of the screen, and look over the categories under "Privacy Settings." Establish the settings you prefer by clicking on each of the subheads and following the instructions:

- Research Surveys
- Connections Browse
- Profile Views
- Viewing Profile Photos

- Profile and Status Updates
- Service Provider Directory
- Partner Advertising
- Authorized Applications

Consider your privacy settings carefully. Find the balance that will keep your information as private as you want it to be, but also allow you to benefit from what LinkedIn can do for you when it shares your information.

ENDNOTES

1. "Anxiety Management," Michigan Technological University, www.counseling.mtu.edu/anxiety_management.html.

2. From Paul D. Nolting, *Math Study Skills Workbook, Your Guide to Reducing Test Anxiety and Improving Study Strategies*, Boston: Houghton Mifflin, 2000. Cited in "Test Anxiety," West Virginia University at Parkersburg, www.wvup.edu/Academics/more_test_anxiety_tips.htm.

Critical Thinking

e lead busy lives and time is a precious commodity.

Columbia Southern University alumnus Rick Lasky knows this all too well.

Over the past 30 years, Lasky has achieved much including teaching for the University of Illinois-Illinois Fire Service Institute and the Illinois Fire Chiefs' Association, receiving the 1996 International Society of Fire Service Instructors "Innovator of the Year" award for his part in developing the "Saving Our Own" program serving as the co-lead instructor for the H.O.T. Firefighter Survival program at FDIC for more than 10 years and writing a book, "Pride and Ownership-A Firefighter's Love of the Job."

Before his retirement in 2011, Lasky served as fire chief of the Lewisville (Texas) Fire Department for 11 years. During his tenure as chief, the Lewisville Fire Department expanded to seven stations and implemented several community-focused programs.

He also finished his associate degree in fire science with CSU in 2011—something he has wanted for many years.

The Illinois-native, who played professional baseball instead of going to college around age 18, has regretted not attending school during his younger years. However, after teaching and lecturing, Lasky said his interest in getting his degree rekindled.

"CSU had the best program for me and my busy lifestyle. Look, I was a full-time fire chief who lectured on my days off.

I have a wife and two children who are busy with sports and activities, too. So I couldn't make the move to take two or four years for college like those who are younger and have time. CSU's online program was perfect for me," said the 50 year old.

However, as Lasky began his endeavor, "my mom got sick and was dying of cancer and my dad was having surgeries," he said. "I had to take a year off, and CSU had no problem with it. They supported me, they helped and they kept checking on me. Not in a pushy way, but concerned. They cared. The faculty and staff were really there for me."

When he returned to classes, Lasky said CSU's personal touch continued.

"My professors were awesome. For something that is online, there is so much more of a personal relationship. You wouldn't think that you would have that kind of relationship online, but it happened. I know I got more support from Columbia Southern University than my son did from a major institution that he was actually at," Lasky added.

Lasky is now teaching and consulting full-time and said his associate degree is helping. "It has enlightened me and made me a better person," he said, adding that he is now working on his bachelor's. "It has given me more confidence. I'm a fairly confident person and it has given me more confidence."

STATUS *Check*

▶ *How developed are your thinking skills?*

For each statement, circle the number that feels right to you,
from 1 for "not at all true for me" to 5 for "very true for me."

▶ I discover information, make decisions, and solve problems by asking and answering questions.	1 2 3 4 5
▶ I don't take everything I read or hear as fact; I question how useful, truthful, and logical it is before I decide whether I can use it.	1 2 3 4 5
▶ I look for biased perspectives when I read or listen because I am aware of how they can lead me in the wrong direction.	1 2 3 4 5
▶ Even if it seems like there is only one way to solve a problem, I brainstorm to think of other options.	1 2 3 4 5
▶ I try not to let the idea that things have *always* been done a certain way stop me from trying different approaches.	1 2 3 4 5
▶ When I work in a group, I try to manage my emotions and to notice how I affect others.	1 2 3 4 5
▶ I think about different solutions before I choose one and take action.	1 2 3 4 5
▶ I spend time researching different possibilities before making a decision.	1 2 3 4 5
▶ I avoid making decisions on the spur of the moment.	1 2 3 4 5
▶ When I make a decision, I consider how my choice will affect others.	1 2 3 4 5

Now total your scores.

Each of the topics in these statements is covered in this chapter. Note those statements for which you circled a 3 or lower. Skim the chapter to see where those topics appear, and pay special attention to them as you read, learn, and apply new strategies.

REMEMBER: **No matter how developed your thinking skills are, you can improve with effort and practice.**

"Successfully intelligent people define problems correctly and thereby solve those problems that really confront them, rather than extraneous ones. . . . [They] carefully formulate strategies for problem solving. In particular, they focus on long-range planning rather than rushing in and then later having to rethink their strategies."

—Robert Sternberg

Why is it important to ask and answer questions?

What is thinking? According to experts, it is what happens when you ask questions and move toward the answers.[1] "To think through or rethink anything," says Dr. Richard Paul, director of research at the Center for Critical Thinking and Moral Critique, "one must ask questions that stimulate our thought. Questions define tasks, express problems and delineate issues. . . . [O]nly students who have questions are really thinking and learning."[2]

As you answer questions, you turn information into material that you can use to achieve goals. A *Wall Street Journal* article entitled "The Best Innovations Are Those That Come from Smart Questions" relays the story of a cell biology student, William Hunter, whose professor told him that "the difference between good science and great science is the quality of the questions posed." Now a physician, Dr. Hunter asks questions about new ways to use drugs. His questions have helped his company reach the goal of developing a revolutionary product—a drug-coated mesh used to strengthen diseased blood vessels.[3]

How can you question effectively?

■ ***Know why you question.*** To ask useful questions, you need to know why you are questioning. Start by defining your purpose: What am I trying to accomplish, and why? As you continue your thought process, you will find more specific purposes that help you generate questions along the way.

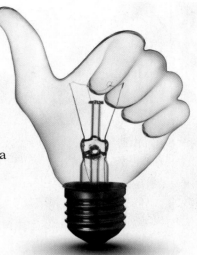

■ ***Want to question.*** Knowing why you are questioning also helps you *want* to think. "Critical-thinking skills are different from critical-thinking dispositions, or a willingness to deploy these skills," says cognitive psychologist D. Alan Bensley of Frostburg State University in Maryland. In other words, having the skills isn't enough—you also need the desire to use them.[4] Having a clear understanding of your goal can help you be more willing to work to achieve it.

■ ***Question in different ways.***

> ▶ Analyze (How bad is my money situation?)
> ▶ Come up with creative ideas (How can I earn more money?)
> ▶ Apply practical solutions (Who do I talk to about getting a job at another company?)

When you need to solve a problem or make a decision, combining all three thinking skills gives you the greatest chance of achieving your goal.[5] This chapter will explore analytical, creative, and practical thinking first individually and then will show how they work together to help you to solve problems and make decisions effectively. Asking questions opens the door to each thinking skill, and in each section you will find examples of the kinds of questions that drive that skill. Begin by exploring analytical thinking.

How can you improve your analytical thinking skills?

Analytical thinking is the process of gathering information, breaking it into parts, examining and evaluating those parts, and making connections for the purposes of gaining understanding, solving a problem, or making a decision.

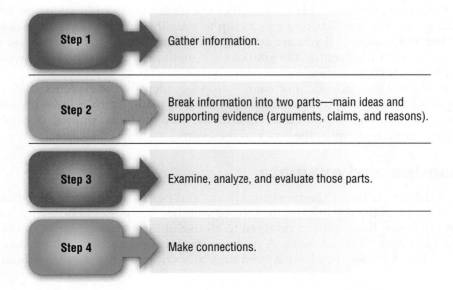

Step 1 Gather information.

Step 2 Break information into two parts—main ideas and supporting evidence (arguments, claims, and reasons).

Step 3 Examine, analyze, and evaluate those parts.

Step 4 Make connections.

Many types of work, such as the elevation drawings this engineering student is working on, involve analytical thinking.
© Shutterstock

Through the analytical process, you look for how pieces of information relate to one another, setting aside any pieces that are unclear, unrelated, unimportant, or biased. You may also form new questions that change your direction. Be open to them and to where they may lead you.

Gather information

Information is the raw material for thinking, so to start the thinking process you must first gather your raw materials. This requires analyzing how much information you need, how much time to spend gathering it, and whether it is relevant. Say, for instance, that you have to write a paper on one aspect of the media (TV, radio, Internet) and its influence on a particular group. Here's how analyzing can help you gather information for that paper:

▶ Reviewing the assignment terms, you note two important items: The paper should be approximately ten pages and describe at least three significant points of influence.
▶ At the library and online, you find thousands of articles in this topic area. Analyzing your reaction to them and how many articles concentrate on certain aspects of the topic, you decide to focus your paper on how the Internet influences young teens (ages 13–15).
▶ Examining the summaries of six comprehensive articles leads you to three in-depth sources.

In this way you achieve a subgoal—a selection of useful materials—on the way to your larger goal of writing a well-crafted paper.

Break information into parts

The next step is to search for the two most relevant parts of the information: the main idea or ideas (also called the argument or *viewpoint*) and the supporting evidence (also called *reasons* or *supporting details*).

ARGUMENT
A set of connected ideas, supported by examples, made by a writer to prove or disprove a point.

▶ *Separate the ideas.* Identify each of the ideas conveyed in what you are reading. You can use lists or a mind map to visually separate ideas from one another. For instance, if you are reading about how teens ages 13 to 15 use the Internet, you could identify the goal of each method of access they use (websites, blogs, instant messaging).
▶ *Identify the evidence.* For each main idea, identify the evidence that supports it. For example, if an article claims that young teens rely on instant messaging three times more than on e-mails, note the facts, studies, or other evidence cited to support the truth of the claim.

Examine and evaluate

The third step is by far the most significant and lies at the heart of analytical thinking. Examine the information to see whether it is going to be useful for your purposes. Keep your mind open to all useful information, even if it conflicts with your personal views. A student who thinks that the death penalty is wrong, for example, may have a hard time analyzing arguments that defend it or may focus his research on materials that support his perspective. Set aside personal prejudices when you analyze information.

The following four questions will help you examine and evaluate effectively.

Do examples support ideas?

When you encounter an idea or claim, examine how it is supported with examples or *evidence*—facts, expert opinion, research findings, personal experience, and so on (see Key 9.1 for an illustration). How useful an idea is to your work may depend on whether, or how well, it is backed up with solid evidence or made concrete with examples. Be critical of the information you gather; don't take it as truth without examining it.

For example, a blog written by a 12-year-old may make statements about what kids do on the Internet. The word of one person, who may or may not be telling the truth, is not adequate support. However, a study of youth technology use by the Department of Commerce under the provisions of the Children's Internet Protection Act may be more reliable.

Is the information factual and accurate, or is it opinion?

A *statement of fact* is information presented as objectively real and verifiable ("The Internet is a research tool"). In contrast, a *statement of opinion* is a belief, conclusion, or judgment that is inherently difficult, and sometimes impossible, to verify ("The Internet is always the best and most reliable research tool"). When you critically evaluate materials, one test of the evidence is whether it is fact or opinion. Key 9.2 defines important characteristics of fact and opinion.

Do causes and effects link logically?

Look at the reasons given for a situation or occurrence (causes) and the explanation of its consequences (effects, both positive and negative). For example, an article might detail what causes young teens to use the Internet after school and

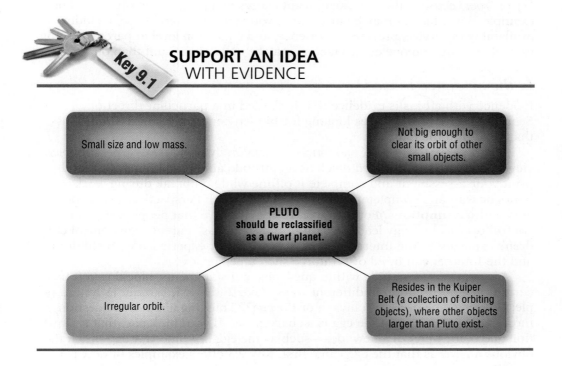

Key 9.1 SUPPORT AN IDEA WITH EVIDENCE

Small size and low mass.

Not big enough to clear its orbit of other small objects.

PLUTO should be reclassified as a dwarf planet.

Irregular orbit.

Resides in the Kuiper Belt (a collection of orbiting objects), where other objects larger than Pluto exist.

EXAMINE HOW
FACT AND OPINION DIFFER

FACTS INCLUDE STATEMENTS THAT . . .	OPINIONS INCLUDE STATEMENTS THAT . . .
. . . deal with actual people, places, objects, or events. Example: "In 2002, the European Union introduced the physical coins and banknotes of a new currency—the euro—that was designed to be used by its member nations."	**. . . show evaluation.** Any statement of value indicates an opinion. Words such as *bad, good, pointless,* and *beneficial* indicate value judgments. Example: "The use of the euro has been beneficial to all the states of the European Union."
. . . use concrete words or measurable statistics. Example: "The charity event raised $50,862."	**. . . use abstract words.** Complicated words like *misery* or *success* usually indicate a personal opinion. Example: "The charity event was a smashing success."
. . . describe current events in exact terms. Example: "Mr. Barrett's course has 378 students enrolled this semester."	**. . . predict future events.** Statements about future occurrences are often opinions. Example: "Mr. Barrett's course is going to set a new enrollment record this year."
. . . avoid emotional words and focus on the verifiable. Example: "Citing dissatisfaction with the instruction, seven out of the twenty-five students in that class withdrew in September."	**. . . use emotional words.** Emotions are unverifiable. Words such as *delightful* or *miserable* express an opinion. Example: "That class is a miserable experience."
. . . avoid absolutes. Example: "Some students need to have a job while in school."	**. . . use absolutes.** Absolute qualifiers, such as *all, none, never,* and *always,* often express an opinion. Example: "All students need to have a job while in school."

Source: Adapted from Ben E. Johnson, *Stirring Up Thinking.* New York: Houghton Mifflin, 1998, pp. 268–270.

the effects that this has on their family life. The cause-and-effect chain should make sense to you. It is also important that you analyze carefully to seek out *key* or *"root" causes*—the most significant causes of a problem or situation. For example, many factors may be involved in young teens' Internet use, including availability of service, previous experience, and education level of parents, but on careful examination one or two factors may be more significant than others.

Is the evidence biased?

Evidence with a bias is evidence that is slanted in a particular direction. Searching for a bias involves looking for hidden perspectives or assumptions that lie within the material.

A perspective can be broad (such as a generally optimistic or pessimistic view of life) or more focused (such as an attitude about whether you should print your assessment and complete it offline while on break during work hours or wait and complete it online in the evening). Perspectives are associated with assumptions. For example, the perspective that people can maintain control over technology leads to assumptions such as "Parents can control children's exposure to the Internet." Having a particular experience with children and the Internet can build or reinforce such a perspective.

Assumptions often hide within questions and statements, blocking you from considering information in different ways. Take this classic puzzler as an example: "Which came first, the chicken or the egg?" Thinking about this question, most people assume that the egg is a chicken egg. If you think past that assumption and come up with a new idea—such as the egg is a dinosaur egg—then the obvious answer is that the egg came first. Key 9.3 offers examples of how perspectives and assumptions can affect what you read or hear through the media.

BIAS
A preference or inclination, especially one that prevents even-handed judgment.

PERSPECTIVE
A characteristic way of thinking about people, situations, events, and ideas.

ASSUMPTION
A judgment, generalization, or bias influenced by experience and values.

Topic: *How teens' grades are affected by Internet use*

STATEMENT BY A TEACHING ORGANIZATION	STATEMENT BY A PR AGENT FOR AN INTERNET SEARCH ENGINE	STATEMENT BY A PROFESSOR SPECIALIZING IN NEW MEDIA AND EDUCATION
"Too much Internet use equals failing grades and stolen papers."	"The Internet use allows students access to a plethora of information, which results in better grades."	"The effects of the Internet on young students are undeniable and impossible to overlook."

Examining perspectives and assumptions helps you judge whether material is *reliable.* The less bias you can identify, the more reliable the information.

After the questions: What information is most useful to you?

You've examined your information, looking at its evidence, validity, perspective, and any underlying assumptions. Now, based on that examination, you evaluate whether an idea or piece of information is important or unimportant, relevant or not, strong or weak, and why. You then set aside what is not useful and use the rest to form an opinion, possible solution, or decision.

In preparing your paper on young teens and the Internet, for example, you've analyzed a selection of information and materials to see how they apply to the goal of your paper. You then selected what you believe will be most useful in preparation for drafting.

Make connections

The last part of analytical thinking, after you have broken information apart, is to find new and logical ways to connect pieces together. This step is crucial for research papers and essays because it is where your original ideas are born—and it is also where your creative skills get involved (more on that in the next section). When you begin to write, you focus on your new ideas, supporting them effectively with information you've learned from your analysis. Use the following techniques to make connections.

■ *Compare and contrast.* Look at how ideas are similar to, or different from, each other. You might explore how different young teen subgroups (boys versus girls, for example) have different purposes for setting up pages on sites such as Facebook or MySpace.

When you think through something with others in a group, the variety of ideas gives you a better chance of finding a workable solution to a problem.
© iStockPhoto

■ *Look for themes, patterns, and categories.* Note connections that form as you look at how bits of information relate to one another. For example, you might see patterns of Internet use that link young teens from particular cultures or areas of the country together into categories.

Come to new information ready to hear and read new ideas, think about them, and make informed decisions about what you believe. The process will educate you, sharpen your thinking skills, and give you more information to work with as you encounter life's problems. See Key 9.4 for some questions you can ask to build and use analytical thinking skills.

ASK QUESTIONS LIKE THESE TO **ANALYZE**

To gather information, ask:	• What kinds of information do I need to meet my goal? • What information is available? Where and when can I get to it? • Of the sources I found, which ones will best help me achieve my goal?
To analyze, ask:	• What are the parts of this information? • What is similar to this information? What is different? • What are the reasons for this? Why did this happen? • What ideas, themes, or conclusions emerge from this material? • How would you categorize this information?
To see whether evidence or examples support an idea, ask:	• Does the evidence make sense? • How do the examples support the idea/claim? • Are there examples that might disprove the idea/claim?
To distinguish fact from opinion, ask:	• Do the words in this information signal fact or opinion? • What is the source of this information? Is the source reliable? • If this is an opinion, is it supported by facts?
To examine perspectives and assumptions, ask:	• What perspectives might the author have, and what may be emphasized or deemphasized as a result? • What assumptions might lie behind this statement or material? • How could I prove—or disprove—an assumption? • How might my perspective affect the way I see this material?
To evaluate, ask:	• What information will support what I'm trying to prove or accomplish? • Is this information true or false, and why? • How important is this information?

Source: Adapted from www-ed.fnal.gov/trc/tutorial/taxonomy.html (Richard Paul, *Critical Thinking: How to Prepare Students for a Rapidly Changing World,* 1993) and from www.kcmetro.edu/longview/ctac/blooms.htm (Barbara Fowler, Longview Community College "Bloom's Taxonomy and Critical Thinking").

Pursuing your goals, in college and in the workplace, requires not just analyzing information but also thinking creatively about how to use what you've learned from your analysis.

How can you improve your creative thinking skills?

What is creativity?

▶ Some researchers define creativity as combining existing elements in an innovative way to create a new purpose or result (after doctors noticed that patients taking aspirin had fewer heart attacks, the drug was reinvented as a preventer of coronary disease).

▶ Others see creativity as the ability to generate new ideas from looking at how things are related (noting what ladybugs eat inspired organic farmers to bring them in to consume crop-destroying aphids).[6]

▶ Still others, including Sternberg, define it as the ability to make unusual connections—to view information in quirky ways that bring about unique results (using a weak adhesive to mark pages in a book, a 3M scientist created Post-it notes).

To think creatively is to generate new ideas that may bring change. Even though some people seem to have more or better ideas than others, creative thinking is a skill that can be developed. Creativity expert Roger von Oech highlights mental flexibility. "Like race-car drivers who shift in and out of different gears depending on where they are on the course," he says, you can enhance creativity by learning to "shift in and out of different types of thinking depending on the needs of the situation at hand."[7]

The following tips will help you make those shifts and build your ability to generate and capture the ideas that pop up. Get in the habit of writing them down as you think of them. Keep a pen and paper by your bed, your smartphone in your pocket, a notepad in your car, or a recorder so that you can grab ideas before they fade.

Brainstorm

Brainstorming is also referred to as *divergent thinking:* You start with a question and then let your mind diverge—go in many different directions—in search of solutions. Brainstorming is *deliberate* creative thinking. When you brainstorm, you generate ideas without thinking about how useful they are, and evaluate their quality later. Brainstorming works well in groups because group members can become inspired by, and make creative use of, one another's ideas.[8]

One way to inspire ideas when brainstorming is to think of similar situations—in other words, to make *analogies* (comparisons based on a resemblance of things otherwise unlike). For example, Velcro is a product of analogy: After examining how burrs stuck to his dog's fur after a walk in the woods, the inventor imagined how a similar system of hooks and loops could make two pieces of fabric stick to each other.

When you are brainstorming ideas, don't get hooked on finding one right answer. Questions may have many "right answers"—answers that have degrees

> BRAINSTORMING
> Letting your mind wander to come up with different ideas or answers.

Analyze a *Statement*

Reread the case study that opens the chapter. Consider the statement below; then analyze it by answering the questions that follow.

> *There's no point in pursuing a career area that you love*
> *if it isn't going to earn you a living.*

Is this statement fact or opinion? Why?

_____
_____
_____
_____

What examples can you think of that support or negate this statement?

_____
_____
_____
_____

What perspective(s) are guiding this statement?

_____
_____
_____
_____

What assumption(s) underlie the statement? What negative effects might result from accepting these assumptions without investigation?

_____
_____
_____
_____

As a result of your critical thinking, what is your evaluation of this statement?

_____
_____
_____
_____

of usefulness. The more possibilities you generate, the better your chance of finding the best one.

Finally, don't stop the process when you think you have the best answer—keep going until you are out of steam. You never know what may come up in those last gasps of creative energy.[9]

Take a new and different look

If no one ever questioned established opinion, people would still think the sun revolved around the earth. Here are some ways to change how you look at a situation or problem:

■ *Challenge assumptions.* In the late 1960s, conventional wisdom said that school provided education and television provided entertainment. Jim Henson, a pioneer in children's television, asked, Why can't we use TV to educate young children? From that question, the characters of *Sesame Street,* and eventually many other educational programs, were born.

■ *Shift your perspective.* Try on new perspectives by asking others for their views, reading about new ways to approach situations, or deliberately going with the opposite of your first instinct.[10] Then use those perspectives to inspire creativity. For a political science course, for example, you might craft a position paper for a senatorial candidate that goes against your view of that particular issue. For a fun example of how looking at something in a new way can unearth a totally different idea, look at the perception puzzles in Key 9.5.

USE **PERCEPTION PUZZLES** TO EXPERIENCE
A SHIFT IN PERSPECTIVE

There are two possibilities for each image. What do you see?

Source of middle puzzle: "Sara Nadar" illustration from *Mind Sights* by Roger Shepard. Copyright © 1990 by Roger Shepard. Reprinted by permission of Henry Holt and Company, LLC.

GET CREATIVE!

Activate Your Creative Powers

First, think about the past month; then list three creative acts you performed.

1. To study, I _____

2. In my personal life, I _____

3. At work or in the classroom, I _____

Now think of a problem or situation that is on your mind. Brainstorm one new idea for how to deal with it.

_____

Write down a second idea—but focus on the risk-taking aspect of creativity. What would be a risky way to handle the situation? How do you hope it would pay off?

_____

_____

Finally, sit with the question—write down one more idea *only* after you have been away from this page for at least 24 hours.

_____

Keep these in mind. You may want to use one soon!

■ *Ask "what if" questions.* Set up imaginary environments in which new ideas can grow, such as, What if I had unlimited money or time? For example, the founders of Seeds of Peace, faced with long-term conflict in the Middle East, asked, What if Israeli and Palestinian teens met at a summer camp in Maine so that the next generation has greater understanding and respect? And what if follow-up programs and reunions strengthen friendships so that relationships change the politics of the Middle East? Based on the ideas that came up, they created an organization that helps teenagers from the Middle East develop leadership and communication skills.

Set the stage for creativity

Use these strategies to generate creative ideas.

■ *Choose, or create, environments that free your mind.* Find places that energize you. Play music that moves you. Seek out people who inspire you.[11]

■ *Be curious.* Try something new and different: Take a course outside of your major, listen to a new genre of music, read a book on an unfamiliar topic. Try something you don't think you will like to see if you have misjudged your reaction. Seeking out new experiences will broaden your knowledge, giving you more raw materials with which to build creative ideas.[12]

■ *Give yourself time to "sit" with a question.* American society values speed, so much so that we equate being "quick" with being smart.[13] In fact, creative ideas often come when you give your brain permission to "leave the job" for a while.[14] Take breaks when figuring out a problem—get some exercise, nap, talk with a friend, work on something else, do something fun.

Take risks

Creative breakthroughs can come from sensible risk taking.

■ *Go against established ideas.* The founders of Etsy.com went against the idea that the American consumer prefers cheap, conventional, mass-produced items. In 2005 they created an online company that allows artisans to offer one-of-a-kind, handmade products to the consumer. The site has also created a community of artists and connects each artist personally to his or her customers.

■ *Let mistakes be okay.* Open yourself to the learning that comes from not being afraid to mess up. When a pharmaceutical company failed to develop a particular treatment for multiple sclerosis, the CEO said, "You have to celebrate the failures. If you send the message that the only road to career success is experiments that work, people won't ask risky questions, or get any dramatically new answers."[15]

As with analytical thinking, asking questions powers creative thinking. See Key 9.6 for examples of the kinds of questions you can ask to get your creative juices flowing.

Creativity connects analytical and practical thinking. When you generate ideas, solutions, or choices, you need to think analytically to evaluate their quality. Then, you need to think practically about how to make the best solution or choice happen.

How can you improve your practical thinking skills?

You've analyzed a situation. You've brainstormed ideas. Now, with your practical skill, you make things happen.

Practical thinking—also called "common sense" or "street smarts"—refers to how you adapt to your environment (both people and circumstances), or shape or change your environment to adapt to you, to pursue important goals. Think about this example.

Your goal is to pass English composition. You learn most successfully through visual presentations. To achieve your goal, you can use the instructor's PowerPoints or other visual media to enhance your learning (adapt to your

ASK QUESTIONS LIKE THESE
TO **JUMP-START CREATIVE THINKING**

Key 9.6

To brainstorm, ask:
- What do I want to accomplish?
- What are the craziest ideas I can think of?
- What are ten ways that I can reach my goal?
- What ideas have worked before and how can I apply them?

To shift your perspective, ask:
- How has this always been done—and what would be a different way?
- How can I approach this task or situation from a new angle?
- How would someone else do this or view this?
- What if . . . ?

To set the stage for creativity, ask:
- Where, and with whom, do I feel relaxed and inspired?
- What music helps me think out of the box?
- When in the day or night am I most likely to experience a flow of creative ideas?
- What do I think would be new and interesting to try, to see, to read?

To take risks, ask:
- What is the conventional way of doing this? What would be a totally different way?
- What would be a risky approach to this problem or question?
- What is the worst that can happen if I take this risk? What is the best?
- What have I learned from this mistake?

environment) or enroll in a heavily visual Internet course (change your environment to adapt to you)—or both.

Why practical thinking is important

Real-world problems and decisions require you to add understanding of experiences and social interactions to your analytical abilities. Your success in a sociology class, for example, may depend almost as much on getting along with your instructor as on your academic work. Similarly, the way you solve a personal money problem may have more impact on your life than how you work through a problem in an accounting course.

Keep in mind, too, that in the workplace you need to use practical skills to apply academic knowledge to problems and decisions. For example, although students majoring in elementary education may successfully quote child development facts on an exam, their career success depends on the ability to evaluate and address real children's needs in the classroom. Successfully solving real-world problems demands a practical approach.

Practical thinking means action

Action is the logical result of practical thinking. Basic student success strategies that promote action—staying motivated, making the most of your strengths, learning from failure,

Take a Practical Approach to Building Successful Intelligence

Look back at your Wheel of Successful Intelligence in Chapter 1 on page 26. Write here the skill area in which you most need to build strength:

_____

Write down two practical actions you can take that will improve your skills in that area. For example, someone who wants to be more creative could take a course focused on creativity; someone who wants to be more practical could work on paying attention to social cues; someone who wants to be more analytical could decide to analyze one newspaper article every week.

1. _____

_____

2. _____

_____

managing time, seeking help from instructors and advisors, and believing in yourself—will keep you moving toward your goals.[16]

The key to making practical knowledge work is to use what you discover, assuring that you will not have to learn the same lessons over and over again. As Sternberg says, "What matters most is not how much experience you have had but rather how much you have profited from it—in other words, how well you apply what you have learned."[17]

See Key 9.7 for some questions you can ask in order to apply practical thinking to your problems and decisions.

How can you solve problems and make decisions **effectively?**

The best problem solvers and decision makers put their analytical, creative, and practical thinking skills together to solve problems and make decisions. Problem solving and decision making follow similar paths, both requiring you to identify and analyze a situation, generate possibilities, choose one, follow through on it, and evaluate its success. Key 9.8 gives an overview indicating the process at each step.

Understanding the differences between problem solving and decision making will help you know how to proceed. Remember, too, that whereas all problem solving involves decision making, not all decision making requires you to solve a problem.

ASK QUESTIONS LIKE THESE
TO ACTIVATE **PRACTICAL THINKING**

Key 9.7

To learn from experience, ask:	• What worked well, or not so well, about my approach? My timing? My tone? My wording? • What did others like or not like about what I did? • What did I learn from that experience, conversation, event? • How would I change things if I had to do it over again? • What do I know I would do again?
To apply what you learn, ask	• What have I learned that would work here? • What have I seen others do, or heard about from them, that would be helpful here? • What does this situation have in common with past situations I've been involved in? • What has worked in similar situations in the past?
To boost your ability to take action, ask:	• How can I get motivated and remove limitations? • How can I, in this situation, make the most of what I do well? • If I fail, what can I learn from it? • What steps will get me to my goal, and what trade-offs are involved? • How can I manage my time more effectively?

SOLVE PROBLEMS AND MAKE DECISIONS
USING SUCCESSFUL INTELLIGENCE

Key 9.8

PROBLEM SOLVING	THINKING SKILL	DECISION MAKING
Define the problem—recognize that something needs to change, identify what's happening, look for true causes.	**STEP 1** **DEFINE**	**Define the decision**—identify your goal (your need) and then construct a decision that will help you get it.
Analyze the problem—gather information, break it down into pieces, verify facts, look at perspectives and assumptions, evaluate information.	**STEP 2** **ANALYZE**	**Examine needs and motives**—consider the layers of needs carefully, and be honest about what you really want.
Generate possible solutions—use creative strategies to think of ways you could address the causes of this problem.	**STEP 3** **CREATE**	**Name and/or generate different options**—use creative questions to come up with choices that would fulfill your needs.
Evaluate solutions—look carefully at potential pros and cons of each, and choose what seems best.	**STEP 4** **ANALYZE** (EVALUATE)	**Evaluate options**—look carefully at potential pros and cons of each, and choose what seems best.
Put the solution to work—persevere, focus on results, and believe in yourself as you go for your goal.	**STEP 5** **TAKE PRACTICAL ACTION**	**Act on your decision**—go down the path and use practical strategies to stay on target.
Evaluate how well the solution worked—look at the effects of what you did.	**STEP 6** **ANALYZE** (REEVALUATE)	**Evaluate the success of your decision**—look at whether it accomplished what you had hoped.
In the future, apply what you've learned—use this solution, or a better one, when a similar situation comes up again.	**STEP 7** **TAKE PRACTICAL ACTION**	**In the future, apply what you've learned**—make this choice, or a better one, when a similar decision comes up again.

Solve a problem

The following strategies will help you move through the problem-solving process outlined in Key 9.8.

■ ***Use probing questions to define problems.*** Ask, What is the problem? And what is causing the problem? Engage your emotional intelligence. If you determine that you are not motivated to do your work for a class, for example, you could ask questions like these:

> ► Do my feelings stem from how I interact with my instructor or classmates?
> ► Is the subject matter difficult? Uninteresting?

Chances are that how you answer one or more of these questions may help you define the problem—and ultimately solve it.

■ ***Analyze carefully.*** Gather information that will help you examine the problem. Consider how the problem is similar to, or different from, other problems. Clarify facts. Note your own perspective and look for others. Make sure your assumptions are not getting in the way.

■ ***Generate possible solutions based on causes, not effects.*** Addressing a cause provides a lasting solution, whereas "putting a Band-Aid on" an effect cannot. Say, for example, that your shoulder hurts when you type. Getting a massage is a helpful but temporary solution, because the pain returns whenever you go back to work. Changing your keyboard height is a lasting solution to the problem, because it eliminates the cause of your pain.

■ ***Consider how possible solutions affect you and others.*** What would suit you best? What takes other people's needs into consideration?

■ ***Evaluate your solution and act on it in the future.*** Once you choose a solution and put it into action, ask yourself, What worked that you would do again? What didn't work that you would avoid or change in the future?

What happens if you don't work through a problem comprehensively? Take, for example, a student having an issue with an instructor. He may get into an argument with the instructor, stop showing up to class, or take a quick-and-dirty approach to assignments. Any of these choices may have negative consequences. Now look at how the student might work through this problem using analytical, creative, and practical thinking skills.

Make a decision

As you use the steps in Key 9.8 to make a decision, remember these strategies.

■ ***Look at the given options—then try to think of more.*** Some decisions have a given set of options. For example, your school may allow you to major, double major, or major and minor. However, you may be able to brainstorm with an advisor to come up with more options such as an interdisciplinary major. Consider similar situations you've been in or heard about, what decisions were made, and what resulted from those decisions.

■ ***Think about how your decision affects others.*** What you choose might have an impact on friends, family, and others around you.

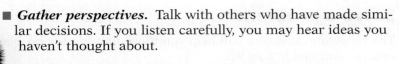

■ *Gather perspectives.* Talk with others who have made similar decisions. If you listen carefully, you may hear ideas you haven't thought about.

■ *Look at the long-term effects.* As with problem solving, it's key to examine what happens after you put the decision into action. For important decisions, do a short-term evaluation and another evaluation after a period of time. Consider whether your decision sent you in the right direction or whether you should rethink your choice.

Keep your balance

No one has equal strengths in analytical, creative, and practical thinking. However, you think and work toward goals most effectively when you combine all three. Staying as balanced as possible requires that you analyze your levels of ability in the three thinking areas, come up with creative ideas about how to build areas where you need to develop, and put them to use with practical action. Above all, believe in your skills as a thinker.

"Successfully intelligent people," says Sternberg, "defy negative expectations, even when these expectations arise from low scores on IQ or similar tests. They do not let other people's assessments stop them from achieving their goals. They find their path and then pursue it, realizing that there will be obstacles along the way and that surmounting these obstacles is part of the challenge."[18] Let the obstacles come, as they will for everyone, in all aspects of life. You can face and overcome them with the power of your successfully intelligent thinking.

Thinking and Researching Online

Although you have undoubtedly had experiences in which you had to research and think things through in your lifetime, researching online requires particular strategies and methods. This chapter covers the most important techniques.

Thinking about course content

Thinking is internally processing the information presented to you. Here are some ways to help you really think about the concepts presented in your class:

▶ Relate the new information to your own experiences or what you've already learned.
▶ Translate the concepts into your own words. What related ideas and information does the new content bring to mind? Be sure to take note of any questions that occur to you regarding the ideas presented in class.
▶ *Do not* parrot the text or the responses of your classmates. Use your own background knowledge and experiences to contribute to what you are reading and learning. How might the concepts being discussed in class apply to you? Keep an open mind.
▶ Try to have a holistic as well as a personal view. How do these ideas impact your life as well as the greater world?

- Pay attention to your thought process. Try to communicate in your writing *how* your ideas progress from one point to the other. Think of working out a math problem. It is helpful for you and others to be able to see the process. This approach not only shows your instructor how you are thinking through the concepts, but it can be helpful to your classmates as an example of a way to approach their learning.
- Ask questions. Seek clarity about the goals of individual assignments and activities, and try to ensure that what you take away from an assignment matches the learning objective.
- We all learn from one another. Pay attention to the comments and insights of your instructor, as well as your classmates. Use their diverse knowledge and perspectives to round out and contribute to your own. Don't forget to give credit to others for their ideas!

Critical thinking

The basis of critical thinking is questioning, which can help you achieve clarity regarding what is being said, as well as why and how. Here are some questions to consider:

- Is this correct?
- Who is saying it and why?
- Who is the intended audience for this information?
- What perspective is being put forward?
- What other perspectives are there that might be relevant?
- What sounds right about this to you and what sounds wrong, and why?
- Why would someone want you to believe this?
- What other questions does this information provoke?

Try to remember not to just take information at face value.

Ask questions

Don't be afraid to ask questions, even if you do not obtain sufficient answers. Just the asking can help you gain clarity about the important concepts. Questioning is also a valuable way to decipher your own views about the information presented in class.

Remember, asking questions does not mean just interrogating your instructor and classmates. It also means being open to letting others question you. It even means questioning your own opinions and preconceived notions, trying to determine their origins truthfully. Responding thoughtfully to others' questions can also clarify your own reasoning.

Internet research

Critical thinking is especially important with regard to Internet research. Thinking about an idea and approaching it from different angles will aid you in doing online searches. Also, being critical of the information presented will help you sift through the vast amount of data on the Web and determine which online sources are relevant and reliable for your purposes.

Search engines

Search engines are the tools you use on the Web to lead you to information. You are probably already familiar with a few of them. Alta Vista, Ask.com, or Yahoo! are some example of search engines.

A search engine typically features a page with a box where you to type in words to describe the information you want. Type in the word(s), hit return, and the 'engine' searches the Internet for mentions of those particular word(s). If you are unfamiliar with search engines, go to Google.com and experiment with searching. Use any tutorials or help information offered.

How and where a particular engine searches can vary. Some search engines look for specific forms of information, such as scholarly materials, while others are more general.

Technically, search engines can be categorized into two types: individual search engines and metasearch engines.

▶ Individual search engines are the most basic ones. They search the whole Web.
▶ Metasearch engines are those that search, and usually organize, the results from other search engines.

Decide what type of search engine is right for your purposes before you begin your research.

Types of online searches

You can do a basic, uncomplicated Web search using an engine such as Google just by directly typing in the relevant terms. There are two tricks to effective searching of this type: language options and persistence.

You need to think critically about your topic and come at it from various angles, using different words and giving yourself language options. Putting together a successful online search is a little like note taking. The best way to do it is not just to copy out exact words from the lecture or text but to grasp the main ideas and restate them in your own language. It is a game in word association, and it helps to have a wide vocabulary, a creative thought process, and a knowledge of synonyms. For instance, say you are searching for information regarding "online learning." Of course, your obvious initial search terms are those words. But try varying the words. What other terms would express the same concept or something closely related? For "online" you might consider *computer*, or *distance*, or even *virtual*. For "learning" you might try *learner*, or *classroom*, or *student*. Mixing up and recombining all these different, but similar terms, will give you some more interesting and diverse search results than just the basic concept you started with. And if you can't think of various terms right away, do that initial search using "online learning," and see what other related terms are included in the results list from that search to give you additional ideas.

The element of persistence comes into the equation in two ways. Try numerous different word combinations before being satisfied with your results. And do not limit yourself to finding information in the first few pages of results that come up. Skim through three to five pages of the results, especially if nothing really relevant seems to have come from the search. Sometimes the good stuff is buried further down the list.

Although you can always do a search as just described by typing any terms into the engine that are relevant to what you want to find, the Internet does offer more complex options. You might need to use a specific type of search method. Two basic types of online searches are "Boolean" and "Wild Card."

Boolean searches

A Boolean search uses the terms *and, or,* and/or *not* to set particular limits on the information being searched. Boolean is the type of logic used in these searches. It defines the relationship among the terms used in the search. Boolean logic takes its name from the British-born Irish mathematician and philosopher George Boole.

The easiest way to envision what you are doing when you use a Boolean search is to show it through Venn diagrams. Observe the following examples:

Using the term OR in a Boolean search

Goal: I would like information about college.

Query: college OR university

In this search, you will retrieve records in which *at least one* of the search terms is present. You are searching on the terms *college* and also *university* because documents containing either of these words might be relevant. Look at the accompanying figure.

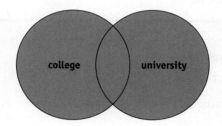

The shaded circle with the word *college* represents all the records that contain the word "college." The shaded circle with the word *university* represents all the records that contain the word "university." The shaded overlap area represents all the records that contain both "college" and "university."

OR logic is most commonly used to search for synonymous terms or concepts. The corresponding table is an example of how OR logic works.

OR logic collates the results to retrieve all the unique records containing one term, the other, or both. The more terms or concepts you combine in a search with OR logic, the more records you will retrieve.

SEARCH TERMS	RESULTS
college	396,482
university	590,791
college OR university	819,214

Using the term AND in a Boolean search

Goal: I'm interested in the relationship between poverty and crime.

Query: poverty AND crime

In this search, you retrieve records in which *both* of the search terms are present. This is illustrated by the shaded area overlapping the two circles representing all the records that contain both the word *poverty* and the word *crime* in the corresponding graphic.

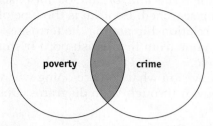

Notice how we do not retrieve any records with only "poverty" or only "crime." The corresponding table is an example of how **AND** logic works.

SEARCH TERMS	RESULTS
poverty	76,342
crime	348,252
poverty AND crime	12,998

The more terms or concepts we combine in a search with AND logic, the fewer records we will retrieve.

Using the term **NOT** in a Boolean search

Goal: I want information about cats, but I want to avoid anything about dogs.

Query: cats NOT dogs

In this search, we retrieve records in which *only one* of the terms is present. This is illustrated in the nearby graphic by the shaded area with the word *cats* representing all the records containing the word "cats."

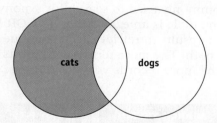

No records are retrieved in which the word *dogs* appears, even if the word *cats* appears there too. The accompanying table shows how NOT logic works.

SEARCH TERMS	RESULTS
cats	86,747
dogs	130,424
cats NOT dogs	65,223

NOT logic excludes records from your search results. Be cautious when you use NOT: The term you *do* want may be present in an important way in documents that also contain the word you wish to avoid.

Wild card searches

In a wild card search, you use a specific character among your search terms in a particular way, to expand the boundaries of your search. The two most common characters used are the question mark and the asterisk (the "?" and the "*").

The question mark ("?") can represent a single alphanumeric character in a search expression. For example, searching for the term "ho?se" would yield results that contain such words as "house" and "horse."

The asterisk ("*") can specify zero or more alphanumeric characters. It can be used in the middle or, more commonly, at the end of a word. Depending on where you place the asterisk, it can signify different words or just different forms of a single word.

For example, searching for the term "h*s" would yield results that contain such words as "his," "homes," "houses," "horses," "horticulturalists," and "herbaceous." Searching for the term "boat*" would yield results such as "boats," "boating," and "boaters." It is usually best to avoid using the asterisk as the first character in a search string.

A search term consisting of a lone asterisk and no other alphanumeric characters will retrieve every record from the database.

The credibility of information online

When you do online research, keep in mind that finding current, accurate information is better than finding lots of information. Just because something is posted online does not mean it is accurate and valid.

Do not take everything you find on the Web at face value. Be critical of the websites you encounter in your research. Plagiarism is rampant on the Web. Many times you can do a search and find numerous sites that contain exactly the same information. You can usually figure out on which site the information originated: the site set up the most professionally, listed as created by a qualified individual that cites references for the information. In general, websites that end in *.gov, .edu,* and *.org* tend to be more reliable than just *.com* and *.net* sites.

Beware of sites that do not account for their sources or have not been updated recently. Be especially critical of wikis, where anyone, regardless of knowledge or qualifications, can contribute to the so-called truth about a subject. Wikis can result in some very well-rounded information, but the information may be inaccurate. When qualified editors do not oversee a website, it may perpetuate inconsistencies, fallacies, and flat-out untruths about the topics discussed.

Primary and secondary sources

The safest source for any information is the *primary source*, the place where the information was first expressed or put into print. In terms of technical research, a primary source is the study itself. If you are looking for information on music therapy, find a journal article describing an actual study on music therapy and the results. This would be your primary source.

Alternately, if you use a book, magazine, or Internet article that summarizes the findings of a number of music therapy research studies, you are using a *secondary source*, one that just restates information from its first occurrence. In general, the further you are from the primary source of information, the more likely there may be errors or oversights in the information.

The more often something is interpreted, the more chance there is of losing some meaning in translation. Never assume the first site to come up in search results is correct and adequate for your needs. Read through as many of the search results as you can. It will help you round out your perspective, as well as identify which sites stand out in terms of quality, readability, and scope of information.

Try the search again using terms that are synonyms. This can be a way to fine-tune your results and maybe find information that is not as obvious.

Do your best to gain a well-rounded view of the information available. Try to find sites that come at the information from different angles.

You may find that after you look at several sites, you can see mistakes in some of them. But you only caught those mistakes because you looked at the big picture instead of just trying to take advantage of the fastest, easiest view.

Academic integrity and plagiarism

Doing research puts you in a position to present views relevant to your topic other than your own. You will discover many interesting ideas. But be sure you keep track of which ideas are your own and which come from other people. You must cite your sources correctly and give credit to others where it is due. That honesty in dealings regarding your coursework is known as academic integrity.

Plagiarism can be defined as "the unauthorized use or close imitation of the language and thoughts of another author and the representation of them as one's own original work" (*Dictionary.com Unabridged*; http://dictionary. reference.com/browse/plagiarism).

In other words, you are plagiarizing when you copy the words or the thoughts of someone else and do not tell your audience that those words or thoughts were not originally your own.

Looking closely at plagiarism

The most important point to consider about plagiarism is not just that it isn't fair to others or can result in serious consequences. It is that if you plagiarize, you are passing up a chance for learning.

What's wrong with plagiarizing?

If plagiarism becomes a tempting option, maybe you need to rethink your priorities. Have you given up on school? If not, then the reason you are here is to *learn*. Doing research, thinking through ideas, and articulating your thoughts in writing are all a big part of that learning experience. You forsake that part when you plagiarize.

There is much more to consider with regard to plagiarism, however. What may seem like an insignificant act can be taken as an indicator of various character traits. For any given instance of plagiarism, any of these might apply:

■ *You are a thief.* You couldn't be bothered to put in the required amount of work in terms of the research, thought, and writing the assignment required. So you used someone else's thought, research, and work, and stole the opportunity to learn from yourself!

■ *You are unimaginative.* You used someone else's words and ideas, instead of paraphrasing or summarizing them, so you couldn't, or didn't bother to, think of new ways to express the information and ideas.

■ *You are dishonest.* You didn't cite the ideas or information that you used properly, so, in effect, you tried to pass them off as your own.

- **You are disrespectful.** You didn't have enough respect for those who conceived the original ideas or did important research on the topic to give them the credit they are due. In addition, you didn't have enough respect for the readers of your work to give them the facts of the situation.

- **You are unprofessional.** Being professional entails extending a certain level of courtesy to others and following the guidelines for a task, as well as acting ethically. By plagiarizing, you broadcast the fact that you do not care about professional standards and are neither courteous nor ethical. Is that the way you want to present yourself? Probably not. So take care not to plagiarize.

What if you plagiarize accidentally?

Maybe you didn't deliberately plagiarize; maybe it was just an accident or an oversight, but ignorance or accident is really no excuse. You will be informed of the proper ways to cite information for your assignments, but if you aren't, it is your responsibility to ask about it. Because plagiarism in itself is dishonest and sneaky, it can be difficult to give people who plagiarize the benefit of the doubt that it was not intentional.

Although the penalties for plagiarism vary widely by instructor and institution, it is always regarded as a serious offense. Students who plagiarize may be asked to redo the assignment. They may receive a failing grade for the assignment or for the course. They may be put on academic probation, or they may even be expelled.

Common instances of plagiarism

Plagiarism occurs when students include a small part of another person's work in their own without giving credit to the source or when students submit an entire paper or project created by another person. It can also occur when a whole paper is made up of small parts of others' work.

There are websites where students can purchase complete papers written on a wide variety of subjects for common courses. Your instructor knows that, too. There are also websites instructors can visit, and just by putting in a small excerpt of text and doing a search, they can find out if a student has misrepresented a part or the whole of the work put forward as his or her own.

In this Internet age, where information is so easy to obtain, it is just as easy to track. So if you ever consider plagiarizing, do not forget it is just as easy for an instructor to run a search on your work as it was for you to commit your crime. But we hope that as a person who values learning—an honest, imaginative, careful, respectful person, with a good work ethic—you will avoid plagiarizing.

Citing sources

The way to avoid plagiarizing is to always cite your sources correctly. Citations are brief notes describing what information sources you used, who originally wrote them and when, and where you found them. They can take the form of footnotes, endnotes, notes within the text, or even a separate resource page that lists all the sources you referred to in your research.

Columbia Southern University requires that all students use the citation style of the American Psychological Association (APA). In this unit, an introduction to the APA format will be provided. A more in-depth look at the format will be provided in English Composition I and English Composition II.

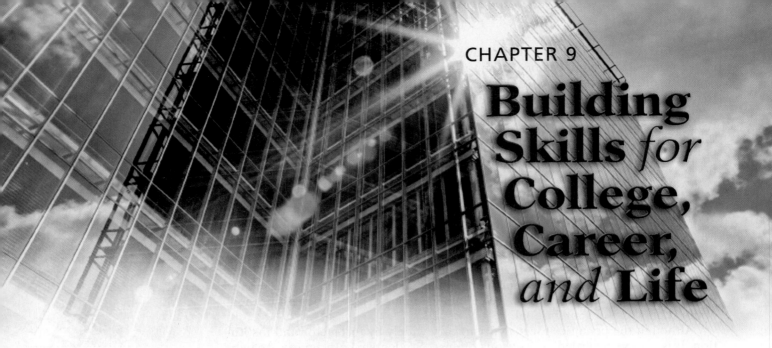

Building Skills *for* College, Career, *and* Life

Steps to Success

Make an Important Decision

BUILD BASIC SKILLS. List the steps of the decision-making process.

_____

_____

_____

_____

TAKE IT TO THE NEXT LEVEL. Think about how you would put the decision-making process to work on something that matters to you. Write an important long-term goal that you have, and define the decision that will help you fulfill it. Example: "My goal is to become a nurse. My decision: What to specialize in."

_____

_____

_____

_____

MOVE TOWARD MASTERY. Use a separate piece of paper to apply the decision-making process to your goal. Use the following steps to organize your thinking.

- *Examine needs and concerns.* What are your needs, and how do your values come into play? What is most needed in the health market, and how can you fulfill that need? What roadblocks might be involved? List everything you come up with. For example, the prospective nurse might list the following needs: "I need to feel that I'm helping people. I intend to help with the shortage of perinatal or geriatric nurses. I need to make a good living."
- *Generate options.* Ask questions to imagine what's possible. Where might you work? What might be the schedule and pace? Who might work with you? What would you see, smell, and hear on your job? What would you do every day? List, too, all of the options you know of. The prospective nurse, for example, might list perinatal surgery, neonatal intensive care unit, geriatric nursing in a hospital or in a retirement community, and so on.

- *Evaluate options.* Think about how well your options will fulfill your needs. For two of your options, write potential positive and negative effects (pros and cons) of each.

    Option 1: _____

    Potential pros: _____

    Potential cons: _____

    Option 2: _____

    Potential pros: _____

    Potential cons: _____

- *Imagine acting on your decision.* Describe one practical course of action, based on your thinking so far, that you might follow. List the specific steps you would take. For example, the prospective nurse might list actions to help determine what type of nursing suits him best, such as interning, summer jobs, academic goals, and talking to working nurses.

An additional practical action is to go to an actual job site and talk to people. The prospective nurse might go to a hospital, a clinic, and a health center at a retirement community. Get a feel for what the job is like day-to-day so that can be part of your decision.

Writing

Build Intrapersonal and Communication Skills

Record your thoughts on a separate piece of paper, in a journal, or electronically.

EMOTIONAL INTELLIGENCE JOURNAL

Make a wiser choice. Think about a decision you made that you wish you had handled differently. Describe the decision and what feelings resulted from it. Then, describe what you would do if you could approach the decision again, thinking about a mindset and actions that might produce more positive feelings and a better outcome.

REAL-LIFE WRITING

Address a problem. Think about a problem that you are currently experiencing in school—it could be difficulty with a course, a scheduling nightmare, or a conflict with a classmate. Write a letter—to an advisor, instructor, friend, medical professional, or anyone else who may help—that asks for help with your problem. Be specific about what you want and how the person to whom you are writing can help you. After you finish, consider sending your letter via mail or e-mail. Carefully assess the effect that it may have, and if you decide that it may help, send it. Be sure to have someone you trust review it for you before you send.

Personal Portfolio

Prepare for Career Success

GENERATE IDEAS FOR INTERNSHIPS

21st Century Learning Building Blocks

- Financial, Economic, Business, and Entrepreneurial Literacy
- Leadership and Responsibility
- Communication and Collaboration

Complete the following in your electronic portfolio or separately on paper.

Pursuing internships is a practical way to get experience, learn what you like and don't like, and make valuable connections. Even interning in a career area that you don't ultimately pursue can build skills that are useful in any career. The creative thinking skills you've built will help you generate ideas for where you might intern at some point during your college career.

First, use personal contacts to gather information about career fields. List two people here:

People whom I want to interview about their fields/professions, and why:

1. _____ Field: _____

Because: _____

2. _____ Field: _____

Because: _____

Talk to the people you have listed and take notes.

Next, look up each of these fields in the *Occupational Outlook Handbook* published by the U.S. Department of Labor (available at the library or online at http://stats.bls.gov/oco/home.htm). To get a better idea of whether you would want to intern in these fields, read OOH categories for each.

Social Networking

CONTROL YOUR COMMUNICATION

Many people these days are overwhelmed by the volume of electronic communication that comes their way each day. Make sure that LinkedIn is more helpful than overwhelming by establishing how you want to be contacted. Sign in to your account and proceed as follows:

- Click on "Edit My Profile."
- Scroll to the bottom, and click on the Edit button next to "Contact Settings."
- Indicate what type of messages you would like to accept on LinkedIn.
- Indicate what kinds of opportunities you are looking to receive from the network you are building.
- If you choose, include advice to users contacting you. (For example, if you feel like it will take too much time to accept InMail as well as manage your regular e-mail, you can instruct users to contact you using your regular e-mail account.)

ENDNOTES

1. Vincent Ruggiero, *The Art of Thinking*, 2001, quoted in "Critical Thinking," http://success. oregonstate.edu/criticalthinking.html.
2. Richard Paul, "The Role of Questions in Thinking, Teaching, and Learning," 1995, www.criticalthinking.org/resources/articles/ the-role-of-questions.shtml.
3. "The Best Innovations Are Those That Come from Smart Questions," *Wall Street Journal*, April 12, 2004, p. B1.
4. Sharon Begley, "Critical Thinking: Part Skill, Part Mindset and Totally Up to You," *Wall Street Journal*, October 20, 2006, p. B1.
5. Matt Thomas, "What Is Higher-Order Thinking and Critical/Creative/Constructive Thinking?" n.d., Center for Studies in Higher-Order Literacy, http://a-s.clayton.edu/tparks/What%20 is%20Higher%20Order%20Thinking.doc.
6. Charles Cave, "Definitions of Creativity," August 1999, http://members.optusnet.com.au/ ~charles57/Creative/Basics/definitions.htm.
7. Roger von Oech, *A Kick in the Seat of the Pants*, New York: Harper & Row, 1986, pp. 5–21.
8. Dennis Coon, *Introduction to Psychology: Exploration and Application*, 6th ed., St. Paul, MN: West, 1992, p. 295.

9. Roger von Oech, *A Whack on the Side of the Head*, New York: Warner Books, 1990, pp. 11–168.

10. J. R. Hayes, *Cognitive Psychology: Thinking and Creating*, Homewood, IL: Dorsey, 1978.

11. Robert Sternberg, *Successful Intelligence*, New York: Plume, 1996, p. 219.

12. Adapted from T. Z. Tardif and R. J. Sternberg, "What Do We Know About Creativity?" in *The Nature of Creativity*, ed. R. J. Sternberg, London: Cambridge University Press, 1988.

13. Sternberg, p. 212.

14. Hayes, *Cognitive Psychology*.

15. "The Best Innovations Are Those That Come from Smart Questions," p. B1.

16. Sternberg, pp. 251–269.

17. Ibid., p. 241.

18. Ibid., p. 128.

chapter 10

Cultural and Global Awareness

To say CSU occupational safety and health graduate and student Julie Carter is passionate might be an understatement.

The corporate environmental health and safety director with The Mundy Companies exudes a sincere love and drive for her work. Carter is very serious and concerned in trying to help others work in a safe and healthy environment. With 25 years of experience in OSH, she works in a complex world of rules, guidelines and procedures which can mean the difference between life and death in some cases.

As she teaches the gospel of safety, her reasoning remains simple and direct.

"I do it because it's the right thing to do," said Carter, who is also the chair of the Construction Division of the National Safety Council. She added that she gets satisfaction from her EHS manager job by "knowing I am making a difference educating people on working safely and preventing injuries and death."

Her passion was evident in her work with the IHNC surge barrier project in New Orleans in 2011 when she worked as the safety manager. Her work with the barrier, which was built to protect the city from hurricanes and named one of the top 2011 engineering projects by Popular Science magazine, was praised by then-supervisor New Orleans District Safety Office senior safety specialist Sherry Scott.

"She was onsite daily covering 36 cranes on barges to ensure that they were in compliance with not only company policy, but with the U.S. Army Corps of Engineers," Scott said. "She adapted to the Corps of Engineers with the high expectations that was required with such a high-dollar, large project as the IHNC Surge Barrier. She took safety beyond what is expected and made it personal."

"Julie goes outside of the box to perform analysis of not only daily job activities but the ones that present a challenge for most safety professionals. She has gained the trust from the common laborer to the superintendent. They have complete confidence in her knowing that she is going to move mountains when it comes to safety for everyone on the team and project," Scott added.

Carter said OSH really chose her.

"I was in the field, as project manager/superintendent, and the opportunity was given to become a safety manager. At that time, I decided to pursue both my degree and certifications to become the best safety manager I could be," the 53-year-old Metairie, La., resident explained.

On the recommendation of a CSU student and learning that the Board of Certified Safety Professionals recognizes CSU programs, Carter decided to pursue an OSH degree with the online university. The student said the courses were in depth and challenging as opposed to other schools—something she would find true and rewarding.

While attending CSU, Carter said she was pleased with the courses "and the personal attention and interaction with the professors. They are truly involved and willing to help, not just 'monitors.'"

Working and going to school was challenging, but Carter pushed to achieve her bachelor's degree in OSH in summer 2010. She also proudly beams when remembering her graduation "walking across the stage and having my dad watch me receive my degree at the graduation ceremony, especially as summa cum laude."

Carter said her CSU degree has allowed her to advance further and gain senior leadership positions. She added that the degree gives her a measure of "educational safety" because some large contractors and facilities now require that the safety managers have a minimum of a four-year degree and certifications.

"I always recommend CSU to people and have all of my site safety personnel enrolled. The curriculum is solid and relevant," Carter said. "In choosing any online education, it is important to do the research into the school. There are several out there who aren't as diligent in ensuring your educational needs are really being met."

Carter decided to meet more of her personal educational goals by re-enrolling in CSU to seek a master's degree in OSH in late 2010.

"CSU met or exceeded my expectations through the bachelor's degree program. I am finding the same to be true in the master's program. The flexibility of distance learning fits my busy schedule, and the coursework stimulates my thinking," she said.

STATUS *Check*

► ## *How prepared am I to be a culturally aware global citizen?*

For each statement, circle the number that best describes how often it applies to you.

1 = never   2 = seldom   3 = sometimes   4 = often   5 = always

► I can define *culture* and *citizenship*.	**1 2 3 4 5**
► I understand the different cultures that affect my growth and development.	**1 2 3 4 5**
► I live, work, or study with people from different cultures.	**1 2 3 4 5**
► I am able to push past my initial assumptions about people.	**1 2 3 4 5**
► I speak or understand at least one language besides English.	**1 2 3 4 5**
► I am comfortable communicating with diverse people.	**1 2 3 4 5**
► I use technology as a means to connect with and understand people from different cultures.	**1 2 3 4 5**
► I am aware of how my daily life depends on products and services from all over the globe.	**1 2 3 4 5**
► I keep the needs of others in mind as I make personal choices.	**1 2 3 4 5**
► I feel responsible for making things better in my corner of the world.	**1 2 3 4 5**

Now total your scores.

Each of the topics in these statements is covered in this text. Note those statements for which you circled a 3 or lower. Skim this text to see where those topics appear, and pay special attention to them as you read, learn, and apply new strategies.

REMEMBER: *No matter how prepared you are to succeed in college, you can improve with effort and practice.*

student profiles

Mariela, a first-generation student who is Hispanic and grew up in a suburban area of Arizona, decided to spend one year of school in China through a study abroad program available at her school. She studied in Shanghai and also spent time in rural areas with a Chinese friend she met through the program. Every setting she experienced—the abject poverty of the rural areas, the intensity of the densely populated city—was unlike anything she had ever seen in her life.

Mariela found most of the people she met to be open, friendly, and extremely diligent and hard-working. She learned from her friend's parents that their experience growing up in Shanghai without cars was vastly different from how the city is now, with so many cars that pollution is a major issue. It brought to mind her grandparents' experience growing up in Guatemala, and how their choice to come to the United States brought them more of both good things (education, technology) and problematic things (pollution, processed foods). She began to think she might want to pursue a career in urban man-agement, or perhaps environmental management.

Raj was raised in Mombasa, India, and came to the United States for college at the age of sixteen. Once in school, he noticed many students who seemed uninterested in their coursework or disconnected from their purpose in school. This amazed him, as he had grown up in a poor family of migrant workers who took education seriously, had earned a scholarship for outstanding research in science, and highly valued the opportunity to study at the college level. At first he did not make time for fun outside of his coursework, distanced himself from other students, and did not often make use of resources offered by his school.

Over the next couple of years, Raj realized that there were positive and negative aspects to both his way of being in school and the culture more common to American students. He found a better balance of school-work and fun by getting a part-time job and developing a circle of close friends. Becoming more comfortable with the language helped—he had studied English since first grade, but using it every day increased his fluency to a level he could not have imagined. He planned to major in education and commu-nications, keeping in mind his goal of returning to India to start an organization to help improve poor children's access to good education.

Technology has changed how peo-ple live and work, creating a world where people and companies interact and work with others all over the world. As new technologies come into use, the rate of change will only con-tinue to accelerate. Think about these two students and their experiences in light of the new global connections. What have they learned about them-selves and the world, and how have they changed? How do you think you might change if you studied for a year in China or went to college in India? What would be challenging for you, and what would energize you? What would you learn about yourself? Our goal is to help you open your mind to new experiences, showing you that appreciating and cooperating with people of all different races, religions, ethnic origins, cultures, economic and life circumstances, and values is essential in the interconnected mod-ern world.

What is cultural awareness?

Every human being belongs to, and identifies with, many cultures. Everywhere you go, you encounter culture—sometimes one in which you feel at home, sometimes one that is completely unfamiliar and even confusing or disturbing to you. Your family has a culture, your school has a culture, your workplace has a culture, and the community in which you live has a culture.

Why do you need to be aware of culture? Culture informs every human action and communication. **For people to communicate and accomplish goals together in any setting, they need to understand and adapt to one another's cultures.** A lone-ranger type worker in an office culture marked by teamwork, for example, might be put off by how often he is dragged into projects, not understanding how the team structure helps this company get things done. A student visiting a friend whose family seems to fight all the time might be intimidated by the atmosphere, not having any idea that in that family's culture, talking that way is a functional form of communication.

Whether you commute, live on campus, or take courses online, college is a time of encountering all kinds of cultures. You are exposed to new cultures through the material you study and through the instructors, students, and other people with whom you interact. The key to getting the most education out of every moment in class and out is to be open to learning about, and from, other cultures. You have an amazing opportunity waiting for you—an opportunity that cultural awareness can help you embrace.

Defining culture

Cultural awareness starts with defining what *culture* is. Think about this definition below:

> ***Culture,*** *noun.* The pattern of attitudes, social customs, and beliefs that characterizes a group of people, transmitted through language, material objects, and institutions.

One way to crystallize this definition is to reduce it to these two questions:

1. How do people from this culture **see** things?
2. How do people from this culture **act**?

Perceptions and actions together communicate the values and beliefs that make up a culture. Ask these two questions of any culture you want to investigate, and the answers will give you a basic picture of what that culture is about.

When you think of culture, the first things that come to mind are likely ethnic and racial groups, religions, and countries. However, any group can have a culture. Consider these examples of distinct cultures:

▶ people living in a particular neighborhood, town, or city (the culture of Tampa, Florida)
▶ families dealing with a particular medical issue (the culture of autism)
▶ employees of a particular company (the culture of Google)
▶ people who work a certain type of job (the culture of public elementary education)

Take a closer look at one of these cultures using the definition you just read. For example, teachers at public elementary schools are likely to share a positive attitude toward public education, have similar customs about how they interact with students in the classroom, and share particular beliefs about what children can learn in a school setting. They use language specific to their knowledge as educators, pass on rituals (both in-classroom and among teachers), and value particular objects (gifts from special students).

There can even be subcultures within a group. For example, the culture of the teachers at a school in rural Oklahoma may differ radically from the culture of the teachers at a school in the Los Angeles metropolitan area, even though both groups belong to the culture of elementary school teachers and will have some cultural characteristics in common.

Four levels of cultural awareness[1]

Now that you have a broader understanding of culture, you might conclude that cultural awareness is simply an awareness of cultures. If so, you would be partially correct. Cultural awareness includes, but moves beyond, being aware of different cultures.

Becoming culturally aware is a journey. Business and culture experts Stephanie Quappe and Giovanna Cantatore discuss four levels of cultural awareness at which people operate (see Key 10.1).

More advanced levels of cultural awareness involve an acceptance of other cultures that enables you to value, and benefit from, what those cultures bring to individual situations. The highest level, although not always reached, is where new cultures can be born out of the interaction of the cultures of all participants.

1. **My way is the only way.** At this first level, people only know about their own culture, and don't even know that there are other ways to live.
2. **I know their way, but my way is better.** The second level brings an awareness of other ways of doing things, but people at the second level believe that their way is always superior to anyone else's.
3. **My way and their way.** At the third level, people are able to both understand and value other ways of being, seeing what other cultures have to offer and not automatically assuming that their way is best. They are able to look at a situation and decide which choice will benefit that situation, regardless of the culture from which that choice emerges.

THE FOUR LEVELS OF
CULTURAL AWARENESS

My way is the only way

I know their way, but my way is better

My way and their way

Our way

4. **Our way.** This fourth, most advanced level makes possible the creation of a new culture. In this level, a group of people from different cultures working toward a goal together can interact in ways that create new language, meanings, and perspectives unique to the situation.

Although these levels are on a continuum, not everyone moves through all of them. Some people stay at one level for life. Some people grow up in a family that operates at the third or fourth level and never experience the previous levels. Depending on family values and life experience, different people may currently operate at any one of the four levels, and therefore will have more or less of a journey to take toward cultural awareness.

Wherever your starting point, how do you increase your cultural awareness? The first step, and a necessary one for those who need to move out of the "my way is the only way" level, is to understand who you are as a cultural being.

Know your culture first

Begin your investigation of culture by becoming more aware of your own culture. How do you *see* things? How do *you* act? Think first about the obvious or visible, and then look beyond it to the invisible. Another way to think it through is to first identify how you are like others around you, and then pinpoint the ways you differ.

Most people belong to a wide array of cultures. For example, someone could be part of a Korean-American family, attend Catholic church, be involved in hospital culture in work as a pediatric nurse, live in an urban setting, have conservative political views, and be an avid knitter—six cultures right there, and there are likely even more (see Key 10.2).

In your investigation, consider the following:

▶ **Race and ethnic origin.** These can also be distinct cultures. For example, someone who identifies as a member of the Asian race can be ethnically Chinese, Vietnamese, Thai, and so on.

▶ **Country of residence, origin, or both.** If your family has lived in the same country for generations, your country of residence and origin may be the same. However, many people live in one country but are part of a family that originally came from another country, and such people often display elements of both cultures. For example, a resident of Chicago whose parents grew up in Egypt may feel connected to both Egyptian and U.S. culture; a child of a German-American mother and an African-American father may have a value system that displays elements of both European-American and African-American cultures.

▶ **Generation.** Various generations can have distinct cultures. The values, beliefs, and practices common to Baby Boomers born in the late 1950s differ from those common to so called Millennials born around the year 2000.

▶ **Religion.** Most religions have a defined set of beliefs and values that you will likely adopt if you are a practicing member. Many religions, of course, share certain values in common.

▶ **Local culture.** The group of people who live in your city or town, your neighborhood, or even on your street or in your apartment building can develop particular customs that they value and practice together.

▶ **Political views.** Where you stand on political issues is often connected with a particular set of values and beliefs.

▶ **Workplace.** Both your job or career in general and your specific place of work have their own culture. Employees in marketing share a culture, for example, but a marketing manager at Macy's and a marketing manager at Nike may experience widely different workplace cultures.

Korean-
American

Political
Conservatism

VOTE

Catholic
Church

City
Living

Pediatric
Nursing

Knitting

▶ **Lifestyle.** Your sexual orientation, family and marital status, and other lifestyle characteristics make you a member of distinct cultures that inform your day-to-day actions.

▶ **Immediate family.** Families often have their own culture, often consisting of a mash-up among all of the different cultures to which the family belongs. To identify your family culture, think about your unique customs, your particular beliefs, even the special terminology that families develop and use over time (nicknames, catch phrases, inside jokes).

▶ **Academia.** In addition to the distinct cultures of individual institutions, higher education has a culture of its own. The ways in which this culture differs from high school culture can pose a challenge for students making the transition. This culture includes:

> ▶ The expectation that you will learn independently, taking responsibility for keeping a schedule, attending course meetings, completing assignments, reading, and studying

► A faster pace and an increased workload
► More challenging, higher-level work
► More out-of-class time to manage
► The need to think critically and move beyond straight recall of information

What can you gain from a careful look at your own culture? First of all, you will develop a broader understanding of cultures and how they affect your beliefs and actions. Secondly, you will be more able to see the variety of cultures around you. The next step to becoming more culturally aware is to explore those cultures that you encounter.

Explore other cultures

One look around you in a crowd, one lunch with co-workers or fellow students, one hour of surfing the Internet will show you that there are many other ways of being outside of your own. Knowing about other cultures is the gateway to understanding, accepting, and valuing those cultures. There are many ways to get to know the different sets of values and beliefs that exist beyond your own culture. Here are a few:

► **Consider family members.** Even within your own family, which often shares a culture, you will find other cultures that are unfamiliar to you. Perhaps a sibling moved to a completely different part of the country or the world; maybe a parent re-married someone from a different race or country; a cousin might have converted to a different religion or might identify with a different sexual orientation than your own.
► **Go local.** Within most neighborhood and school circles you can find a wide array of cultures—different professions, languages, interests, ethnicities, and so on. Visit unfamiliar places, eat in unfamiliar restaurants, and go to unfamiliar events.
► **Read and view.** Books, newspapers, online articles, movies, television, and other media can introduce you to almost any culture in the world.
► **Learn from friends.** Open your mind to learning about the cultures of your friends. Ask them about their traditions. Notice their values and customs. Eat something unfamiliar that a friend likes to cook, or read something new that a friend recommends.

Be receptive and respectful

Being receptive to new cultures and maintaining an attitude that all cultures are worthy of respect are the next ingredients in your progression toward cultural awareness. Even if you spend a period of time at Level 2—"I know their way but my way is better"—what you've learned about other cultures gives you the raw material with which to move ahead to Level 3—"My way and their way"—where you can place cultures on an even playing field.

Being receptive literally means being *able to receive*. Therefore, it requires an openness and a willingness to receive information about other ways of being. It can be challenging to resist our human tendency to shut the mental door against unfamiliar ideas and practices. However, that mental door is the gateway to successful interaction with others, because accepting and valuing others depends on your ability to learn about them.

Being respectful depends on being receptive. Although it is possible to respect people you know nothing about simply because they are human, the deeper respect that fuels successful relationships has its roots in knowledge.

Developing cultural awareness is an ongoing process. First of all, cultures will continue to emerge and change. Secondly, throughout your life you will continue to encounter new cultures as you meet people, go places, change jobs, move into different stages of life, and have new experiences. Here are two keys to being receptive and respectful:

1. **Assume differences.** It's human to look for the similarities in people you meet. Make the effort to assume that there are differences as well—and look for them. Even as you search for common ground with a study partner, for example, notice that he has a different native language and that he dresses, takes notes, and interacts with the instructor differently than you do.

2. **Avoid judgments.** When you find those differences, stop short of judgment. Accept the reality of those differences. Know, for example, that the way your study partner dresses, speaks, takes notes, and asks questions is not better or worse than yours—just different. Of course, different ways of being might be better for one person and not a good choice for another—but whether a choice is good or bad for one person does not change that the choice has value and deserves respect.

The value of cultural awareness

Why be culturally aware? Understanding the benefit of cultural awareness comes down to understanding how much your success depends on others. You will interact with cultures visible and invisible in school, at work, and in your personal life. The more aware and accepting you are of these cultures, the more effectively you will:

▶ Communicate with others
▶ Achieve goals on work teams with others
▶ Solve life's problems with others
▶ Find and use products and help from people around you

You can make these things happen by putting cultural awareness into practice. You might refer to cultural awareness in action as *cultural competence*.

How can you build cultural competence?

Diversity refers to the differences among people and among groups that people are a part of. As with culture, some differences are visible, such as gender, skin color, age, and physical characteristics; others are less visible but no less significant, such as education, marital and parental status, sexual orientation, socioeconomic status, and thinking and learning styles. Some differences, like religion, are visible in some situations (such as with people who dress or wear their hair a certain way in accordance with religious law), but not in others (such as with people whose religion has no visible identifier). It is the incredible diversity among people that makes understanding, tolerance, and competence necessary.

As all people do, you have your own personal diversity. This encompasses all of the visible elements of who you are in addition to invisible elements such as your personality traits, learning and working styles, natural talents, interests, and challenges.

When you with all your differences encounter others with all their differences, it takes cultural competence to interact effectively in order to achieve goals. Having *cultural competence* means understanding and appreciating the differences among people and adjusting behavior in ways that enhance relationships

Expand Your Perception of Culture

The ability to respond to people as individuals requires that you become more aware of the diversity of culture that is both visible and invisible. Start by looking at what is unique about you. Brainstorm ten words or phrases that describe you. Here's the challenge: Try to keep references to visible details (brunette, Arab-American, wheelchair-dependent, and so on) to a minimum, and fill the rest of the list with characteristics others can't see at first glance (easygoing, 25 years old, guitar player, marathoner, interpersonal learner, and so on).

1. _____

2. _____

3. _____

4. _____

5. _____

6. _____

7. _____

8. _____

9. _____

10. _____

    When you are done, pair up with someone else in your class, preferably a student you do not know well. List on a separate sheet of paper any characteristics know about him or her—chances are most of them will be visible. Then talk with the person. In your conversation, talk about what you've listed, and add to your list using what you discover as the conversation unfolds. Finally, answer two questions:

1. What stands out to you about what you learned about this classmate, and why?

_____

_____

2. What within your description of yourself would you like people to pay more attention to and value more, and why?

_____

_____

and communication. Keep in mind: *Developing cultural competence does not require you to go against your principles, and it does not mean that you have to agree with everyone.* The effort to understand and work with others should not result in changing who you are. In fact, your exploration of other cultures and ideas may reinforce your understanding of what you believe and why. It can also lead to an adjustment or enhancement of those beliefs from what you've learned.

Consider this story: A pizza addict who ate pizza nearly every single day took a trip to an area in India where no pizza was available. For two weeks, he ate the food cooked by the family with whom he stayed. Once back home, he was thrilled to eat pizza again, but also began to incorporate other foods into his diet, even coming up with an Indian-style pizza featuring saag paneer as a topping. Without giving up his love for pizza, he enhanced his diet, his health, and his flexibility by exploring another way to eat.

The National Center for Cultural Competence identifies five actions that make up cultural competence:[2]

1. Value diversity
2. Identify and evaluate personal perceptions and attitudes
3. Be aware of what happens when different cultures interact
4. Build knowledge about other cultures
5. Use learning to adapt to diverse cultures

By putting these five actions to work, you can have what you need to edit a memo with a co-worker, build a water purifier in the Sudan, create a presentation with a study group, make a personal decision with a parent, or accomplish any other goal that requires the efforts of more than one person.[3] See Key 10.3 for an example that shows the five stages of cultural competence.

Action 1: Value diversity

The first action—to value diversity—is to have both a respect for what is different among people and an understanding of what is valuable about those differences. This action takes you beyond the first level of cultural awareness, helps you surpass the second level, and puts you well on your way to reaching the third level.

Note that respecting and valuing others does not require that you like them or adopt their ideas as your own. You don't have to be someone's best friend to respect the person and value the diverse ideas he or she brings to a problem-solving or goal-setting process. Valuing diversity means accepting without judgment. Furthermore, it means seeing the benefits that diversity brings to a situation and embracing teamwork so that you can enjoy those benefits.

Action 2: Identify and evaluate personal perceptions and attitudes

As with cultural awareness, understanding others begins with examining yourself. The second action requires that you look carefully at your own feelings about others and how they may affect you and others. Many people may value the idea of diversity, but have problematic attitudes toward certain differences that get in the way of accomplish goals with diverse people. Usually these attitudes show up in the form of prejudices and stereotypes.

Prejudice

Defined as "a preconceived opinion formed without just grounds," prejudice is widespread. Almost all people prejudge others based on characteristics such as

BUILDING CULTURAL COMPETENCE

Jordan, a first-year college student, is put in a study group with three other students—a young female Muslim student who wears a head scarf, a woman in her late 40s, and a male student who is gay.

STAGE OF CULTURAL COMPETENCE		ONE PERSON'S EXPERIENCE
Valuing diversity		Anticipating that he might experience some challenges working with this group, Jordan makes an effort to give everyone an equal measure of respect at their first meeting. He works to listen actively to the different ideas presented and consider what is valuable about them.
Identifying and evaluating perceptions and attitudes		Outside of study group time, Jordan thinks over his perceptions and attitudes about age, religion, and sexual orientation. He identifies any prejudicial thinking or stereotypes, and evaluates them by comparing them against what he is learning about the individuals in his group.
Being aware of what happens when cultures interact		At weekly meetings, Jordan notices when interactions are affected by problematic attitudes. He tries to get the conversation back onto the coursework without insulting anyone.
Building knowledge		After one of the meetings, Jordan goes for a cup of coffee with the student who is older. He calls the student who is gay to go over information from class. Curious about Muslim traditions, about which he knows nothing, he reads information online.
Using learning to adapt		Jordan is consciously making different choices. He avoids references to jokes that may offend a gay person. He explains, rather than judging, when he makes reference to something that the older student may not be familiar with. He interacts with the Muslim student without physical contact, in an effort to respect her religious tradition.

religion, disability, gender, skin color, and so on. Factors that lead to prejudice include:

▶ **Family and cultural influence.** Ideas and attitudes are spread within families and cultural groups. If your parents have a prejudiced idea about a particular type of person, for example, you are likely to hold the same belief—at least until you are old enough to question it and think critically about it.

▶ **Experience.** One experience with a particular person can lead to a negative or incorrect judgment about other people from a similar background.

▶ **Ethnocentrism.** This human tendency to see one's own group or culture as superior leads naturally to judging other groups or cultures as inferior.

Stereotypes

A stereotype is defined as an assumption made without proof or critical thinking, about the characteristics of a person or group. What leads to stereotyping?

▶ **Looking for logic and understanding**. Human nature leads people to try to find easy ways to explain and categorize, resulting in stereotypical labels and generalizations. It is more complicated and time-consuming to understand each person individually than it is to categorize them using stereotypes.

▶ **Unfamiliarity**. Humans often respond to the unknown with fear. The labels that stereotyping provides can help to alleviate that fear by making the unknown seem known.

▶ **The media**. The more you see a stereotypical image on TV or in the movies, such as the funny overweight person or the nerdy intellectual, the more likely you are to believe that the stereotype is universally true.

Stereotypes hinder communication because they make it tough to connect. If someone has pasted an inaccurate, stereotypical label on you, you aren't likely to put effort into building a relationship with that person. Positive stereotypes, as complimentary as they may seem, can put just as much of a block on getting to know the real person underneath as a negative stereotype can. See Key 10.4 for some examples of positive and negative stereotypes.

Be aware that even if you have grown up in a family or atmosphere that works to reject prejudice and stereotypes, you are not immune to developing them. People commonly adopt stereotypes or develop prejudicial thinking in high school and young adulthood as they are figuring out where they fit into the social structure. As important as it is to belong to social groups, it is crucial to make sure those connections are not built on the shifting sands of prejudice.

Evaluating yourself

Everyone prejudges and stereotypes at one time or another. Investigating your perspectives and attitudes for prejudice and stereotyping requires you to ask yourself questions like these:

▶ When I see people with a certain characteristic (race, lifestyle, weight, and so on), what stereotypes come to mind? Are they accurate?
▶ How do I prejudge people based on personal characteristics? Is that fair?
▶ What prejudices or stereotypes do my family and friends believe or use? Do I share them?
▶ What harm can my prejudices and stereotypes cause?

Building your understanding of how you react to differences and cultures builds your cultural competence that much further. The next step is to examine and understand interactions among people of different cultures.

STEREOTYPES CAN BE POSITIVE OR NEGATIVE— AND INACCURATE EITHER WAY

POSITIVE STEREOTYPE	NEGATIVE STEREOTYPE
Women are caring and nurturing.	Women are not strong enough emotionally for tough business situations.
Latinos are family oriented.	Latinos are too focused on their families.
People with disabilities have strength of will.	People with disabilities are bitter.
Older people are wise.	Older people are set in their ways.
White men are successful in business.	White men are cold and power hungry.

Action 3: Be aware of what happens when cultures interact

As you know from the definition of culture, different cultures have different values and make different choices. Thinking about this, it makes sense that intercultural interaction often creates issues and conflict. If handled effectively, the differences among the cultures can be understood, discussed, and dealt with productively. However, even a quick look at history shows that this doesn't always happen, and that problems large and small can arise from a lack of mutual understanding and respect.

Intercultural conflict

On the "small" side, problems can be as simple as a disagreement between two parents based on the different values each grew up with (one prefers to spend only what cash is on hand, the other uses credit cards liberally). Any type of difference of opinion or misunderstanding between cultures can result in some level of conflict. The first tool necessary in working through this conflict is cultural awareness—understanding what the differences are and where they come from. The rest of the toolbox is filled with communication strategies, which appear later in this section.

Bigger issues

When problems that result from intercultural clashes escalate, discrimination and hate crimes can result.

■ **Discrimination.** Basically, *discrimination* happens when people act on negative feelings they have about a particular population. It can be defined as denying equal access to employment, educational, and housing opportunities or treating people as second-class citizens. Discrimination is against the law; according to federal statute, you cannot be denied basic opportunities and rights because of anything to do with your race, creed, color, age, gender, national or ethnic origin, religion, marital status, potential or actual pregnancy, or potential or actual illness or disability (unless the illness or disability prevents you from performing required tasks and unless accommodations are not possible).

■ **Hate crimes.** When someone acts violently toward a person out of hatred of a specific characteristic thought to be possessed by that person (usually race, ethnicity, or religious or sexual orientation), the act is labeled a *hate crime*. Because victims fearful of being targeted again may choose not to report incidents, statistics probably do not reflect the true number of hate crimes that occur.

With an awareness of what can happen, good and bad, the next step to cultural competence is to build knowledge.

Action 4: Build cultural knowledge

The modern world brings you into day-to-day contact with different people and cultures in a variety of ways—in person, through social networking or other communication technology, through the media, and through consumer activities (goods and services that you purchase). To make the most of these interactions, you have a responsibility to learn about those people and cultures. What can help?

▶ Read in order to learn about different perspectives—consult books, newspapers, magazines, and websites.

- Ask people questions, online or in person, about their traditions, values, and perspectives.
- Observe—with a nonjudgmental mind—how people dress, behave, eat, and interact with others.
- Nurture friendships with people you meet at home or in the academic arena who differ from you. Learn from the conversations and time you spend connecting with these people.
- Share your own culture with friends, fellow students, and coworkers.

Building cultural knowledge is not something finite that you can do and be "done" with. You will encounter people from different cultures throughout your life. Interacting successfully with people in and out of the workplace demands that cultural learning become a lifelong skill. Because people are always changing and growing from what they learn and experience, there is always something more to know about a person, even when you have known that person for many years.

Action 5: Adapt to diverse cultures

This last stage is where you put your cultural competence into action toward the goal of successful communication and teamwork. Here are some of the actions you can take:

▶ **Make the effort to get to know the whole person.** Look past external characteristics. Someone with a disability may also be a journalism major, a parent, a wrestling fan, a blogger.

▶ **Move beyond your assumptions and perspectives.** Notice how you think about people and cultures you encounter and whether prejudices and stereotypes come to mind. Acknowledge your thoughts, considering the potential harmful effects they could have on how you communicate. Then push past them to improve the chance that you will be able to interact productively.

▶ **Try out other perspectives.** If you can put yourself in other people's shoes, you are more likely to understand where they are coming from. Ask questions to build your understanding.

▶ **Adjust your behavior.** Changing how you behave in order to make someone from a different culture more comfortable shows respect and fosters communication. If someone needs more personal space, maintain a reasonable distance. If an online study partner dislikes strong language, avoid it when you interact.

▶ **Address language barriers.** Choose your language carefully when speaking to people in a language they don't know well, just as you would expect them to do for you if the tables were turned. Ask and answer questions to make sure you are getting your point across. Fill in with body language where spoken language isn't getting the job done.

▶ **Fight discrimination, prejudice, and hate.** The first line of defense is to make sure that you don't participate yourself. After that, if you witness these negative actions, find safe ways to get help and to get things moving in a more positive direction. Show your support for organizations that promote tolerance.

▶ **Focus on your common ground.** Everyone, everywhere, has the same basic needs. Every human being hopes, fears, loves, and thinks. Keep in mind that you are united with all people through your essential humanity.

The most crucial area in which to use your cultural competence is in communication. How well you can navigate cross-cultural communication can make or break your success in anything that requires interaction with other humans, whether in person or through technology.

The cultural components of communication

Culture expresses itself in every aspect of communication—what you say, how you say it, to whom you say it, when you say it, and in what setting you say it. To understand the effects of culture on communication at a more detailed level, consider these ten cultural components of communication. Key 10.5 shows how some of these components might operate in two contrasting cultures.

■ *Age* Depending on age, people have different expectations of the level of formality in communication. In some cultures, older people command a great deal of respect and are addressed formally. Age also affects how you are perceived as a communicator. When you are communicating with people your own age, you may get a different reaction than when you are communicating with people older or younger than you are.

■ *Gender* Although gender equality has been a focus in the United States for some time, many cultures have strongly defined gender roles. Some cultures, for example, forbid men and women to interact in public and have rules about how men, women, or both should dress.

■ *Family* Family has a different level of value in different cultures. In some cultures, family is so important that it is crucial to ask about a person's family when you come into contact with that person. For other cultures, personal questions may be perceived as intrusive.

■ *Religion* Different cultures have different levels of religious practice, and how much value is placed on religion affects how people communicate. When religion is not a priority, it has little effect on communication. However, as with certain cultures where religion permeates all aspects of home and work, it informs factors such as when you do and do not conduct business, what you wear, and what you eat.

■ *Language fluency* When communicating with others, you need to be aware of their level of fluency in your language. Those who understand you easily will not need many accommodations. With others, it may be necessary to slow down and to avoid slang or idioms that may not be familiar to non-native speakers. In particular, *idioms*—phrases whose meaning is not predictable from their elements—can be problematic for non-native speakers, because it is easy to take them literally. See Key 10.6 (p. 17) for examples.

■ *Greeting behavior* Good greeting behavior strongly influences that important first impression. Should you shake hands, hug, kiss, bow? Bring a gift or take off your shoes when visiting a home? Remember that people generally take about 30 seconds to make up their minds about someone they've met, so choose how you use your time carefully.

■ *Business and public behavior* With what title should you address people in a work setting, and how should you greet them? Should you look them in the eye, or is it more respectful not to? Should you get right down to business or make small talk first about personal matters? Observe and consider culture as you make these decisions.

■ *Eating behavior* What do people of a particular culture eat or not eat? How do they eat—with their hands, one hand, utensils? Some religious cultural practices forbid the eating of certain meats or all meat, the mixing of certain foods, or the consumption of certain foods on particular days. Even if you do not belong to the culture, breaking cultural eating rules in front of those who belong to that culture can be disturbing or insulting to them.

■ *Personal space* Different cultures have different levels of *personal space*—in other words, how close you can stand next to someone without making them

COMPONENTS OF COMMUNICATION
VARY FROM CULTURE TO CULTURE[4]

	NORTHEASTERN UNITED STATES	SAUDI ARABIA
Gender	No restrictions on what men and women wear or how they interact.	Socializing is usually same-sex. Most men wear long white garments that fall below the knee, and in public women must cover all but the face, hands, and feet.
Family	Extended families often separate when work goals or personal needs lead individual family members to move.	Extended families tend to be close and family responsibilities are a high priority.
Religion	No official connection between the state and any one religion. Individuals follow a variety of religious traditions. Most religious activities happen on weekends.	All Saudis practice Islam and are obligated to pray five times a day. All businesses close on Fridays (the Muslim holy day).
Greeting and public behavior	Men and women shake hands or, if they are more familiar with one another, may hug or kiss.	Unrelated men and women do not greet one another in public.
Eating behavior	Very few rules about eating. Behavior depends on the food consumed and the location. People talk while eating.	People eat with the right hand. Meals are often served family-style and on the floor. Although socializing happens before the meal, not much conversation takes place while eating.
Personal space	Varies with the person, but moderate personal space is generally needed.	People tend to stand very close when talking (not much personal space needed).
Business behavior $\$ \, €$ $¥ \, £$	Businesspeople tend to restrict relationship building to a brief exchange of pleasantries before focusing on the task at hand.	Businesspeople tend to go through a lot of relationship-building conversation about family and health before moving to business topics.

KNOW IT

How Can I Become More Culturally Competent?

In each of the five areas of cultural competence, you will first give yourself a "score," consisting of the total of three questions for each area (a score of 12–15 indicates you perceive you are highly developed; 7 to 11 moderately developed; and 3 to 6 minimally developed). Then, analyze how you want to develop in each area, coming up with an action to which you can commit in the next six months.

ANALYZE YOUR LEVEL OF DEVELOPMENT

Please rate your development in each area from one to five, with 1 being "not developed" to 5 being "highly developed":

AREA OF CULTURAL COMPETENCE	QUESTION	SCORE				
Value diversity	I see the value of human diversity and of being exposed to different ideas and perspectives.	1	2	3	4	5
Value diversity	I go beyond tolerance in order to accept diversity.	1	2	3	4	5
Value diversity	I actively pursue teamwork and friendship with people who differ from me.	1	2	3	4	5
Identify perceptions	I can identify and evaluate my personal perceptions and attitudes.	1	2	3	4	5
Identify perceptions	I notice the personal perceptions and attitudes in others.	1	2	3	4	5
Identify perceptions	I address prejudice and stereotypes in my own thinking.	1	2	3	4	5
Be aware of interactions	I am aware of what can happen, both positive and negative, when cultures interact.	1	2	3	4	5
Be aware of interactions	I work to make sure my thoughts and actions do not contribute to discrimination.	1	2	3	4	5
Be aware of interactions	When interactions involve conflict, I try to help resolve them calmly and productively.	1	2	3	4	5
Build knowledge	I am well-informed about my own culture.	1	2	3	4	5
Build knowledge	I know a fair amount about cultures other than my own.	1	2	3	4	5
Build knowledge	With an understanding that there is always more to know, I read and ask questions to continue to learn about other cultures.	1	2	3	4	5
Adapt to cultures	I put myself in other people's shoes.	1	2	3	4	5
Adapt to cultures	I look past external characteristics and try to get to know the real person underneath.	1	2	3	4	5
Adapt to cultures	I am committed to helping and working with others no matter how different they may be from me.	1	2	3	4	5

1. Value diversity. Your score: _____

2. Identify perceptions. Your score: _____

3. Be aware of interactions. Your score: _____

4. Build knowledge. Your score: _____

5. Adapt to cultures. Your score: _____

PLAN TO BUILD CULTURAL COMPETENCE

Look at the two areas that you want most to develop. For each, determine a helpful action that you could take in the next six months. For example, if you wanted to know more about other cultures, you could find a particular novel to read or friend to get to know better; if you wanted to adapt more effectively, you could determine a way that you could help others in your community who differ from you culturally.

Cultural competence area: _____

Specific action I will take and my reason why: _____

_____

_____

Cultural competence area: _____

Specific action I will take and my reason why: _____

_____

_____

TAKE ACTION

Choose one plan that you will put into action at some point within the next 30 days. Think carefully and select the one that is most do-able for you right now. In the space below, describe the goal of your action as well as the specifics of what you will do and how you will do it.

_____

_____

_____

_____

uncomfortable. Some people are comfortable standing or sitting close together, whereas for others, this is undesirable or even forbidden depending on the gender of the people involved.

■ *Perception of time* Consider how important punctuality is to the culture of the person with whom you are interacting. In some cultures, being on time is important, and chronic lateness is considered disrespectful. In others, there is no value judgment placed on being a few minutes or even up to an hour late, and lateness is therefore common and even expected.

As you approach any situation where you are communicating in person—or even through technology—with another person, consider these cultural components as you make decisions about when, where, and how to communicate. Whether you are able to pay attention to these details will determine how successful your interaction will be.

CHOOSE THE CLEAREST POSSIBLE WORD OR PHRASE

SLANG OR IDIOM	THE CLEARER ALTERNATIVE
Let's chill out.	Let's stop working and relax for a few minutes.
Dicey	Questionable, unsure
You are off the hook.	You are not responsible for that task.
Lame	Ineffective, inadequate
I'm down with that.	That is fine with me.

Barriers to intercultural communication

Communicating across cultural lines is often a challenge, and several types of barriers tend to get in the way. Here they are, with information about how to address them.

■ *Ethnocentrism* This "my way or the highway" attitude—the belief that your own culture is superior to all others and that the beliefs and values held by that culture are correct—automatically demeans anyone outside that culture. Ethnocentrism practically guarantees anger and misunderstanding on a person-to-person level. Furthermore, it causes challenging conflicts at an institutional or national level. Dangerous and destructive things tend to happen when one culture or country decides that its way of doing things is superior to that of all other cultures or countries.

▶ *Jump this barrier:* First, understand that no culture is superior to another. Even if some ways of thinking and acting work better for you, it does not mean that they are universally better for all people. Whatever culture you identify with, refrain from putting its attitudes and practices ahead of those of other cultures. Furthermore, remember that the United States is not the center of the universe. It is simply one country among many, and its attitudes, primary language, and behaviors are not the only acceptable ones in the world. Finally, learn about other ways of thinking, being, and doing. The more you know, the less ethnocentric you are likely to be.

■ *Assumptions and stereotypes* An assumption is defined as a judgment, generalization, or bias influenced by experience and values. A student whose study partner fails to show up for work sessions, for example, might assume that all students from the same race, gender, ethnic group, etc. are irresponsible. However, the assumption would be dead wrong. Even though everyone makes assumptions from time to time, they have a negative impact on how people perceive others and therefore on relationships and communication. Assumptions are often born out of stereotypes. If you know a stereotype about a particular culture, you are more likely to assume that everyone from the culture fits the stereotype.

▶ *Jump this barrier:* Be aware of your thoughts when you encounter someone from another culture. Observe what assumptions come to mind and set those thoughts aside. Work to get to know each individual without resorting to stereotypes.

Did You **Know?**

Only 9 percent of Americans speak a second language, and only 23 percent have a passport.[5]

■ *Language differences* This may be the most obvious barrier to successful communication. If two people are trying to communicate but do not speak the same language, they will have trouble understanding each other. Most Americans expect everyone to speak English and do not speak a second language themselves. Nonnative English speakers may be fluent in the language but not comfortable with slang or dialects, or they might be in the process of learning English. People tend to make the mistake of speaking loudly or talking down, as to a child, when communicating with someone who does not speak their language well. This feels demeaning and reinforces the barrier that already exists.

▶ *Jump this barrier*: Here are tips for communicating across a language barrier.

- Speak clearly, avoiding slang, contractions, and "filler words" such as "um," "you know," and "like."
- Repeat important points and give clear examples
- Use appropriate body language
- Use straightforward language and avoid slang
- Avoid speaking loudly or using a parental tone
- Never assume you have been understood—ask for feedback so that you can determine whether you were heard correctly
- Be patient and respectful, especially when a person is struggling to get a point across
- Choose your format of communication carefully—although in-person communication can be better for building rapport, e-mail and written communication make details and specifics clear and accessible[6]

■ *Closed-mindedness* Having a closed mind—in other words, not being open to different perspectives and choices—is related to ethnocentrism. When you believe that your culture is best, you aren't likely to open your mind to consider other cultures. Closed-mindedness basically short-circuits communication with people from any culture other than your own. Without a willingness to understand and accept other cultures, you can't respectfully exchange ideas with anyone from those cultures. You are less likely to make new friends, eat new foods, and seek out new experiences—and the boundaries you set up around yourself can sharply limit your potential.

▶ *Jump this barrier:* Choose to open your mind to new ideas and experiences. Depending on the person, this is easier said than done. One way to push yourself in the direction of open-mindedness is to put an unfamiliar experience on your schedule—a restaurant, arts performance, book, visit to the home of someone from a different culture, and so on. Exposure to differences tends to open your mind bit by bit.

■ *Lack of knowledge* If you don't know about a culture, you have no understanding of its values and customs. This causes conflict in relationships because it can result in your unknowingly behaving in disrespectful ways. If an American woman tries to shake hands with a man from a culture where men and women don't make contact in public, for example, she will be embarrassed at the least, and at the worst may shut down the interaction.

▶ *Jump this barrier:* The cure is education. Be informed. If you do something that makes a bad impression on someone from another culture, politely ask for information on the acceptable way to behave, and keep it in mind for next time so you don't repeat your mistake. If you know you will encounter people from a particular culture either at school, at work, or while traveling for business or pleasure, read up on how to dress, greet people, and behave in public—and what to avoid doing or saying.

■ *Fear* It is human to fear people and ideas that are unfamiliar to you. It is also problematic. Fear of differences can make you uncomfortable around others, leading you to avoid interacting with them. Without spending time with people, respectfully hearing what they have to say, and understanding their point of view, inaccurate judgments and prejudices arise, making it impossible to communicate or work together successfully. Think of it this way: trying to listen to someone through your fear is like trying to have a meaningful conversation with loud music blaring. Emotions can block comprehension just as loud music makes it tough to hear.

▶ *Jump this barrier:* The main antidotes to fear are education and experience. As you learn more about different people, you become more aware of your common humanity. As you log positive experiences with different people, you become more comfortable with them, and your fear lessens over time. Think, too, about what others have feared about you. Have you ever been the "different" one wanting to be understood and accepted? How did it make you feel? Even if you have never been that in position, try putting yourself in someone else's shoes so that you can understand more about how it feels and the effect it has on human interaction.

In the modern world, people cross real and virtual paths with individuals from other cultures more and more every day. With the cultural awareness and competence you have explored, you will be as prepared as possible to receive your passport as a global citizen.

What is global citizenship?

A message sent over digital phone systems, e-mail, or Facebook goes from Singapore to Germany in seconds, or even milliseconds. A work team made up of people living in New York, Ohio, Arizona, and California has meetings over the phone and on Skype and accomplishes its goals much as it would if team members worked in adjacent cubicles in one office building. Businesses based in one country hire and manage employees who live and work in other countries and time zones. These changes and others like them have forged new connections among people from around the globe, and have led to the idea that everyone in the world is a member of a *global community*.

Defining community

First, before we discuss that definition any further, we need to take it a step further back and define the word *community*.

Community, noun.
   1. A social group of any size whose members reside in a specific locality, share government, and often have a common cultural and historical heritage.
   2. A social, religious, occupational, or other group sharing common characteristics or interests and perceived or perceiving itself as distinct in some respect from the larger society within which it exists.[7]

So community can be defined by geography and shared citizenship and heritage, or it can be created based on any set of shared characteristics or interests. Examples of communities range widely and include:

- ▶ Competitive skateboarders
- ▶ Residents of Tokyo, Japan
- ▶ Seasonal workers who travel from Mexico to the United States to bring in crops
- ▶ Transgendered individuals
- ▶ Parents of multiples
- ▶ Converts to Buddhism
- ▶ Members of the NRA
- ▶ Students at Essex County Community College in New Jersey
- ▶ Attendees at the Mormon Tabernacle in Washington, DC

You get the picture—the number and types of communities are nearly endless. Additionally, there is no rule restricting how many communities you can belong to. Each individual has a myriad of personal characteristics, values, and beliefs, and those can lead to any number of communities. Take a look at Key 10.7 to see a visual representation of the communities of just one person.

What links people together as members of a community? The definition illustrates that two primary factors are at work:

- ▶ Interaction
- ▶ Shared interests

Over most of human history, up until a few hundred years ago, the primary factor determining whether people were able to interact and build

Key 10.7   PEOPLE ARE MEMBERS OF **MANY COMMUNITIES**

communities was geography. Without fast transportation methods or modes of sending communication, people primarily interacted with and formed communities with those who lived nearby. This gradually changed with the development of motorized transportation and communication by mail, telegraph, and telephone.

However, even those momentous changes have been dwarfed by the technological advancements of the last thirty years. Now you can interact with people all over the globe, any time of day or night, using methods that transport your communication in the blink of an eye. You can even speak face-to-face with people anywhere in the world using technology, without having to physically travel to where they are. Things have come a long way from the nearly ten-day trip made on the first run by the Pony Express, in 1860, to bring mail to California from the midwest.

Even fifty years ago, you were unlikely to feel a sense of community with anyone outside of your family, town, and workplace. Now, being able to interact with and do business with people all over the globe has pulled people together, allowing them to build all kinds of new communities—and giving every person a new status as members of the *global community*.

The global community

Exactly who or what is a member of the global community? An organization called Global Community Earth Government offers one broad definition of the term:

> "The Global Community is defined as being all that exists or occurs at any location at any time between the Ozone layer above and the core of the planet below."

By this definition, everything that lives in the air, on the earth, and below the earth's surface is part of the global community, and all of these living things are connected one to the other.[8]

Interaction within a community of any type or size creates a cause-and-effect relationship among community members. When you come into contact with someone or something in your day-to-day life, your actions have an effect—positive or negative—on them, and vice-versa. Throwing cell phone batteries into the trash instead of recycling them, for example, can put the batteries into a landfill where acids can leak out and cause damage to plant and animal life in the area, potentially leaching into your food supply (negative effect). Making sure your sidewalk is shoveled after a heavy snow storm helps children who pass by your house on their way to school walk more safely, and keeps you from being subject to fines or even a lawsuit (positive effect).

This cause-and-effect relationship is as true for individuals as it is for larger entities such as colleges, businesses, and countries. For example, a U.S. food company that relies on shipments of rice from India will be affected by the weather in India where the rice is grown, the health and welfare of the people who cultivate the rice, and the work ethic of the people who pack and transport the rice overseas.

Being a global citizen

To define global citizenship, we first offer a definition of citizenship.

> *Citizenship,* noun: Having the rights, privileges, and duties associated with membership in a particular society or community.

It is key to note the two sides of citizenship:

1. What you *receive*, that is, rights and privileges
2. What you *give*, that is, duties and obligations to others

Global citizenship, therefore, is being a member of the global community, and having both the benefits (rights and privileges) and the obligations (duties) that come with that membership. Inherent in this definition is the idea that global citizens should choose actions with awareness of the needs of others and appreciation of how those actions might affect others in the world. What are some examples of ways that your everyday actions might have a positive effect on others in the global community?

▶ Using your own shopping bags and water bottles means fewer plastic bags and bottles in landfills, rivers, and oceans all over the world, resulting in less money spent on cleanup and greater survival of marine life.
▶ Purchasing food from nearby growers invests in your local community and means less fuel is burned transporting food from far away.
▶ Tutoring a foreign student in English improves his chances for success at school and at work, making it more likely that he will earn a steady income, which can in turn improve the lives of his family members and give them better chances to achieve their goals.
▶ Donating to an organization working to prevent HIV infection in southern Africa helps to improve the health of citizens there, allowing those countries to allocate more resources for the growth and development of industry and education rather than the care of citizens with AIDS.

This is just the tip of the iceberg. You can trace nearly any action of yours back many steps and find the effects it has, good and bad, on people and environments near and far. Each person's actions have consequences that ripple across the globe.

The scope of global citizenship goes beyond individual people. Each school, company, organization, and nation can be seen as a global citizen, enjoying the privileges of the global community while being obligated to consider the needs of other people, schools, companies, organizations, and nations when choosing actions.

How can I take action as a global citizen?

First of all, know this: you *are* a global citizen. Your citizenship comes by virtue of living in the modern world, even if you have never set foot outside of one of the fifty states. As a global citizen, you have rights and privileges as well as obligations and duties, as Key 10.8 illustrates.

Note: The rights and priviliges of a global citizen are the basic rights of every human being, as set out in the United Nations' Universal Declaration of Human Rights.[9]

Every duty or obligation can have a positive effect. One statement that puts all of these obligations in a nutshell is to say that as a member of the global community, you have a responsibility to make things better—or, at the very least, not to make things worse.

BEING A GLOBAL CITIZEN
CARRIES BOTH RIGHTS AND OBLIGATIONS

RIGHTS AND PRIVILEGES INCLUDE...	DUTIES AND OBLIGATIONS INCLUDE...
Life, liberty, and security	To protect the rights of other members of the global community
Status as a person before the law	To consider the needs of others when making decisions
Freedom of movement within and without one's own country	To act in ways that do not harm others
Freedom of opinion and expression	To choose actions that have a positive effect on other members
Freedom of peaceful assembly and association	To choose actions that protect the environment
Freedom to work and to rest	To respect other members of the global community
Education	To build multicultural knowledge

With every action, you have a choice. It is human, and has been common, to make choices with one's own needs as the primary consideration. However, that narrow of a focus is becoming more and more problematic as the connections among all living things grow stronger and more defined. Although global citizens should not ignore their own needs, they should broaden their decision-making processes to consider the needs of others in the global community. The benefit of this consideration will be shared across the board. Here are two factors that strongly influence your decision-making process.

▶ **Personal values**. Often, values set off the chain of events leading to the effects—positive or negative—that a person has on the environment, because values guide everyday behavior. Think about what values anchor your daily life and how you can extend them into active global citizenship. If you grew up helping your parents give unused clothing and household items to local charitable organizations, for example, you became aware of the needs of others. This may have led to your doing the same thing as an adult, and perhaps extending the value with bigger actions like organizing a shoe collection for a town in Africa or a clothing drive for a midwestern town ravaged by a tornado.

▶ **Cultural awareness**. Look back to the section on becoming more culturally aware. With an awareness of the different people in and out of your immediate communities and how your actions affect them, you will be more able to make decisions that give you what you need while not harming, and possibly even helping, others. For example, there are many ways to dispose of your trash that accomplish the goal of getting rid of waste in your environment. However, each way may have a different set of effects on the people and environment around you. Thinking through those effects can lead to a decision that gets you what you need while having a positive effect on others.

Global communication strategies

The success of any community, from local to global, depends largely on the ability of its citizens to communicate. What you already know about the cultural components of communication and jumping barriers to intercultural communication will help you decide how to speak, write, and act in ways that will help you connect effectively. Here are a few additional guidelines about how to communicate with, and respect, your fellow global citizens.

Become familiar with the primary language spoken

If you learn some useful words and phrases from another language and put them to work when talking with someone for whom it is a primary language, you show that you are interested in another culture and willing to meet others halfway. Pay attention, though, to how your efforts are received. Although many people may feel positive and grateful, some may not appreciate your efforts, and in those cases you may be better off sticking to straightforward conversation in your native tongue.

Listen actively

When speaking in person to a nonnative English speaker, the person may be using different words, putting words together in ways unfamiliar to you, or speaking with an accent. Listen carefully, letting the person finish the entire message, and ask for clarification if you need it. With focus and attention, you should be able to figure out what the speaker means. Even with a native English speaker who comes from a culture different from yours, you need the same active listening skills. Regional dialects and slang, different perspectives, or different generations have strong effects on word choice and communication style.

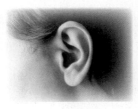

Unlock curiosity

The world is full of extraordinary diversity of people, places, and things. Take the time to learn about some of them. Take elective courses in areas such as sociology, religion, and history that focus on other cultures. Read books, watch movies and television, and explore the Internet. Information about other cultures comes in all kinds of packages, from a movie like *Shine* (showing life with a disability) to a television show like *No Reservations*, featuring chef Anthony Bourdain's international adventures with food and culture.

Keep written messages simple

When communicating on paper or using electronic means, stay clear and simple using these tips:

- ▶ Use correct and complete punctuation and capitalization
- ▶ Avoid texting shortcuts and acronyms
- ▶ Use clear language, and keep sentences and paragraphs concise
- ▶ Avoid contractions (can't, won't) in favor of full-length words or phrases (cannot, will not)
- ▶ Use correct salutations (to investigate the salutations that are appropriate for different cultures, explore websites such as Executive Planet)
- ▶ Be clear with dates and numbers—for example, Europeans use a day-month-year order when they write dates, rather than the month-day-year order used by most Americans

Use technology safely

Now that messages, photographs, and videos can be sent around the world in the blink of an eye, it is crucial that you keep control of what you generate and where it goes. Follow these safety tips:

WRITE IT

Personal Journal and Real-Life Writing

Record your thoughts on a separate piece of paper, in a journal, or electronically

CONSIDER PREJUDICE AND STEREOTYPES

As human as it is to prejudge and stereotype, so it is possible to set these tendencies aside. Describe an experience of holding a prejudiced or stereotypical thought that was proven wrong. What did you think? What effects did it have on you and on others? What happened to prove your perspective inaccurate? Discuss what you have learned from the experience and how it informs your day-to-day life now. Finally, if anyone has had a thought about you that was wrong, describe the situation. What did the person think? How did it make you feel? What other effects did it have?

GLOBAL CITIZENSHIP IN YOUR CAREER

You are likely to have thought about your career in terms of what it can do for you, and depending on the career area, you may also have thought about what it can do for others (deliver products, provide services, and so on). However, you might not have thought about how you could act as a global citizen in the context of your career or how a company in your career area might take on global citizenship. Choose someone who can give you perspective on your chosen career area, like an instructor or professional with whom you have contact. Draft a polite inquiry to this person, asking for information about how you can be a responsible global citizen in this career. Ask about particular jobs for which you can look, individual companies that are focused on making a difference, and actions that you can take on the job no matter where you work.

Send your letter over e-mail or regular mail. If you receive a response, keep it in mind as you make decisions about how you will pursue your career.

▶ Protect your e-mail and social networking accounts with strong passwords (use seven or more characters and mix numbers and letters).

▶ When communicating in an educational or professional setting, use e-mail and social networking account names that identify you clearly and neutrally (note: even if a playful e-mail address doesn't seem problematic to you, it might be offensive to a colleague from another country for reasons you are not aware of).

▶ Use discretion when sending photographs. Once a digital image is out of your hands, it can be sent to anyone. Furthermore, images sent from a cell phone have GPS labels showing their origin. Here's one rule of thumb: Don't send any photograph you wouldn't want your mother, your instructor, and your boss at work to see.

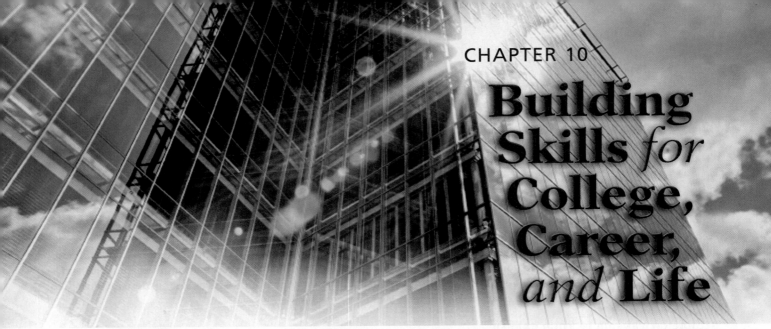

Building Skills *for* College, Career, *and* Life

Steps to Success

Act as a Responsible Citizen of Your Communities

First, on a separate sheet of paper or computer file, brainstorm a list of communities to which you belong. Don't limit yourself—look at your values, your activities, and the cultures with which you identify, and write down as many as you can think of that apply to you. This includes but is not limited to your family, cultural, neighborhood, religious, spiritual, educational, organizational, and social communities.

Next, if there are any ways in which you have already helped any of these communities through volunteer service, service-learning, internship, or employment, list them.

Finally, plan to carry out your obligation as a local and global citizen—to *make things better in some way*—in two different communities from your list. Choose one that is small and close to home and one that has a larger reach. You may plan to continue service you have performed in the past, or you may decide to do something totally new.

My close community (examples include your family, work team, a group of students from a course you take):

_____

A goal for an improvement I can make:

_____

_____

_____

A group that needs help within the larger community (examples include the town where you live, your institution, the company where you work, a business or organization):

_____

A goal for an improvement I can make:

_____

_____

_____

1. A specific action or set of actions
2. A date on which, or by which, you intend to accomplish action(s)
3. A person who you can partner with to check on you to make sure you have taken action
4. A list of potential issues requiring cultural awareness and competence that could arise from this experience (differences in values or ethics, gender roles, family interactions, and so on)

Here is an example:

Goal: To donate business clothing to Dress for Success, an organization that provides professional attire and support to women who need extra help as they seek employment.

1. **Actions:** First, sort through my own wardrobe to see what I can donate. Next, e-mail my networks—friends, fellow students, family—to see if anyone else has clothing, and have them give it to me. Then, contact the local Dress for Success chapter and set up a delivery date. Finally, deliver clothing.
2. **Dates:** Sort through wardrobe and contact others by the end of this week. Contact Dress for Success the next week. Finalize the clothing donation by the end of the month. First week of next month, deliver clothing.
3. **Partner:** My best friend. I will have her put all of my due dates on her electronic calendar and tell her to text me every time one is coming up to see how I'm doing.
4. **Potential cultural issues:** Have to think carefully about what we donate. Some clothing may not be considered appropriate by women of other cultures, and they would not be able to use it. Or, if employers of other cultures didn't approve of the clothing, that would hinder a woman's chance of getting a job.

Now make these improvements happen. Write down your goals and the actions in a calendar on the date that you've set. Communicate with the person who will check on you about your plans. Then take action. Finally—and importantly—evaluate the experience afterward and consider how to carry your efforts forward so that this is not just a one-time "flash in the pan." Did you accomplish your goals? How did you feel? Would you take action again in a similar way? Would you do something different? How will you continue to make a difference in the future?

Writing

Build Intrapersonal and Communication Skills

Record your thoughts on paper, in a journal, or electronically.

EMOTIONAL INTELLIGENCE JOURNAL

Your experience with prejudice. Have you ever been discriminated against or experienced any other type of prejudice? Have you been on the other end and acted with prejudice yourself? Describe what happened and your feelings about the situation (if you have no personal experience, describe a situation you have seen or heard about). Outline an emotionally intelligent response that you feel would bring something positive or helpful out of the situation.

REAL-LIFE WRITING

Improve communication. Few students make use of the wealth of ideas and experience that academic advisors can offer. Think of a question you have—regarding a specific course, major, or academic situation—that your advisor might help you answer. Craft an e-mail in appropriate language to your advisor, and send it. Then, to stretch your communication skills, rewrite the same e-mail twice more: once in a format you would send to an instructor and once in a format appropriate for a friend. Send either or both of these if you think the response would be valuable to you.

Personal Portfolio

Prepare for Career Success

WRITE A JOB INTERVIEW COVER LETTER

21st Century Learning Building Blocks

- Communication and Collaboration
- Financial, Economic, Business, and Entrepreneurial Literacy
- Leadership and Responsibility

Complete the following in your electronic portfolio or on separate sheets of paper.

To secure a job interview, you will have to put your communication skills to the test—on paper—by creating a cover letter to accompany your resumé. With this key communication tool, you can pull your best selling points out of your resumé and highlight them to a potential employer.

For your portfolio, write a one-page, three-paragraph cover letter to a prospective employer, describing your background and explaining your value to the company. Be creative—you may use fictitious names, but select a career and industry that interest you. Use the format shown in Key 10.9.

Introductory paragraph: Start with a statement that convinces the employer to read on. You might name a person the employer knows who told you to write or refer to something positive about the company that you read in the newspaper or on the Internet. Identify the position for which you are applying, and tell the employer that you are interested in working for the company.

Middle paragraph: Sell your value. Try to convince the employer that hiring you will help the company in some way. Center your "sales effort" on your experience in school and the workplace. If possible, tie your qualifications to the needs of the company. Refer indirectly to your enclosed resumé.

Final paragraph: Close with a call to action. Ask the employer to call you, or tell the employer to expect your call to arrange an interview.

Exchange your first draft with a classmate. Read each other's letter and make marginal notes to improve impact and persuasiveness, writing style, grammar, punctuation, and spelling. Discuss and then make corrections. Create a final draft for your portfolio.

Social Networking

FILL OUT YOUR PROFILE

LinkedIn helps you see how much of your profile you have completed. Use the information it gives you to make your profile even more complete—and therefore more useful. Plus the closer you get to your goal (completing the profile), the less stress!

- Sign in to your account and click on "Profile."
- Look at the bar on the right side of the screen that shows "profile completeness." Note your percentage.
- Below that, read the list of "Profile Completion Tips" that it recommends.
- Click on "Why do this?" to get an even better idea of how the site can help you.
- Finally, act on LinkedIn's recommendations to increase your profile completeness percentage. With the knowledge that a higher percentage may help you grow your network more effectively, aim to hit 75 percent or higher.

First name Last name
1234 Your Street
City, ST 12345

November 1, 2008

Ms. Prospective Employer
Prospective Company
5432 Their Street
City, ST 54321

Dear Ms. Employer:

On the advice of Mr. X, career center advisor at Y College, I am writing to inquire about the position
of production assistant at KWKW Radio. I read the description of the job and your company on the
career center's employment-opportunity bulletin board, and I would like to apply for the position.

I am a senior at Y College and will graduate this spring with a degree in communications. Since my
junior year when I declared my major, I have wanted to pursue a career in radio. For the last year I
have worked as a production intern at KCOL Radio, the college's station, and have occasionally filled
in as a disc jockey on the evening news show. I enjoy being on the air, but my primary interest is
production and programming. My enclosed resumé will tell you more about my background and
experience.

I would be pleased to talk with you in person about the position. You can reach me anytime at
555/555–5555 or by e-mail at xxxx@xx.com. Thank you for your consideration, and I look forward to
meeting you.

Sincerely,

Sign Your Name Here

First name Last name

Enclosure(s) *(use this notation if you have included a resumé or other item with your letter)*

1. Stephanie Quappe and Giovanna Cantatore, "What is cultural awareness, anyway? How do I build it?" November 2, 2007, www.culturosity.com/articles/whatisculturalawareness.htm.

2. National Center for Cultural Competence, "Conceptual Frameworks/Models, Guiding Values and Principles," 2002, http://gucchd.georgetown.edu//nccc/framework.html.

3. Information in the sections on the five stages of building competency is based on Mark. A. King, Anthony Sims, and David Osher, "How Is Cultural Competence Integrated in Education?" Cultural Competence, http://cecp.air.org/cultural/Q_integrated.htm.

4. Kwintessential, "Saudi Arabia: Language, Culture, Customs, and Etiquette," http://www.kwintessential.co.uk/resources/global-etiquette/saudi-arabia-country-profile.html.

5. http://globalcitizenyear.org/2011/04/gcy-featured-in-the-christian-science-monitor/

6. Kate Berardo, "10 Strategies for Overcoming Language Barriers," 2007, www.culturosity.com/pdfs/10%20Strategies%20for%20Overcoming%20Language%20Barriers.pdf.

7. Dictionary.com Unabridged based on the Random House Dictionary, "Community," 2011, http://dictionary.reference.com/browse/community.

8. Global Community WebNet Ltd, "The Global Community Concept and the Global Governments Federation," February 6, 2006, http://globalcommunitywebnet.com/gceg/Act2006.htm#chapter4draft.

9. General Assembly of the United Nations, "Universal Declaration of Human Rights," December 10, 1948, www.un.org/en/documents/udhr/index.shtml.

10. Steve Connor, "Forty Years Since the First Picture of Earth from Space," January 10, 2009, www.independent.co.uk/news/science/forty-years-since-the-first-picture-of-earth-from-space-1297569.html.

11. Jason Ables and the Foundation for Global Community, "The Wombat," 2005, www.globalcommunity.org/flash/wombat.shtml.

12. National Institute for Environmental Health Sciences, "Reduce, Reuse and Recycle," October 28, 2010, http://kids.niehs.nih.gov/recycle.htm.

13. http://blog.communicaid.com/cross-_cultural-training/measuring-the-benefits-of-cross-cultural-awareness-training/

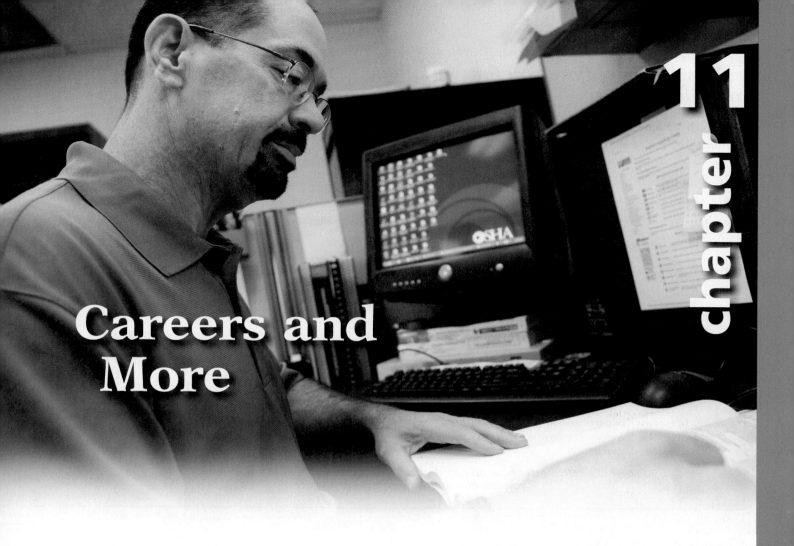

Careers and More

*a*fter being laid off from a job he held for more than 12 years, Marc Greenfield applied for numerous jobs in occupational safety and health. He was turned down many times and was told by employers that they felt more confident hiring a person with the degree, even if Greenfield had more experience than that candidate.

The former risk management worker decided to make a crucial career decision: He would get an occupational safety and health degree. After researching schools online, Greenfield chose CSU.

Greenfield said he was attracted to the online university's self-paced, flexible class schedules and competitive tuition rates.

"It was very convenient for me. I was able to complete my classwork according to my schedule. I was working as much as 62 hours a week when I first started at CSU," he explained.

"Going to traditional classes would have been impossible for me."

He was further pleased with the 10 percent tuition discount he received via the CSU Learning Partnership Program and the textbooks at no cost grant. "No other school offered that," he added.

Shortly before Greenfield graduated from CSU, he was hired by the Occupational Safety and Health Administration. "I believe the fact that I was going to graduate soon with a degree in OSH helped me get hired."

And now he is very happy with job and the benefits of attending CSU. "The most important thing that I am most thankful to CSU for is that it helped me to get hired into the best and most satisfying job I have had in my adult life," Greenfield said.

STATUS *Check*

▶ *How prepared are you for workplace and life success?*

For each statement, circle the number that feels right to you, from 1 for "not at all true for me" to 5 for "very true for me."

▶ I have thought about different careers that seem to suit my personality, interests, and abilities.	1 2 3 4 5
▶ I have looked into majors that match up with my career interests.	1 2 3 4 5
▶ I have, or intend to get, hands-on experience in a particular field through an internship, job, or volunteer work.	1 2 3 4 5
▶ I understand the qualities that today's employers value most.	1 2 3 4 5
▶ I save and update contact information for people I network with about career advice or job possibilities.	1 2 3 4 5
▶ I am familiar with major online job search and career planning sites.	1 2 3 4 5
▶ I know how to write an effective cover letter.	1 2 3 4 5
▶ I have a current resumé for sending out to prospective employers.	1 2 3 4 5
▶ I am prepared to give a good impression in interviews.	1 2 3 4 5
▶ Knowing how quickly the modern workplace changes, I'm ready to be flexible if a job or career choice doesn't last.	1 2 3 4 5

Now total your scores.

Each of the topics in these statements is covered in this chapter. Note those statements for which you circled a 3 or lower. Skim the chapter to see where those topics appear, and pay special attention to them as you read, learn, and apply new strategies.

REMEMBER: **No matter how prepared you are to succeed in the workplace and in life, you can improve with effort and practice.**

"Successfully intelligent people realize that the environment in which they find themselves may or may not enable them to make the most of their talents. They actively seek an environment where they can not only do competent work but also make a difference."

—Robert Sternberg

How can you prepare for career success?

Whether you have a current career, a work history of various different jobs, or no workplace experience at all, college is an ideal time to take stock of your career goals. The earlier in your college education that you consider career goals, the more you can take advantage of using college to help prepare you for work, in both job-specific and general ways.

Your career reflects your values and talents and provides the income you need to support yourself and your family in the years ahead. Choosing a career requires knowledge of yourself, your economic situation, and where you want to be in the future. Because of the personal nature of these questions, it's important to remember that the "right" career can mean something different to everyone. As you read this section, keep in mind that all of the skills you acquire in college—thinking, teamwork, writing, goal setting, and others—prepare you for workplace success, no matter what career is right for you.

Consider your personality and strengths

Because who you are as a learner relates closely to who you are as a worker, your assessment results will give you helpful clues in the search for the right career. The multiple intelligences assessment (Multiple Pathways to Learning) points to information about your natural strengths and challenges, which can lead you to careers that involve these strengths. Look at Key 11.1 to see how those intelligences may link up with various careers.

The Personality Assessment profile is equally as significant, because it focuses on how you work best with others, and career success depends in large part on your ability to function in a team. Look for your strengths and decide what you may want to keep in mind as you search. Look also at areas of challenge, and try to identify ways to boost your abilities in those areas. Even the most ideal job involves some tasks that are not in your area of comfort.

Use the information in Key 11.2 as a guide, not a label. Although you may not have all the strengths and challenges indicated by your dominant area, thinking through them will still help you clarify your abilities and interests. In addition, remember that you are capable of change, and with focus and effort you can develop your abilities. Use ideas about strengths and challenges as a starting point for your goals concerning how you would like to grow.

Taking courses in an area of interest can help you see how well a job in this area might suit you.
Courtesy of Shutterstock

Finally, one other way to investigate how your personality and strengths may inform career choice is to take an inventory based on the Holland theory. Psychologist John Holland theorized that personality was related to career choice, and he came up with six different types that identify both personality and career area: Realistic, Investigative, Artistic, Social, Enterprising, and Conventional (together known as RIASEC).[1] Holland developed two interest surveys that allow people to identify their order of preference for the six types and help them link their stronger types to career areas. Ask your career center about these surveys—the Vocational Preference Inventory (VPI) and the Self-Directed Search (SDS).

Be strategic

With your knowledge about your talents and strengths, focus on making a practical, personal plan to achieve your career goals. First, create a timeline to illustrate the steps you plan to take toward a specific career goal. Working with an advisor, career office employee, or mentor, establish a time frame and write your steps by when they should happen. If your plan is 5 years long, for example, indicate what you plan to do by the fourth, third, and second years, and then the first year, including a 6-month goal and a 1-month goal for that first year. Your path may change, of course; use your timeline as a guide rather than as an inflexible plan.

After you establish your time frame, focus on details. Make specific plans for pursuing the jobs or careers that have piqued your interest. Set goals that establish whom you will talk to, what courses you will take, what skills you will work on, what jobs or internships you will investigate, and any other research you need to do. Be proactive in finding opportunities.

Build knowledge and experience

It's hard to choose the right career path without knowledge or experience. Courses, internships, jobs, and volunteering are four great ways to build both.

MULTIPLE INTELLIGENCES MAY **OPEN DOORS** TO CAREERS

Key 11.1

MULTIPLE INTELLIGENCE	CAREERS
Bodily-Kinesthetic	• Carpenter or draftsman • Physical therapist • Mechanical engineer • Dancer or actor • Exercise physiologist
Intrapersonal	• Research scientist • Computer engineer • Psychologist • Economist • Author
Interpersonal	• Social worker • Public relations or human resources rep • Sociologist • Teacher • Nurse
Naturalistic	• Biochemical engineer • Natural scientist (geologist, ecologist, entymologist) • Paleontologist • Position with environmental group • Farmer or farm management
Musical	• Singer or voice coach • Music teacher • Record executive • Musician or conductor • Radio DJ or sound engineer
Logical-Mathematical	• Doctor or dentist • Accountant • Attorney • Chemist • Investment banker
Verbal-Linguistic	• Author or journalist • TV/radio producer • Literature or language teacher • Business executive • Copywriter or editor
Visual-Spatial	• Graphic artist or illustrator • Photographer • Architect or interior designer • Art museum curator • Art teacher • Set or retail stylist

■ *Courses.* Take a course or two in your areas of interest to determine whether you like the material and can excel. Find out what courses are required for a major in those areas and decide if you are willing to study this material during college. Check out your school's course catalogue for detailed information on the courses involved. Also, consider talking with professors to gain more insight into the field.

■ *Internships.* Internships provide supervised practical experience in different professional fields. Your career center may list internship opportunities. For more comprehensive guides, check out reference books like those published by Vault and Internet sources like www.internships .com and www.princetonreview.com.

> → INTERNSHIP
> A temporary work program in which a student can gain supervised practical experience in a particular professional field.

■ *Jobs.* You may discover career opportunities while earning money during a part-time job. Someone who takes a legal proofreading job to make extra cash might discover an interest in law. Someone who answers phones for a newspaper company might be drawn into journalism.

■ *Volunteering.* Helping others in need can introduce you to careers and increase your experience. Many schools establish committees to organize volunteering opportunities or sponsor their own groups. The federal government encourages volunteerism through AmeriCorps, a federal clearinghouse that awards its volunteers money to pay tuition or student loans. You may even be able to find opportunities that mesh with an area of interest. For example, if you are studying accounting, donating your time as a part-time bookkeeper in a shelter will increase your skills while you help those less fortunate than you. Many employers look favorably on volunteering.

■ *Service learning.* The goal of service learning is to provide the community with service and students with knowledge gained from hands-on experience.[2] Students in service learning programs enroll in for-credit courses in which volunteer service and related assignments are required. Service learning builds a sense of civic responsibility, helps students learn useful skills through doing, and promotes values exploration and personal change. If you are interested, talk to your advisor about whether your school offers service learning programs.

Investigate career paths

Career possibilities extend far beyond what you can imagine. Ask instructors, relatives, mentors, and fellow students about careers. Explore job listings, occupation descriptions, assessments, and other information about careers and companies at your school's career center. Check your library for books on careers or biographies of people who worked in fields that interest you. Look at Key 11.2 for the kinds of analytical questions that will aid your search. Keep the following in mind as you look.

Courtesy of Shutterstock

▶ *A wide array of job possibilities exists for most career fields.* For example, the medical world consists of more than doctors and nurses. Administrators run hospitals, researchers test drugs, pharmacists prepare prescriptions, security experts ensure patient and visitor safety, and so on.

▶ *Within each job, there are a variety of tasks and skills.* For instance, you may know that an instructor teaches, but you may not realize that instructors also write, research, study, design courses, give presentations, and counsel. Take your career exploration beyond first impressions to get an accurate picture of the careers that interest you.

▶ *A variety of occupations pay well.* Rewarding jobs go beyond law, finance, and medicine. According to data from the U.S. Labor

What can I do in this area that I like and do well?	Do I respect the company or the industry? The product or service?
What are the educational requirements (certificates or degrees, courses)?	Does this company or industry accommodate special needs (child care, sick days, flex time)?
What skills are necessary?	Do I need to belong to a union? What does union membership involve?
What wage or salary and benefits can I expect?	Are there opportunities near where I live (or want to live)?
What personality types are best suited to this kind of work?	What other expectations exist (travel, overtime, and so on)?
What are the prospects for moving up to higher-level positions?	Do I prefer the service or production end of this industry?

Department, careers with comfortable earnings include electricians, aircraft mechanics, and more.[3] Look up the U.S. Bureau of Labor's *Occupational Outlook Handbook* or see http://salary.com for information on average salaries in different fields.

Know what employers want

When you apply for a job, it is important to realize that prospective employers look for particular skills and qualities that mark you as a promising candidate. Most employers require you to have a **skill set** that includes specific technical know-how, but in this rapidly changing workplace, general life skills and emotional intelligence may be even more crucial to your success.

SKILL SET
A combination of the knowledge, talent, and abilities that are needed to perform a specific job.

General skills

In the modern workplace, workers will hold an average of ten jobs through their productive working years.[4] The high rate of job and workplace change means that abilities such as successful thinking and teamwork are crucial to workplace success. Many of these general skills can also be described as *transferable* skills—general skills learned through job or life experience that you can use with (or transfer to) a new and different job or career. For example, you will need teamwork and writing skills for almost any job. Key 11.3 describes transferable skills that employers look for.

Emotional intelligence

Employers are also drawn to emotionally intelligent job candidates, as you learned in Chapter 1. Your emotional intelligence has an impact on your effectiveness. Consider this scenario: You arrive at work distracted by a personal problem and tired from studying late the night before. Your supervisor is overloaded with a major project due that day. The person you work most closely with is arriving late due to a car problem. In other words, everyone is strung out. What does an emotionally intelligent person do? Remember the three actions of emotional intelligence:

▶ *Tune in to everyone's emotions first.* You: Tired and distracted. Your co-worker: Worried about the car and about being late. Your supervisor: Agitated about the project.

EMPLOYERS LOOK FOR CANDIDATES WITH THESE **IMPORTANT SKILLS**

SKILL	WHY IS IT USEFUL?
Communication	Good listening, speaking, and writing skills are keys to working with others, as is being able to adjust to different communication styles.
Analytical thinking	An employee who can analyze choices and challenges, as well as assess the value of new ideas, stands out.
Creativity	The ability to come up with new concepts, plans, and products helps companies improve and innovate.
Practical thinking	No job gets done without employees who can think through a plan for achieving a goal, put it into action, and complete it successfully.
Teamwork	All workers interact with others on the job. Working well with others is essential for achieving workplace goals.
Goal setting	Teams fail if goals are unclear or unreasonable. Employees and company benefit from setting realistic, specific goals and achieving them reliably.
Cultural competence	The workplace is increasingly diverse. An employee who can work with, adjust to, and respect people from different backgrounds and cultures is valuable.
Leadership	The ability to influence and motivate others in a positive way earns respect and career advancement.
Positive attitude	Other employees will gladly work with, and often advance, someone who completes tasks with positive, upbeat energy.
Integrity	Acting with integrity at work—communicating promptly, being truthful and honest, following rules, giving proper notice—enhances value.
Flexibility	The most valuable employees understand the constancy of change and have developed the skills to adapt to its challenge.
Continual learning	The most valuable employees take personal responsibility to stay current in their fields.

▶ *Understand what the emotions are telling you.* Making the deadline that day might be more challenging than anticipated. Everyone is going to need to set aside distracted, negative thinking and maintain an extra-focused and positive state of mind to get through it.

   ▶ *Take action toward positive outcomes.* You come up with several ideas.

- Prioritize your task list so that you can concentrate on what is most pressing.
- Put a memo on your supervisor's desk saying that you are available to support her as she nails down the loose ends on her urgent project.
- Call your co-worker on his cell phone while he settles the car problem and let him know the status at work, preparing him to prioritize and to support the supervisor.
- Ask another co-worker to bring in a favorite midmorning snack to keep everyone going on what looks to be a long day.

The current emphasis on teamwork has highlighted emotional intelligence in the workplace. The more adept you are at working with others, the more likely you are to succeed.

Expect change

The working world is always in flux, responding to technological developments, global competition, and other factors. Think about the following as you prepare for your own career.

■ *Growing and declining career areas.* Rapid workplace change means that a growth area today may be declining tomorrow—witness the sudden drop in Internet company jobs and fortunes in 2001. The U.S. Bureau of Labor keeps updated statistics on the status of various career areas. For example, for the period 2008 to 2018, of the ten fastest-growing occupations identified by the bureau, six are related to health care.[5]

■ *Workplace trends.* Companies are hiring more temporary employees (temps) and freelancers. Temporary and freelance jobs offer flexibility, few obligations, and often more take-home pay, but they have limited or no benefits. Also, in response to changing needs, companies are offering more "quality of life" benefits such as telecommuting, job sharing, and on-site child care. You can track these changes by reading hard copy or online versions of business-focused publications such as *Fortune, Business Week,* or the *Wall Street Journal.*

■ *Personal change.* Even difficult personal changes can open doors that you never imagined were there. For example, after being diagnosed with Parkinson's at only 30 years old, actor Michael J. Fox found new passions in life as a best-selling author and advocate for others suffering from the degenerative disease.

Adjusting to changes, both large (leaving an industry for a new career) and small (changing the software you use daily on the job) means putting successful intelligence to work. With the information you collect from newspapers and magazines, Internet sites, and television news, you can analyze what you are facing in the workplace. Based on your analysis, you can create options for yourself, either within your own workplace or elsewhere, and take practical action.

With what you know about general workplace success strategies, you can search effectively for a job in a career area that works for you.

How can you conduct an effective job search?

Whether you are looking for a job now or planning ahead for a search closer to graduation, you have choices about how to proceed. Maximize your success by using the resources available to you, knowing the basics about resumés and interviews, and planning strategically.

Use available resources

NETWORKING
The exchange of information or services among individuals, groups, or institutions.

Use your school's career planning and placement office, your (networking) skills, classified ads, and online services to help you explore possibilities for career areas or specific jobs.

Your school's career planning and placement office

Generally, the career planning and placement office deals with postgraduation job opportunities, whereas the student employment office, along with the financial aid office, has information about working during school. At either location you might find job listings, interview sign-up sheets, and company contact information. The career office may hold frequent informational sessions on different topics. Get acquainted with the career office early in your college career.

Courtesy of Shutterstock

Networking

The most basic type of networking—talking to people about fields and jobs that interest you—is one of the most important job-hunting strategies. Networking contacts can answer questions regarding job hunting, occupational responsibilities and challenges, and salary expectations. You can network with friends and family members, instructors, administrators, counselors, alumni, employers, co-workers, and people you meet through extracurricular activities, as a few ideas.

Online social networking can also help you in your job search. Tools like Facebook, Twitter, and LinkedIn allow members to create personalized pages and connect with other individuals through groups, fan pages, and similar interests. During a job search, these sites can be used to meet potential employers through your contacts and showcase portfolio pieces. A word of caution: Your online presence is public. Before you post anything, remember that if you wouldn't want a potential employer (or your parents, instructor, or religious leader) to see it, don't put it online.

CONTACTS
People who serve as carriers or sources of information.

Online services and classified ads

Although classified ads are still helpful when looking locally, the Internet is capable of storing tons of information without any cost in paper and ink. Therefore, more employers post through online job boards, and those listings are often more detailed than the two- or three-sentence ads you'd find in a newspaper. In addition to a job description and salary information, most online postings will contain company information and a link to where you can submit an application. Use the following tips to make the most of your virtual resources:

Take advantage of career fairs sponsored by your school or town. These career fair attendees pick up useful information and applications from different employers.
© Adam Lau/AP Images

- ▶ Look up career-focused and job-listing websites such as CareerBuilder.com, Monster.com, America's Job Bank, BilingualCareer.com, JobBankUSA.com, or futurestep.com. Many sites offer resources on career areas, resumés, and online job searching in addition to listings of openings.
- ▶ Access job search databases such as the Career Placement Registry and U.S. Employment Opportunities.
- ▶ Check the Web pages of individual associations and companies, which may post job listings and descriptions.

If nothing happens right away, keep at it. New job postings appear, and new people sign on to look at your resumé. Plus, sites change all the time. Search using the keywords "job sites" or "job search" to see what sites come up (quintcareers.com has a listing of the top fifty best job sites).

Use an organized, consistent strategy

Organize your approach according to what you need to do and when you have to do it. Do you plan to make three phone calls per day? Will you fill out one job application each week? Keep a record—on 3-by-5 cards, in a computer file or smartphone, or in a notebook—of the following:

- ▶ People you contact plus contact information and method of contact (e-mail, snail mail, phone)
- ▶ Companies to which you apply
- ▶ Jobs for which you apply, including any results (for example, a job that becomes unavailable)
- ▶ Responses to communications (phone calls to you, interviews, written communications), information about the person who contacted you (name, title), and the times and dates of contact

Keeping accurate records enables you to both chart your progress and maintain a clear picture of the process. If you don't get a job now but another opens up at the same company in a few months, well-kept records will enable you to contact key personnel quickly and efficiently.

Your resumé, cover letter, and interview

Information on resumés, cover letters, and interviews fills entire books. To get you started, here are a few basic tips on giving yourself the best possible chance.

Resumé and cover letter

Design your resumé neatly, using a current and acceptable format (books or your career office can show you some standard formats). Make sure the information is accurate and truthful. Proofread for errors and have someone else proofread it as well. Type it and print it on high-quality paper (a heavier bond paper than is used for ordinary copies). Include a brief, to-the-point cover letter that tells which job interests you and why the employer should hire you.

Prospective employers often use a computer to scan resumés, selecting those containing *keywords* relating to the job opening or industry. Resumés without enough keywords probably won't even make it to the human resources desk, so make sure to include as many keywords as you can. For example, if you are seeking a computer-related job, list computer programs you use and other specific technical proficiencies. To figure out the keywords for your field, check out occupation descriptions, job postings, and other current resumés.[6]

Interview

Be clean, neat, and appropriately dressed. Choose a nice pair of shoes—people notice. Bring an extra copy of your resumé and any other materials that you want to show the interviewer. Avoid chewing gum or smoking. Offer a confident handshake. Make eye contact. Show your integrity by speaking honestly about yourself. After the interview, no matter what the outcome, follow up right away with a formal but pleasant thank-you note.

Being on time to your interview makes a positive impression—and being late will almost certainly be held against you. If you are from a culture that does not consider being late a sign of disrespect, remember that your interviewer may not agree.

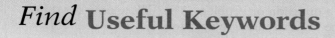

GET PRACTICAL!

Find Useful Keywords

Name two career fields that you would consider pursuing:

1. _____

2. _____

Research resumé keywords that employers in these fields look for. On your chosen search engine, enter the words *keyword, resume,* and a word or phrase related to the field ("chemical engineering," "criminal justice," etc.). Fill in the list with ten keywords for each field. Keep them on hand to tailor your resumé for a job in either one of these fields.

Field _____

1. _____   6. _____

2. _____   7. _____

3. _____   8. _____

4. _____   9. _____

5. _____   10. _____

Field _____

1. _____   6. _____

2. _____   7. _____

3. _____   8. _____

4. _____   9. _____

5. _____   10. _____

How can you continue to activate your successful intelligence?

Throughout this text you have connected analytical, creative, and practical thinking to academic and life skills. You have put them together in order to solve problems and make decisions. You have seen how these skills, used consistently and with balance, can help you succeed.

You are only just beginning your career as a successfully intelligent learner. You will continue to discover the best ways to achieve goals that are meaningful to you. According to Sternberg, successfully intelligent people apply the following techniques.[7]

1. *Motivate themselves.* They make things happen, spurred on by a desire to succeed and a love of what they are doing.
2. *Learn to control their impulses.* Instead of going with their first quick response, they sit with a question or problem. They allow time for thinking and let ideas surface before making a decision.
3. *Know when to persevere.* When it makes sense, they push past frustration and stay on course, confident that success is in their sights. They also are able to see when they've hit a dead end—and, in those cases, to stop pushing.
4. *Know how to make the most of their abilities.* They understand what they do well and capitalize on it in school and work.
5. *Translate thought into action.* Not only do they have good ideas; they are able to turn those ideas into practical actions that bring ideas to fruition.
6. *Have a product orientation.* They want results; they focus on what they are aiming for rather than on how they are getting there.
7. *Complete tasks and follow through.* With determination, they finish what they start. They also follow through to make sure all the loose ends are tied and the goal has been achieved.
8. *Are initiators.* They commit to people, projects, and ideas. They make things happen rather than sitting back and waiting for things to happen to them.
9. *Are not afraid to risk failure.* Because they take risks and sometimes fail, they often enjoy greater success and build their intellectual capacity. Like everyone, they make mistakes—but they tend not to make the same mistake twice.
10. *Don't procrastinate.* They are aware of the negative effects of putting things off, and they avoid them. They create schedules that allow them to accomplish what's important on time.
11. *Accept fair blame.* They strike a balance between never accepting blame and taking the blame for everything. If something is their fault, they accept responsibility and don't make excuses.
12. *Reject self-pity.* When something goes wrong, they find a way to solve the problem. They don't get caught in the energy drain of feeling sorry for themselves.
13. *Are independent.* They can work on their own and think for themselves. They take responsibility for their own schedule and tasks.
14. *Seek to surmount personal difficulties.* They keep things in perspective, looking for ways to remedy personal problems and separate them from their professional lives.
15. *Focus and concentrate to achieve their goals.* They create an environment in which they can best avoid distraction to focus steadily on their work.
16. *Spread themselves neither too thin nor too thick.* They strike a balance between doing too many things, which results in little progress on any of them, and too few things, which can reduce the level of accomplishment.
17. *Have the ability to delay gratification.* Although they enjoy the smaller rewards that require less energy, they focus the bulk of their work on the goals that take more time but promise the most gratification.

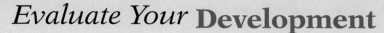
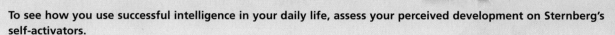
Evaluate Your Development

To see how you use successful intelligence in your daily life, assess your perceived development on Sternberg's self-activators.

1	2	3	4	5
Not at All Like Me	Somewhat Unlike Me	Not Sure	Somewhat Like Me	Definitely Like Me

Please circle the number which best represents your answer:

1. I motivate myself well.   1 2 3 4 5

2. I can control my impulses.   1 2 3 4 5

3. I know when to persevere and when to change gears.   1 2 3 4 5

4. I make the most of what I do well.   1 2 3 4 5

5. I can successfully translate my ideas into action.   1 2 3 4 5

6. I can focus effectively on my goal.   1 2 3 4 5

7. I complete tasks and have good follow-through.   1 2 3 4 5

8. I initiate action—I move people and projects ahead.   1 2 3 4 5

9. I have the courage to risk failure.   1 2 3 4 5

10. I avoid procrastination.   1 2 3 4 5

11. I accept responsibility when I make a mistake.   1 2 3 4 5

12. I don't waste time feeling sorry for myself.   1 2 3 4 5

13. I independently take responsibility for tasks.   1 2 3 4 5

14. I work hard to overcome personal difficulties.   1 2 3 4 5

15. I create an environment that helps me concentrate on my goals. 1 2 3 4 5

16. I don't take on too much work or too little.   1 2 3 4 5

17. I can delay gratification to receive the benefits.   1 2 3 4 5

18. I can see both the big picture and the details in a situation. 1 2 3 4 5

19. I am able to maintain confidence in myself.   1 2 3 4 5

20. I balance my analytical, creative, and practical thinking skills. 1 2 3 4 5

When you complete the assessment, look back at pages 22–23 for your original scores. What development do you see? List three changes that feel significant to you:

1. _____

2. _____

3. _____

As you grow, there is always room for improvement. Choose one characteristic that you feel still needs work. Analyze the specific reasons why it remains a challenge. For example, if you are still taking on too much work, is it out of a need to please others? Write a brief analysis on a separate sheet of paper or electronic file, and let this analysis guide you as you work to build your strength in this area.

18. *Have the ability to see the forest and the trees.* They are able to see the big picture and avoid getting bogged down in tiny details.

19. *Have a reasonable level of self-confidence and a belief in their ability to accomplish their goals.* They believe in themselves enough to get through the tough times, while avoiding the kind of overconfidence that stalls learning and growth.

20. *Balance analytical, creative, and practical thinking.* They sense what to use and when to use it. When problems arise, they combine all three skills to arrive at solutions.

These characteristics are your personal motivational tools. Consult them when you need a way to get moving. You may even want to post them somewhere in your home, in the front of a notebook, or as a note in your smartphone.

How will your learning in this course bring success?

You leave this course with far more than a final grade, a notebook full of work, and a credit hour or three on your transcript. You leave with a set of skills and attitudes that open the door to success in the 21st century.

Lifelong learning and the growth mindset

With knowledge in many fields doubling every 2 to 3 years and your personal interests and needs changing all the time, what you learn in college is just the beginning of what you will need to discover throughout your life to succeed. With a growth mindset—the attitude that you can always grow and learn—you are as ready to achieve the goals you set out for yourself today as you are to achieve future goals you cannot yet anticipate.

Courtesy of Shutterstock

If you look back at Key 1.5 and at the 21st Century Building Blocks in each Personal Portfolio exercise, you will see that you have built skills and knowledge in each quadrant of the 21st Century Learning grid.

The attitudes and skills you have acquired this term are your keys to success now and in the future. *As you continue in college, remind yourself that you are creating tools that will benefit you in everything you do.*

Make learning a habit for life by strengthening your growth mindset in ways such as the following:

▶ *Investigate new interests.* When information and events catch your attention, take your interest one step further and find out more. Instead of dreaming about it, just do it.

▶ *Read, read, read.* Reading expert Jim Trelease says that people who don't read "base their future decisions on what they used to know. If you don't read much, you really don't know much."[8] Open a world of knowledge and perspectives through

ATTITUDES AND SKILLS ACQUIRED IN COLLEGE ARE TOOLS FOR **LIFELONG SUCCESS**

ACQUIRED SKILL	IN COLLEGE, YOU'LL USE IT TO . . .	IN CAREER AND LIFE, YOU'LL USE IT TO . . .
Investigating resources	. . . find who and what can help you have the college experience you want	. . . get acclimated at a new job or in a new town—find the people, resources, and services that can help you succeed
Knowing and using your learning styles	. . . select study strategies that make the most of your learning styles	. . . select jobs, career areas, and other pursuits that suit what you do best
Setting goals and managing stress	. . . complete assignments and achieve educational goals; reduce stress by being in control	. . . accomplish tasks and reach career and personal goals; reduce stress by being in control
Managing time	. . . complete course work on time, juggle school and work, turn in assignments when they are due, plan study time	. . . finish work tasks on time or before they are due, balance duties on the job and at home
Analytical, creative, and practical thinking	. . . think through writing assignments, solve math problems, analyze academic readings, brainstorm paper topics, work through academic issues, work effectively on team projects	. . . find ways to improve product design, increase market share, present ideas to customers; analyze life issues, come up with ideas, and take practical action
Reading	. . . read course texts and other materials	. . . read operating manuals, work guidebooks, media materials in your field; read for practical purposes, for learning, and for pleasure at home
Note taking	. . . take notes in class, in study groups, during studying, and during research	. . . take notes in work and community meetings and during important phone calls
Test taking	. . . take quizzes, tests, and final exams	. . . take tests for certification in particular work skills and for continuing education courses
Writing	. . . write essays and reports	. . . write work-related documents, including e-mails, reports, proposals, and speeches; write personal letters and journal entries
Building successful relationships	. . . get along with instructors, students, and student groups	. . . get along with supervisors, co-workers, team members, friends, and family members
Staying healthy	. . . stay physically and mentally healthy so that you can make the most of school	. . . stay physically and mentally healthy so that you can be at your best at work and at home
Managing money	. . . stay on top of school costs and make decisions that earn and save you the money you need	. . . budget the money you earn so that you can pay your bills and save for the future
Establishing and maintaining a personal mission	. . . develop a big picture idea of what you want from your education, and make choices that guide you toward those goals	. . . develop a big picture idea of what you wish to accomplish in life, and make choices that guide you toward those goals

reading. Ask friends which books have changed their lives. Keep up with local, national, and world news through newspapers, magazines, and Internet sources.

▶ *Keep on top of changes in your career.* After graduation, continue your education both in your field and in the realm of general knowledge. Stay on top of ideas, developments, and new technology in your field by seeking out continuing education courses. Sign up for career-related seminars. Some companies offer additional on-the-job training or pay for their employees to take courses that will improve their knowledge and skills.

▶ *Spend time with interesting people.* When you meet someone new who inspires you and makes you think, keep in touch. Form a book club, get a

CONTINUING
→ EDUCATION
Courses that students can take without needing to be part of a degree program.

GET CREATIVE!

Think Fifty Positive Thoughts

List twenty-five things you like about yourself. You can name anything—things you can do, things you think, things you've accomplished, things you like about your physical self, and so on. (Use a separate sheet of paper or an electronic file.)

Next, list twenty-five things you would like to do in your life. These can be anything from trying Vietnamese food to traveling to the Grand Canyon to working for Teach for America. They can be things you'd like to do tomorrow or things that you plan to do in 20 years. At least five items on the list should involve your current and future education.

Finally, come up with five things you can plan for the next year that combine what you like about yourself and what you want to do. If you like your strength as a mountain biker and you want to explore a state you've never seen, plan a mountain biking trip. If you like your writing and you want to be a published author, write an essay to submit to a magazine. Be creative. Let everything be possible.

1. _____

   _____

2. _____

   _____

3. _____

   _____

4. _____

   _____

5. _____

   _____

pickup basketball game together, or join a local volunteer organization. Learn something new from everyone you meet.

▶ *Talk to people from different generations.* Younger people can learn from the broad perspective of those from older generations; older people can learn from the fresh perspective of youth. Communication builds mutual respect.

▶ *Delve into other cultures.* Invite a friend over who has grown up in a culture different from your own. Eat food from a country you've never visited. Initiate conversations with people of different races, religions, values, and ethnic backgrounds. Travel internationally and locally. Take a course that deals with cultural diversity. Try a term or year abroad. Learn a new language.

▶ *Nurture a spiritual life.* Wherever you find spirituality—in organized religion, family, friendship, nature, music, or anywhere else—it will help you find balance and meaning.

▶ *Experience the arts.* Art is "a means of knowing the world" (Angela Carter, author); "a lie that makes us realize truth" (Pablo Picasso, painter); a revealer of "our most secret self" (Jean-Luc Godard, filmmaker). Through art you can discover new ideas and shed light on old ones. Seek out whatever moves you—music, visual arts, theater, photography, dance, performance art, film and television, poetry, prose, and more.

▶ *Be creative.* Take a class in drawing, writing, or quilting. Learn to play an instrument. Write poems for your friends or stories to read to your children. Concoct a new recipe. Design and build something for your home. Express yourself, and learn more about yourself, through art.

Lifelong learning is the master key that unlocks so many of the doors you encounter on your journey. If you keep it firmly in your hand, you will discover worlds of knowledge—and a place for yourself to continue growing within them.

Flexibility helps you adapt to change

As a citizen of the 21st century, you are likely to move in and out of school, jobs, and careers in the years ahead. You are also likely to experience important personal changes. How you react to change, especially if it is unexpected and difficult, is almost as important as the changes themselves in determining your future success. The ability to "make lemonade from lemons" is the hallmark of people who are able to hang on to hope.

Your thinking skills will help you stay flexible. As planned and unplanned changes arise, you analyze them, brainstorm solutions, and take practical action. With these skills you can adapt to the loss of a job or an exciting job offer, failing a course or winning an academic scholarship.

Although sudden changes may throw you off balance, the unpredictability of life can open new horizons. Margaret J. Wheatley and Myron Kellner-Rogers, leadership and community experts, explain: "Unpredictability gives us the freedom to experiment. It is this unpredictability that welcomes our creativity."[9] Here are some strategies for making the most of changes:

▶ *Focus on what is rather than what is supposed to be.* Planning for the future works best when you accept the reality of your situation.
▶ *Use your planning as a guide rather than a rule.* If you allow yourself to follow new paths when changes occur, you'll be able to grow from what life gives you.
▶ *Be willing to be surprised.* Great creative energies can come from the force of a surprise. Instead of turning back to familiar patterns, explore new possibilities.

With successful intelligence and a growth mindset, you will always have a new direction in which to grow. Live each day to the fullest, using your thinking skills to achieve your most valued goals. Challenge yourself to raise the bar and vault over it by seeking to improve and grow in the ways that are most meaningful to you. By being true to yourself, a respectful friend and family member, a focused student who believes in the power of learning, a productive employee, and a contributing member of society, you can change the world.

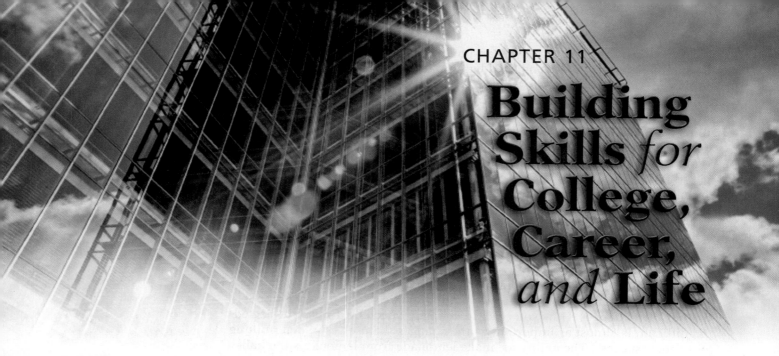

Building Skills *for* College, Career, *and* Life

Steps to Success

Become a Better Interviewee

BUILD BASIC SKILLS. Think about the questions that a job applicant would typically hear in an entry-level interview. Recall questions from job interviews you've had, look up questions using online sources such as www.quintcareers.com, or consult books on job interviews. On a separate sheet of paper or electronic file, list fifteen to twenty questions.

TAKE IT TO THE NEXT LEVEL. Imagining yourself as the interviewer, brainstorm some more creative questions to add to your list. Think about learning styles, life experiences, learning from failure, role models, and more as you ponder. Write five additional questions here:

1. _____
2. _____
3. _____
4. _____
5. _____

Writing

Build Intrapersonal and Communication Skills

Record your thoughts separately on paper, in a journal, or electronically.

EMOTIONAL INTELLIGENCE JOURNAL

> ***Revisit your personal mission.*** Look back at both the personal mission you wrote and the three career priorities that you felt most effectively matched up to your mission. Thinking about how you

298   KEYS TO LEARNING STRATEGIES FOR SUCCESS

feel now at the end of the term, and considering what has changed about the outcomes you want to make happen in your life, write an updated version of your mission. Incorporate one or more of those career priorities into your mission statement.

REAL-LIFE WRITING

Create a resumé. Start with a brainstorm using two sheets of paper or a computer file. On one electronic page or sheet of paper, list information about your education (where and when you've studied, degrees or certificates you've earned) and skills (what you know how to do, such as use various computer programs or operate certain types of equipment). On another, list job experience. For each job, record job title, the dates of employment, and the tasks you performed (if the job had no particular title, come up with one yourself). Be as detailed as possible—it's best to write down everything you remember. When you compile your resumé, you will make this material more concise. Keep this list and update it periodically as you gain experience and accomplishments.

Using the information you have gathered and Key 11.5 as your guide, draft a resumé. There are many ways to construct a resumé; consult other resources for different styles (try www.resume-help. org or www.howtowritearesume.net). You may want to format your resumé according to an approach that your career counselor or instructor recommends. If you already have a specific career focus, that field may favor a particular style of resumé (check with your career counselor or an instructor in that area).

Keep this resumé draft in hard copy and on a computer hard drive or disk. When you need to submit a resumé with a job application, update the draft and print it out on high-quality paper.

The list of general tips provides useful help for writing a resumé:

- Always put your name and contact information at the top. Make it stand out.
- State an objective if appropriate—when your focus is specific or you are designing this resumé for a particular interview or career area.
- List your postsecondary education, starting from the latest and working backward. This may include summer school, night school, seminars, and accreditations.
- List jobs in reverse chronological order (most recent job first). Include all types of work experience (full-time or part-time work, volunteer experiences, internships, and so on).
- When you describe your work experience, use action verbs and focus on what you have accomplished, rather than on the description of assigned tasks.
- Include keywords that are linked to jobs for which you will be applying.
- List references on a separate sheet. You may want to put "References upon request" at the bottom of your resumé.
- Use formatting (larger font sizes, different fonts, italics, bold, and so on) and indent selectively to help the important information stand out.
- Get several people to look at your resumé before you send it out. Other readers will have ideas that you haven't thought of and may find errors you have missed.

Personal Portfolio

Prepare for Career Success

REVIST THE WHEEL OF SUCCESSFUL INTELLIGENCE

21st Century Learning Building Blocks

- Initiative and Self-Direction
- Critical Thinking and Problem Solving

Complete the following in your electronic portfolio or separately on paper. When you have finished, read through your entire career portfolio. You have gathered information to turn to again and again on your path to a fulfilling, successful career.

Désirée Williams

237 Custer Street, San Francisco, CA 94101 • 650/555-5252 (w) or 415/555-7865 (h)
• fax: 707/555-2735 • e-mail: desiree@zzz.com

EDUCATION

2009 to present   San Francisco State University, San Francisco, CA
Pursuing a B.A. in the Spanish BCLAD (Bilingual, Cross-Cultural Language Acquisition Development) Education and Multiple Subject Credential Program. Expected graduation: June 2012.

PROFESSIONAL EMPLOYMENT

10/10 to present   **Research Assistant, Knowledge Media Lab**
Developing ways for teachers to exhibit their inquiry into their practice of teaching in an online, collaborative, multimedia environment.

5/09 to present   **Webmaster/Web Designer**
Work in various capacities at QuakeNet, an Internet Service Provider and Web Commerce Specialist in San Mateo, CA. Designed several sites for the University of California, Berkeley, Graduate School of Education, as well as private clients such as A Body of Work and Yoga Forever.

9/09 to 6/10   **Literacy Coordinator**
Coordinated, advised, and created literacy curriculum for an America Reads literacy project at Prescott School in West Oakland. Worked with non-reader 4th graders on writing and publishing, incorporating digital photography, Internet resources, and graphic design.

8/09   **Bilingual Educational Consultant**
Consulted for Children's Television Workshop, field-testing bilingual materials. With a research team, designed bilingual educational materials for an ecotourism project run by an indigenous rain forest community in Ecuador.

1/09 to 6/10   **Technology Consultant**
Worked with 24 Hours in Cyberspace, an online worldwide photojournalism event. Coordinated participation of schools, translated documents, and facilitated public relations.

SKILLS

Languages: Fluent in Spanish.
Proficient in Italian and Shona (majority language of Zimbabwe).

Computer: Programming ability in HTML, Javascript, Pascal, and Lisp. Multimedia design expertise in Adobe Photoshop, Netobjects Fusion, Adobe Premiere, Macromedia Flash, and many other visual design programs.

Personal: Perform professionally in Mary Schmary, a women's a cappella quartet. Have climbed Mt. Kilimanjaro.

Without looking at these same assessments or the wheel from Chapter 1, analyze where you are after completing this course by taking the three assessments again.

ASSESS YOUR ANALYTICAL THINKING SKILLS

For each statement, circle the number that feels right to you, from 1 for "not at all true for me" to 5 for "very true for me."

1. I recognize and define problems effectively.   1 2 3 4 5

2. I see myself as a "thinker," "analytical," "studious."   1 2 3 4 5

3. When working on a problem in a group setting, I like to break down the problem into its components and evaluate them.   1 2 3 4 5

4. I need to see convincing evidence before accepting information as fact.   1 2 3 4 5

5. I weigh the pros and cons of plans and ideas before taking action.   1 2 3 4 5

6. I tend to make connections among bits of information by categorizing them.   1 2 3 4 5

7. Impulsive, spontaneous decision making worries me.   1 2 3 4 5

8. I like to analyze causes and effects when making a decision.   1 2 3 4 5

9. I monitor my progress toward goals.   1 2 3 4 5

10. Once I reach a goal, I evaluate the process to see how effective it was.   1 2 3 4 5

Total your answers here: _____

ASSESS YOUR CREATIVE THINKING SKILLS

For each statement, circle the number that feels right to you, from 1 for "not at all true for me" to 5 for "very true for me."

1. I tend to question rules and regulations.   1 2 3 4 5

2. I see myself as "unique," "full of ideas," "innovative."   1 2 3 4 5

3. When working on a problem in a group setting, I generate a lot of ideas.   1 2 3 4 5

4. I am energized when I have a brand-new experience.   1 2 3 4 5

5. If you say something is too risky, I'm ready to give it a shot.   1 2 3 4 5

6. I often wonder if there is a different way to do or see something.   1 2 3 4 5

7. Too much routine in my work or schedule drains my energy.   1 2 3 4 5

8. I tend to see connections among ideas that others do not.   1 2 3 4 5

9. I feel comfortable allowing myself to make mistakes as I test out ideas.   1 2 3 4 5

10. I'm willing to champion an idea even when others disagree with me.   1 2 3 4 5

Total your answers here: _____

ASSESS YOUR PRACTICAL THINKING SKILLS

For each statement, circle the number that feels right to you, from 1 for "not at all true for me" to 5 for "very true for me."

1. I can find a way around any obstacle.   1 2 3 4 5

2. I see myself as a "doer," the "go-to" person; I "make things happen."   1 2 3 4 5

3. When working on a problem in a group setting, I like to figure out who will do what and when it should be done. 1 2 3 4 5

4. I apply what I learn from experience to improve my response to similar situations. 1 2 3 4 5

5. I finish what I start and don't leave loose ends hanging. 1 2 3 4 5

6. I note my emotions about academic and social situations and use what they tell me to move toward a goal. 1 2 3 4 5

7. I can sense how people feel and can use that knowledge to interact with others effectively. 1 2 3 4 5

8. I manage my time effectively. 1 2 3 4 5

9. I adjust to the teaching styles of my instructors and the communication styles of my peers. 1 2 3 4 5

10. When involved in a problem-solving process, I can shift gears as needed. 1 2 3 4 5

Total your answers here: _____

After you have finished, fill in your new scores on the blank Wheel of Successful Intelligence in Key 11.6. Compare it with your previous wheel on page 26. Look at the changes: Where have you grown? How has your self-perception changed?

- Note three creative ideas you came up with over the term that aided your exploration or development:

Idea 1: _____

_____

Idea 2: _____

_____

Idea 3: _____

_____

- Note three practical actions that you took that moved you toward your goals:

Action 1: _____

_____

Action 2: _____

_____

Action 3: _____

_____

Let what you learn from this new wheel inform you about what you have accomplished and what you plan to accomplish. Continue to grow your analytical, creative, and practical skills and use them to manage the changes that await you in the future.

Social Networking

ADD YOUR RESUMÉ

Add your current resumé to the tools on LinkedIn that can help you achieve career goals. Make sure your resumé is accessible (from the hard drive or another source such as a flash drive) on the computer you are using. Sign in to your account and click on "Edit My Profile." Click on the "Import your resume" button on the right side of the screen, and follow instructions.

USE THIS NEW **WHEEL OF SUCCESSFUL INTELLIGENCE** TO EVALUATE YOUR PROGRESS

With your new scores in hand, create the most updated representation of your thinking skills. In each of the three areas of the wheel, draw a curved line approximately at the level of your number score and fill in the wedge below that line. Compare this wheel to your previous wheel and note any change and development.

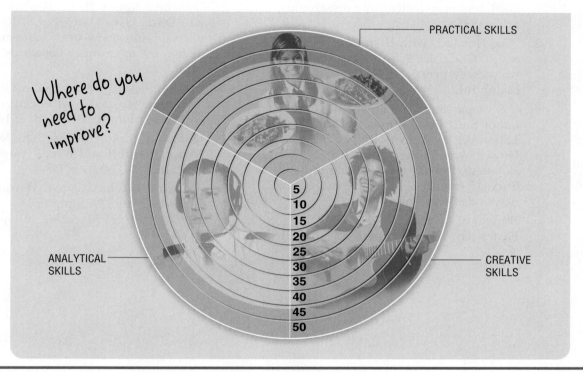

Source: Based on "The Wheel of Life" model developed by the Coaches Training Institute. © Co-Active Space 2000.

As you move ahead in college and life, continue to build, adjust, and use the LinkedIn profile you have built throughout this course. Make it a tool for success.

Social Networking

GET RECOMMENDED

LinkedIn has a feature that can help you show recommendations from valued contacts. Users with recommendations are more likely to be picked up by employers searching LinkedIn for possible employees. Sign in to your account and proceed as follows:

- Click on "Edit My Profile."
- Under "Recommended," click on "Get Recommended."
- Follow the three steps to contact people who you think would have positive and helpful things to say about you. (Choose what you want to be recommended for, decide who you'll ask, and create your message.) Keep in mind that the more credible the sources, the more useful your recommendations will be. (A family member saying you are a great person is not as effective as a former teacher or employer talking about your skills.)
- Finally, click "send" and keep an eye out for recommendations coming in.

ENDNOTES

1. Self-Directed Search, www.self-directed-search.com.

2. National Service Learning Clearing-house, "Service Learning Is . . . ," May 2004, www.servicelearning.org/article/archive/35.

3. "The Hot Jobs with High Pay," February 2007, Career Prospects in Virginia, www.careerprospects.org/Trends/salary-high.html.

4. U.S. Department of Labor, Bureau of Labor Statistics, "Number of Jobs Held, Labor Market Activity, and Earnings Growth Among the Youngest Baby Boomers: Results from a Longitudinal Survey," August 25, 2006, www.bls.gov/news.release/pdf/nlsoy.pdf.

5. Bureau of Labor Statistics, "The 30 Fastest Growing Occupations Covered in the 2008–2009 Occupational Outlook Handbook," December 18, 2007, www.bls.gov/news.release/ooh.t01.htm.

6. Job Interview and Career Guide, "Resume: Keywords for Resumes—Keywords List," December 8, 2009, www.job-interview-site.com/resume-keywords-for-resumes-keywords-list.html.

7. List and descriptions based on Robert J. Sternberg, *Successful Intelligence,* New York: Plume, 1997, pp. 251–269.

8. Quoted in Linton Weeks, "The No-Book Report: Skim It and Weep," *Washington Post,* May 14, 2001, p. C8.

9. Margaret J. Wheatley and Myron Kellner-Rogers, "A Simpler Way," 1997, *Weight Watchers Magazine,* 30, no. 3, pp. 42–44.

Maintaining Your Online Success

chapter 12

The feeling of completion is a powerful one. Just ask CSU graduate Cindy Watts.

"My bachelor's degree has given me a feeling of completion like no other," the Foley, Ala., police officer said. "Earning the degree was not an easy thing to do, but the accomplishment and feeling of completion is amazing!"

Watts added, "The most important thing to me was not just the degree and the completion of it, but the fact that I did my best. When I received the actual certificate in the mail, I wanted to rearrange my room with a new desk just so I could hang it up properly."

She graduated in 2011 with a bachelor's degree in criminal justice administration and a 4.0 grade point average all the while raising a son alone and working a stressful job.

However, Watts, who has been in law enforcement since 1996, sees her work as very rewarding. "I love it. I really enjoy helping others."

Because of her job and family, Watts found CSU's flexible course schedule to be a good fit for her lifestyle.

"You are able to study at your own pace, which in our line of work, is necessary," she explained. "There were many times court dates would be an issue, but knowing that I could do the work on my own, when I'm ready to do it, was great."

This proved very beneficial for the 45-year-old when she had to have surgery. "Before I had surgery, I was able to work ahead knowing that I was going to be in bed for a week or so," Watts said.

"Another reason she enjoyed her education with CSU "was that the staff helped me through each and every step from transcripts to financial aid to registration. If the 'Live Chat Now' was a telephone number, it would have been on my speed dial."

While her interaction with faculty and staff was frequent, Watts said the service she received was always helpful, informative and prompt. "I just can't say enough good things about my experience with CSU."

And good things later arose from her education with CSU. Within six months of graduation, Watts said her degree and coursework were instrumental in her promotion to corporal. "The written portion of the test for promotion covered the same material that I have taken in my classes."

As the new corporal takes on her supervisory duties, she is continuing her studies with CSU as she seeks a master's degree in emergency services management. She said she plans to graduate before her son does from high school.

Based on her determination and desire for completion, she can and she will.

In closing, we talk about continuing your education. You will see that beginning is easy. You have heard people talk about the "honeymoon period" or how the "newness wears off," and these stages may apply to you as you go through your program.

When you begin school, you will be full of excitement and drive, and that alone can keep you going for the first few classes. But the truth is, at some point in your program you may feel down and discouraged about how much more there is to do. You may wonder if it is all worth it, and you may even consider not continuing. This chapter addresses what it takes to maintain your online success and continue when you feel like hanging it up.

Staying organized

As you progress through the program and each class, your knowledge will grow. But so will the number of textbooks and electronic documents you have to keep track of. Staying organized will help you stay efficient.

Computer files

We suggest you set up a filing system to store important documents. You may choose to use a hard-copy filing system, but we recommend that you save work on the computer as much as you can. It will save both space and paper.

Use your desktop and create folders. Ideally you have a folder for each class, and in that folder you store all the documents you created for the class.

Take the time to develop your own logical system of filing. Be sure you use brief but descriptive names for all your documents, and even numbers when it is called for. Logical naming of folders helps you easily determine their content after the memory of the particular assignment has faded. The first time you do a large paper with multiple drafts, you will be glad you chose a relevant title for the document and saved the versions using numbers 1 to 4.

You may not see the need for multiple files at first, but as work piles up, you will wish you had it carefully marked and stored. It will make locating the files in the future so much simpler.

We suggest you keep everything: your assignments, your in-depth posts, your answers to discussion questions. You cannot be sure now what may come in handy later. You may be able to build on what you have done for future assignments and posts. For example, if you decide in your business program to focus your papers on Wal-Mart, you could use the same introduction with the company history for each paper. You may also find other bits of information you could reuse.

Textbooks for future reference

When you finish a class, you may be tempted to sell your books. There may be compelling reasons to do so. Perhaps you need the money or they take up too much space. However, keep in mind that you are in an academic program and the concepts and ideas will often be related or build on one another. You may find the books from previous classes useful for resource material. By continuing to use your books as references, you reinforce your memory about the concepts you learned in those classes.

You may also discover that certain books can become valuable references well beyond your academic career: You might talk to people who work in your chosen field to find out what books they have found helpful in their work. All of your textbooks might not be worthy of becoming lifetime references. But consider which ones might, and keep them on hand.

Emergency backup

As you progress through the program, always have a plan to back up your work. You need to consider what would happen if your computer were to crash or be infected with a destructive virus, or if a natural disaster occurred.

We all know the computers are not completely reliable. *We strongly recommend that you back up your documents periodically.* You could do this by

- ▶ Using a whole drive designed specifically for the purpose.
- ▶ Using a small portable thumb or flash drive.
- ▶ Saving documents on backup disks.
- ▶ Printing hard copies and keeping them in a safe place.
- ▶ E-mailing copies to an alternative e-mail account.

If you use a machine backup, make sure the backup system itself contains enough memory to hold everything you need to save.

Whichever option you choose, back up regularly. Weekly is usually good, and daily is better. This kind of planning is easy to dismiss or overlook but can save your life, if not your sanity.

You will work hard completing assignments as you move through your program. Do not let some unforeseen glitch cause your hard work to be lost.

The master juggler: You

You will have so much to manage while you are completing your academic program. Acquiring an education while working and trying to stay involved with family and friends is a juggling act. You will find yourself trying to figure out what you can give up and what you must keep in order to survive.

Planning ahead

You will always need to be looking ahead and calculating your time constraints and how they can be managed. For example, if you have children and they are out of school for the summer, you may not want to take a challenging class at that time. You might want to wait until the fall when everyone's lives are more structured. It may be easier then for you to fit in more time for class.

The holidays can also lead to increased stress. You are busy in school as well as trying to step up to all the commitments that come along with the holidays: social obligations, family gatherings, and shopping, for example. As you select your courses and plan your schedule for the semesters ahead, be sure to consider all the possible factors that can make demands on your time.

One of your authors remembers some of the conflicts between family and school. In particular, she recalls how classes fell during a few holiday seasons. She once had a class that ended December 23, the day before Christmas Eve. She had a huge paper due. She had to finish it because the policy at the school was that all assignments had to be in when the class ended. It was stressful, but it was worth it to be done before the festivities started.

Another year, she had an assignment due, but the class was not ending; it would continue after a two-week break over Christmas. She ended up submitting the assignment late and taking a hit on the points, but she was okay with that because it was more important for her to be sane and available for her kids over the holidays.

As you can see, it is a matter of give and take, determining what is best for each situation and adapting to the circumstances. Strategize for success and determine what will work for you at any given point.

One class follows another and another

As you are nearing the end of your first class, in fact, any time you are nearing the end of a class, consider what you need to do to prepare for the next class.

What are the enrollment policies at your institution? You will need to find out whether you are automatically enrolled in your next class or whether you are responsible for enrolling yourself.

You will need to know what materials are required. As we have already advised, order your books early, so you can begin working on the next class as soon as possible.

If you have a break between classes, take time to relax and enjoy the reprieve, but do not become too comfortable or you may not want to go back to school. Studies show the longer you are away from school, the harder it will be to go back. If you are concerned about that, gather your books and start reading and preparing for the next class. Get a jump start on it!

As you finish one class and close that door, remember you are starting from square one again in your next class. You have to study the syllabus. You have to learn the faculty member's idiosyncrasies. It is up to you whether you make the same mistakes or learn from your past experiences in subsequent classes. Remember, each instructor is different, so do not expect things to play out as they have before. Adaptability and an open mind are key characteristics to cultivate as you progress through your program.

Celebrate your achievements

As you finish a class, reward yourself for a great accomplishment. If you can afford to take yourself out to lunch or dinner, that's great. But if all you can do is reach your own arm around to pat yourself on the back, then that's enough. Acknowledge your continued success. You deserve it. Do not forget and let it slide. Do not undermine the importance of a reward.

One student we know told us that every time she finished a class, she and her husband would go to happy hour for a cold beer and chicken wings. It was her little treat for a job completed. Plus, it allowed her time to reconnect with her husband before jumping into the next class. Do not overlook the importance of taking the time to appreciate your own effort and sharing your success with those close to you.

Good luck!

This book has been filled with tips. We do not think it covers everything at all. We continue to learn and to think of new ideas.

Online learning is dynamic, which makes creating tips for this environment ever changing too. You will learn new ideas and apply different strategies as you progress through the program, which is what will make you successful. Each of us has to discover our own recipe for success.

Further, we live in an ever-changing landscape: of technology, of obligations, and of individual circumstances. So we have to be flexible and remember what worked at one point in our life may not work at another point, even with school.

You will probably be in school for two years or more. Children will get older, jobs may come and go, you will have both happy and sad times, and through it all, school will go on. You have to stay flexible and figure out how to accomplish your goals. Just as a tree bends in the wind, you will become a stronger and better person for the experience of completing your degree.

Following are some closing thoughts for your education. What can you add?

- ▶ Going to school is not easy, but it should be invigorating. You should be excited.
- ▶ Keep a journal and record your thoughts when you finish a class. When you feel down, read those thoughts and remind yourself why you are doing this.
- ▶ You are worthy of this experience. You have made some sacrifices, and there are more to come, but you will emerge a better person: more experienced, more educated, more confident. Surround yourself with supportive people who will be there just to listen and encourage you.
- ▶ Work hard, but remember, you have a life too. Do not neglect yourself or the special people in your world. Strive for balance.
- ▶ Be a good listener, ask questions, and keep an open mind. Stick to your goals, and do not be afraid of failure. Sometimes it can teach you as much, if not more, than success.
- ▶ Always enjoy the education. Worry less about the final product, and enjoy the new ideas, concepts, and people that you are being introduced to through your classes.
- ▶ *Appreciate the journey.* Believe in yourself and believe in your potential for success. We do!

We hope we have confirmed your desire to attend school online and perhaps even made it stronger. Going to school is both a privilege and the opportunity of a lifetime. We wish you the best!

More Power To You

Now is your chance to explore this chapter's topics further. Check out the sites listed here. Enjoy expanding your knowledge and *more power to you!*

If any of these websites are not available or you wish to seek out additional information, we encourage you to do your own online search. Consider the concepts covered in the chapter that are most important to you, and think of various keywords that could be used to describe them. For this chapter, some potential keywords to search include:

> *organizing computer files*
> *lifelong learner*

When searching online, consider different ways to express ideas. Remember to use synonyms and related words. Try phrasing things in different ways. And always review more than the first few pages of search results.

APPENDICES

Writing a research paper or essay involves planning, drafting, revising, and editing.

Planning

The planning process involves six steps that help you think about the assignment. It now takes you from beginning practical questions, to research, to a working outline.

Pay attention to logistics

Practical questions will help you decide on a topic and depth of coverage:

1. *How much depth does my instructor expect and how long should the paper be?*
2. *How much time do I have?* Consider your other courses and responsibilities.
3. *What kind of research is needed?* Your topic and purpose may determine this.
4. *Is it a team project?* If you are working with others, determine what each person will do.

Brainstorm topic ideas

Start the process of choosing a paper topic with *brainstorming*—a creative technique to generate ideas without judging their worth (see Chapter 9):

▶ Begin by writing down anything on the assigned subject that comes to mind, in no particular order. Tap your multiple intelligences for creative ideas. To jump-start your thoughts, scan your text and notes, check library or Internet references, or meet with your instructor to discuss ideas.

▶ Next, organize that list into an outline or think link so you can see different possibilities.

Use prewriting strategies to narrow your topic

Strategies such as brainstorming, freewriting, and asking journalists' questions[1] help you decide which possible topic you would most like to pursue. Use them to narrow your topic, focusing on the specific sub-ideas and examples from your brainstorming session.

▶ *Brainstorming.* The same creative process you used to generate ideas will help you narrow your topic. Write down your thoughts about the possibilities you have chosen, do some more research, and then organize your thoughts into categories, noticing patterns that appear.

▶ *Freewriting.* When you *freewrite*, you jot down whatever comes to mind without censoring ideas or worrying about grammar, spelling, punctuation, or organization.

▶ *Asking journalists' questions.* When journalists start working on a story, they ask Who? What? Where? When? Why? How? Asking these questions will help you choose a specific topic.

Prewriting helps you develop a topic that is broad enough for investigation but narrow enough to handle. Prewriting also helps you identify what you know and what you don't know. If an assignment involves more than you already know, you need to do research.

Conduct research and take notes

Research develops in stages as you narrow and refine your ideas. In the first brainstorming-for-ideas stage, look for an overview that can lead to a working thesis statement. In the second stage, track down information that fills in gaps. Ultimately, you will have a "body" of information that you can evaluate to develop and implement your final thesis.

As you research, create source and content notes to organize your work, keep track of your sources, and avoid plagiarism.

■ *Source notes.* Source notes, written on index cards, are preliminary notes that should include the author's name; the title of the work; the edition (if any); the publisher, year, and city of publication; the issue and/or volume number when applicable (such as for a magazine); and the page numbers consulted. Notes on Internet sources should reference the website's complete name and address, including the universal resource locator (URL), which is the string of text and numbers that identifies an Internet site. Include a short summary and critical evaluation for each source.

■ *Content notes.* Content notes, written on large index cards, in a notebook, or on your computer, are taken during a thorough reading and provide an in-depth look at source material. Use them to record needed information. To supplement your content notes, make notations—marginal notes, highlighting, and underlining—directly on photocopies of sources.

Write a working thesis statement

Next, organize your research and write a *thesis statement*—the organizing principle of your paper. The thesis declares your specific subject and point of view and reflects your writing purpose (to inform or persuade) and audience (your intended readers).

Consider this to be your *working thesis,* because it may change as you continue your research and develop your draft. Be ready and willing to rework your writing—and your thesis—one or more times before handing in your paper.

Write a working outline or think link

The final planning step is to create a working outline or think link to guide your writing.

Drafting

You may write many versions of the assignment until you are satisfied. Each version moves you closer to saying exactly what you want in the way you want to say it. You face the following main challenges at the first-draft stage:

- ▶ Finalizing your thesis
- ▶ Defining an organizational structure
- ▶ Integrating source material into the body of the paper to fit your structure
- ▶ Finding additional sources to strengthen your presentation
- ▶ Choosing the right words, phrases, and general tone
- ▶ Connecting ideas with logical transitions
- ▶ Creating an effective introduction and conclusion
- ▶ Checking for plagiarism
- ▶ Producing a list of works cited

Don't aim for perfection in a first draft. Trying to get every detail right too early may shut the door on ideas before you even know they are there.

Freewriting your draft

Use everything that you developed in the planning stage as the raw material for freewriting a draft. For now, don't think about your introduction, conclusion, or organizational structure. Simply focus on what you want to say. Only after you have thoughts down should you begin to shape your work.

Writing an introduction

The introduction tells readers what the paper contains and includes a thesis statement, which is often found at the end of the introduction.

Creating the body of a paper

The body of the paper contains your central ideas and supporting evidence, which underpins your thesis with facts, statistics, examples, and expert opinions. Try to find a structure that helps you organize your ideas and evidence into a clear pattern, such as one of the several organizational options presented in Key A.1.

Writing the conclusion

A conclusion brings your paper to a natural ending by summarizing your main points, showing the significance of your thesis and how it relates to larger issues, and calling the reader to action or looking to the future. Let the ideas in the body of the paper speak for themselves as you wrap up.

Avoiding plagiarism: Crediting authors and sources

Using another writer's words, content, unique approach, or illustrations without crediting the author is called *plagiarism* and is illegal and unethical. The following techniques will help you properly credit sources and avoid plagiarism:

■ *Make source notes as you go.* Plagiarism often begins accidentally during research. You may forget to include quotation marks around a quotation, or you may intend to cite or paraphrase a source but never do. To avoid forgetting, write detailed source and content notes as you research.

■ *Learn the difference between a quotation and a paraphrase.* A *quotation* repeats a source's exact words and uses quotation marks to set them off from the rest of the text. A paraphrase, a restatement of the quotation in your own

FIND THE **BEST WAY TO ORGANIZE** THE BODY OF THE PAPER

ORGANIZATIONAL STRUCTURE	WHAT TO DO
Arrange ideas by time.	Describe events in order or in reverse order.
Arrange ideas according to importance.	Start with the idea that carries the most weight and move to less important ideas. Or move from the least to the most important ideas.
Arrange ideas by problem and solution.	Start with a problem and then discuss solutions.
Arrange ideas to present an argument.	Present one or both sides of an issue.
Arrange ideas in list form.	Group a series of items.
Arrange ideas according to cause and effect.	Show how events, situations, or ideas cause subsequent events, situations, or ideas.
Arrange ideas through the use of comparisons.	Compare and contrast the characteristics of events, people, situations, or ideas.
Arrange by process.	Go through the steps in a process: a "how-to" approach.
Arrange by category.	Divide topics into categories and analyze each in order.

words, requires that you completely rewrite the idea, not just remove or replace a few words.

■ *Use a citation even for an acceptable paraphrase.* Credit every source that you quote, paraphrase, or use as evidence (except when the material is considered common knowledge). To credit a source, write a footnote or endnote that describes it, using the format preferred by your instructor.

■ *Understand that lifting material off the Internet is plagiarism.* Words in electronic form belong to the writer just as words in print form do. If you cut and paste sections from a source document onto your draft, you are probably committing plagiarism.

Key A.2 will help you identify the types of material that instructors regard as plagiarized work.

PLAGIARISM TAKES MANY FORMS

Instructors consider the following types of work to be plagiarized:

- Submitting a paper from a website that sells or gives away research papers
- Handing in a paper written by a fellow student or family member
- Copying material in a paper directly from a source without proper quotation marks or source citation
- Paraphrasing material in a paper from a source without proper source citation
- Submitting the same paper in more than one class, even if the classes are in different terms or even different years

Students who plagiarize place their academic careers at risk, in part because cheating is easy to discover. Increasingly, instructors are using anti-plagiarism software to investigate whether strings of words in student papers match material in a database. Make a commitment to hand in your own work and uphold the highest standards of academic integrity.

Citing sources

You may be asked to submit different kinds of source lists when you hand in your paper:

- ▶ *References list.* Only the sources actually cited in your paper (also called a *List of Works Cited*)
- ▶ *Bibliography.* All the sources you consulted, whether or not they were cited in the paper
- ▶ *Annotated bibliography.* All the sources you consulted as well as an explanation or critique of each source

Your instructor will tell you which documentation style to use, commonly one of the following:

- ▶ The Modern Language Association (MLA) format is generally used in the humanities, including history, literature, the arts, and philosophy.
- ▶ The American Psychological Association (APA) style is the appropriate format in psychology, sociology, business, economics, nursing, criminology, and social work.

Consult a college-level writers' handbook for an overview of these documentation styles, or read about them online at www.mla.org and www.apa.org.

Get feedback

Talk with your instructor about your draft, or ask a study partner to read it and answer specific questions. Be open-minded about the comments you receive. Consider each carefully, and then make a decision about what to change.

Revising

When you *revise,* you critically evaluate the content, organization, word choice, paragraph structure, and style of your first draft. You evaluate the strength of your thesis and whether your evidence proves it, looking for logical holes. You can do anything you want at this point to change your work. You can turn things around and present information from the end of your paper up front, tweak your thesis to reflect the evidence presented, or choose a different organizational structure.

Engage your critical thinking skills to evaluate the content and form of your paper. Ask yourself these questions as you revise:

- ▶ Does the paper fulfill the requirements of the assignment?
- ▶ Do I prove my thesis?
- ▶ Is each idea and argument developed, explained, and supported by examples?
- ▶ Does the introduction prepare the reader and capture attention?
- ▶ Is the body of the paper organized effectively?

- ▶ Does each paragraph have a topic sentence that is supported by the rest of the paragraph?
- ▶ Are my ideas connected to one another through logical transitions?
- ▶ Do I have a clear, concise writing style?
- ▶ Does the conclusion provide a natural ending without introducing new ideas?

Check for clarity

Now check for sense, continuity, and clarity. Focus also on tightening your prose and eliminating wordy phrases. Examine once again how paragraphs flow into one another by evaluating the effectiveness of your *transitions*—the words, phrases, or sentences that connect ideas.

Editing

Editing involves correcting technical mistakes in spelling, grammar, and punctuation, as well as checking for consistency in such elements as abbreviations and capitalization. If you use a computer, start with the grammar check and spell check to find mistakes, realizing that you still need to check your work manually. Look also for *sexist language*, which characterizes people according to gender stereotypes and often involves the male pronouns *he*, *his*, or *him*.

Proofreading, the last editing stage, involves reading every word for accuracy. Look for technical mistakes, run-on sentences, spelling errors, and sentence fragments. Look for incorrect word usage and unclear references. A great way to check your work is to read it out loud.

Your final paper reflects all the hard work you put in during the writing process. Ideally, when you are finished, you have a piece of work that shows your researching, writing, and thinking ability.

ENDNOTE

1. Analysis based on Lynn Quitman Troyka, *Simon & Schuster Handbook for Writers*, Upper Saddle River, NJ: Prentice Hall, 1996, pp. 22–23.

Social networking refers to interacting with a community of people through an online network such as Facebook, MySpace, forums (message boards), or chat rooms. *Social media* are the types of media people use to share information online (examples include Web logs or "blogs," podcasts, websites, videos, and news feeds). Social media allow participation through comments and ratings. The people who provide social media content range from experts to amateurs, which means the content will not always be accurate or trustworthy.

In general, social networking and media make three things possible:

1. Communicating information about yourself to others
2. Connecting with people who have similar interests
3. Networking with others to accomplish goals

Social networking has grown rapidly worldwide through sites like the following:

▶ **Facebook** enables users to set up personal profiles and communicate with other users through profile updates, public or private messages, games, and photos
▶ **Twitter** enables users to send or receive short text updates, or "tweets," to other users signed up on their accounts
▶ **Skype** enables users to make calls over the Internet

How they can help you in college

Use social networking and media to:

▶ *Connect with peers to achieve academic goals.* Students might create groups that correspond to courses, study together on an Internet call, or post course-related questions and comments on a message board or chat room used by the class. (Try: Facebook, Skype)
▶ *Manage coursework and projects.* Particular sites can help you search for information, study, and ask questions. When doing a group project, social networking can help you collaborate in an online format. (Try: Evernote, Google Docs, EtherPad, Wikidot)
▶ *Network with students who have shared interests.* A student might start a blog on an academic topic and hope to attract interested readers, or look for groups or Internet forums. (Try: Facebook, MySpace, forums on specific topics)
▶ *Adjust to college.* Ask other students at your school about local issues (bus schedules, library hours), or ask students anywhere in the world about more general concerns (test anxiety). You can even use social media to stay organized. (Try: Twitter, Facebook, GradeMate, Backpack)
▶ *Focus on career development.* Put your qualifications and career goals out there for others to peruse, and build a network that may lead you to job opportunities. (Try: LinkedIn, Zumeo)
▶ *Stay connected to loved ones.* Students might tweet or blog happenings to family and old friends, post updates, or make free phone calls. A budgeting bonus: Most social networking tools cost nothing to use as long as you have Internet access. (Try: Twitter, Facebook, Skype)

► *Share your opinion.* Blogs allow you to communicate to an audience on a regular basis, and creating a blog is usually free. Another tool, the forum or message board, encourages individuals to come together and discuss a common knowledge or experience. (Try: Blogger, MySpace)

Ten strategies for success

Follow these guidelines to get the most from your time and energy on social networks and with social media.

1. *Control your personal information.* Read the privacy policy of any network you join. Adjust security settings, indicating what information, photos, and so on you want to be visible or invisible. Know what will always be visible to users.

2. *Control your time.* One quick check of your e-mail can lead to hours spent online that you should have spent getting something else done. To stay focused and in control:

   • Create a separate e-mail for alerts from your social networking sites.
   • Set your status to "offline" or "do not disturb" when you are studying.
   • Set up goals and rewards. Try doing a defined portion of your homework and then rewarding yourself with ten minutes on your favorite social networking site.

3. *Be an information literate critical thinker.* Evaluate what you read on social networking sites or social media with a critical eye. Use the CARS test (p. 141) to check Credibility, Accuracy, Reasonableness, and Support of any source or statement.

4. *Keep career goals in mind.* With anything you write, think: How will this look to others who may evaluate me in the future? Also, choose and post photographs carefully, because some employers use social networking sites for background checks.

5. *Use caution with forums and chat rooms.* There is no way to know who is posting on a forum or in a chat room. Consider using a name that differs from your legal name or regular e-mail address. Remember, too, that everything you write can be copied and saved.

6. *Watch your temper.* Wait, and think, before you post on emotional topics. Forums can turn into hostile environments. Snarky tweets and updates can come back to haunt you if they are viewed by potential employers, instructors, or others who may judge you by them.

7. *Separate the personal and the academic/professional.* You probably don't want an employer seeing that crass video your cousin posted on your page. Consider having two profiles on a network if you want to use one to communicate with students or advance your career.

8. *Show restraint.* Although it's easy to get carried away, keep your purpose in mind. For example, if one goal is to keep up with friends using Facebook, you are defeating your purpose if you have so many friends that you can't possibly stay up-to-date with them.

9. *Understand what a blog or website requires.* Blogs need updating at least weekly if not more often, and require time and motivation. Websites can be even more labor-intensive.

10. *Network with integrity.* Treat others with respect. Search for, and use, information legitimately. Cite sources honestly.

Index

Abbreviations in email messages, 57
Accountability, 6
Action-oriented listeners, 153
Action verbs, 214
Active listening, 164
Active reading, 121
Advertisement, Cigna, 25
Analogies, 227
Analytical process, 221–227
Analytical thinking, 13, 176, 182
    assessing, 38
    developing, 221–227
Approach failure, 17
Argument, 222
Asking questions, 237
Assumptions, 224, 267
Audio strategies for studying, 185
Auditory learning style, 109

Backup system, 307
Bard, Carl, 8
Barnes, Tracy, 1
Basic needs, hierarchy of, 21–22, 34
Bias, 224
Bloom, Benjamin, 99, 130
Bloom's Taxonomy, 130, 132–133
Bodily-kinesthetic intelligence, 105
    for careers, 284
    for learning styles, 144
    for memory, 181
    for note-taking, 160
    for reading, 140
    for test preparation, 207
Boldness, 5
Boolean searches, 239–240
Brain
    chemical process for learning,
        99–100
    natural learning power, 98–99
Brainstorming, 227
Briggs, Katharine, 109
Briggs-Myers, Isabel, 109
Brown, Les, 27
Buren, Abigail Van, 31
Burka, Jane B., 77
Buscaglia, Leo, 6, 35

Capital letters in email messages, 57
Career areas, changes in, 288
Career paths, 285–286
Career success, 7–8
    building knowledge and experience for,
        283–285
    continuing education and, 294–297
    preparing for, 282–288
    role of personality and strengths, 282–283
    skill set and, 286–287
    strategies for, 320
Carter, Julie, 248–249
Challenges in college study, 3
Chunking, 183
Churchill, Winston, 34
Citing sources, 243
Closed-mindedness and culture, 268
Cognitive mental action, 98
College course, potential of, 2–3
College culture, 3–4
College education, skills gained from,
        8–9
College readiness, assessing, 2
College self, 14
Color in email messages, 56–57
Communication skills, 147
Community, definition of, 269–270
Computer skills, 5
Confidence, 5
Connections with people, making, 18
Contacts, 289
Contaminated people, 29
Content-oriented listeners, 153
Continuing education, 5, 295
Cornell note-taking system, 159, 161
Covering letter, 290
Cramming, 202–203
Creative ideas, strategies to generate,
        230–231
Creative thinking, 13
    assessing, 39
    developing, 227–231
Credit rating, 5
Critical thinking, 13, 221, 237
Critical thinking skills, 5
Cue column, 159

Cultural awareness
  defined, 251–252
  developing, 255–256
  investigation of, 253–255
  levels of, 252–254
  value of, 256
Cultural competence, 256–269
Cultural components of communication, 263–266
Cypin (sigh-pin), 100

Decision making, 235–236
Deficiency needs, 21
Delay gratification, 85
Desirable employee, 4
Dictionary, 125
Digital revolution, 9
Divergent thinking, 227
Dominant intelligence, 102
Drafting, 314–317
Dweck, Carol, 11–12, 17

Ebbinghaus, Herman, 174–175
Editing, 318
Education level
  employment and, 10
  income earned and, 10
Eighth intelligence, 102
E-mail
  communication guidelines, 56–59
  managing, 79–80
Emoticons, 57
Emotional intelligence (EI), 35, 286
  abilities of, 19
  journal, 37–38, 92, 117, 147, 169, 194, 216, 245, 277, 298–299
  success and, 18–19
Emotions and listening, 155–156
ENFJ type person, 114
ENFP type person, 113
ENTJ type person, 114
ENTP type person, 113
ESFJ type person, 114
ESFP type person, 113
Essay questions, 213
ESTJ type person, 114
ESTP type person, 113
Ethnocentrism, 267
External motivation, 20
Extroverts, 112

Fears, overcoming, 16, 26–27, 269
Feelers, 112

Filing system, 306
Fill-in-the-blank questions, 212
First-generation students, 21–23
Fixation, 127
Fixed mindset, 15
Flash cards, 184–185
Fonts in email messages, 56
Forgetting, 174–175
Formal outlines, 158
Formulas, 137
Friedman, Thomas, 9
Frierson, Tem, 197
Fu-tse, Kung (Confucius), 99

Gainful employment, skills for, 7
General education requirements, 137
Global citizenship, 269–272
  definition of, 271–272
  rights and obligations, 272–273
  scope of, 272
Global communication strategies, 273–275
Global community, 271
Global Community Earth Government, 271
Goal-related tasks, scheduling of, 71–73
Goals
  defined, 64
  long-term, 66–67
  setting, 64–69
  short-term, 67
  SMART goal-achievement plan, 67–70
Gordon, Greg, 171
Greenfield, Marc, 281
Growth mindset, 13–17, 35, 294
Guided notes, 159

Hearing, 151–153
Higher-level thinking, 3
Highlighting, 131
Hightower, Tifani, 119
Holistic learning, 98
Holland, John, 283
Horne, Lena, 28
Human relation skills, 6

"I CAN'T" Syndrome, 28–29
Independent learning, 3
INFJ type person, 113
Informal outlines, 158
Information processing model of memory, 172–174
INFP type person, 113

Intelligence
multiple, 102–104, 140, 144, 160, 181, 207
naturalistic. *See* naturalistic intelligence
Intelligence measurements, 11–12
Intercultural communication, 267–269
Internalizing, 20–21
Internal motivation, 20
Internet research, 237–241
Internships, 285
Interpersonal intelligence, 105
and careers, 284
for learning styles, 144
for memory, 181
for note-taking, 160
for reading, 140
for test preparation, 207
Interview, 290
INTJ type person, 113
INTP type person, 113
Intrapersonal intelligence, 105
and careers, 284
for learning styles, 144
for memory, 181
for note-taking, 160
for reading, 140
for test preparation, 207
Intrapersonal skills, 147
Introverts, 112
Intuitive, 112
IQ (intelligence quotient), 11
ISFJ type person, 113
ISFP type person, 113
ISTJ type person, 113
ISTP type person, 113

Jester, Brock, 42
Job-hunting strategies, 288–290
Job search, 288–291
Jobs, Steve, 133, 135
Journalists' questions, 175
Judgers, 112
Jump-start creative thinking, 232
Jung, Carl, 108

Kellner-Rogers, Myron, 297
Knowledge work, 9
Kushner, H., 29

Language differences and culture, 268
Lao-Tse, 99
Lasky, Rick, 219

LEAD (Learning Evaluation and Assessment Directory), 107
Learned helplessness, 24
Learning
formal *vs* informal, 98
holistic, 98
Learning from failure, 16–17
Learning management system (LMS), 48–49
Learning process, steps, 100–102
Learning style (LS), 96, 102, 106, 109, 114–115
reading strategies for, 143–144
strategies, 185
Learning through ages, 99
Leno, Jay, 126
Lifelong learner, 35, 294
Lifelong success, attitude and skills for, 295
LinkedIn, 60
Listening
active, 164
Chinese and, 151–152
constructive, 153
defined, 151–152
importance of, 150–151
objective, 152
obstacles in, 154–156
styles, 153–154
vs hearing, 151–153
with a purpose, 152
Literature, reading strategies for, 139
Locke, John, 99
Logical-mathematical intelligence, 105
for careers, 284
for learning styles, 144
for memory, 181
for note-taking, 160
for reading, 140
for test preparation, 207
Logodaedalian, 124
Long-term goals, 66–67
Loyalty, 4

Mariela, 250
Maslow, Abraham, 21, 98
Matching questions, 212
Math anxiety, 203–204
Mathematics and science subjects, reading strategies for, 137
McCornack, Steven, 153
McGraw, Tim, 32
Memorization, 172, 182
of math and science material, 186–187

Memory
    evaluating, 193–194
    information processing model of, 172–174
    long-term, 173–174
    short-term, 173
Mental walk strategy, 188–189
Metacognition, 96
Mindful concentration, 126
Mind map, 162
Mirror neurons, 17
Mission statement, 65–66
Mnemonic devices, 187–191
    acronyms, 189–191
    developing, 188
    songs or rhymes, 191
    visual images, 188–189
Moreno, Mike, 95
Motivation, 13
    first-generation students and, 21
    internal *vs* external, 20–21
    Maslow's theory, 21
    strategies to improve, 24–34
Motivators of success, 13–17
Multiple-choice questions, 210–211
Multiple intelligence (MI), 102–104
    for careers, 284
    for learning styles, 144
    for memory, 181
    for note-taking, 160
    for reading, 140
    for test preparation, 207
Multitasking, 5
Musical-rhythmic intelligence, 105
    for careers, 284
    for learning styles, 144
    for memory, 181
    for note-taking, 160
    for reading, 140
    for test preparation, 207
Myers-Briggs Type Indicator, 109

Naturalistic intelligence, 105
    for careers, 284
    for learning styles, 144
    for memory, 181
    for note-taking, 160
    for reading, 140
    for test preparation, 207
Networking, 288–289
Neuroplasticity, 100
Newman, Randy, 26
Nielsen, Jakob, 54

Noneducational computer time, management
    of, 80–81
Note-taking
    developing shorthand for, 164–166
    format, 157
    for multimedia presentations, 163–164
    skills, 156–157
    strategies, 157–163

Objective questions, 208
Online communication concerns, 58–59
Online courses
    assignments, 48
    discussion forum, 48, 80–81
    group projects in, 48
    quizzes and exams, 48
    resource management, 80
    time management in, 79–83
    types of, 47
Online information, credibility of, 241–242
Online learning
    asking for help, 55–56
    benefits of, 44–45
    developing discipline and accountability for,
      51–52
    emotion and thought management, 54–55
    facts and fictions of, 45–47
    friendships and career networking opportunities
      in, 52–54
    practices of successful, 49–56, 60
    schedule for, 50–51
    setting priorities for, 51
Online reading challenges, 141–143
Online searches, 238
Online social networking, 41
Openmindedness, 6
Optimists, 24
Outlaw, Frank, 24
Outlines, 158–159

Pace of study, 3, 82
PAP (Personality Assessment Profile), 110–111
Partnership for 21st Century Skills, 9
Passive reading, 121
Paul, Richard, 220
Payne, William, 149
Peck, Scott, 150
People-oriented listeners, 153
Perceivers, 112
Perception puzzles, 229
Perfectionism, 77
Personal guiding statement, 31–32

Personality Assessment, 283
Personality type, 102
Personal mission, 65–66
Personal reading rate, 121–124
Personal time profile, developing, 70
Perspectives, 224, 229
Pessimist, 24
Peter, 143
Piaget, Jean, 98, 99
Picasso, Pablo, 100
Pink, Daniel, 9
Pitino, Rick, 15
Plagiarism, 242–243
Planner, using a, 71–75
Planning for future, 307–308
Plato, 99
Plutarch, 99
Poe, Edgar Allan, 98
Positive thoughts, 296
Practical thinking, 13
    assessing, 39
    developing, 231–234
Prejudging and listening, 154
Prejudice, 52–53
Pretest, 200
Primary group, 146
Primary sources of information, 241–242
Prioritizing, 74, 82
Priority management, 5
Problem solving, 233–235
Procrastination, 75–78, 81
Profile assessment, 283
Psychological need, 21

Q-stage questions, 128–131
Qualifiers, 208
Question– read–recite cycle, 128–135
Questions, formulating, 128–131

Reading
    ingredients for successful, 121
    online, 141–143
    specific subjects, 137–139
    stating point for, 131
    strategies for different learning styles, 143–144
Reading skills, college-level, 120–121, 126–127
Reading style, 121–122
Realistic, Investigative, Artistic, Social, Enterprising, and Conventional (RIASEC), 283
Reciting, 135, 184
Rehearsing, 184
Resumé, 290, 300

Reviewing techniques, 135–137
Revising draft, 317–318
Rousseau, Jean-Jacques, 99
Routine, establishing a, 81–82
Rucha, 53

Sara, 163
Schedule preferences, establishing, 71
Schuller, Robert, 26
Search engines, 238
Secondary group, 146
Secondary sources of information, 241–242
Self-actualization, 21
Self-assessment
    of skills and preferences for online learning, 43–44
    of success, 36–37
Self-defeating behavior, 24, 25
Self-Directed Search (SDS), 283
Self-esteem, 15
    characteristics of, 34
    strategies to enhance, 33–35
Self-management skills, developing, 63
Self-portrait, 117–118
Sensing, 112
Sensory registers, 173
Sentence completion questions, 212
Service learning, 285
The Seven Habits of Highly Effective People, 65
Shorthand for note-taking, 164–166
Short-term goals, 67
Short-term memory, 173
Skills needed for college graduates, 4–6
SMART goal-achievement plan, 67–70
Social groups, 146
Social media mistakes, avoiding, 5
Social networking, 41, 60, 93, 118, 148, 170, 195, 218, 246, 278, 302–303, 319–320
Social sciences and humanities, reading strategies for, 138–139
Socrates, 99
Spelling and punctuation in email messages, 57
SQ3R reading strategy, 127–138, 200
Statement of fact, 223
Statement of opinion, 223
Stereotypes, 53–54, 267
Sternberg, Robert, 2, 11–12, 36, 83, 96–97, 220, 282
Strategies for lifetime success, 24
Strengths, assessment of, 102
Stress, assessment of, 83–84
Stress management, 83–88

Stressors in life, 85–87
Study
    managing children and, 179
    purpose of, 178–179
    strategies for, 179–186
    what to, 178–179
Study location, 177
Study materials, evaluation of, 178–179
Study plan, 183
Study strategies, 191–192
Subjective questions, 208
Successful intelligence, 12, 234, 291–293
    assessing, 38
    importance of, 13
Summary, 159
Surveying, 128

Tactile learning style, 106–107, 109
Talking and listening, 155
Terry, Anthony, 62
Test anxiety, managing, 203–205
Test day strategies, 205–208
Test performance
    cramming, 202–203
    physical preparation for, 200–202
    preparation for, 198–203
    reading and studying strategies, 200
    study schedule and checklist, 199–200
    time strategies, 204–205
Test questions
    predicting, 199
    types of, 208–214
Textbooks as valuable references, 306
Thinkers, 112
Thinking skills, 220
    contribution to goal achievement, 13
    types of, 12–13
Think link, 162
Thought process, 236–237
Tim, 79
Time management, 69–78, 87–92
Time-oriented listeners, 153
Time wasters, 78
T-note system. See Cornell note-taking system
To-do lists, 73–74
Topic sentence, 133
True/false questions, 211
Trustworthiness, 4

21st Century Learning, 9, 11, 38, 217, 278, 299

Values
    developing, 64
    life experiences and, 64
    role in achieving goals, 63
Verbal-linguistic intelligence, 104
    for careers, 284
    for learning styles, 144
    for memory, 181
    for note-taking, 160
    for reading, 140
    for test preparation, 207
Visual aids for reading, 141
Visual learning
    skill, 106–107
    style, 109
Visual-spatial intelligence, 104, 107
    for careers, 284
    for learning styles, 144
    for memory, 181
    for note-taking, 160
    for reading, 140
    for test preparation, 207
Vocabulary, developing, 124–125
Vocational Preference Inventory (VPI), 283
Volunteering, 285

Wallpaper/settings in email, 56
Watson, J. B., 99
Watts, Cindy, 305
Westside Test Anxiety Scale, 206
What to study, 178–179
Wheatley, Margaret J., 297
When, where, and who of studying, 176–177
Wild card search, 241
Word web, 162
Working memory, 173
Workload in colleges, 3
Workplace
    skill development, 9
    trends, 288
The World Is Flat, 9
Writing, 184
Writing a research paper or essay, 313–318

Yuen, Lenora M., 77

Credits

Pages 4–8; 20–34; 98–113; 120–124; 126–127; 141; 150–155 contain content from *Cornerstones for Career College Success*, Third Edition by Robert M. Sherfield and Patricia G. Moody.

Pages 43–55; 79–82; 141–144; 163–164 contain content from *Keys to Online Learning* by Kateri Drexler, Carol Carter, Joyce Bishop, and Sarah Lyman Kravits.

Pages 249–277; 280 contain content from *Keys to Learning Strategies for Success: Cultural Awareness and Global Citizenship* by Carol Carter and Sarah Lyman Kravits.

Pages 56–59; 236–243; 306–309 contain content from *Power Up: A Practical Student's Guide to Online Learning* by Stacey Barrett, Catrina Poe, and Carrie Spagnola-Doyle.

Images and personal stories found at the beginning of each chapter are used with courtesy of Columbia Southern University.

All other content is from *Keys to Learning Strategies for Success: Building Analytical, Creative, and Practical Skills*, Seventh Edition by Carol Carter, Joyce Bishop, and Sarah Lyman Kravits.